Like a Summer wi...  y's: Collect... from Dave and Stu... 008.

Publisher: Bread and Circuses 2016

www.breadandcircusespublishing.com

ISBN: 9780993475719

Cover design: Anthony Gerace

http://a-gerace.com

Book layout/design: Louise Kentell

seahorse design

Like a Summer with a Thousand July's: Collected Writings from Dave and Stuart Wise, 1978 – 2008.

Contents

Introduction	4
The End of Music *(1978)*	8
Once Upon A Time There Was A Place Called Notting Hill Gate *(1982)*	51
Like A Summer with a Thousand Julys *(1982)*	125
Ralph Rumney: Hidden connections, ruminations and rambling parentheses *(Dave Wise: 2007)*	227
Nietzsche, Revolutionary Subversion and the Contemporary Attack On Music *(Stuart Wise: 2007)*	245
Alex Trocchi's Hour Upon The Stage *(Dave & Stuart Wise: 2008)*	253
Comparisons: From Mass Observation to King Mob - The changing face of revolutionary elites from the 1930s to the late 1960s and ever after *(Incomplete: Stuart Wise: 2007)*	270
On What Happened at Selfridges *(Dave Wise. Spring 2007)*	290
Reflections on the lump: Dave Lamb *(Solidarity :Britain, 1974)*	293
Some thoughts on the pamphlet by Dave Wise - for the use of "Wildcat" in Germany: *(March, 1997)*	298
Reflections on Brendan Ward's Builders' Remembered *(1984)* and "Builders, Chancers and the Crack" *(1985)*	319
'King Mob: The Posters, Leaflets, Cartoons' *(2000)*	332

Introduction

Now into their late 60's, and still working with the same gang of skilled / unskilled labourers, chippies, sparks and plumbers on the London building sites that they've been working on since the late 70's, key King Mob faces Dave and Start Wise reply simply and straightforwardly to a question about coping with the decades long aftermath to the "death of the social revolution" in the late 60's, a death that left them initially isolated and adrift, two working class insurrectionists and dreamers slowly drowning in a sea of desertion and recuperation : "it's the crack, 10 of us, all on equal pay, equal status, working together, no tension, getting jobs done, ideas and conversations drifting back and forth between equals. It creates an energy..."

Outside of the sites, and long after King Mob had ended, the Wise brothers never stopped the writing, thinking or agitating, and this, a companion volume to last years' warmly received 'King Mob : A Critical Hidden History' pulls together some of the best of their polemics, reflections, and righteous rants from the last thirty years.

The subject matters range far and wide, but the gaze remains steady, underpinned by an unwavering ideological perspective that firmly rejects the stasis of the post war 'revolutionary left', just as it recoils in disgust at encroaching Neo Liberal barbarism.

Starting with the piece that lends the book it's title, 'Like A Summer With A 1000 July's' takes an extensive, sideways look at the wave of urban insurrection that swept inner city UK in 1981, as "the four corners of England... were exposed to a force 10 gale of youthful class fury."

As often with the Wise's writings, we get glimpses at the margins, shards of surrealism cutting through : the assault on art "in the great mod battle of Keswick, when a travelling theatre was again torched" or the Dadaist guerrilla flavoured August 1981 bank holiday attack when "the model railway station at Brighton was molotoved by white youths."

But on a far wider scale, he looks beyond the idea of the 1981 urban riots representing simply a black youth rebellion against hard times (with white and Asian working class youth happily weighing in) digging down into the role of the 'soft state' that emerged out of the recuperated but unresolved socio-political frustrations of the post 68' generation, as those post 68' radicals became the teachers, urban planners, youth workers, family court officials, neighbourhood liaison officers, radical lawyers:

"They drew up Community Strategies, set up local development projects and rebranded 'alienation' to signify 'unneighbourliness', full of hope of fulfilling their political dreams at localised levels whilst quietly nurturing career ambitions."
The contradictions running through later stage capitalist economies and creating fissures in the cities were "artfully rebranded in pathological terms suited to remedial treatment: delinquency, crime, deprivation, children at risk, problem families." The explosion of urban anger in 1981 put an end to those post 68' dreams, and Wise argues that this must be seen as much as a defeat for the post 68' liberals as it was for the boys in blue and their political paymasters.

In his definitive work on Punk, 'The End Of Music' *(1978)*, Wise debunks the cosy idea that Punk, with King Mob associate and pro situ fan Malcolm McLaren at the helm of the Pistols, was a situationist inspired assault on the sterile, ossified sub-pop culture of the 1970s', arguing that it was in fact capital (pop culture dept.) responding to the, by then, flatlining cultural economy, using situationist critique and the rebel spectacle to reinvigorate a decrepit rock industry, and forcefully remove the Rick Wakeman platform boot threatening to stamp on youth cultures bloated face, forever.

"At such an impasse where to turn? Part of the answer came from a not totally unexpected quarter. The most revolutionary critique of the late 1960s - that of the Situationists - suddenly had a raison d'etre for capital. After being suitably doctored, such a critique could be used as a force able to keep pop music kicking as pacification agent of the young proletariat both in terms of channelling energy into hierarchical aspiration, fake liberation from drudgery and the goal of a higher level of wage slavery with all its alluring but alienated sexual appeal."

Wise looks at parallel recuperation and exploitation of rebel music movements in Cuba via the Castroist Neuva Trova (1969 onwards), and the wholesale co-opting of Reggae / Bob Marley into Michael Manley's PNP political circus in Jamaica during the febrile 1970's, quoting Gianfranco Sanguinetti in conclusion. "All rebellion expressed in terms of art merely ends up as the new academy".

As for the future / No Future: "Only when the planet is rid of commodities will music cease to fall well short of our desires; but then can we be sure it will be called music? Until that beautiful dawn, down with musicians! And while we are at it, down with all art and artists. It has been said before but its comeback is long overdue."

Tracing punk and McLarens ideological lineage back to a possible primary source, 'What Happened at Selfridges In 1968' *(2004)* takes a brief, but definitive look at the glorious prank immortalised in McLarens' 1991 mini film 'the Ghosts of Oxford Street', when Dave Wise, McLaren, Fred Vermorel (later Pistols diarist / PR) and a few King Mob associates infamously dressed up as Santa Claus in Selfridges toy dept (Xmas 1969), handed out toys from the shelves to the hordes of expectant children and "watched the chaos of consumerism unfold before them" as crying children had the King Mob freely-gifted toys wrenched from their arms by confused and desperate security guards.

Wise points out that it wasn't McLaren in the Santa suit as he later claimed (that was "Peter 'Ben' Trueman, builder, hooligan, never a student... out of his head on speed,") but rated his performance highly on the day: "Malcolm McLaren had dash and audacity, and proved to be very plucky and imaginative, darting here, there and everywhere during the battle for Selfridges."

Away from any ghosts in Oxford Street, in 'Reflections on Brendan Ward's' 'Builders Remembered' and 'Builders, Chancers and the Crack' 1984) the Wises look at these (now very hard to find) first person narratives from the casual Irish labourers who built post war London, and in 'Reflections on The Lump' *(1987)*, at the struggles and tensions between casual labourers, rank and file building workers, union bureaucrats, and revolutionary leftist interventionists. With 30 years + experience as radical building workers, the uniqueness of perspective offered by the Wise brothers here throws up insights that won't be easily found elsewhere.

Beyond the buildings, the Wises' gaze wonders far and wide across the post war political, economic and (sub) cultural / landscape. In 'Alex Trocchi's Hour Upon The Stage' *(2008)*, Dave Wise looks at one of the two founding members of the English branch of the Situationist International: original beatnik, infamous junkie and renowned author - from a personal and political vantage point. Wise reminisces about waking up in bed, late, with Trocchi's cleaner, listening to her fending off her irate employer. He charts the then young authors attempts to "transcend cultural specialisms and dissident cultural milieus", rejecting commodified art and "the literary industry", before mourning Trocchi's subsequent "embrace of vapid notoriety" and "descent into creative stasis, bohemian high society and heroin".

'Nietzsche: Revolutionary' *(2005)* looks at the much debated / revered / contested philosopher as 'a reluctant communist', 'proto ecologist' and 'brother Hegelian', and questions the attempts to reclaim him / his work by the likes of Georges Bataille for "the radical revolution envisaged by the International Lettrists, the Situationist International, King Mob and the Motherfuckers and others in America" and then later the "Stalinoid rehabilitation of Nietzsche led by Louis Althusser".

'In Once Upon A Time There Was A Place Called Nothing Hill Gate...' *(1988)* long time W11 resident Wise looks at the "anti-work ambience, cheap lodgings, shabby bedsits, private and council, which later turned into squats", the transition from comfortable post WW1 arty milieu, to 1940's/50 bohemia, to 60's alternative / drop out culture and the birth place of the Angry Brigade and King Mob : Notting Hill of the 60's / 70's, and where, Wise argues, "real issues and real conflict are instantly spectacularized for media consumption", where " phoney classlessness" rules the roost.

Spanish and Portugese refugees celebrating the downfall of fascism and the death of Franco in their respective homelands within 12 months of 1974, Czech spys running cake stalls on Portobello Road, Irish Ceiledh at the Tabernacle one night, on another Anarcho-Syndicalist union, "the revived CNT, sunk in a glorious past" showing Durrutti films, with "Durruti as the heroic, benign, great liberator."

And most off all, Wise attempts to scrape off the "the radical veneer to community politico claptrap" and examine at full glare the outbursts of street resistance that marked the growth and subsequent repression of carnival over the decades.

From working class whites standing alongside their black neighbours against marauding but underprepared Met coppers in 76', to the death of old Carnival in 1987', as the sound systems get turned off at 8.30pm, and the battle lines go up once again. Any resistance to the latest waves of gentrification were now over, the Notting Hill set who were to head up the Tory govt of 2010-15 were no doubt away at their country estates as tooled up Robocops ended carnival that bank holiday Monday, but their hold on the area was to be uncontested from that point on.

'King Mob : The Posters, Leaflets, Cartoons' *(2000)* takes a quick look at the visual legacy. From the iconic : "Same – Thing – Day – After Day – Work – Tube – Dinner – Armchair " graffiti piece that adorned the Hammersmith & City line at Westbourne Park for a couple of decades "before being obliterated by tag banality", through the many pieces from "the caring, penniless, hurt guy... Richard 'Irish' Bell" that played a key part in influencing Jamie Reid and McLaren in the years to come, the LSE occupation leaflet that was suppressed by the Trots / OG intersectionalists for alleged sexism, Charlie Radcliffe's infamous Disney detournement, and more.

Finally, In 'Ralph Rumney: Hidden Connections, Ruminations And Rambling Parentheses' *(2007)* "Wise reflects on the life and times of Rumney, co-founder of the International Situationists in 1957, artist, psychogeographer, lover of Michelle Bernstein, one time communist and conscientious objector, drinker, and lifelong artist (despite everything: 'Rumney really did believe in art')."

Along the way, Wise imagines conversations between Rumney and EP Thompson, (who'd given the young army refusenik and fellow Communist Party comrade Rumney a bed for a while after he'd gone on the lam following a local media scandal in the late 50's), and wonders how much each influenced each other in subsequent years, as EP went on to publish his Making of the English Working Class, and Rumney on to form the SI.

And as the collection ends, we find Wise looking back at the Rumney / Guy Debord / Michelle Bernstein triangle through the prism of first hand experience :

"Guy and Michele broke up around 1970. Hardly surprising as everybody's relationship did, including my own; a break up, may it be said, I never got over and I've thought about my beloved Anne Ryder every day of my life since. These break-ups weren't about sexual difficulties or inadequacies nor about not being able to relate or even love, but finally about history and how the most profound revolt ever experienced failed so utterly, and the essential by-product of such failure was a psychosomatic pain so desperate it seemed in need of therapeutic treatment; a treatment simple warm cuddling and quiet affection couldn't match. We stormed and smashed open the gates of paradise to let in every exploited nutter who cared to join in... yet on the brink of utopia we were refused entry and where, just where, could you go from such a point of no return?"

THE ORIGINAL: The End of Music

PUNK ROCK, NEW WAVE, REGGAE - A CRITIQUE.......

"A taste for change, satisfied by a change of taste." *(Vaneigem)*

"For sale anarchy for the masses" *(Rimbaud, Clearance Sale)*

Punk rock / new wave or something similar had inevitably to come about. Pop music was getting jaded and many people from the record consumer to the journalist wordsmiths of the musical trade papers were aware of that. The wordsmiths breathed a sigh of relief – their jobs were no longer in jeopardy for another season at least - as the record buying public were consuming again with something like enthusiasm. In retrospect what is amazing is that the insipidness, (within of course its own terms) of early to mid 1970s rock, didn't produce an active revolt against the musical spectacle but merely the urge to update it.

There had been similar downturns in rock history, but this time around, it took ex-revolutionaries from the late 1960s to make the spectacle compelling again, and some, moreover who had embraced one of the most radical revolutionary perspectives of the late 1960s, that of the Situationists.

Punk coincides with the long, protracted end of post second world war capitalist re-construction. The relatively affluent base of previous rock eras is no longer there. Primary poverty is returning with a vengeance after an epoch of capital expansion when it was thought that there was no end to a surfeit of commodities. Hence the-critique of the poverty of abundance in the 1960s, which was a major factor in the potentially revolutionary explosions of the late 60's among, alienated youth (though not necessarily of the productive working class, where, combating productivity deals played a greater part as subversive departure, than, immediate aesthetic / ecological objections to frozen chickens, Mini cars and TV shows.)

Punk, like previous rock movements, is based upon youth, but a youth which has in increasing numbers been thrown out of work, and has become part of the growing surplus population which is allowed only sparingly to consume, through welfare relief and various scrounges. Punk rock uses the desperation of this social base, but only finally to reinforce this desperation. As long as the spectacle lasts, it will equally be superceded by something different but which sounds really very familiar; probably, more desperate and schizoid, if only more frantically to try and hold some attention.

Who knows? Megadeath rock / Happening-cum-suicide rock where the lead guitarist slowly electrocutes his cock to cinders and a splendid media sensation and total sacrifice to an art, long since thoroughly colonized by capitalism? And what an exit for a very highly paid wage labourer!

Through its acts and lyrics, punk music has caused a furore but largely as a fight between various representatives of the bourgeoisie. Journalists at odds with each other - some praising, some blaming - with MP's, council bureaucrats, managers of chain stores, generally united in condemnation.

Because of the sound and fury, (also signifying nothing) the left have been forced to take note of punk but with differing degrees of emphasis. The Communist Party with its fossilized commitment to archaic forms of art has again missed the boat and its paper, the Morning Star, following the legacy of Milton, Marlowe, Shakespeare and Eng Lit snobbery, still retains a greater coverage of theatre than any other art form just at the very moment theatres are thankfully being closed by capital through cuts in state expenditure. Privately however, the Communist party is grieved by its failure to make any headway among yout, but recently, because it has recruited into its ranks, disillusioned radicals - now quiet reformists from the late 1960s (both theoretically and practically), the cultural image has been given a facelift. Thus, The Soft Machine was billed alongside Santiago Carrillo (boss of the Spanish CP) in the Communist party's People's Jubilee at Alexandra Palace. But hippy music was no longer even then the trend and those late 1960s ex-revolutionaries wallowing in nostalgia cannot put a Communist party Humpty Dumpty back together again, even if, being hip to racism, they at least had the savvy to bring the reggae band Aswad from Ladbroke Grove. But to really grab the centre stage, they should have taken a cue from those other ex-revolutionaries who processed punk.

The Trotskyists, particularly the Socialist Workers party, quicker off the mark and more hipply opportunist, rushed to recruit punk by setting up front organizations, like Rock Against Racism, accompanied by appallingly banal photo news sheets, such as Temporary Hoarding and Rentamob, to bring together punk and reggae in a pathetic pseudo attempt to combat racism, seeing that blues drenched rock stars like Eric Clapton were sounding off about "wogs". The libertarian, ultra left quickly grabbed the content of punk lyrics and the movement was discussed with approval in the pages of Social Revolution. But the common factor, which seemed to underlie the debates from the left to the ultra-left, was the fear of fascism, which again is making a re-appearance amidst all the modernizing tendencies in post 1968 capitalism.

After having first gagged at the image of punk, the left and ultra left quickly realized that the content was all about lousy social conditions and therefore OK. (After all the photo of The Clash on their first CBS recording suggested all the complex trajectories of the 1970s; a kind of melange of the Russian Red Army mixed in with Manchester United's football club's Red Army - "we're the worst behaved supporters in the land" and who can at times even give off an aura of Ernst Rohm's Storm Troopers). The common denominator on the left was the anti-fascist alliance, which of course, the ultra-left quite rightly scorns, but in both camps, the material processes behind punk and reggae consumption were left without comment. That is the quantitative technical changes in the mode of production of the music in the 1970s, its form of capitalization, (the relation / antagonism between small and big capital) and marketing outlets. As usual, the left concentrated on the content of the lyrics and not the form of production, and what makes them even more pathetic was their pitiful analysis of the source of the content. The spectacle cannot be changed in its essential dictatorship but it can and is constantly altered.

Periodically, pop music has floundered into no-go periods, but it did seem as if it had reached an ideological, if not economic dead-end in the I970s. It was the most severe ideological rock crisis ever and the next will be even better for us. The Golden Age of protest - at $5 dollars a throw - of Dylan, the Stones, Sly and the Family Stone etc., had come to an end. The large music companies, with their periodic sclerosis had again turned their backs on innovation even within a recuperated capitalist framework. More fundamentally, the revolutionary hopes of the 1960 s lay in schizoid turmoil with some hesitant forward movement.

 Some of the most famous superstars lay dead, (read: some of the most sacrificial, fucked over and naive victims of capital) – Janis Joplin Mama Cass, Jim Morrison, Jimi Hendrix etc. Others had simply cracked up and were trying to play some fine tricks on madness, John Lennon, Bob Dylan, Brian Wilson, Mick Jagger etc. But amidst this grave yard-cum-asylum, some aspects of capital, particularly film, were willing to explore with a greater objectivity, the structural relations vis-à-vis exploitation in musical capitalism. Stardust accurately portrayed the musician as a highly paid, surplus value producing worker (perhaps part of a new labour aristocracy) who is virtually forced to sell every part of the self to the company and is suicided by this total alienation.

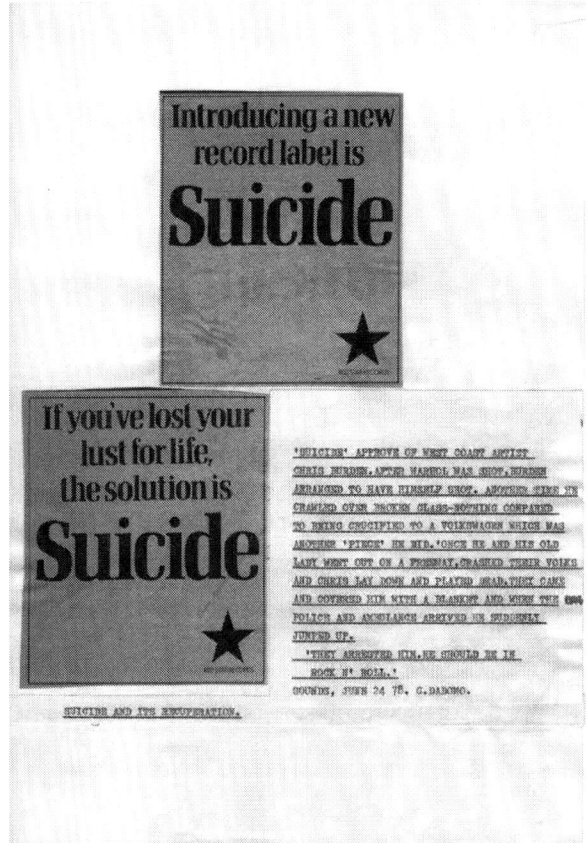

"Any person in today's music scene knows that rock, classical, folk and jazz are all yesterday's titles"

Sleeve cover remark on Ornette Coleman's 'new' LP Dancing in your Head

Even such a jazz superstar has been forced to accept some of the inevitable but leaves a suitable opening back into the artistic fold and like so many artists, is unable to recognise in the self activity of the proletariat the only authentic creativity left. Was the beginning of such a realization confusedly present when Albert Ayler threw himself off Brooklyn Bridge in 1970? Perhaps he sensed jazz was dead and that improvisation was moving onto another terrain - towards unlimited revolutionary improvisation - ultimately freeing daily life from the shackles of bourgeois political economy? Certainly there can occur at such fundamental juncture an impasse, which an individual cannot immediately supersede, an impasse resulting in desperate madness. Perhaps Ayler didn't know which way to turn apart from a downturn into the black waters of the Hudson River? Like so many of his colleagues, he could have withdrawn; settling for the null business Jazz had become and as substitute produced relatively unimaginative political music. The reggae superstars were to do no less, but in so doing neglected "the recovery through transfer" (Marx) which the essence of subversive creativity now historically demands.

At such an impasse where to turn? Part of the answer came from a not totally unexpected quarter. The most revolutionary critique of the late 1960s - that of the Situationists - suddenly had a raison d'etre for capital. After being suitably doctored, such a critique could be used as a force able to keep pop music kicking as pacification agent of the young proletariat both in terms of channelling energy into hierarchical aspiration, fake liberation from drudgery and the goal of a higher level of wage slavery with all its alluring but alienated sexual appeal.

A musical situationism was born in the dressed up rebel imagery of punk and new wave. While, the Situationist influence can only be thoroughly credited in the one specific instance of the Sex Pistols, the rebellion of modern art forms, first expressed pictorially and in literature, though now recuperated, has been increasingly applied to the production of music through intermediaries like The Velvet Underground and Lou Reed. Antecedents from the old cultural avant-garde run into and feed the musical new. Ms Patti Smith, 'radical' star, all the way from New York to Barcelona, quotes on the cover of her LP Radio Ethiopia, Andre Breton's clarion call in Nadja, "Beauty will be convulsive or not be at all." After being phased out from a radio broadcast because she said "fuck", Patti Smith wrote in The Yipster Times March / April 1977, "the political awareness of the 1960s was a result of the political repression of the 1950s. The 70s have represented the merging of both..... political – artistic / activism expression."

And the emphasis is on bourgeois representation - precisely that which turns against proletarian realization. With all the panache of a Yippee sale and perhaps a bourgeois about turn, a detournement of Black Mask's, "We seek a form of action which transcends the boundary between art and politics. it is the act of revolution", Patti Smith plays a clever, lethal game more deadly than the relative naiveties of earlier phases of pop consumerism. These new stars are doubly dangerous because someone as sophisticated as Patti Smith will in all probability have access to real revolutionary material and the skill to market it with a few essential lobotomies. Not that Patti Smith wants to transcend either art or politics, for she has a great respect for bourgeois specializations. Where would her money, audience, bogus rebel charisma be without it? Take the following: "The colonial year is dead. Rock and Roll is not a colonial art. We colonize to further the freedom of space." Well, for sure this is pure mumbo jumbo as Patti Smith colonises the imagination of wage slaves, to limit the freedom of space. Not that Patti Smith is a stranger to the real owners of capital. A backer of the film version of William Burrough's Junky in which Patti Smith will star was Stern de Rothschild, heir to the Rothschild fortune.

"Nihilism idealizes in the direction of disgust" - *Nietzsche, The Will to Power*

Part of the genesis of punk goes back 10 years to the English section of the Situationists and the subsequent King Mob group, a loose affliation (hardly a group) of disparate though confused revolutionary individuals in England in 1968.

King Mob lauded and practised active nihilism. In desperation one of them said and wrote, "Revolutionaries, one more effort in order to be nihilists" thus upturning the familiar De Sadian comment deployed by the Situationists in their heyday, though for good reason as by 1969 we felt that the praxis of active nihilism should be directed against the pseudo-revolutionary pretensions of the extreme left of capital especially marked by those who insisted on abiding by a straight job. A tremendous interest was shown in the praxis of deviants: psychotics, the mentally collapsed, (it was somewhat hip to have been through a mental asylum) and petty crooks. The most deranged manifestations of hate against the present organization of society were greeted with fascination - Jack the Ripper, child killer Mary Bell, John Christie – we even sprayed up a big Christie Lives slogan opposite the former Rillington Place mews where he lived in Notting Hill.

Just look at these monstrosities produced by bourgeois society – isn't that sufficient to condemn the golden afternoon of hippy ideology? There was a greater emphasis on such horrific negatives than the revolutionary negative. Socialism or barbarism? Rosa Luxembourg's stark choice was giggled at - better barbarism. Better to be horrible than a pleasant, altruistic hippy, as a kind of un-dialectical over-reaction to hippy. Chris Grey had the idea of creating a totally unpleasant pop group, those first imaginings, which were later to fuse into The Sex Pistols, plus writing a spoof, hip, in depth, sociological report of utter degeneration in the sub-cultural milieu to be published by Penguin books and then exposed for the farce it was.

Ideas were mooted in 1968 that were sufficiently tasteless to horrify the prevalent hippy ideology and its older more, conservative forms like romantic English pantheism. For instance the dynamiting of a waterfall in the English Lake District was suggested together with a message sprayed on a rock saying, "Peace in Vietnam" not because there was a deep on-going interest in the war like there was in the United States but because the comment was an absurdist response to ruralism and the revolution had to be aggressively urban. There was a suggestion to blow up Wordsworth's house in Ambleside, alongside a Delphic comment, "Coleridge Lives". Inevitably, ideas for action also produced the psychotic suggestion: why not hang the peacocks in west London's Holland Park. That much beloved brilliantly plumed bird of the aristocracy, (largely now nationalized) would thus be found hanging on a rope in front of a huge graffiti, "peacocks is dead". But the inverted detournement of this psychically maimed, active nihilist critique was to be found within itself, that of a tranquillising agency as laughing at the nature-mystique was also combined with a subconscious love for it. The lines from Coleridge's, Ode to Dejection graffitted on a wall in Moorhouse Rd, London W 11 already contained the seeds of a passage back into rural romanticism; "a grief without a pang, void, dark and drear, a stifled drowsy unimpassioned grief". With the degeneration of King Mob, (at the instigation of Chris Grey playing the songs of Leonard Cohen) a tranquillizing acceptance largely won out, bringing about a delayed fusion with hippy ideology and junkie clamouring, of Aleister Crowley cum the Brethren of the Free Spirit, all heading in the direction of the new mysticism. Even rain on a window pain was fetishized as conceptual art.

In terms of revolutionary critique however, no sound basis was there and neither did one gradually unfold. History was too frowned upon and the spontaneous act was sufficient unto itself. The name King Mob itself, came from the Gordon Riots in London in the late 18th century when on the walls of the newly built gutted prison of Newgate the signatories of the insurgents, "His Majesty King Mob" were placed. On the one hand, King Mob applauded uncritically the black riots and the activities of the Motherfuckers in the USA while on the other hand, opportunistically collaborated with a whole consortium of Trotskyists and Maoists, (Maoist spontaneists) under the umbrella of the Vietnam Solidarity Committee. The actions only could have, (and did have) reformist conclusions. Powis Square in Notting Hill was aggressively opened up as a children's playground though in reality it was a kind of King Mob guerrilla theatre bringing imagination to the assistance of social democracy. Such activity was well recuperated in advance, supplying the muscle against the cops for the benefit of the Labour left and providing a cunning debut for the future careers of Adventure Playground Leader. In themselves, adventure playgrounds' limit and contain a youthful sense of play, (as vandalism or whatever) to an area designated by the social worker-cum-artist under the guidance and money of local councils and charities.

King Mob's hysterical over emphasis (without adequate explanation) on violence, whether Futurist or contemporary hooligan outbursts, played into the hands of a charismatic romanticism of deeds that mistakenly equated genuine theoretical development with the dead hand of academia. Without such a distinction the way was open for the grotesque return of English philistinism and the renewed acceptance of the university salon. It was energy itself that was needed, an excess of energy, which fostered an apocalyptic fear of the imposed extending passivity; the big sleep, the hunkering down under, the steady job. Fear too, that this fate lay around the corner for each individual who wasn't seen to be radiating personal energy. Do Something: it didn't matter that you carried Vaneigem in one pocket, while the other contained a manual on the 'new' participatory social democracy, (peoples' associations, law centres, neighbourhood 'soviets' in twilight areas, all coupled with a 'militant' market research manual cum con for finding out "the wishes of the people") .In any case one could always threaten bombs and call for the arming of the working class. The superman / woman militancy and the subsequent terrorism came with the tragic loss of the sense of game and vandalism through theoretical and practical confusion caused by having to confront a fresh series of problems.

From the breakdown of King Mob, other tendencies developed. One trying to live out the ideologies of a politically conscious hippy life style, somewhat akin to the American Yippees, the more honest became openly terrorist (the tragedy of' the Angry Brigade), others became careerists in the university set up. Those university arseholes, The Sociology of Deviancy, were able to maintain Trotskyist connections (mainly Socialist Workers' Party) and dealt – (and still deal) - with all kinds of issue problems generated by capitalism (modern or otherwise): sabotage, survival in high security prisons, drug taking, thieving, suicide, soccer violence, Weatherman bombing,(uncritically clapped on the safer sidelines) with dubious paradigms derived from the Chicago Sociology School.

It's an academic sociological situationism there to promote reforms, to awaken top state functionaries to their own glaring insufficiencies, and more pointedly keeping sociologists on relative sinecures as intelligence spies of the state. Others settled for obscurity, but even as they accepted lowly positions, they reproduced capital's status quo as low-grade social workers, teachers, shop stewards, production managers - even though they were all suffering from schizophrenia. Only a small minority avoided recuperation and they were mainly women in a one parent family situation.

Chris Grey continued with the same opportunisms but on a well-publicised level, as his charisma was very appealing to dippy rich women whom he could then part from their wealth in smart parts of the city. Although maintaining independence from state institutions of ideology, to keep up his image when the revolutionary passion faded, Chris Grey increasingly glamorised, forms of breakdown and vandalism before moving into a neo-religion which put together, Reich, Vaneigem, some aspects of Eastern religions and business. Vandalism became promoted like the sales hype for a vacuum cleaner, and by picking on certain moneyed freaks who were into a bit of destruction (before settling down into some professional role) were held up as examples to the more proletarian voyeurs of a now jaded King Mob leadership to faithfully mimic themselves even though they had been veterans of many acts of spontaneous vandalism years previously.

But this was working class vandalism and therefore not blessed with the same quality. A certain tendency towards the ideology of individualism manifest in Vaneigem was incorporated into the old petite bourgeois perspective of the "self made man". now hip entrepreneur. Chris Grey preferred to cover up the social relations involved with his invocation of how great it is to be a "self made man" and, as always upset – with the immediate straight forward come back, "No, he's a capitalist". The small entrepreneurial capitalist extended in this milieu from Benny Gray's Antique Emporium, Alan Marquason and his carpet business, "we're only ripping of the rich" quite forgetting who made the carpets, the small Reichian mystical firm, "here's mud in your third eye" to the situationist turned semi spiv McLaren (though there are others).

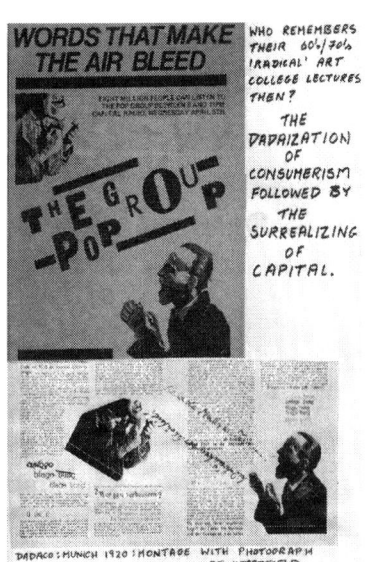

This form of hip capitalism coming from the overt recuperation of a bowderalized Situationist critique in the UK was really the capitalizing of active nihilism inherent in the activities of King Mob, continuing to exist as a nostalgic, dearly beloved memory, static and un-self critical. In the case of punk, it meant returning active nihilism to a consumed passive nililism via rock venues. King Mob eventually gave an extra fillip to the marketing of disintegration, and ironically, became more noticeable in the late 1970s than in the late 1960s because of the sale of the mass market artistic anti-art, with pop music gone Futuristic / Dadaistic (e.g. Eddie and the Hot Rods use of Crowley's photo of himself wearing Mickey Mouse ears looking like a pervy Oxford Don).

Malcolm McLaren, manager of The Sex Pistols had been friendly with individuals versed in the Situationist critique in England and had picked up some of the slogans and attitudes of that milieu. He fairly quickly realised not much money was to be made through revolutionary subversion and after taking over Goldsmith's College of Art union and freely distributing national union of students cards to whoever needed them, (like some mini situationist 1966 Strasbourg university scandal) and heckling James Baldwin as "the black man's Billy Graham", by the early 1970s McLaren had turned to the sale of a chic sado masochism, which was a growing market, with the1970s accelerating sexual chaos and the flip side to earlier Reichian therapy relaxation sessions. His shop SEX was opened up in Kings Road, Chelsea which sold T shirts on which were stencilled, "Be reasonable demand the impossible", or "Take your desires for reality", *(slogans from Paris 1968)*, which now meant, buy some of my kinky gear - that rubber suit on your left for example - and help make me a rich man.

Capitalizing on all the miseries of fucked up sexuality and love, McLaren nevertheless had a mission. Under the guise of an ostensible 'liberation', he wanted to promote repressive de-sublimation, voyeuristically. Get your repression out on the street for everyone to have a look at with the aid of various sexual commodities. Loosen up repressive de-sublimation and give it a more rebel image vis-à-vis more archaic forms of sexual sublimation and practise. Make your alienated privacy into a public thoroughfare, but don't try to supersede repression, as that would not be good for business.

The Sex Pistols were merely the musical extension of SEX. McLaren spotted the kid who was to become Johnny Rotten loafing around next to the jukebox in SEX. In addition to that McLaren was no stranger to avant-garde pop and before owning the shop, he managed briefly The New York Dolls, still flashing on about the Situationists. Also two pro-situ's who had worked on Surburban Press in south London's Croydon, (a marginally better underground paper which had printed texts of Lefebvre and Vaneigem) became roadies for the Sex Pistols. Among the other pro situ's were Jamie Reid, responsible for the bands artwork and imagery, and Fred Vermorel, the press preson, who had once produced the intelligent and witty International Vandalism and amusing one off Gestetner sheets.

Rotten and Co were fed lyrics from this formidable source now having slid over to the side of reaction. The title of the Pistols first EP, Anarchy in the UK, is a vinyl Ravachol blaring out a message of destruction, though in fact it was the opposite of destruction, and was lifted straight from the title of a defunct anarchist magazine. Iggy Pop's No Future the B side to God Save The Queen was fronted by a snarling, "Here's a sociology lecture, a neurology lecture, Fuckology" read, 1960s subversion of specialisms and the lecture bazaars turned into the music of salesmanship. A subversion that was lived directly, active though confused, had been turned into its opposite, a consumerism for a passive audience and no longer an incitement to the destruction of the university , but an adjunct to the university as Saturday night entertainment. The ambience neatly fits in with the present conformism of students scared by the presence of high unemployment.

Posters advertising Sex Pistols' records were imitative of the Situationist comic strip. The EP, Pretty Vacant was promoted through a poster campaign displaying cut out photos of long distance coaches heading for BOREDOM and NOWHERE and lifted straight from the pages of Point Blank, the now defunct American situationist group. Holidays in the Sun, is the musical cache of the bubble speak of the SI pamphlet Ten Days that shook the University, ten years on. Accurate revolutionary comments, "Culture, ugh, the one commodity which helps sell all the others, no wonder you want us all to go for it" become culture again, the raison d'etre behind bubble diversion now lost in a welter of meaningless bubbles.

"Wanna see some history cos I got a reasonable economy" (????!!?!????)

"I don't want a holiday in the sun, I wanna go to the New Belsen" (huh, you what???)

The only reasonable line is the last one:

"A cheap holiday in other people's misery"

The sleeve cover itself is decorated with an almost straight lift from an early situationist drawing, reproduced in Free Fall's publication, Leaving the 20th Century.

McLaren, having a situationist pedigree, knew only too well that the image of the Sex Pistols should be as against other punk groups. Anti traditional academia, he snidely said, "The Stranglers will work well on the college circuits", probably because they are 'good' accomplished musicians for 'good' accomplished students. Anti intellectual, as befits a capitalist inclined pro-situ, McLaren chides The Clash for being the intellectuals of the movement. There's only one real forte left after that: and its spontaneity. For McLaren, the Sex Pistols are disturbing because "their spontaneity is something people feel a little threatened by", (all quotes from New Musical Express, March 19th, 1977) no matter that it is another variation of spontaneous substitutionism so well described by John Barker, theoretical protagonist of The Angry Brigade ,even as he was trapped by a further substitutionism, terrorist substitutionism. Re, The Who, Barker had said, "We contemplate other people destroying the environment we want to destroy" (Birmingham, Radical Arts magazine, 1969.

The society of situationism is in the process of appearing in the Anglo American world, largely through recent tendencies in pop music, academic situationism in sociology and art history, the new religions, (Sri Bagwhan and the insertion of Vaneigem into Taoism, the sexuality which says anything goes). In production, the mystique of 'self management' and workers control which the experiences of the last few years (the Clyde shipyard work-in, the Lip watchmakers work-in and the Portuguese 'revolutionary' co-operatives between 1974-77) has called into question and affects the validity of workers councils, at least as they have been previously conceived e.g. the Workers Parliament in Russia, and the broadly social democratic content of all previous workers councils. Unlike, France or Italy, there are no Vaneigem-ist town planners or Debord-ist economists writing for influential journals or ensconced in the state apparatus. But no matter, their practise will be broadly the same, that is some kind of modernism whether their forlorn inspiration comes from "small is beautiful" Schumacher or Debord. The extent of the recuperation is slowly emerging in spite of the economic crisis, which one mistakenly assumed would have curtailed such experiment. The gaps in previous revolutionary critique are becoming painfully obvious.

Punk is the admission that music has got nothing left to say but money can still be made out of total artistic bankruptcy merely acting as a surrogate substitute for creative self-expression in our daily lives. Punk music, like all art, is the denial of the, revolutionary becoming of the proletariat. When the Situationists said, "art is dead" they weren't wrong, merely, that the capitalization of music wasn't developed as a critique, preferring instead to concentrate on The Angry Young Men rather than Bill Haley and his Comets.

Indeed "Art is dead" had something of the aura of revolutionary nostalgia about it, encompassing the Dada period and the failed German revolution of 1918-20, Russian constructivism and early Surrealism. With the Situationists, the critique of art had developed from traditional activities confined to the studio or garret, to include the film maker of nouvelle vague persuasions, the Happener, the Architect, the Town Planner but music was left without explanation. Perhaps this can be explained by the fact that France and Italy were effectively insulated from the rock 'n' roll craze of the 1950s and 60s. But such neglect did mean that pro-situ's in Anglo / America could flirt with rebel musicians of the spectacle and enjoy the romantic posturing of the latest American films like Pat Garret and Billy the Kid, Easy Rider, The Wild Bunch which had an effect on the style of active nihilism and on The Angry Brigade.

Intervention against music was almost totally absent, as far as can be ascertained. Frank Zappa at the London School of Economics was heckled and disrupted, to the point where he could no longer perform and shouts of "Up against the Wall Mothers" in Newcastle-Upon-Tyne were heard. An insurgent Billy Howell, in 1973, for more subconscious reasons, put Zappa in hospital for a few weeks at the Rainbow, Finsbury Park. One bloodthirsty leaflet hinted at assassination, The Death of Art spells the Murder of Artists and called for imitations of Valerie Solonas's shooting of Andy Warhol, together with a rub-off list of choice targets including (among others),

Bob Dylan and John Lennon. Although the leaflet had shock value, it was basically two faced, (notwithstanding the hermetic terrorisms no assassination was remotely intended) because Dylan, along with The Who, and the Rolling Stones and particularly The Velvet Underground, were regarded as something meaningful in this radical milieu.

In this identification, the participants were still marked by the pop era. A number of pro-situ's hung for a while expectantly around Max's Kansas revue bar in New York, venue of Lou Reed and The Velvet Underground. There was no desire to negate music, ("great music falls short of our desire"- Rimbaud) merely to make it free, but leaving intact the antagonistic structure which turns audience against performer, creator against consumer and vice versa in a relationship of near reciprocal alienation. The violent clashes at rock concerts (e.g. the Isle of Wight, 1970) were attempts to have the commodity without the cash nexus, so it wasn't really an active critique of the capitalization of music. Only now, is a more developed critique shaping up.

THE NON-POLITICS OF MUSICAL RECUPERATION

("Yeah, like man, I do think Baader Meinhof should be given independence")

Although, Situationist theory was a general theory of subversion against world capitalism, as a movement, it nevertheless did not encourage any investigation of particular differences vis-à-vis national capitals. It's long been recognised but never developed, that English revolutionaries influenced by the Situationists should develop a critique of the peculiarities – the swamp - of English society. Failure to have done so is precisely what helps punk acquire rebel status with minimal contestation of that status.

The much lauded punk politics is more accurately an attempt to update the mores of a fossilized bourgeois structure in the UK through a form of guerrilla tactics in music, (placed in terms of the capitalist mode of production) which is meant to shake awake England's dreaming. Vinyl violence bred its predictable mirrored response in everyday life. Thus, although Johnny Rotten had his faced slashed by Queen and Country mobs and Paul Cook had to spend time in hospital with head wounds received from thugs wielding iron bars, it is still a movement through trends in consumption for modernizing capitalism, which even Tom Nairn with his desire for an efficient, meritocratic capitalism in the UK shouldn't find that amiss. Basically punk is an attack by capital against "the enduring quintessentially English archaisms".

How is this expressed? It is expressed, not only in rebellion against the influence of the aristocracy (God Save the Queen)but pretends to contest the cachet of social provenance and its fall out, the-know-your-place, lurid class fetishisms of the English obsession with genealogies', which usually is an effective barrier to a scientific analysis of class structure. As punk is populist spectacle, the popular responses are reflected there too, even though the demagogic anti-county, anti horse and hounds bias is merely good rhetorical cover for punk musicians to head in the very direction they criticize, thus making a mockery of clear-cut class vengeance. Expressing venom against public schools, inherited privilege based on birth, accent, manner and pleasant behaviour, can in a minority of instances be the entrance ticket to that very domain.

Initially, punk expressed itself as a musical class-in-itself, ouvrierism encapsulated by capital. Ironically, even in the beginning, it was already typical demagogic ouvrierism, as the musician who emphasized class the most, Joe Strummer of The Clash went to public school. Punk is merely another response, this time in terms of art, to the complex miseries of the 'social apartheid' in the UK. Working class is middle class; middle class is working class in this tortured state of affairs. At one and the same time class is emphasized in order to promote career stridently, through resentment of the more traditionally cultured and secure middle and upper classes, who are prepared to give way to, be turned on to, the new members to their ranks with all their slovenly habits, natty dress and accents, because these new members have relinquished all desire to rid society of classes and the wages system and therefore their ouvrierism can be acknowledged as exciting entertainment.

On the other hand, the loudly proclaimed working class emphasis while one is in fact, middle class - in whatever profession - is often used as a rhetorical gambit to confuse the proletariat, keeping them in their place through manipulation. One of the more subtle, subjective reasons for the success of the present 'social contract', and the management of increasing austerity since the Labour government came to power, has been PM's Callaghan's often repeated comment - like some subliminal ditty - that he is working class himself because he came from a working class background.

A critique of the monarchy and the aristocracy in general, is not irrelevant, because as a class fraction, it is still the focal point of privilege in the UK. The snooty, Oxbridge, amateurish ways, a Civil Service of Eng Lit persuasions and, most importantly, the Official Secrets Act, which is there to protect the public school product from any public scrutiny, floats free from its social base and spreads throughout the whole fabric of society enforcing secrecy and deviancy everywhere throughout English life. Ironically, the Sex Pistols, God Save the Queen though banished by the state, did more to harm the image of the monarchy in Jubilee Year than any of the campaigns of the left, which again demonstrates their nullity when in competition with a rebel spectacle they invariably support. The banning of God Save the Queen on radio and TV (both private and state) even caused a ripple of interest on the continent where it was sometimes said that the function of the British Monarchy applied to other European monarchs. The comparisons were arbitrary for the simple reason that European monarchs present themselves more as the common people, thus, the Swedish and Norwegian monarchs queue at bus stops.

Gut hostility against the aristocracy outside of the UK produces more incomprehension than anything else. Even American anglophiles find it difficult to understand, and even a knowing musician like Randy Newman said, "Why get worked up about a goddam Queen anyway" and apropos of Rotten and Co, "I thought it was funny for anyone to come on that vicious" *(New Musical Express, Sept 24th 1977).*

For the West Indians things are different. Gut hostility against the aristocracy is well understood but through the refracting lens of an old ultra-colonialist perspective, which helps the rebel reggae spectacle on its way, emphasising past roots and slavery which is now a sentimental cultural diversion from the real problem, the abolition of wage slavery which could never be conceived of in terms of 'progressive' racial identification. In Third World's, Slavery Days, the taught, sleek and spare voice of English upper class command is imitated, "Prices are at an all time low, I think we should free them niggers actually" piss take on that accent, the demagoguery is again to the fore for the reggae artists, like professional spokesmen / women at black meetings in Britain, grieved by the bone hard hierarchies of the fossilized, almost pre-bourgeois superstructure in the UK, which will not fully accept them.

In parenthesis however, this musical nostalgia must be seen also in terms of a democratization of the music market, where many different types of "Roots" culture has been recently promoted to keep the near corpse of rock 'n' roll alive by countless blood transfusions. A near corpse that moreover, will try anything to keep interest in sales alive, like bringing punk and reggae together in a fine gesture of anti-racist sales hype. But this democratization must be seen in terms of world changes in capitalism and the necessity of finding ever new consumer markets. When Island Records looks to the Nigerian market with African hopefuls, it is not out of whimsy but because advanced Black African nations with growing and powerful working classes, (e.g. Ghana and Nigeria) have experienced a consumer take off, which could take them out of the category of third world countries.

Although punk is political, it has hardly been used as such, excepting the Trotskyist, Rock against Racism - a Socialist Workers party front organization – who, for example, arranged a gig in Wigan Casino, Lancashire on Sept the 8th 1977, to coincide with the arrival of the Right to Work march on their way to the TUC conference at Blackpool. Fossilized protest and fossilized rock together - 800 marchers with 800 boppers. But this use of white rock by politicians, or aspiring politicians, is in its infancy when compared with reggae. Where would the clever and cunning, social democratic PM of Jamaica, Michael Manley be without reggae? As Manley said, "reggae is much more accurate than a political machine when it comes to gauging mass reaction."

In the 1972 election campaign, Bob Marley and the Wailers, like the majority of Jamaica's musicians supported him - a factor enabling him to win at the polls and Marley's campaign song was, Better must come. The same was true for the 1976 election where one of Marley's concerts was scheduled to take place in front of the Presidential Palace before the December election in Jamaica. The gesture was reciprocated and one of Michael Manley's political tactics was to watch a whole reggae concert, clearly visible and without protection at the Cayamanas, race track so the vast crowd could dig his courage.

In 1976, Marley's election song was Under Heavy Manners - the phrase used by Manley and repeated ad nauseam - when he introduced his draconian security measures in 1976 against the gunmen. There had been 300 political murders before the bill was passed. The use of the term "gunmen" was quite arbitrary - it didn't matter if you were left, right or revolutionary. Marley acted as faithful apparatchik:

"This is a State of Emergency in a Jamdown.
Gunmen, you better change your plans"

Bob Marley paid the price with a bullet in his head but he wasn't the only reggae musician to be tailed by a hit man. Jah Stitch working in Marley's Tuff Gong record shop was also shot in the head. Both recovered. This seemed like the realisation of leftist wish fulfilment- artists for radical politics, even to the death. Despite the real ferment below, which found its musical recuperation through reggae, the violent conflict in Jamaica is between two formations of capital. One, the Jamaican Labour party supported by the United States and the CIA, the other, Manley's Peoples' Progressive Party, which seems more 'independent' with its programmes of social democratic, state capitalist nationalizations and increased monetary benefits for the huge and growing surplus population. It's a social democracy which is attractive to the economically deprived Rasta base from which reggae has largely drawn its audience. Manley merely uses the music for his own electoral ends as his strongest constituency support comes from a combination of those Jamaican middle classes supporting an emotionally nationalistic, primitive anti-imperialist perspective and (more importantly) the surplus population. Inevitably, the latter are more drawn to him than the Jamaican middle classes who may now prefer a more right wing solution. Manley has no choice but to use reggae as a ploy to keep in with the surplus population, precisely because reggae cannot be a revolutionary force and is only Rastafarian chic sold under the guise of Dread rebellion. For example, capital was made out of the shooting of Jah Stitch by his promoter Bunny Lee who even produced a record of the event to boost Stitch's record sales, "No Gun Can't Dead a Man Wid A Dread Pon Him Head" (Oh really.) Drama must never be taken at face value and for good measure, the dub group; The Revolutionaries are in every way pillars of the reggae establishment.

SLEEVE COVER FOR RIP REGGAE E.P. ALL THE'RE' DESIGN HAS HISTORICAL PRECEDENTS AND THE PHOTOGRAPHER KNOWS HIS RAY BAY-THE ONELY ANGLED PHOTO LIKE A BRANCUSI SCULPTURE WITH THE BASE CHOPPED OFF.

Rebel music has been inserted into the state apparatus of Jamaica – more or less - as a stabilizing ingredient, even though the production of the music continues to remain in private hands. Until recently, maximum surplus value was often extracted from Jamaican musicians who frequently didn't get paid (c/f Perry Hensel's film The Harder They Come). This manipulation by the state of rebel music is without precedent in western type social democracies but in the more thorough going totalitarian state capitalist regimes like Mao's China and Castro's Cuba it's fairly common.

Consider the use Castro has made of subversive music - trova cubana - and note how a form can be turned into its opposite by skilful manipulation. The following is from El Pais 24th of July 1977.

"La trova cubana, commenced some years ago when popular singers lacking the means to get a piano, (the dominant instrument of the epoch) made their own guitars cut mostly from materials as basic as boxes of packing. Going from town to town like real troubadours inventing a song for each bend in the road utilizing the particular materials and themes of the places through which they passed. This music was a mixture of African that was imported with slavery and Spanish themes, (above all Andalusian) that came with colonization. These first troubadours had never complied with the general public that was under the sway of the demoralizing effects of melodramatic songs called La Habana. But in spite of it, the first troubadours introduced new forms - its basic innovation was the "filin" (degeneration of the English word "feeling") Filin was marked by popular language and was slow in being accepted by fashionable singers."

With Castro's putsch, things changed. On the cultural terrain, spectacular advances were made. *[El Pais ibid]*

"Singers like other branches of the arts came to be considered as elements of cultural dynamization, receiving a fixed salary and having access to the mass communication media. Many troubadours applied themselves henceforth to singing about the revolution and its successes……. the great majority threw themselves into this new employment utilising the same colloquial expressions and the same expressive simplicity as always."

In reality of course, the troubadours were helping cement together the fabric of a Cuban society which was to become more totalitarian and oppressive than Batista's Cuba (C/F Sam Dolgoff's, Cuba, a Critical Perspective, despite the anarcho-syndicalist illusions.) Cuba's army managed state capitalism, along with its countless spies, to maintain the illusion of social revolution and the troubadours assisted in this image making. In 1967, a festival was held in Havana named "Protest song get together" which resulted in the creation of a movement by young Cuban authors and singers that has called Nueva trova which uses new styles of Latin American songs, jazz and El Rock -while retaining the same 'radical' content in love songs and elegies to fallen revolutionaries.

In terms of social democracy, reggae fulfils something of the same function in Jamaica – rebellion becomes pacification agent. It was so, even before reggae was used by the political machine. Marley's first record, Simmer Down was a tranquilliser for unemployed Kingston "rude boys" A few years later, Curfew asked, "How many bridges do I have to cross, before I get to talk to the boss" even though the chorus was for "a burnin' and lootin' tonight". Lacking a theory of structures, Marley's records are now regarded as a "sell out" by Rasta youth who formulate their dislike by objecting to Marley's Swiss bank account and his refusal to invest his money in Jamaica. On a similar footing is the naïve bitterness of JA writers like Henderson Dalyrmple who object to Marley moving from Trenchtown to hilly, wooded, uptown Kingston to join the likes of Noel Coward and Ian Fleming. Both are in a quandary through their romantic personalizing of structures which are lost to capital in the first place, which they think can be magically changed by radical 'black' personnel. Rasta

base will move on from Marley to apparently more radical, ethnic, roots bands that presumably won't "sell out". It's one of the oldest and saddest illusions of all.

Pop musicians through their super star status and wealth defend the spectacle. Nevertheless when under contract with recording companies, the structure is that of musician worker producing wealth for a capitalist. Often too, the degree of exploitation is much higher than that of an industrial worker selling his labour power to an industrial enterprise. Elvis Presley in his working life produced a massive amount of surplus value (in terms of profit, $160 million for the record companies plus $30 million for the film companies) He will probably produce as much again through his death with the re-cycling of Elvis product.

Between musician and owner, the bitter antagonism of capital and labour is again reproduced. Socially however, the hyped musician is isolated within the reality of exploitation and to achieve success must defer to capital more than a mass of industrial workers gaining confidence through collective action. Thus the revolt against capital by the pop stars is more bizarre and histrionic (e.g. the endemic freak out, or clandestine obtuseness like Eric Clapton refusing to play until his recording contract ran out, guitarist Jimmy Page dropping out onto a building site.) The frustration has never been expressed as a direct, generalized assault on musical capital as such. In all probability, it never will be because the function of art in modern day capitalism is pivotal and this 'new' labour aristocracy, should it successfully revolt against its employers, will also have to revolt against its own role. As Gianfranco Sanguinetti said, "All rebellion expressed in terms of art merely ends up as the new academy".

Punk and reggae are merely the latest recruits to enter the new academy.

THE ECONOMIC AND MORAL STATE VERSUS 'REBEL' MUSIC

Fossilized representatives of capital tried to silence punk. Who are they? Various formations of the State apparatus - the British Broadcasting Corporation / The Greater London Council, Local Councils in the provinces and Parliament where MP's like Marcus Lipton said, apropos of God Save The Queen, if pop music is going to destroy our established institutions, then it ought to be destroyed first. In truth punk was against certain fuddy-duddy attitudes embodied in some institutions, though accepting others that are rooted in capital. Who else tried to silence punk? Well, various distribution outlets in influential private hands, the International Buyers Association (IBA) / the chain store of WH Smith's and some venue ballrooms.

While the state is necessary for business, it is generally so for Dept I *(Das Kapital)* - the production of the means of production (heavy machinery etc). Exceptions of course are giant monopolies like British Leyland, Rolls Royce etc, which fall into the category of Dept II - the production of the means of consumption. Often however, state functionaries are at loggerheads with some tendencies which they regard as distasteful in the arena of consumer capital. Punk and pornography are two examples. In spite of the hysteria which spills over into the media, it is still an internecine conflict between bourgeois archaisms and those modernizing representatives of capital who are more daring in terms of marketing lurid possibilities.

An appearance to the contrary, the state is always fighting a losing battle. As Marx said, in a different context, (that of the industrial bourgeoisie against feudalism) "profit is a born dissenter" and punk is profit. Zombies in the UK state apparatus finally have to recognise the real interests of an important fraction of capital, even if it is marketing the disintegration of moral values. As Al Clarke, press officer for Virgin Records said on November 9th 1977, with reference to Never Mind the Bollock's, "The LP was released 11 days ago. It brought in £250,000 before it was even released and went straight to no 1 in the charts."

Punk was initially suppressed through a moral force present in the UK state apparatus. No law in Parliament was needed after the moral outrage of some mainly Labour party MPs who ensured through their diatribe that the English puritan consensus was respected. This morality was faithfully driven home by intermediary bodies of the state, hypocritically using safety regulations to ban punk concerts in local council halls, virtually ensuring that insurance companies could no longer financially cover concerts in private halls. But what a loud silence, as punk music got a wider and wider audience and the more the thumbscrews were turned, the more the cash registers jingled. The UK state, once able to enforce bans on music it regarded as popularly subversive, (C/F the fate of calypso and festivals in the Caribbean prior to 1850) was made a mockery of.

Now, in spite of real threats, the state lost because music has become more capitalized since the early phases of industrial capitalism. With the unprecedented development of the production of the means of consumption after the second inter-imperialist world war, the state cannot maintain any effective ban on a musical style which is capitalized by private companies. Only if a state has full control over marketing and distribution outlets can pop music be silenced. In Czechoslovakia where the state has far greater control over pop music than in the west, the pop group, The Plastic People has been silenced through the cover of a smear campaign, suggesting that pop musicians are against communist society (e.g. potential fascists etc.)

Punk rock has been promoted by small entrepreneurial record companies like Stiff Records / Anchor / Berserkely / Polydor / etc. These are companies in a kind of semi-competition with the big monopolies like EMI (Electric & Musical Industries Ltd), CBS, (Columbia Broadcasting System) WEA, (Warner Bros / Electra Records / Atlantic Records) etc, who tend to handle the record distribution of the smaller companies through superior servicing outlets (c/f the arrangement between United Artists and Island Records). Thus competition is more in terms of hip image promotion, with the small record companies winning hands down because they have their ears to the ground, unlike the cumbersome, bureaucratic ways of the large companies. As companies, they seem more liberal and hip, but when the going gets tough the tough get going. Biba's was a trendy clothes boutique catering for 1960s swinging London. Once class conflict erupted in the early 1970s in the UK and the fall of sterling had made "the right little, tight little island", the troublesome sick man of Europe, Biba for safeties sake, moved to the calmer situation of Brazil where fascism rather more abruptly guaranteed profits.

However they end up, small capital is generally the innovator, but the big companies don't remain outside of the mad scramble for long. CBS quickly signed up The Clash, and United Artists signed up The Stranglers and The Buzzcocks. EMI, in chagrin after their cold feet and the aborted contract with the Sex Pistols promoted the Tom Robinson Band - of all the new wave bands the most obviously leftish - supporting George Ince, (a gangland guy framed for a murder he did not commit) Gays and Blacks.

Punk managers want to modify the superstar system, but they can only do so in terms of the spectacle itself. Some of their more sophisticated apologists confront the problem of the spectacle, but in a very halfhearted way. After all, their jobs would be at stake if they went any further. Rock wordsmith Charles Shaar Murray said in New Musical Express, July 9th 1977."We have a new kind of rock star now, and like all other new kinds of star it arose out of an attempt to break down the star system". He goes on to note what the star system does to those caught in its "veritable Pandora's box" and it's the predictable, frightening conclusion (but without analysing the essential compulsion which drives individuals to become stars.)"So its not surprising that people get pissed off with stars, except it was exceptional naivety to believe that those folks who hit the Stardom Jackpot wouldn't get affected by it." *(Murray,ibid)*.

Then the big comedown

"That radio, television, movies, rock and roll, politics and sport alike all create stars by their very natural stardo is implicit and unavoidable. To talk of destroying the star system is completely and utterly utopian." *(ibid)*

On the contrary, what is demonstrated is CS Murray's utopian cum-social democratic perspective, because he does not recognise the spectacle as an historical category, which will be superseded by a communist mode of production. Like all previous modes of production, the society of the spectacle exists as an historical finite and there's nothing eternal about its existence.

The spectacle is in flux, and because capitalist society has become direr, its image reflects this misery and questioning. Thus, the new superstars must somehow be ordinary people - e.g. Elvis Costello isn't allowed by Stiff Records managers to have a fan club as it would look like an earlier era of rock 'n' roll. Nor would it fit in with the contemporary superstar populism of dole queue artists. Because of these glaring contradictions manifested in the spectacle effect - in the programmed marketing of an image schizophrenia, punk / new wave, is literally forced into being more dishonest than any other previous rock 'n' roll epoch. They must be poverty stricken but necessarily rich. They ride in Rolls Royce's' and wear bin liners. If the new stardom is too obviously into conspicuous consumption, they'll lose the support of a no longer marginally affluent social base in comparison to the 1960s.

Already, the recuperated fallout from 1968 had made its impact before the dawn of punk. Chris Jagger informed big brother and his radical chic partner, Bianca (famous daughter of Nicaraguan Latifundista / Paris barricade fighter and new friend of Princess Margaret, Rhoddy Llewellyn) of the subversive use of graffiti in '68. Mick Jagger, (in admiration) then hired down and outs to promote his new record; It's only Rock an' Roll. With the birth of record company graffiti, many musical con stars followed, I fought the Law / Whatever happened to Slade, etc. Punk promotion followed on from this tendency but with a DIY kit. Punk musicians had to be more sacrificial and do their own street wall graffiti promotions. They were forced into being the living embodiment of image rebellion. Thus Joe Strummer ended up in a Kentish Town magistrate's court for spraying The Clash on a wall in Camden Town.

Why was punk / new wave greeted with such hysteria? Indeed, the UK state reared itself up in a frenzied religio-secularized frothing at the mouth at the excesses of a licentious and amoral capitalism over which it pretends to preside. What greeted punk was not a critique of its pro-capitalist role but a quintessentially English moral outrage, which unites in uneasy alliance, state functionaries, managers of record companies, hip musicologists, journalists and ex-revolutionaries gone respectable. Although the American record companies were for the Sex Pistols, i.e. CBS and WEA, their local English managers were not, obviously realizing they would offend the morality of the English state. In spite of the fact that the major record companies are international corporations, they nevertheless have to take into account national ideologies.

Punk gave aspects of capital an illusory radicalism again. Small record retail businesses-owned by Virgin records were unsuccessfully prosecuted by the state for exhibiting Never Mind the Bollocks in shop windows. Dusty laws were brought from out the statute books - the 1889 Indecent Advertisement Act and in Notting Hill and Marble Arch; managers of record shops (owned by Virgin) were charged and cleared with contravening the indecent advertisement section of the 1824 Vagrancy Act. Victorian morality? It points to the state's antediluvian character as a moral, if not as an economic force, in the era of state capitalism. However, with the disintegration of values, the state must insist on the antediluvian to make the fabric of bourgeois society appear intact, as it must also act economically to maintain many an archaism.

State capitalism has moved into the arena of culture. Once various arts companies can no longer survive economically through the aid of trusts, private donations and charities, the state then becomes the most important benefactor. Artistic forms that are entering into a social and historical demise (Opera / Theatre etc) have then a preservation order taken out on them by the state, artificially arresting their decline. (Sadler's Wells, The Royal Court Theatre, Glynbourne etc) These artistic events must be maintained in the major metropolitan centres if not in the provinces. If the state adhered to its logic (always somewhat ideological anyway) laissez faire capitalism would have allowed them to die an artistic death, but the state confronted with the decay of bourgeois - and even pre-bourgeois - aesthetics, has a moral necessity to maintain their existence and the semblance of a higher aesthetic order. The state and state capitalism generally and ineffectually opposes changes in the mode of artistic production (e.g. the opposition to rock 'n' roll). Moreover, the state must try and enforce the separation between high and low art, but often has great difficulty in so doing.

Consequently, private capital is credited with the image of rebellion in the arts because it operates as a subversive force against more traditionally bourgeois attitudes. It is this tendency that holds the attention of youth, (Elvis Presley, pirate radio stations and now new wave / Reggae.) Absolutely contrary to the leftist faith in state capitalism, culturally it is private capital, which is the progressive force, as it records more accurately the bankruptcy and potential of supercession at the heart of the last phase of bourgeois society. Is it therefore not surprising, that leftist parties like the Communist party and the Trotskyists with a large theatrical / artistic membership, support culturally archaic etatist tendencies.

The modern state oscillates between acknowledging the revolt of artistic forms encompassing the 20th Century and suppressing them. Is it possible that a highly developed modern state thoroughly abandons outmoded art forms and emphasizes modernist forms like Jamaica? We will have to wait and see. As it stands, entrepreneurial capital will more readily acknowledge the void at the centre of modern survival if it is good for business. Perhaps a paradigm may be drawn from Yves Klein selling "the void" of a pocket of air - drawn with his finger- at $300 a throw.

The state subsidizes avant-garde experiments, but rather more in the period of capitalist expansion than in the present period of economic crisis. Only those states with a greater economic power, (West Germany / America and Japan) can still with something like aplomb, finance the nothing exhibition (C/F Kassel 1976 and the construction of expensive earth works funded from the proceeds of taxation). But precisely because these exhibits are not directly profit making and largely act as a drain on that part of accumulated surplus value deposited in the coffers of the state, the fury expressed over such events is more successful in preventing follow ups, than journalist-cum-TV diatribes against a profit making punk rock, such as the Genesis P Orridge / Cossi Fanni Tutti "Prostitution in the Mall " exhibition at the ICA, (the Institute of Contemporary Arts). The ensuing campaign in the media and Parliament, centred around the frittering away of tax payers moneys, re: 'good' and 'bad' causes for state funding, was effective in curbing the funding of such future ventures by that state aesthetic body, the Arts Council. Here media persecution worked in suppressing avant-garde events, whereas for private capital, scurrilous persecution of avant-garde commodities generally acts as incitement to surplus value realization.

Why do youth continually fall for the myth of stardom in rock, its recurring attraction? Because it seems more exciting than most other things, because it appears to breakdown accepted patterns of socialization? What has to be reckoned on is the enormous attraction of Punk / new wave, and glib dismissals of its ability to grab', will leave the traditional revolutionary perspective tailing the dominant spectacle.

"In England, in response to every little emancipation from theology, one has to reassert one's position in a fear-inspiring manner as a moral fanatic….. For the Englishmen, morality is not yet a problem". Nietzsche: The Twilight of the Idols.

To what extent has punk put English morality into a tighter corner than it has been in for some time? Moreover, has it really put morality in a corner, or is it really making chic play of the horrible? Isn't the anti-morality staged managed as a new sales gimmick, the 'bad' language, the cheapo clothes, the recuperated revolutionary contempt for the audience and journalists and the presentation of states of mind of the deranged 1970s psyche. And doesn't the blistering, almost psychotic nihilism encountered everywhere - no fun, no feelings and savage dreams of mayhem - even towards those closest to you - becomes the language of cash registers? Bourgeois society has bred its monsters. It objects to them at the same time as it makes money out of their deformations. Punk / new wave blandly accepts sado-masochistic sexuality almost as a riposte to the leftists who denounce it with such moralistic vehemence. Militant feminism and red puritanism have ironically added to this syndrome by 'purging' the repressions through a noisy moral outrage which has merely succeeded in burying repressions deeper and as a fallout, ironically, increasing S/M compulsions.

Though at loggerheads with each other, there is a connection between Victorian morality a la Mary Whitehouse and the moralism of militant feminism. In their methods both want the state to act against sex exploitation - a de facto recognition of the state and the excesses of the capitalization of fantasy (the capitalization of fantasy being an important factor in Dept II - the production of the means of consumption). Even one or two lapsed militant women, have finally recognised vis-à-vis English moralism that the acceptance of pornography with all its attendant alienations is better than old time English moralist hypocrisy. The problematic of sado masochism and fetish sexuality is extremely complex and ever changing nuancing seems to move in terms of epochs too.

The late 1960s and the potential revolutionary upheavals glimpsed the overcoming of repression. Punk is part of the 1970s return of the repressed and the return of fetish. As against, the idealist, almost Feuerbachian concept of love, of hippy mythology, S/M is recognised though it is not explained essentially as the savagery of commodity relations promoted visually. S/M, in major or minor manifestations is a form of sexuality that imperfectly adapts itself to commodity society, at the sametime, as the bourgeoisie must denounce it as a form of sexual 'sickness'. (It is to be noted in passing, that Freud never used the term 'sick' except with reference to those physically ill precisely because it was a too morally loaded a term.) While the left must retain their hip image and support the latest trends, they feel somewhat uneasy about the S/M characteristics of punk and the manipulation of 'depraved' tendencies outside of conscious self control. It clashes too starkly with the purified sexuality of the Christ dyed red, socialist martyr syndrome, which in reality of course, testifies to the existence of a powerful masochistic momentum, which must have at times, a sexual manifestation, if only in fantasy. It's not a question of being for or against S/M in major or minor manifestations but recognising a powerful determinant in bourgeois society, which is difficult to transcend. While it may be contested in theory, in practise, the difficulties are enormous. Marcuse in his book Eros and Civilization recognised some of the basis of a free sexuality in the complex conflict between Eros and Thanatos. In parenthesis – this is merely a hypothesis - possibly it can be said that the 1960s was Eros and a life-in-death, the 1970s, death-in-life and Thanatos. For sure, the 1970s is an epoch where the revolts of the 1960s in the loosening of everyday life, (marriage etc) has reached something of an impasse.
A growing number in the highly developed world are coming to the conclusion that all relationships are now virtually un-workable whether of the old or new varieties. While such a position may encourage a false despair, it should not be dismissed lightly as it could perhaps be the negative frontier of new fulfilments. Certainly militant lesbianism and women's separatism have revealed their limitations when the same

violent dominated / dominating syndrome of orthodox heterosexual relationships has been reproduced in the supposed avant-garde of sexual relationships. Revolutionary love will be something different but we can only know what that that will feel like with either a prolonged break with existing conditions or a general insurrection.

Dialectically too, the failure of the new experiments and more terribly, the failure of the new love could be a fact or in scraping together an insurrection (C/fF, the written introduction by the Surrealists to the film L'Age D'Or). Generally however, failure in love and its shattering pain brings nothing but the wistfulness of unrequited longing, which were the despair of the romantic poets and the misery of their many kitsch but no less real successors.

Although, punk has reflected the changing status of women in bourgeois career possibilities and their greater integration-cum-independence largely in and through the professions, it has done so with no subversion in view. In new wave, there are more women pop groups than in previous rock 'n' roll eras and not just a la Diana Ross and the Supremes. These new women's' groups have taken the commodity in all its barbarity at face value e.g. The Slits) and at one and the same time, accepting economic feminism whilst still ensconced in the brutality of the commodity.

How can the moralism which Women's Lib uses with such crusading zeal and which is a factor in creating punk notoriety, be explained..... A moral force that's become an inherent part of the state apparatus in the UK, which has rarely to resort to law though there recent exceptions like what happened at Gay Lib News.)

What is the source of this moralism? Seeing the Church is now (and has been for a long time) a weak institution morally in the English state apparatus, there has developed throughout the last 100 years or so, a formation of self appointed guardians of public morality. Though these powerful individual presences from Ruskin to Carlyle to Firmin and Muggeridge have no statutory force, they nevertheless influence those who do like local government bosses and the chiefs of WH Smiths, etc. There is therefore some collusion between these mighty secular priests. Typically in the Jubilee year, they all took offence at the Sex Pistols,God Save the Queen. What they protect is a traditional, inflexible morality - a secularised absolutism which though very formidable, is still not as inflexible as Catholic morality. Those few thinkers who have commented upon this morality - Nietzsche being perhaps the most incisive – have only made profound observations and have never gone onto formulate a theory of this stifling phenomenon. Part of its basis is in John

Ruskin and the doctrine of good works, incorporating attractive labour and skill which he's carried over into the ideology of the Labour aristocracy, the most important foundation of morality in the UK and the backbone of the Labour party. Thus it is important to focus on this general tendency and not on the cranky individuals of far right persuasions like Mary Whitehouse - the left's bete noire - which so often functions as nothing more than a noisy smokescreen for their own acceptance of a modified moral consensus. On the contrary, the over-publicity afforded to the rightist cranks means this self appointed elite which aims for the heart of the official representatives of the Labour movement is let off the hook.

This elite, which generally holds leftist sentiments garnished with Christian sympathy, cannot be separated from moral control of the aesthetic, which is why, apropos of certain developments in Dept II - the production of the means of consumption - they react with such vehemence against visual "pollution" in advertising, banning sex shops and cinema front displays, etc. Basically, this elite wants a moral austerity in consumer habits, as against a consumption which is 'vulgar'. Their psyche is one of salacious puritanism, together with a romantic feudal idyll of anti-consumerism that is popularly translated into a predilection for craft now transformed into DIY, as against passive, laid back entertainment e.g. a haughty dismissal of TV. It's really a patrician transmission of English aristocratic values to the literate / skilled working class which keeps alive the moral skill equation. (What role does Methodism play in this conjuncture?) This transmission and class extension of the puritan revolution, applied to industrial capitalism is one of the main factors in keeping together the austerity of the social contract in the present epoch, as well as a force which can try to obstruct developments in consumer capital like for instance, the CBS workers' strike in London who downed tools against producing God Save the Queen.

In all its recuperated display, punk / new wave in the consumer musical-cum-fashion syndrome has again upset the seemingly intractable English moralist dualism of good / evil, ugly / beautiful, right / wrong, etc. Bad taste has again been promoted in a country obsessed with the 'good'. Then the continent of Europe and the United States has periodically delighted in the pleasures of bad taste expressed most lucidly in Andre Breton's comment, "In the bad taste of my epoch, I wish to go farther than anybody" Why does bad taste have such subversive potential? Surely because it reduces ideological standards and the social base of these standards plus the pretence of state ideologists and professionals like teachers who insist on good English, etc. A leveller, it reduces elitism and the vanity of vanguardist theories of revolution (a la Lenin / Trotsky and the residual forms of Jacobinism in Marx and Bakunin) and thus helps to reduce self-appointed leaders of the proletariat to ashes. More broadly bad taste is a factor undermining the obsession with craft so dear to moralist olde Englande - an obsession that extends from craft trade unionism to technically expert guitar playing so beloved of musical moralists like Charlie Gillet.

"I kind of hate the way the Sex Pistols remove all musical standards" *Randy Newman NME, Sept 24th 1977*

Punk has been termed "minimalism" by that slippery opportunist Mick Farren– ex leader of The White Panthers, strike breaker at the New Musical Express, musician, (punk and otherwise) and promoter of grotty, gestetnered mags which complain about the official music press. Although an accurate description in so far as it consciously equates minimalism in the plastic arts of the 1960s to the one minute, three chord performance of some punk bands, as usual, the description remains at the level of empiricism. Not minimalism, but a theory of artistic dilution is needed, and how and if it parallels dilution of skill in the industrial working class. While there may be similarities technically, in terms of personal mystique, there is a great deal of difference; art is "sexy" in spite of its anti-art overtures, while skilled work (say on a lathe) is decidedly un-glamorous. When, Marcel Duchamp said in the early years of the 20th Century, there's no point in creating a "work of art unless it shocks" he had the minimalism of the ready-mades and the concept of "aesthetic inertia" in mind. Music had yet to shock in terms of the mass consumer market – Rock was still 40 years away - and when it came, it was to be more policed than any previous historical art form (the live rock venues which no doubt could provide a good subject for some aspiring sociologist). Punk is the most extreme form of dilution in the trajectory of rock 'n' roll, even more so than skiffle.

Malcolm McLaren was right when he said, "Christ if people bought the records for the music this thing would have died the death long since". Youth listens to punk for the attitude and not for the quality of performance, But it is the capitalisation of rebel 'attitude' and in terms of surplus value, is a bowderlised realisation of Lautreamont's maxim: "poetry must be made by all and not by one". Anyone can be a punk musician but (the Catch 22 and the bourgeois detournement) only those singled out for promotion will take advantage of the Career Opportunities on offer.

The effect of modern art experiments on pop music has become of increasing significance. By the 1960s, pop musicians were finally beginning to experiment with techniques which avant-garde artists had used in other fields of artistic expression years earlier, though for a more isolated coterie, (isolated in terms of the mass consumer market). Natural sounds used by John Cage appeared in Beatles / Pink Floyd recordings and Hendrix imitated the sound of the machine gun etc. It has however been in the 1970s that technical innovation in the mode of musical production has made the greatest strides, making manual dexterity on an instrument the legacy of a prior historical period. It has also eroded the difference between the black musical 'genius' and the poor white musical imitator.

Sounds have been produced in the 1970s which nearly bear comparison with Hendrix's skill, (e.g. the reggae reverb ricochet) and increasingly, records are processed which use all the techniques of a recuperated Dada montage like say, David Bowie borrowings from William Burroughs. Mixing, dubbing and tracking are gradually becoming more necessary than individual genius, with the production managers having a more central function in music. The electronics expert has become more of a musician at the same time as the musician has to become more acquainted with electronics. The greatest impetus to this development has come through the evolution of reggae in Jamaica where the processed recording has played a greater part than live performance.

Dub grew from the mobile discos and sound systems. King Tubby, one of the first innovators, was originally, by trade, an electrical engineer who built sounds systems and was able to use the essentials of bass and drums, keyboards and vocals and drop them in and out of the mix in random sequence shot through with massive voltages of reverb, echo and ricochet. No wonder, black kids in the UK are more interested in sound systems than in becoming musical artists themselves, and in contradictory ways have already left behind the concept of the artistic individual.

Moreover, in terms of artistic dilution, the development of synthesizers has played a hidden and subtle role. Now a novice can make a sound like a skilled musician in 15 minutes, even with a one finger melody. Inevitably, the Trade Fairs promote these technological developments. For instance, the Skywave Synthesizer was launched on August 17th in London at the British Musical Instruments Trade Fair. The guy who designed the Skywave also developed an instrument called the Bio Activity Translator which translates plants natural electrical signals into sound and was exhibited at the Festival for Mind and Body at Olympia, London, in the spring of 1977. (How about a new thing, minimalist plant music with a beat???) Dealers can now customize organs to suit individual needs such as those customised by Thomas Musical Instruments in California. In a sense, music already heralded its own demise. In jazz, the importance of sound was favoured much more than the actual music as such (e.g. Coltrane's later music), when under the influence of African music, it was necessary for the music to follow the pitches of the language. Now music has to follow the pitches of voltage and musicians can sound entirely different according to which producer mixes the product.

The more pop music experiences and repeats the conflicts of modern art (Duchamp's double barrel effect) and the more it is processed by the application of scientific technique to a musical mode of production which is capitalized, the more the possibility is there for pop music to move to the point of negation. This time, it will no longer only be of relevance to the private affairs of an aesthetic elite but through its extensive capitalization in the mass music market, the end of music will be of relevance to the mass of the proletariat.

The Critique of Unemployment

The social base of punk and reggae is largely the unemployed. Marx in his analysis of the surplus population divides the unemployed into three categories.

A. "The floating population" which relates to the periodic lay offs experienced by the industrial working class.

B. "The latent population" -agricultural workers who are thrown out of work or displaced (c/f today, emigration from the Iberian peninsula to the North European states.)

C. "The stagnant population" those under the rubric of "domestic industry" which grows proportionally in comparison to the other two categories. Those involved in the farming out of work, (e.g. Conway Stewarts use of cheap labour in the Welsh Valleys) disabled employment and most importantly, those people who "succumb to their incapacity for adaptation due to the division of labour". *(Marx, Capital 1)*

It's a pointed sentence and one which relates to a huge social crisis of roles which goes beyond the actual surplus value producing proletariat. often concomitant with a stultifying repetition, (e.g. the routine of the detail worker) which "cripples to the point of abnormality" *(Capital: The Working Day)* and extends to a huge role rejection of the agencies of capital and the final trajectory of state capitalism - roles which mystify the proletariat, (teacher, lecturer, ad man, foreman, artist, town planner, social worker, etc). The crisis is so pervasive that there is not a single role, paid up or otherwise and / or the subtler manifestations in the arena of personal relationships, that is immune from revolutionary critique.

The stagnant population is on its way to becoming a permanent welfare proletariat. However, to add to the complexity, subversive careerism often begins within the stagnant population where there's a whole branch of capital which feeds off its negative social standing, (its loser position). It's here that The Clash's,Career Opportunities, "the one's that never knock" knock at last. There's nothing like the complaint of bitter resentment to help you get on in the world.

The process of formation of a permanent welfare proletariat means that a group of 'marginals' are being formed who will either never work in their lives or will work very infrequently. These marginals are no longer in the great urban areas a source of labour power, loafing around and being a general nuisance as a rowdy, bawdy, riotous mob, (rather like the participants who were the core of London's Gordon Riots in 1780) in the interregnum before coercion into the mechanistic drudgery of the factory routine, but are now a permanent characteristic of the final phase of capitalism as much as plumbing is to a building.

The more intelligent bourgeois economists have in the last few years begun to see this as a disturbing reality (for them). For even if capital partakes of a partial economic upswing, fewer workers will be needed in newly built, capital-intensive plant. Marx suggests that there is no definite certainty as regards numerical reduction in the working class in terms of the valorization of surplus value. However, the history of capitalism has provided adequate evidence (with the advent of relative surplus value) that fewer workers are needed to produce the requisite surplus value, and their exploitation increases (c/f Solidarity and the labour shake out in the new Ford plant in Valencia). Such a process of capital formation is truer of the West with its greater technological developments than at present in the East where extensive exploitation of the proletariat -rather than intensive exploitation - is the rule. Over the years, extensive exploitation has combined increases in productivity of labour with a shortening of the working day. Any renewed Stakhanovism in Russia would be an embarrassment to the bureaucrats, where going slow on the job has given way to gangs of painters and decorators working so minimally that many sleep three quarters of the day on the job.

In the more highly developed economies of Europe and the USA, that famous, beautiful slogan of the Situationists, "never work" acquires a harsher reality because of the economic penalties involved, though this penalty is virtually eliminated in those countries where earnings related benefits are up to 90% of the previous wage.

However "never work", is no longer the trajectory of voluntaristic anti-work of the English hippy and pro-situ milieu of the late 1960s and early 1970s, but a never work imposed by the dictatorship of a capitalist economy in severe crisis. "Never Work" as practised by the English Situationist elite was merely an extension of class privilege, and moneys from rich parents. Money from the fruits of exploitation gave them space to look ultra radical and not for these situationist gentry the humiliation of the Labour Exchange. In reality, it was more a cultural challenge, with its antecedents in La Boheme, even though it was flung as a challenge to capital and propagandized as such.

In Notting Hill Gate, Rimbaud's, "Oh we shall never work, Oh seas of fire" was sprayed on a wall and as quickly painted out by a property conscious owner-occupier. "Never Work" was never thought through and as practised by the Situationists in the UK, it was experienced as a highhanded gesture. One cannot doubt the radicalism inherent in the never work perspective, as such a refusal does not reproduce capital unlike the working class submitting slavishly to the boss, but there is a difference between the proletarian non-workers and those who have been cushioned from the despotism of capital through being directly in receipt of surplus value through family inheritance.

Such refusal of work can however be open to all kinds of manipulation through intermediary bodies of the state, such as becoming the unpaid, voluntary social worker, (particularly intense now with the cuts in state expenditure), and concomitant with the show people their rights syndrome. Through the use of guilt - that great panacea of presumptuous leftist state bureaucrats and the aristocratic and imitative aristocratic, feminist Pollyanna's of social work – and a guilt which merely benefits liberal aspects of the state, you are coerced into falling into line. Unfortunately, the sheer marginality of those forced into the surplus population / 'never work' positions make them particularly prone to the pseudo involvement of community politics. The commendable inability and refusal to cope with alienated social roles, which often expresses itself in a kind of delirium, can be slightly pacified by the many faceted aspects of community politics, which so often traps those with the beginning of a negative perspective into unwittingly becoming, often through naivety, fifth column social workers. This is often the trap laid for the ex-educated members of the surplus population.

The stagnant population is also one of the formations where 'bogus' alternatives make their appeal and where "small is beautiful" schemes find their mug workers, with, for example, the ruralisation of the inner cities (C/F Ed Burnham's county type, cabbage patch in Camden Town). In Notting Hill, Meanwhile Gardens was built by cheap labour from the surplus population who built their hippy-cum-OD park with wages almost at the level of pauperisation.

Capital does not want a permanent welfare proletariat, and where possible, is prepared to go to considerable lengths to conceal the evidence. Thus President Carter's proposals for the creation of social work type would be more likely to kick - rather than help - old ladies across the street. Here economic imperatives are not to the fore as it costs the treasury of the state more than expenditure on welfare. In the UK, because of the economic crisis, expenditure is more limited, but the Queen's Jubilee year (1977) provided a few paternalist gestures like the making of Portobello Green by a largely Black labour force. However, the most important factor for the state is to instil the work discipline into youth and the long term unemployed in order to renew in the workless proletarian, the necessary submission demanded by capital vis-à-vis, its regular time schedules. The employment state subsidies, (job creation schemes, etc) although meant to provide a pseudo labour intensive work experience is, in fact, merely cosmetic surgery, unlike in under-developed capitalist economies where subsidized jobs, are of necessity labour intensive, (e.g. in Jamaica, where some of the unemployed are used on sugar plantations). Consequently, in the highly developed economies, reactions of work nihilism are bound to increase. For example, youths daily clean up Sunderland beach, even when there's no rubbish to be disposed of.

The logic of capital is however to try and 'do' something for the unemployed, particularly, the young unemployed before they become a revolutionary force, or before they become an overtly tragic, vandalistic-cum-suicidal fraction of the proletariat. Either outcome will not do much for the promotional image of capital. At the moment, the unemployed are a disintegrating force in capital, prone to looting, mugging and more generally, an important factor in precipitating a break down of the fetishism of law so dear to Olde Englande and the tiresome rituals of workers lobbying parliament. Having no definite target to react to everyday - unlike the wageworker - the situation of the workless is often chaotic, and they can easily take their aggressions out on each other when the commodity is not there to hit at clearly. For instance, the shutters on all the big supermarkets in the Notting Hill Carnival riot of 1977 was one of the main factors which turned the battle against the police in 1976 into the sad inter-personal fracas with heavy black racist overtones of 1977.

There is a third possibility for capital, apart from growing unemployment amidst the sop of job creation schemes and that is, job sharing. But, this will involve many difficulties not the least of which would be the unlikely acceptance of wage cuts by the unemployed. If proposed, it would be a tacit recognition by capital that the long working week is historically complete.

The permanent welfare proletariat is no longer the "industrial reserve army" of productive workers, or "the floating population" forced out of the factory because of periodic economic crisis, but also those middle class, unproductive wage labourers, forced into the surplus population because of cuts in state expenditure. Also, it is essential to recognise the hidden unemployment of many aspects of higher education (a friend cynically accurate called the art schools, a cross between the Labour Exchange and Tesco's supermarket). The unemployed do not suddenly become an undifferentiated mass with a shared identity or common aim. The ex-middle class often remain the same by becoming new elites as claimants' union organizers, left party cadres at dole offices and even aspiring punk rook journalists. The Blacks have a similar elite of pukha Locksmen and pukha Natty Dreads and have spawned the growth of black social worker agencies, run no longer by Johnny too Bads but Johnny DO Goods (e.g. the Black People's Information Centres).

The present unemployed are however ambiguously staged for capital. Either the system has to reluctantly recognize them as workers or as the harbingers of anti workers. These workless proletarians, although prone to recuperation on other levels, (social work, job creation, punk and reggae music) are forced to claim social security, and wherever possible, to augment the meagre offerings of the state, work on the side and off the insurance cards. They are therefore, (along with many others) fighting for a living wage but under a criminal guise where there are often less restrictions placed on them like in the trade union policed workaday world but because of their petty criminal position re: the state and the resultant paranoia, open communication, even among themselves, is hindered. The rule rather than the exception is who's a cop, who's going to shop me to the Inland Revenue etc. Consequently foci of friends discuss their position with each other but are quite legitimately afraid to open up communication with other proletarians because of the ever-present fear of the nark. It is a socio economic position, which acts as a dampner on forthright proletarian anger, as no one wants to get busted by the states' welfare detection agencies, whose main aim is the maintenance of the smoke screen from the authorities. Many wiles are forthcoming. The constant changing of names has become a feature of the surplus population, and was even reflected in the punk spectacle, as Mark Perry (Sniffin Glue) and Gaye Advert were busted by the SS (before they made the big time and could look on such practises as juvenilia) for earning money on the side as punk artists. The supercession of such paranoia is necessary, but it cannot be done through an idealistic ignoring of the obstacles. The material and subjective basis must be there.

For instance, one of the commendable effects of cuts in state expenditure, and of use to the proletariat, has been the redundancy notices meted out to Social Security visitors and detectives. Furthermore, the process of criminalization of the employed proletariat is also developing. Due to inflation and the social contract, many workers have taken second jobs where there are no tax or insurance cards. Increasingly too, members of the armed forces have been forced to do the same and will thus help to break down the separation between a professional army and the proletariat - a factor which could have great weight in an insurrection. There's no accurate statistical record of how many workers are involved in such rackets but it's obviously a large movement, and workers quite rightly are reluctant to come forward and tell those plain clothes cops of state accountancy - the statisticians - just how they earn their money.

The subjective factor is more difficult to evaluate within the proletariat as a whole. For workers to lose any identification with trade unionism would, of course, open up all the possibilities for real dialogue between the employed and the unemployed over work / non work, the possibilities of large scale automation, unrestricted pleasure etc. Increasingly, the objective position is there, now that the trade unions have become a state monopoly of variable capital, (of wages). A rather more favourable terrain has been created for this historic conjuncture between the waged and the unwaged because increasingly, trade unions will be identified with the state as boss. But that is only so theoretically. Practically, for now, the gap between the waged and the un-waged has never been so wide. The employed are hostile to the unemployed and vice versa. Hostile, because the employed see the unemployed as having an easy time, because they are more cushioned by welfare benefits than in previous eras of mass unemployment. On the other hand, the unemployed are hostile to the employed because they view them as straight, caught in the web of capitalist drudgery and hardly able to distinguish between the exploited and the exploited. All are mugs therefore and worth mugging. Mugs because they have no sense of riot and adventure, lack spontaneity and the grand passions, which lefties narrowly see as self-destructive. On the contrary, so-called self-destruction is often a prerequisite for a higher, more lucid grasp of life. Many of the employed undoubtedly have genocidal fantasies towards the unemployed, perhaps because they jealously resent their negative perspective. When long termers sign up for Xmas post, the regular workers increasingly give them a hard time, and are often particularly vindictive to the ex-middle class, (only economically speaking) who have dropped out from a professional role because generally, the working class still has some respect left for the professions.

Workers in this process of re-orientation must lose all sense of social democratic moralism, something much easier said than done. It's been one of the major factors in hindering their attempts at self activity in the past. A moralism about money must be superceded in the productive working class as it has had such a deforming effect upon insurgent perspectives when accepted as a permanent historical reality. Take one example. A lot of the venom in the building workers strike in 1972 was directed against The Lump by shop stewards who said that Lump workers depressed the earnings of unionized workers. By this ploy, the stewards were able to whip up a false aggression against the Lump, which really was nothing other than a foil for their own respectability yearnings because the building trade was held in such contempt by various fractions of the bourgeoisie, in particular the trade unions. The number one reason in the declamations against the Lump and writ large on agitational posters, was that Lump workers did not pay taxes and were little better than criminals. That the Lump was often divisive, and a counter tendency to unified class action was really not part of the strike strategy and action of UCATT (United Construction & Allied Technical Trades) in 1972 shows only too typically the tendencies in the early 1970s to redirect strikes onto the terrain of social capital and statifications by leftist aspiring politicians who demagogically insisted that taxation was primarily for the subsidizing of the welfare state.

In the building workers strike of 1972, a typical comment of a shop steward organizer of left labour persuasions was "workers must put their own house in order first by paying taxes correctly before we can fight capitalism and the tax havens for the rich." (Mac: chief shop steward, Barbican Building Site) The idealism is terrifying because bourgeois political economy is accepted with the Keynesian face-lift, and which is now no longer possible to practise coherently the managers of capitalism. When will it become obvious to the proletariat, that tax revenues are used only in small part for the welfare state, (about 5% of taxes) and the rest is spent on the repressive state apparatus, (the police, servants, politicians etc,) and more importantly supplies the necessary extra revenue required by the huge corporations to fund their long term investment programmes, guided by state technocrats with the aim of making British capital competitive again on the world market. But this moralism is not only an English phenomenon, because the trade union structure worldwide exhibits similar moralisms. In the West German state, it has probably been a factor which has grimly termed those forced into a position of social marginality, as "schwartz arbeiters" (black workers) with all its suggestions of black-legging and strike breaking. Precisely because the unemployed are no longer quite the moral force to be pitied as they were before the Second World War, certain breaks with past traditions have been made.

These breaks are one of the reasons why The Right to Work marches have got nowhere, (in fact, rather less than The Right to Work EP by punk group Chelsea) and working on the side is experienced as a better deal than job creation. The musicians cannot show the way for the unemployed. Delroy Washington's, The Streets of Ladbroke Grove, is a Rasta Jarrow March set to music. "Give them their fair share, Give them what is theirs", which ironically buttresses that great English social democratic fairness ideology again. Until all those factions who make up the unemployed, recognise that their common interest lies with all those consigned to surplus oblivion, (young and old alike) and are able to overcome their reactive, futile opposition to the employed and grasp the potential of the revolutionary becoming of the industrial working class, their potential radicalism will defeat itself in a plethora of media charged false oppositions, of which music is the blackest dead end.

The unemployed must become part of the revolutionary movement against the commodity and wage labour but at the moment in the UK, the unemployed are sorting out a deviant survival, are low profile, (excepting black youth) and remaining well-laid back. For the unemployed white youth, this is surprising, considering punk's emphasis on energy but not surprising when seen that punk energy is more stage style than a living factor within the social base, which is more withdrawn in terms of self-expression and more contained than the hippy base of ten years ago. But the unemployed have a long way to go in comparison to their Italian counterparts, who are increasingly tending to refuse all mediators and representatives and where anonymity is proclaimed. Truly, unlike The Stranglers, no more heroes. Although, somewhat lost in a yearning for the idyll of crafts, small co-operatives, a utopianism about money, ("wages for laziness") and an elaborately garnished language reminiscent of Yippee / Motherfucker poetics, the marginalized Italian insurgents are now an ever present violent and armed threat to the very existence of the Italian state.

YOURS, JOE SOAP INTELLECTUALS

New Afterword to The End of Music (2007)

(To be included in a La Felguera, Spanish publication)

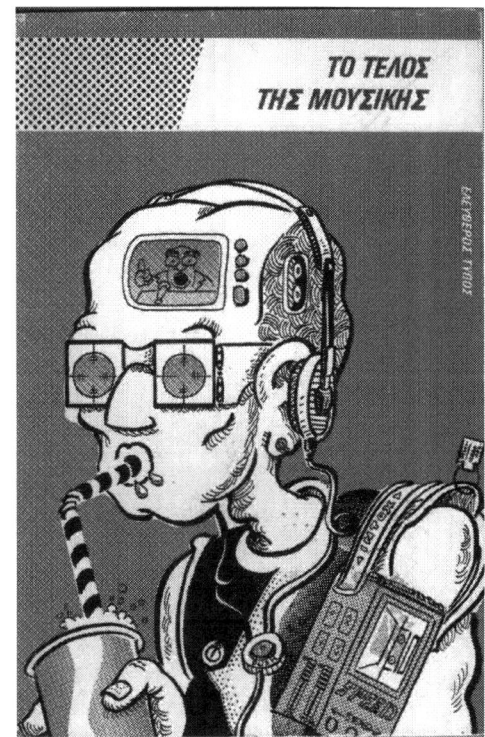

Above Left: *The original Glasgow, Calderwood 15 publication, 1981.*
Above Right: *A Greek publication of The End of Music from the late 1980s.*

This pamphlet from the late 1970s is indeed an attack on music and the need for supersession of this time honoured mode of entertainment (admittedly often profoundly moving entertainment). More than that it was also recognition that music had meant so much in shaping and changing our lives especially that music that was breaking through the limits of form and which pleasurably littered particularly the 20th century with profound future possibilities.

This re-shaping of our lives, this deep, passionate involvement didn't just come from high-end avant-garde (e.g. atonality) mixed-in with ingredients from Debussy, Satie through Russian Futurism to John Cage, etc. but the Mississippi blues and the latter day glories of Be-bop, some rock 'n' roll and then, alas, no more!

To take one example, we had at the age of 12 transferred the call and response of the southern American rail track laying / cotton fields / penitentiary work songs to our local white pit communities in northern England and in no time via our skiffle group we'd got the whole town a callin' and a rockin'.

Well, kind of. However, By the mid 1970s, post the revolutionary explosions of the late 1960s we were looking for the music that had no name, the sound that had transcended itself in the creativity made by all and not by one and the sound that enmeshed with a profound peoples' uprising; a sound (for want of a better description) inseparable from a renewed everyday life that had transcended the audience / performer fulcrum – that essential passive cash consumer nexus that still must be subverted and destroyed. In a way a post-situationist like Chris Shutes in California had put this conundrum better vis-a-vis 'rebel' music which he described as "teasing with rebellion". That's just the point, it's a hide 'n' seek rebellion and we at the 'passive' audience' receiving end have no choice but to be so much more unflinchingly against what we increasingly saw as musician's guile.

The End of Music quotes Rimbaud, "Great music falls short of our desire" but as bro' later said this is a wrong translation relying as we did on an apology of a translation in a Penguin Classics. It should have read, "<u>Knowing</u> music falls short of our desire". Yes, that was it! We knew the history of contemporary music on all levels, were impassioned by it as we also finally desired a more profound transcendence, one which it ineluctably pointed to. Later something of a similar drift also appeared in an introduction done between ourselves and Pete D during the early 1990s or rather what became the Afterword for a new publication of BAD - that remarkable autobiography of Black Panther James Carr's Californian situationist influenced account of his life – whereby we reckoned that the Los Angeles riot of 1992 was more than hinted at via contemporary rap lyrics. We made the obvious (yet also not so obvious) distinction that real destruction was something entirely different........

The thrust of the pamphlet was centered on the need to drop out from art and a now inseparable, stratospherically expensive art market. Recognising full on the process of artistic dilution we knew we had to push on through all vestiges of the artistic / anti artistic paradigms. What hopefully lay before us – getting ever clearer – was a new vision of an individual based communality. No messing about; we had to take the plunge while being pragmatic about everyday realities. In no time the prospect of a communal co-operative on the buildings quickly fell into place and for nigh on 45 years we have kept that reality going.

That process revolved around one central axis – equal wages for everybody - whether young or old, women or men, though beyond that diktat the gang was extremely fluid and un-dogmatic. It certainly wasn't a model for a new society though a step in that direction. Moreover, in the mid-1970s, such a builders' cooperative wasn't that unusual and over the next few years we worked together with others committed to the same principles. Sadly –and almost immediately – these everyday 'ordinary' survival organisations started to disappear as the horrendous neo-liberal economic experiment kicked-in and we, along with other insurgents, described as old fashioned "dinosaurs". At the time, transient though it was, this hoped for new communality overflowed borders. It could be said that The End of Music marked this search for new, meaningful subversive friendships; a communal expression emanating often as not only from small building sites but enhanced through working side by side with enough clued-in likeminded individuals contributing to patterns of thought as we knocked out the shit. (In fact later these building scenes were satirised on a hip TV comedy programme as the protagonists talking of Heidegger and Hannah Arendt etc, interspersing their scaffolding conversation with traditional vulgar sexist wolf whistles to all the gals passing below). Actually the main protagonist in our work based conversations at the time was a firm friend of Michel Prigent's name of Nik Holliman, who made many an eco contribution far better than those a Greenpeace or Friends of the Earth activist could deliver and two and a half decades later is still making such contributions most recently on the Principia Dialectica website.

Moreover the contributions were initially anonymous and what became known as The End of Music was basically a collective creation. Initially the pamphlet was done under the signatory of Joe Soap Intellectuals indicative of our new space doing jobs which had that necessary low ideological content and profile meaning you were free to cut to the chase without comebacks like you'd be up against in academia, journalism and / or cultural professions. Remember too, that Joe Soap was rhyming slang for dope and during world war one was sung to the tune of the hymn Onward Christian Soldiers, "Forward, Joe Soap's army, marching without fear, with our brave commander, safely in the rear."

The other central theme running through The End of Music is its emphasis on the lobotomisation of the "most revolutionary critique of the 1960s that of the situationists." We were right about that but in the late 1970s that process was still in its infancy in comparison to today where, especially during the noughties and beyond, a point of nullity has been reached as an excellent subversive praxis, now grotesquely acadamised has become little more than a slightly daring offshoot of specialised cultural studies, professional journalism and what have you. Still we did outline – and with real hatred - what was beginning to happen within the dregs of general culture, art and academia noting the growing "mass market of artistic anti art" as active nihilism instead of providing a springboard to total revolutionary critique, gave way to passive nihilism and the status quo. We rightly said we had to refuse all career opportunities and at least we have stayed true to that subversive necessity. And as one door closed on us so did another.....

"More fundamentally, the revolutionary hopes of the '60s lay in schizoid turmoil." Too true and that – now elongated fulcrum - and loss still remains with us despite a lot of trouble throughout the world comprising of troughs and possible peaks (e.g. the unfulfilled possibilities hinted at during 2011) yet capitalism remains supreme and relatively undisturbed as it heads at the very least towards an ecological abyss, though surely an economic abyss is equally just as likely. Indeed both seem to be are happening in disjointed tandem and things can only get more catastrophic.

Did we get any responses to The End of Music either in its original scrappy format or the more polished Glasgow edition? Most likely the pamphlet would have disappeared without trace if it hadn't been immediately picked up by the Leninist New Left Review-ists who in the meantime had put together an exhibition in London's ICA gallery curated by Peter Wollen which then seemed to tour the world and quotes from the pamphlet were writ large on wall exhibits sadly attended by the likes of Michelle Bernstein, Debord's ex partner.

We never attended the exhibit, never even looked inside its walls or picked up the catalogue. We simply scorned this abhorrent spectacle, this marker down the path which Ken Wark and his academic cohorts still tread, this neo-Leninisation of the original situationist revolutionary perspective which finds such a ready market today. Nonetheless we got letters through our former BM Blob box number though mainly from would be musicians. We were hoping for correspondence on a higher level that would clarify and develop subversive possibilities. Instead we got letters from hoped for new pop groups saying they were into authentic music making and could we help them out with recording / mixing suggestions!! Obviously we'd really gotten through to people! Beyond that we knew it had created a stir in the hip musical arena and ever after, Joe Strummer of the Clash would look away in a kinda of shame cum despair when one of us passed him on the street; McLaren on the contrary put on an angry face but didn't say anything. On the real level however, apart from provoking interesting discussions in Leeds there was little or no creative feedback. Indeed, the only helpful and long written contribution came from Phil Meyler who was still living in Portugal after the publication by the British Cardinite Solidarity group, of his excellent book, Portugal: The Impossible Revolution? Indeed without our financial help through proceeds from building work, Solidarity wouldn't have had the funds to publish.

Furthermore, again it can be said with some certainty that The End of Music would also probably have disappeared without much of a trace it the pamphlet hadn't been the first 'radical' effort to have put something together on King Mob in any depth. Today re-reading that analysis brings on some grimaces and embarrassments as certainly enough off-the-cuff reminiscences weren't nuanced enough as hastily cobbled together in a far too superficial way. In fairness though remember this collage / montage was a preliminary pasting together for discussion purposes and in itself, partially based on other notes and texts which had been typed up – ready for re-working – which were then be set aside for the famous "criticism of the mice". Today these texts have been posted, very belatedly, on the Revolt Against Plenty web especially Memories of the Portuguese Revolution in the mid 1970s though one is still missing, a text with a pompous title, The Chimera of a Campaign with a few Suggestions and Ramblings on the anti deportation agitation around the Lotta Continua, Italian militant, Franco Caprino and an appraisal that focussed on the 'new' social workers and the colonisation / pacification of children's' play.

In a way too, this first re-evaluation of King Mob was too despairing even at times, irksome. Yes, King Mob was "aggressively urban" even grossly dismissive of nature and what goes by the name of "the countryside" in general. Yes, we were woefully short on eco critique only for some of us since to encompass the latter's absence on a massive scale though with a great emphasis on the potential glories inherent on sites of industrial dereliction since remarkably enriched by a fecund bio-diversity. Yes, we were sick of hippy passivity but then we tended to foolishly attack anything craft based even attacking Ruskin's "doctrine of good works". We hated machine based modernism and its production line components, its cut and dried city and urban landscapes but then we hated the Olde Englande of crafts and cottage industries not seeing a possible revolutionary third way through this muddle. (This is particularly true of Memories of the Portuguese Revolution of the mid 1970s). It was only later, much later, that we saw the possibility in a renewed artisanal contribution in the moment when art has lost all semblance of creativity. In fact for us we saw crafts hopelessly colonised by an English moralism we despised so much eagerly quoting Nietzsche on the subject in our defence, though more about the central specifics of that hideous moralism later.

At the time we had hoped this cobbled together critique could be the first among many such recollections from other participants but that wasn't to be the case. In reality the pamphlet merely provided the cue for an easing back into the culture we abhorred, especially music, so much so, that to Google King Mob today is to Google the King Mob pop group made up of ex Sex Pistols' Glen Matlock, Martin Chambers of The Pretenders and Chris Spelling, ex John Cale and Roxy Music. Beneath the drop down listings you then find Kind Mob Clothing, which is all copyrighted (we were and still are ardently anti copyright) so much so that you cannot even copy and paste images to reproduce them here.... The predatory arseholes.....

What all this amounts to is little beyond changes in surface appearances. More often than not the musical scene is a brief interlude before the real nitty-gritty kicks in as we learnt a few years later bumping into ex-musician after ex-musician who had finally opted for a life on the buildings. Even one of our best friends, a scaffolder called Kev used to sing along with Rod Stewart and sure enough cuddly photos of Kev have sentimentally appeared as bessy mates in Rod Stewart's Autobiography though Mr Rod forgot to mention that this tough guy had given him sometime later a right hammering for becoming a shite hawk.

As is well known the dropout ranks are legion so there's only need to mention a few here. Thus Brian Poole of the Tremoloes worked in a butcher's shop after quitting the music scene and Jet Harris after drifting from The Drifters became a bus conductor and then a repair electrician for Space Invaders. As for Mark P ofSniffing Glue and punk group Alternative TV, he later trained as a male nurse. Most tragically love for some worthless user of a middle class white woman broke another of our best friends on the buildings, Ray from the Caribbean, who played alongside Steve Cropper. Turning to smack and crack he killed himself. Oddly enough only rarely did these (kind of) ex-stars we knew speak of their past though occasionally they'd say they couldn't take the spotlight again as it had become so truly alien for them. The one's we didn't know like Jet Harris and Brian Poole never stayed the course and, giving up the ghost, tried again to embrace the alienation of the musical scene but to look at them on TV or film somehow you can see etched on their faces that performance was now something they endure rather than believe in.

The background to The End of Music took place after sojourns in Italy Spain, & Portugal, when the latter two countries were erupting socially after their long fascistic night immediately transcending the boundaries of a simple social democratic, anti-fascist perspective. Autonomy loomed but it all ended with little than promising beginnings followed by prolonged sadness. The pamphlet, as previously mentioned, was a composite effort, though more than that, it was a self-composite effort, as parts were 'stolen' from other tracts that I had written, or contributed to throughout those lost years clouded with one drinking binge after another especially a tract on Portugal which never saw the light of day and wasn't read by anybody even at the time. Finally that tract, Memories of the Portuguese Revolution in the mid 1970s was never published until belatedly posted on the RAP web in 2012. This overlapped with another composite long text, Chinese Takeaway, A Critique of Western Maoism put together by ourselves and Phil Meyler which also chimes with The End of Music and which again lay dormant, even unread, until posted on the RAP web in the same year.

Some of the notes that were to make their way into The End of Music first saw the light of day in a pre-punk era pension in Barcelona stimulated by an article in the then youthful El Pais daily newspaper which could and did throw in apt one liners from Gianfranco Sanguinetti such as "All energy expended on art merely ends up as the new academy" rather than dealing with a more rounded discuss ions of his theories. I say "youthful" because which liberal newspaper in the UK would even have known who Sanguinetti is and was and that's as true today as back in the mid 1970s. Nonetheless, we weren't fooled by surface appearances and in no time we also began nicknaming El Pais, El Piss, simultaneously as some of our French friends also began deploying exactly the same piss take.

However, this background European wide information leaves out another much more local ambience that of Leeds in the north of England a little later which briefly became home to an influx of ex Situ's and ex Cardinite Solidarity individuals often in flight from London and possibly attracted by the strikes and rebellion of the employed working class which had a kind of fulcrum in south and west Yorkshire, though truth to tell there was no real geographical fulcrum as the strikes, often wildcat, were everywhere. These strikes were exhilarating, semi autonomous, pointing towards hope and yet without focus as to what the shape of a new world might possibly be. Be that as it may there was a certain ambience in the air and area and most of the 35 gestetnered copies of a text initially lumbered with the dullish title of Punk & Reggae; A Critique were handed out in Leeds, a text which was unfinished – up for discussion - and which later became known as The End of Music. Indeed there was a kind of mini ultra leftist ferment in Leeds at the time, one defiantly anti the new conformist leftism which had gained ground in the city pro-moed by such dismal pamphlet's as Life Beyond Leeds which for us rapidly morphed into Is there Life Beyond Leeds? Most of the contemporary isms of the time were given a fair old pounding in particular a certain reductive puritanical feminism which inevitably and understandably had gained a wide response in a city reeling from the horrors perpetrated by the yet to be caught Bradford based Yorkshire Ripper. On a broader level the ground was being prepared for Leeds based groups such as Infantile Disorders and the longer lasting, Here & Now, both of which we contributed to in different ways.

But then it could be said why in The End of Music is there such an emphasis on the Caribbean especially Jamaica? The essential backdrop to all of this was much more organic, more visceral, living as I did on a west London street with a very high Afro-Caribbean profile, a situation whereby I gradually became one of the few palefaces around. In no time the street became infamous for its atmosphere of almost day to day, permanent riot. 'Infamous'? On the contrary it was fascinating what with the ingredient of something like a permanent police clamp down and "swamp operation." I can never forget the hilarious moment when cops – without asking permission and without a warrant – burst into my flat, presumably on a drugs raid, only to find me covered in Daz soap suds after a really mucky day on the buildings. Surprised all the cops could do was double-up with laughter and left within seconds, mission abandoned....

In these evolving circumstances, a slower, rounder analysis evolved and one with a substantial theoretical interest in the way recuperation was changing its face especially re the pacification of rebellious youth in Jamaica under the new social democratic presidency of Michael Manley, especially the way 'rebel' music was used to buttress the status quo. Out of the blue a stunner then fell into my lap in the name of None Shall Escape, an LP put out by a situationist inspired Jamaican workers' group which I found compelling and although it was accompanied by reprints of classic situationist texts by Raoul Vaneigem and Mustapha Khayati there was some vivid originality here. A spoken – not musical LP – None Shall Escape was a description and analysis of authentic self initiatives plus a major wildcat strike at Western Meat Packers which took place in the strike torn Jamaican province of Westmoreland; a perspective moreover that was critical of alternative unions, various opportunistic Leninists and a sundry collection of leftist bigwigs in general. In no time other friends were discussing somewhat abstractedly the adventures of Fundi, a Rasta influenced refrigeration mechanic who with others set an inspiring subversive example. And then we heard no more so we now eagerly await a new book, Workers' Self-management in the Caribbean coming our way soon which it seems is a collection of Fundi's writings?

A further essential ingredient in the pick 'n' mix has to be acknowledged, an overlap with Michel Prigent and his magazine, The Catalyst Times some time après Michel had splashed up slogans on Westbourne Park Rd in west London, like Punk =Pound Notes. Indeed it was Michel Prigent who shoved The End of Music pamphlet in my hands bumping into him sometime in late 1981(?) which was then followed by friendly banter and a stroll across London's Hyde Park. I forget what we said but I went back to my flat and immediately wrote to Glasgow asking them to destroy the publication as it had been altered somewhat from the grubby, photocopied texts I'd initially handed out. In retrospect it was a response that was well over the top as the changes were somewhat acknowledged and wasn't the new title The End of Music for better, far more appropriate, even if other things weren't? For instance the original contained no footnotes and the Glasgow production tilted the pamphlet towards a more academic presentation. So included in this latter-day offering is the original text though not all the original 35 or so copies contained the montages on display here. And jeez, was it difficult to unearth rummaging through a chaotic filing system that had hardly seen the light of day for decades! And yet again, reflecting on self-plagiarisation, parts in the meantime had been lifted and planted into Like a Summers with a Thousand Julys that pamphlet on the splendid country wide UK riots of 1981 a few years later especially all that relates to Jamaica, honing in on the crossover between Jamaica's PM Michael Manley and reggae musician, Bob Marley. Interestingly, for both pamphlets the common dominator from immediate critical commentaries coming in from all sides revolved around "intransigence" notably academic Sadie Plant's digs against Like a Summers with a Thousand Julys saying Mclaren's self recuperation of situationist theory made much greater sense.....

Moreover, The Catalyst Times tub-thumping had brought back into focus past friendships I had had with Malcolm McLaren and Fred Vermorel during the latter days of King Mob. But then there had been a distancing between us as bro' and myself descended down over into full time survival more or less on the buildings, together with periods of voluntary dole subsidised unemployment, entering into a very different world as we gave up on any petty careerist pursuits etched with a stern goodbye delivered to anything like professional status in art, writing, music, academia or anything similar.

On the contrary McLaren and Vermorel ditching their initial radical subversion were onto a new kind of on the make in journalism and entrepreneurial activities. Seeing them in the streets of central London in the mid 1970s looking in bookshop windows and I knew I had nothing to say. There could be no embrace, no glad hello, as I pondered "Why are you looking in fucking book shop windows." A great gap had opened up and I instantly realised that all flow, all camaraderie had evaporated and I knew it would be impossible to talk about what was really on my mind.

But there is another insistent undertow / theme – call it what you will in the text - one previously suggested and that is English moralism. The real crux of English moralism still fundamentally remains a sexual one, which in its essence is hypocritical, often salacious and as gully low and horrendous as ever. It's fundamentally about destroying reputations. Today, former media super stars are attacked for gross sexualised child abuse not so much because it is foul practise but as a deflected way of attacking the celebrity system itself without openly saying so as bankers, bosses and other big wigs go unscathed for the same sexual offences which are still committed in there thousands on an everyday basis. However in The End of Music we noted that English moralism tended to define the first wave of a revived English feminist movement; a thesis refracted through emphasis on Marcuse's concept of repressive desublimation, Eros and Thanatos, Death-in-life or Life-in-death. At the time we still rated Herbert Marcuse seeing him as a 'clean' academic wondering why there weren't more like him only decades later to learn that he had quite outrageously lifted many a concept from Gunther Anders, a brush hand working in Hollywood studios! It seems an academic's leopard's spots hadn't changed and have been with us much longer though minus the crescendo of recuperation which descended on us after the late 1960s.

For sure The End of Music was also about sex, albeit the lack of sex in any real meaningful sense; a situation leading up to a "Love is Dead" brick wall set against the backdrop of a vanilla, commonplace, stock-in-trade S/M having spread everywhere; sex like an end of art, art, becoming central to a capitalist reproduction and nothing more with pornographic social / personal relations as backdrop. The pamphlet was also written on the cusp of the sex positive feminism of the late 1970s in revolt against the early 70s feminist wave. At first this tendency was greeted with a sigh of relief though one that proved to be a short-lived sigh as it quickly became obvious that this change marked little more than the transition from global social democracy to the neo liberalism of sex and the city. Sex was becoming the sex of ponzi schemes, of casino capitalism, of mis-selling everything, of debt and derivatives dressed up (sexed-up) autism revolving around unfeeling, go-getting lifestyles. Much of this was simply intuited at the time and was, more clearly elaborated in detail by the likes of Annie Le Brun especially in Lachez Tout which is still a book that is regarded as shocking by the English speaking part of the world. English moralism was emphasised as something horrific in The End of Music and there's been no change on that score which in many respect is essentially worse than ever in its blatant hypocrisy that Nietzschian "fear inspiring moral fanatici". Annie Le Brun was affirmative regarding pornography at that time – just as The End of Music was to a lesser degree - only later to distance herself from such affirmation as she gradually saw something really dark appearing on the horizon. At the same time Annie could never transcend her Andre Breton mimicked writing style as equally she still cannot make those essential moves beyond art.

Inevitably by the late 1970s we were realising the later Marx, the Marx concerned with a more painstaking fundamental critique of political economy had to be profoundly re-evaluated. This was no easy task and we knew it and were somewhat overwhelmed as a theoretical / practical interregnum loomed. Therefore the engagement with Marx in The End of Music is tentative rather than profound; somewhat pedestrian and certainly not penetrating to a necessary essential core though there are more than hints of this in the discussion on the surplus population, those "surplus to requirements." This however doesn't get to grips with the increasing insubstantiality of capitalist valorisation at the heart of a disintegrating law of value, of "labour without value"; that moment when labour for capital becomes meaningless and fiat money through inflation swallows itself alive as capitalism is ending in a series of devastating, intractable economic crises which no new bubble will finally be able to rescue; a situation which will culminate in either total social revolution or ultimate barbarism. However, the Calderwood 15 in Glasgow who initially published the pamphlet didn't like this turn towards a greater understanding and reading of Marx; a factor which also helped bring about an impasse which Solidarity never recovered from although there were also other more significant factors, such as an extremely weak critique of culture and stultifying professional roles and last but not least, the growing counter revolutionary nightmare.

In many respects the text marked an interregnum on the cusp of a great change. The classical workers' movement was ending as globalisation was imposing impotence from below the likes of which the world had known as former national frameworks - essentially the arena of the increasingly blinkered and useless trade unions – just couldn't get to grips with. The workers thus downgraded had become an object of media inspired scorn, little more than slobbering, stupid chavs gateway to a mass society of ever increasing alienation. A mass society endlessly morphing down to ever lower common denominators displacing The Lonely Crowd of the sociological American early 1960s with a sub individual solipsism marked by increasing confinement in what seems like separate prison cells. This is the new Inferno and Hades combined also marking the moment when art and finance capital have become inextricably enmeshed, burying us in a vast shroud everywhere.

Yet, contradictorily the pamphlet is marked by growing class hatred just at the moment the working class was losing all position and profile though also subtly noting, "Expressing venom against public schools, inherited privileges based on birth, accent, manner and pleasant behaviour, can in a minority of instances be the entrance to that very domain." If you like the spectacle was democratising though with the appearance of largely upwardly mobility! And what a crazy situation was to ensue; no more blatantly from the late 1980s onwards when bizarrely we learnt that Manchester Moss Side gangsta drug barons were sending their kids to public schools! Then my own great puzzle: at the moment when class is dead, I was developing the most terrible class hatred – just at the moment there seemed to be no obvious social base to it when such base was becoming increasingly hidden, when officially "the workers" no longer existed. Nonetheless, The End of Music rails against "the pre-bourgeois superstructure in the UK". Now that was real insight as over the next few decades this trajectory has become so much clearer with the local death of the industrial working class concomitant with the rise of something like a neo-feudal plutocracy cum kleptocracy as we at the sharp end morph into surly neo-churls post the depredations of something like a metaphorically speaking, renewed Norman Conquest!!! For certain there's still structural flexibility which is one of the reasons you have to constantly have the guts to refuse such compromise...and increasingly that takes some doing.

The pamphlet also marks its time through an occasional emphasis on the old formation of the working class in the UK located in big numbers in medium or large enterprises, hence the term "the productive working class". We weren't to know it at the time but the UK was on the cusp of becoming the first major experimental arena for the neo-liberal agenda which would involve the dispersal of the classical working large in large parts of the 'west' with a globalisation experiment where much of the former productive working class was to be re-located in south east Asia. This process has been pushed to extremes in the UK whereby a massive parasitic economy now reigns with 40% of the economy based on financial services and another 40% based on housing with a mere 14% or so given over to industry and manufacturing.

Relying on a Marx inspired analysis of productive and unproductive labour, much of the pamphlet revolves around a discussion of the surplus population "which is allowed to minimally consume" and fed with distractions, or if you like, variants of what Orwell had decades previously referred to as "prole food". Though recognising the importance of an unstoppable automation in the productive process, The End of Music balks at defining this surplus as "surplus to requirements" with the attendant horrors this can imply under capitalism whereby a barbaric outcome could mean a holocaust of the surplus the likes of which the world has never known; one far more sophisticated in applying methods of extermination than the crudities of concentration camps and gas chambers, one's that could be digitally (and secretly) invoked by turnkey.

But then the pamphlet was at times too woodenly 'Marxist' and a phrase elsewhere on the need for a "scientific analysis of class structures" brings on blushes. Elsewhere, though not equally cringe worthy there's mention made of "the communist mode of production" which while containing undeniable truths is one of those so over-used categorisations that's lost all veracity, a mere dull and lifeless phrase, shorn of utopian astonishment which will surely mark any transition from suicide capitalism as we take experimental steps beyond the law of value.

Of more relevance - and one that still is very much to the point today – is the questioning of the role and validity of workers' councils noting that they tended to lack real cutting edge revolutionary content. However, all this was jammed packed together, something of a quick overview and said in passing; simply too crowded. Obviously all this was in desperate need of elaboration despite being an addition to recuperative mechanisms that went beyond narrower definitions of cultural recuperation which was at the very core of the pamphlet's purpose. The backdrop to all of this had more to do with Yves Le Manach's growing disdain for workers' councils' as expressed in his 1975 Champ Libre book Bye Bye Turbin plus the pedestrian experience of events like the occupation of Fisher Bendix on Merseyside and the Clydeside shipyard work-in during the early 1970s than any high handed, ultra-leftist like, party-like, Bordiga-like, dismissal of say the Spanish Revolution of 1936-8 which we still remained inspired by remembering with pleasure that childhood eureka moment at the age of eight as Co Durham railway workers in our parent's house on Christmas Day talked of the POUM, disdaining the Communist party, our parents having for years almost refused to nod and say hello to the depressed and even suicidal Communist party signalman living next door.

Curiosity aroused we asked questions and were replied to as if we were young adults and as it should be and the conversation powerfully struck home in our innocent child minds. Come the mid 1970s we still wanted to see the vision of a new world emerge from such base (and basic) organisations like the POUM together with such child-like innocence but where was this vision in practise, where were the workers today criticising their own often stupefying, useless roles or, their own unquestioning submission in manufacturing largely useless products? A much wider vision was needed.....

Perhaps also in The End of Music there's too much glib use of a term like state capitalism borrowed too glibly from some variations of Trotskyism, Socialisme ou Barbarie, Situationists etc, together with too much received populist, social democratic wisdom when such abstractions needed more questions asked than answered especially, when unbeknown to ourselves, the world was on the brink of neo-liberalism, that hoped for free market whereby the state would be pushed more and more into the background as financial markets were leveraged almost everywhere.

Yes indeed this was a leveraged buy-out and not a classical capitalist boom but whatever hopes there were at its inception, 30 years later, post "the banking crises of 2007-8," the concept lay in ruins, despite the fact that the banking crises was merely the surface of more fundamental flaws in capitalist reproduction re the creation of adequate new value. The state through the Fed, the Bank of England, and the European Central Bank etc has since become more powerful than ever with a socialised largesse for the super rich ("high value net worth individuals") and neo-liberal medicine for the rest of us. In short a state capitalism unlike its social democratic forbear, one geared increasingly towards the absolute pauperisation of what's left of both the middle and working classes. It really cannot be otherwise in a situation where debt can only become ever more pronounced whereby capitalism has used up its future to such an extent, that a recovery is no longer possible. As Kurz says, "In a manner that is unprecedented in the history of capitalism, the future creation of surplus-value is already mortgaged" and that's an awesome conclusion.

The End of Music was inevitably a product of its time. It seemed as though a richer vein of subversion was just around the corner but alas, what was heralded was an increasing void of nothingness as amidst increased global warming a real ice age almost bereft of practical subversion dawned, one which still continues and continues......... If culture was bankrupt, it nevertheless again somehow became the only game in town even though sinking into an ever deepening abyss. Indeed we can look with nostalgia on the punk era in comparison with what was to follow as stadia rock in the following decades became ever more ludicrously sensationalised and vacuous as all shock value expressed through the dregs of culture wasted away, never to return.

Since then there's been nothing but machine product, promo, managerial style, what Michel Prigent called "the noise machine" as making one escape attempt after another we always end up drifting down the same one way street. Today, all we have are leftovers littering the flickering screen of every hand held tablet computer and / or related gadgetry, those bleak substitutes for our increasingly absent lives; a tendency that can only become more pronounced as we become more disoriented, locked down, imprisoned within our digital selves. The original pamphlet was an attack on 'rebel' music as a form of faking it, of fake creativity, yet today in these ever more reactionary, dire times why doesn't some kind of rebel music exist? Increasingly perplexed, a lot of people are asking that question without coming up with any insightful contribution as to why the 'music' burnt out for good in the late 1970s? Yet, when pushed against the wall always but always they come out with the same platitude: it's there if we can but find it! This ignores the inescapable truth that the time lapse between what was regarded as cultural creativity and the academy, pace Sanguinetti's previously quoted comment, has become so telescoped it's reached the point of absurdity. Indeed it could be said that the spectacularised rebel music of the late 1970s was the first moment of a now vast syndrome: Lights / Cameras / Performance / Revolution – with hardly any real revolutionary subversion encountered anywhere! It's as if a mix of expiring cultural forms together with ever more relentless capitalisation has put paid to every representation especially those that authentically once emanated from the oppressed masses leaving us more bereft than ever.

The times now cry out for a deeper truth-in-action, the final overthrow of the audience / performer nexus including all pseudo participatory alternatives. Only the total overthrow of the capitalist mode of production can achieve this creating the basis for a genuine lifestyle beyond value, simultaneously anti aesthetic and anti commercial.

© *Revolt Against Plenty* 2014

Once Upon A Time There Was A Place Called Nothing Hill Gate...

A critical history of the Notting Hill Carnival,

Notting Hill Gate as a whole and beyond.....

 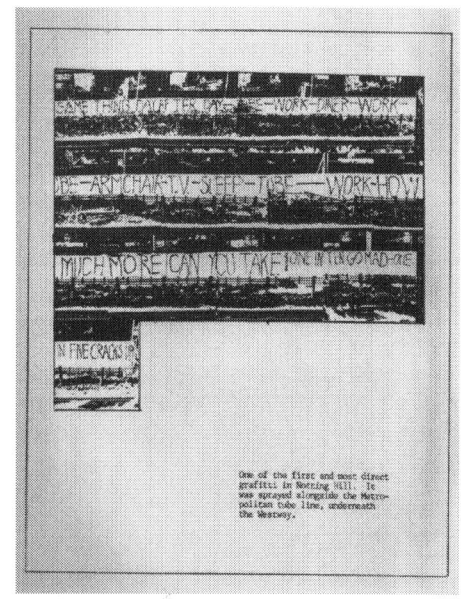

Front & back cover of A4 pamphlet

Preamble

The following is a personal account covering a more or less twenty-year period in Notting Hill Gate (also called North Kensington and colloquially known as "The Gate".) It is sketchy here but detailed there focusing, on the main event: the Notting Hill Carnival, particularly the 1987 riot and the years of conflict on All Saints Road. It's also full of generalities that apply elsewhere too. One could have gone into an immense amount of detail concerning different situations but the length of the text, cost and time involved would have been prohibitive. It therefore has no pretensions at all to being a definitive critique. Its function is finally a pointer what might be by taking a drag at the fag ends of the past.

More generally it would be a good idea if others, independently minded individuals, in particular situations (e.g. other London areas, other UK regions or cities or particular workplace, hospitals, mills, print, pits, building sites, offices, black economy, community programmes, job training schemes and ethnic minorities - could put together some kind of critical document of their own experiences. If nothing else, simply as a guide to those who are fresh in there now or will come after, peering in from the outside or just plain nosey. Although one's own experiences may not seem that interesting to the one telling the tale the fact is such documents would in all likelihood be not just fascinating but also help in clarifying the unknown substance of revolution conceived in a microcosm. "Be global, act local" as the Americans say. In a sense too, the one great autobiography (sort of) this century -Ciliga's, The Russian Enigma - reading like a revolutionary travelogue you can't put down - is also a great indictment of Bolshevism as revolutionary ideology.

A good part of the following was written before the great collapse on the world's stock markets. The first rough draft ended with a prediction that the crash was coming. However this was no different from what many others (including Labour party hacks) had been saying, although the interpretation of what it could mean was quite different. What was important though was that this great event did in fact mean that some of the emphasis of the original had to be changed somewhat. No longer did Notting Hill and London generally seem to be a future of property prices estate agents and yuppies. Thus a kind of postscript is a series of speculative meanderings of what may be in store for us more generally in the UK as a whole. More concrete than such speculation is seeing where this wheel has been. Or, less metaphorically, seeing what has been the history of Notting Hill that has nurtured its present contradictions. In attacking the present we reveal the past. In making our own history we reveal how much, and in what ways, past history was not our own, or that of our class. This therefore is the tale and as the Irish adage goes: "if there's a lie in it, well, let it stand." not that a lie is intentional but one must remember that all theoretical explanation is provisional and mistakes are inevitably made. Blob's done more than a few. There's bound to be more in what follows, particularly as it has been produced at the beginning of a new period of great changes waiting their turn in the wings.

"...But Notting Hill is the tyrant ---that they try to meddle with everyone, and rule everyone, and civilize everyone and tell everyone what is good for him."

G.K. Chesterton: The Napoleon of Notting Hill *(1904)*

Notting Hill was always an immigrant community. The development of the railway network and a changed policy towards cheaper fares in the mid 19th century onwards, meant the centre of London was evacuated in order to become more or less a pure commercial space facilitating the circulation of commodities. As the population was decanted to the peripheral areas between 1830 and 1880, London became the first dead city centre we have now become accustomed to the world over. These areas were then often just fields and pastures and were built up from scratch. Notting Hill was one of them, freshly created and colonized by people from central London, then elsewhere in the UK and finally from the rest of the world. This movement of the poor was accompanied by a similar movement, (though not enforced like that of the poor) of the wealthy from central London who generally took the fresher air of the higher ground of the Hill proper. From its inception the rich and poor lived cheek by jowl with each other affronted by each other's unwanted presence. Indeed the whimsical, light fantasy, The Napoleon of Notting Hill is partially about an earlier resistance to gentrification, although basically the novel is about the richer parts adjacent to Embassy-belt territory and not about the darker, desperate underbelly of "The Gate" proper. In retrospect however, one likes to think that some of Chesterton's paradoxes. ("If a job's worth doing its worth doing badly", " work is the ruin of the drinking classes" etc) which attracted the approval of the French

Surrealists may have been a subconscious assimilation of "the Gate's", often rich, low life.

Notting Hill's special interest as regards the UK and elsewhere is of more recent origin. Whatever importance it may have from a revolutionary perspective is what is highlighted here. What follows is not a funk History Workshop. Its central theme is simple. Far more than elsewhere the lower slopes of Notting Hill sponsored the entrance of post-war 'anarchism' - more precisely an anarchic sentiment - into the political arena and party system. Lacking in rigour from the start its eventual kaleidoscopic dispersal covering an enormous range of issues) acted finally as a buttress supporting the nation state.

A WALK BACK INTO NOTTING HILL

Over the past few decades, Notting Hill has been looked upon as something of an unusual area both in London and the rest of the UK. It had (and to some degree still has) a libertarian ambience though the word is not used as it might be used to describe say the past, and maybe even the present of the Spanish workers' movement. It could be described as a kind of tolerance of freewheeling attitudes, behaviour and dress. Flourishing and revolving around the formerly large private rented sector of bed-sits (and later squats in private and state sector) the 9 to 5 grind got the thumbs down every time. It was a place of refuge; a place to escape away from the insufferable constraints of the family background, away from entrenched working class prejudices or career mindedness and a too straight laced world altogether. Single parent mothers (before it became commonplace) could exist without too much fear of persecution and criticism from neighbours. Social Security snoopers from the DHSS tried to make up for this absence though. Easy too for Lesbians and Gays when these words were still whispered elsewhere. But above all, Notting Hill breathed an anti-work atmosphere and nobody came on too heavy for just dossing about with no aim in life, even in the long-gone days of full employment.

Closely related to this anti-work ambience, indeed possibly encouraging it was a certain bohemianism linked to art. In this respect, Notting Hill was an offshoot of Chelsea Arts. Though lacking in money, prestige and tradition, it was a place where these poor cousins, unable to make it in the bogus Chelsea pantheon of art could reside. It was from cheap lodgings off the Portobello Rd in the early 1930s, that a shabby genteel George Orwell sallied forth to experience being Down and Out in London. Though Orwell wincingly and somewhat pompously proclaimed himself as a 'writer' nonetheless throughout his books there is a constant undercurrent disparaging art that is quite obviously related to the fact that he was always short of cash. It seemed however that the more one climbed the moneyed Hill proper the less art became something to be questioned (and this was as true of Orwell as anyone else). The Sitwell's would look with disdain from their Holland Park mansion down Ladbroke Grove, which partially because of very basic economic insecurity, had more than a whiff of arts transcendence to it.

It was sometimes more than a whiff but only just. Max Ernst stayed for a short while in the late 1930s and Kurt Schwitters, the German Dadaist in exile from Nazism, before moving to the Lake District lived in Notting Hill (from his bed-sit he perhaps began to satirize English obsessions with tea drinking, the weather, etc. "When I am writing about the weather I know what I am writing about.") In the 1930s, the widow of that not quite revolutionary theorist of culture, Walter Benjamin, also resided in the area. More generally it became a place for people with a measure of artistic pretension, unable finally to believe whole-heartedly in art and lacking therefore the push to make it. It would stop short at the abandoned painting and a few scribbled pages of a novel never quite up to grasping the connection between half-hearted artistic fumbling and a critique of capitalism. Any mention of historical antecedents which were critical of art, would be met with a vague acknowledgement but not much more.

This is a common enough occurrence in highly developed countries because authority has consciously set about fostering amnesia when it comes to an appraisal of radical tendencies surpassing art, in the revolution of modern art (1)

Footnote (1): This mustn't be too over-emphasized however, because more generally, inculcating a collective amnesia has become one of the prime strategies of the state. In other matters, the UK state has been singularly unsuccessful in accomplishing this. Big events (e.g. the miners' victory in 1972 at Saltley Depot) are quickly and vividly recalled by many at the sharp end of exploitation.

Until Punk, which marked the on-set of modernist recuperation in the UK, English conservatism could effectively be relied on to do the job, stifling outbreaks at source. As regards the national cultural scene no re-write of the facts ever proved necessary. Indeed most of the avant garde when fleeing fascism found the United States more congenial. Schwitters it must be remembered also had been criticized by fellow German Dadaists for his petit bourgeois behaviour (e.g. evicting an upstairs tenant who just happened to be in the way of one of his expanding Merzbau's). The point is plain enough; a relevant critique of modem art was simply lacking in the UK and there was nothing in the country's post First World War history (unlike in France for example) that could have been used as a springboard. In places like Notting Hill especially in its 'counter culture' period this absence was sorely missed. You might as well have talked to a brick wall as attempt to explain the death of art to this rapidly decomposing La Boheme. Talk of changing life produced a ready response all right. The only trouble was that art was looked on as changing life and not a manifestation on the most basic level of an aspect of the same deadly survival sickness, where the distraction of interesting products (and increasingly today interesting but essentially role-bound behaviour), mediates and substitutes for lifeless, uncreative reality.

It was however a La Boheme with a common touch overlapping continually with local people who weren't made to feel unwanted as had happened recently with the yuppie colonization. Besides, their economic circumstances were often not all that different doing similar jobs in Lyons corner houses and the like and always behind with the rent. The more avant garde cultural careerists found it profitable to market people's fascination with this marginal life-style which has always seemed so different. Notting Hill is the background example, to the 1950s film, The L-Shaped Room in which a pregnant French girl running from her parents moves into a crummy bed-sit. In the sub-divided house there is a black trumpeter, an ever-aspiring novelist, a dragon of a landlady, a prostitute, an understanding dyke who liked to dress up in military uniform and her cat. This was also the setting for the novels of Colin McInnes who despite all his liberal and cultural garbage did emphasize the historically unprecedented post war working class affluence and innovative sub-cultures partly associated with it - Jazz, Teds, blacks and smoking dope. (Why else call one of his efforts Absolute Beginners?) Developments from these initial sub-cultural experiments were of course, to become in later years an explosive ingredient in riots. (2)

Footnote (2): This bohemian, artistic ambience was very different from a neighbouring area like Kilburn with more than a dash of lyrical-talking Irish and a popular respect for the Irish poet. There work was looked on as a central, inescapable necessity; the curse of Adam, which even rivers of Guinness after work, could never cleanse the memory of. (c/f that anti-building company song of the Building Trade ,"McAlpine's Fusiliers", written in a bed-sit down Lymington Rd in the adjacent West Hampstead area) .And where laid-back, loafing, Notting Hill, trying to do as little as possible, was simply a stop on the number 31 and 28 bus routes where engaging weirdos hung out.

Notting Hill's bohemian heyday was in the 1950s. A decade later, the area became the focus of the alternative, underground, hippy, dropout syndrome. Despite its palpable bullshit it did push a few things to the fore. Inevitably the contradictions implied in practising art became more finely stretched the more obvious its banal, unalterable role became in ratifying the status quo. A clearer headed attack on art and one inseparable from a total revolutionary critique came into focus.

The first pro-situationist group to appear in the UK in the late 1960s, King Mob was based in Notting Hill. The delphic slogans which they spray canned on the walls of the area pre-dated those in Paris1968 (also continuing after that) but rarely were as acute and definitely not as consequential. In fact the all-too-obvious flirtation with literature in these slogans was only too appealing to the local counter-cultural poets who just loved them. Their merit lay in remaining anonymous. No one was quite sure who wrote what, nor was it done with an eye to promoting the group (unlike the anarcho-politicos of today, who sign their graffiti, no matter how bad!) In fact graffiti as promo was taken up several years later by groups like the Rolling Stones and others*(3) while the honourable tradition of anonymity was continued in slogans like "Joyless work causes cancer", "We teach all hearts to break" on a school etc. But their revolutionary core poetised though it often was generally remained a dead letter in the area despite the fact that the anonymity and increased incidence of graffiti suggested otherwise. Blake's "The Road of Excess leads to the Palace of Wisdom" was changed to "Willesden" (a nearby area) -a fitting and knowing response to the pretence of having sprayed it up in the first place.

But what was to follow was even direr as Heathcote Williams, the alternative playwright, took up the spray can. The earlier graffiti at least was striking and gave one food for thought even in its un-amended version. But whatever the ubiquitous "Remember the Truth Dentist" slogan meant, Mr Williams alone knows. True it was an ad for one of his rubbishy plays but it had all the hallmarks of that deliberate and elitist obscurantism which passes itself off as profundity. Or for that matter was his word play on Max Bygraves, Sing alonga Max ("Wankalonga Max") really worthy of practically an entire gable-end wall? * (3) Revolt was turning into that "crab like movement sideways" (Tom Nairn) as subversion was replaced with a more compatible and time-honoured eccentricity, which teased rather than indicted. In the process, Eng Lit rather than society, became ripe for renewal as Heathcote Williams sought to update old acting traditions (e.g. in Derek Jarman's outré film of Shakespeare's, The Tempest which was also featured in The Sunday Times colour supp.) Or, giving a new lease of credibility for example to a stodgy rep theatre in Harrogate with his own play, Hancock's Last Half Hour. Indeed "Hancock Lives" was one of his few Notting Hill graffiti that reminded people that here was a comic who despite performing on stage and in front of TV and film cameras could still just about say something. But sadly being trapped in the vicious circle of success and failure in society's terms, which in many ways he was so able to parody, was undoubtedly the most important reason for him making sure he had nothing further to say. And for certain Hancock was not contrasting the untutored comic in everyday situations (who really does have an effect) with the comic entertainer who performs to rote. (4)

Footnote (3): With punk and after graffiti became an acceptable free method for bands to advertise themselves or their records, doing it themselves or getting their fans to do it seemed like progress (self-advertising) from the crudely capitalist way "It's only Rock 'n' Roll" forced itself on the walls of London. Now, with books and books on graffiti - raking in a packet for their authors - graffiti has also become a devalued form of communication.

Footnote (4): The subversive joker is the opposite of those comedians of daily life whose only purpose is arbitrary provocation, who provide the inspiration for many professional humourists. We are talking about the winder-uppers who delight in making anybody feel small so as to inflate themselves. Their put-downs never wish to subvert a person's petrifactions, change a situation, but merely act as a cynical way of displaying their aggressivity, of dressing themselves up in the seductive image of someone prepared to challenge anything, including peoples' genuine integrity, to confront everything, including the truth. The witty insult, devoid of direction, is particularly prevalent in London now, as more and more people try to make up for their increasingly desperate uncreative impotence and isolation with an assertive image of creative potency, a form of art more subtle and immediate than art obviously dominated by economic criteria but hardly less demoralizing.

King Mob didn't really attempt to come to grips with the brute realities outside the door. Its self- questioning, pitifully small, remained a jumble of good insight and utter incoherence. Within two years it was riven to shreds by lack of clarity, the onset of economic crises and by the class archaisms of the UK that almost effortlessly, it seemed to reproduce. Its leaders (and like those of so many groups today, despite protestations to the contrary), quite quickly fucked off for the bright lights and back to the boorjuice from whence they came.

As for many of the rest, the way up not down proved too alluring once their youthful hi-jinks were played out; the way up becoming part of the post 1968 new middle classes. Some (e.g. McLaren,) achieved national renown, their 'misspent youth' contributed to giving them an easy advantage over their staider rivals. It's depressing because they were so promising and if they'd stuck with their original insights/life -and necessarily deepened them - they would have helped lighten the increasing gloom instead of adding to it. Individuals can and do have an effect even though one must be wary of exaggerating that effect. A scant few, cut to the quick, by this shabby behaviour, especially when it involved former close friends, never copped out. In the long night of reaction that is still with us booze, manic-depression and a beckoning madness were their constant companions even though they comprehended that their reactions were reflex responses to the raving needs of a commodity economy gone mad anyway. In a sense they were among the first to ever burst into that silent sea, forced to play many a fine trick on madness - a madness that has plagued the downturn of every major revolt since.

However to return to the early 1970s. One of the initial reactions, apart from cynicism, to the shabby quick compromises of the King Mob milieu was terrorism -which appeared in the form of The Angry Brigade. Fleet footing in and out of "the Gate", the almost ontological warrior strength they projected made others feel inadequate and contemptible - on purpose one suspected. However, to be generous, although in no way justifying their spectacularised substitionism (which, of course denied being substitutionist) one is obliged to recognise The Angry Brigade as the most avant garde terrorist group in Western Europe and one that fortunately wasn't used by the state like the Red Brigades in Italy or Action Directe in France. The potential as in all terrorist groups was there but their early capture prevented this. Also a certain disdain for a too rigid hierarchy and order taking may have made the task of state infiltration more difficult. However one has to be careful in making suppositions like this. Suffice to say that their manifestoes still have a ring of modernity to them despite much of their wooden, tub-thumping tone. They are refreshingly unlike the quasi-Stalinist/unadulterated blood curdling leftisms of Action Directe or Red Brigades communiques. Perhaps this is the reason why their manifestoes are still reprinted and The Angry Brigade is still held in a certain esteem threatening a second coming like the heirs of the Resistance in Italy or France.

Left to ponder on who were the losers in the long run - us or them - the scale of the co-optation was such that the term" revolutionary" became a prime casualty. It's possible to assign different periods to this response beginning with an early 1970s derisive rejection of militancy. A cartoon at the time showed a typical Notting Hill street scene. Someone has stopped underneath a budding tree. "Hark" he says, "The call of the first militant of spring." By the 1980s a person's worth was valued for how they lived their life and not for the quality of the revolutionary phrase mongering. So many revolutionaries without a revolution when one wanted a revolution without revolutionaries. Later in the 1970s this garbled revolutionism was to be squeezed back into the recuperative rebel music of punk, which got at least some of its edge from the Notting Hill experience over the years. The Clash formerly the 101ers of 101, Walterton Rd - an off-shoot of the Elgin Avenue squat – and spawned in the spit and sawdust, Irish-dominated Chippenham pub, were named after the 1976 Carnival clash with the cops. Minder, the TV serial of cockney low life in the late '70's/early 1980s and which began to popularise more than ever cockney rhyming slang and accent throughout the UK (e.g. Bradford Asians occasionally slipping in a cockney phrase and accent etc.) was often shot on location in Notting Hill and its environs. The Mangrove restaurant appeared in one episode with a local, instantly recognisable giant of a Rasta playing a heavy bit part. Possibly even the fragmentary but ever present anti-art rhetoric, rubbed-off on one episode where a rich, eccentric DJ, shouted, "Death to Music". It's also interesting to note that some of the actors who first found their feet in the Merseyside soap for interlectshooals Brookside can be seen quite regularly on the streets of Notting Hill. Brookside was a media fall-out of Liverpool insurgency, particularly Toxteth in 1981. But the name itself goes back to the Shrewsbury trial arising out of the national building workers' strike of' 72 When, Ricky Tomlinson, a Liverpool building worker, (later to become the Brookside actor) was sent to jail, with two others, accused of really cutting-up untidy on a scab building site. The name of the site? Brookside!

The Clash's first album cover montaged the 1976 Notting Hill riot on the sleeve cover. Music of course -along with the rest of the areas cultural-junk pretensions has been high profile and the list of pop musicians resident or passing-through is endless: Van Morrison. The Pogues. Hank Wangford. Motorhead. Peter Kossoff. Amazulu, George Melly, Kilroy Washington, etc, etc. Though some of this can be diverted within another context (e.g. Motorhead painted into New York style, naive but often funny, anarcho pro-situ murals in Catalunya in the Spanish spring of 1987) there's another point worth making. One would have thought the often rich low-life atmosphere of inner-city Notting Hill would have stimulated some original edgy blues. Instead that incisive expression of black experiences funnelled through the UK's originally white social apartheid -at the moment of rock's brief late summer -came from some dull and uninspiring few acres in London's Surrey suburbia, which spawned Jeff Beck, Ritchie Blackmore and Eric Clapton. At their best they weren't so short of Hendrix's guitar licks ...It goes without saying that these are comments about a recent past and of no relevance to the present situation when music has nothing to say except turn the lights off and "go to sleep."

Liverpool is the most artistically conscious of northern cities. Going back to the 1920s and 1930s its main bent was literary, then literary/musical in the 1950s and 1960s. Since the First World War, the art that has stamped the city has always been 'committed' ears pinned back to catch the sharp turns of phrase Liverpool is noted for. It has at frequent intervals obliquely raised the question of 'art and revolution' but has persistently shunned radical critiques. It is an observation as true of John Lennon as it is of Jamie Reid, the pro-situ recuperator and thief of other people's leaflets and stickers who is now a friend of Mersey actors. The fact that Brookside actors are turning up in "The Gate" merely serves to underscore the similarity in outlook and ambience between the artistic scene in "The Gate" and the one in Liverpool - except of course "the Gate" is incomparably wealthier and closer to the real centers of power and influence in TV/film and theatre. (5)

That's Notting Hill in a nutshell: real issues and real conflict instantly spectacularized for media consumption. With regard to recuperation a point must be made about Notting Hill. Here recuperation is instant, clever and quite out of synch with a more laggardly, even archaic means elsewhere in the UK.

Footnote (5): Compare for instance the lives of Jack Common and George Garret, one from Tyneside the other from Liverpool. Garrett, a docker, sailor, tugboat man and beachcomber went to New York where he became a Wobbly before deported back to Liverpool. Increasingly attracted by theatre and literature he took to writing short stories and plays about Liverpool in the 1930s. He died a tugboat man and not an artist. Due to structural changes in capital since – which needs art for its own reproductive ends - a Garrett today would necessarily have to cease being a worker and join the well rewarded, professional world of finks like Willy Russell and Bleasdale. Even in Garrett's day however Common - unemployed for much of the 1920s before moving south - developed the outlines of a strikingly original ~ radical critique of art. It was only after World War Two and the dashing of his revolutionary hopes that he took to writing factual accounts which had the appearance - but note only appearance - of novels.

A Half Way Libertarianism.

However given the areas general libertarian ambience, finding toes to tread on wasn't difficult. Try and be more rigorous and concrete and you were really courting ostracism. Its phoney classlessness was not really to be questioned. The issue of class was always fudged, ignored and a muddle-headed liberal individualism could so quickly turn into a disregard for basic human needs and a helping hand which more solidly working class neighbourhoods give priority too - though less and less so in London. Moreover there was a tendency to disregard those subtle changes of attitude amongst workers. Passing almost unnoticed it meant that a lot of the old prejudices (get a good job, get married, honour the nuclear family, racism etc) were being thrown off. Partly this was happening in response to the high degree of visibility this somewhat elitist libertarian scene gave to scanning such prejudices.

Escaping the constraints of an overbearing family was fine but then to have no back up whatsoever was also often a recipe for mental breakdown and suicide, which happened only too often. The only other alternative at hand were hard drugs, especially heroin, which in Notting Hill was initially spectacularized as romantic, daring and free and the ultimate 'junk' commodity - at once spoof and liberation -surpassing the philistine need to acquire a car, nice carpets and go on a package holiday. Not being able to take our desires for reality heroin ran a close second. But this was well before its extension into working class communities became commonplace and where its destructive, pacifying, function was only too obvious. Indeed, King Mob, constructed a float for the 1969 Notting Hill Carnival on which a girl "Miss Notting Hill 1969" sat with a jumbo sized jacking iron sticking out of her arm from which ketchup was pouring. Sure it was meant to be a tasteless, disenchanted comment but one that refused to sit in judgement. It was a comment on the fact there was junk and junk, the hard stuff or the heroin of mindless routine and consumption. To condemn one without condemning the other, was simply pissing in the wind and when some thirteen years later, smack was more explicitly condemned (because now it was a mass problem), some of the slogans which appeared had, all the abstract poetic dash one had come to associate with the district: "The junkies you've created are committing slow-motion suicide." Others however, were less so: "cheap heroin - the cure for unemployment."

Inevitably, the libertarian element in Notting Hill was expressed in sexual encounters of all kinds. Not only did whites and blacks meet here but gays, lesbians and others in a unique blend. Marriage and the closed family unit were and still are sneered at. But neither was it entirely liberating. In fact, liberation was the exception not the rule.

Though talk of class was frowned on, there was (and is) a lot of rough trade - that typical sexual expression of class. Bohemian middle class meets the working class freak. Given the class-obsessed nature of the UK it's an explosive mix. Both attractive and ruinous as each try to point-score and get their own back on each other. For the patrician bohemian, a means of consciousness-raising and turn on by a wild animal. For the freak, a sexually demagogic dictatorship of the proletariat, even if rarely expressed with this degree of clarity. Inevitably these relationships would break up in bitter mutual recrimination, as libertarianism shaded into decomposition. A former actress of the Maria Aitken rather than the Julie Walters School, her affectations and composure becoming frayed through too many gins, would go on the game looking for some ready dosh. When it comes to naming a shop and independent record label (and which was to become one of the UK's most successful recording labels) Rough Trade was just right for the area.

Plus Multi-Ethnicity and Work.

Alongside the areas attraction to an art/anti-art bohemia, (which in the last analysis ended up in the art game) Notting Hill has acted as a magnet for immigrant peoples. In fact that was to be the areas special stamp: bohemianism and multi-ethnicity. The Caribbean peoples' who started to arrive in large numbers in the 1950s are obviously the most well known. There were also the Spanish and Portuguese escaping unemployment and fascism in the Iberian Peninsula. After the Portuguese coup of April 25th 1974 many local and legless Portuguese celebrated the event in what seemed every pub in the area. The Spanish took their turn eighteen months later on hearing of Franco's death. It goes without saying the Irish are everywhere in Notting Hill because Inner London in total is very much an Irish city - if not the biggest in all but name. Bit by bit there were all the other nationalities to be found in Notting Hill probably numbering around 30.

They were always, always escaping something: sad, ever so sad looking Hungarians unable to forget 1956 in Budapest, Poles excited about the Polish August of 1980, Ukrainians' reminiscing about Kiev but so pleased to have landed safely in the UK's social security system, never to do a stroke of work again. Downing pints of lager in pubs opposite the Brunel Estate (council housing estate) they were coming round to thinking the British state every bit as bad, if not worse than the Russian! And then there are the stateless Czechs hiding from 'their' Embassy a mile away. All of them a bag of nerves, they would crack black jokes about their predicament. Three Czechs together and one must be a spy! One reputed spy ran a cake stall, for a short while on Portobello Rd. Pullover on back to front he seemed to be perpetually drunk. The word got round that he had a flat in the centre of Prague .His cover was blown and Czech home cooking disappeared from Portobello Road. As his former friends said, anybody who can get a flat in the centre of Prague was for certain a spy. Of all the East Europeans in the area though, the Czechs were (perhaps are?) the most aware. They want some autonomous councilist system disliking the Western lefties too. Hating state bureaucracy so much one preferred to remain stateless. On the night the LP of the Czech pop group, Plastic People was released, several of them went wild, insisting the English police were liberal and you could kick them up the arse before they would do anything. It never got as far as this. Throwing gallon jars onto a main road from top story windows was sufficient to get them nicked. Taken to Notting Hill cop shop one of them when asked if he'd ever been arrested before replied: "hundreds of times -by the Russians"!

Many of the immigrants weren't of course, so inspiring or nice – either being deeply conservative and sometimes even worse. In The Earl Percy pub one evening, a former - or so he said- Latvian SS guard drunkenly lamented that he hadn't killed enough Jews! His eyes bloodshot through drink and maybe lack of sleep, he took a perverse pleasure in being offensive. Maybe he was bullshitting; maybe he was acting out a tasteless piece of street theatre for an audience and therefore more fool enough than elsewhere to fall for 'living theatre'.

But as a rule the libertarian feel of the area undoubtedly spread its glow over all ethnic groupings and cramping traditions quickly broke up. A Filipina gal would shack-up with a Ukrainian. A Moroccan youth would leave the prayer mat for the ganja, while his Dad started to carry on with the Irish barmaid, who was having a few hot flushes about not going to Mass. Not forgetting the first Asian supermarket on the corner of Westbourne Park Road and All Saints Road: staffed by drunken Pakistanis (how did they square this with Islam?) who let shoplifters do as they pleased because they were having secret tipples all day from the shelves. A few months later they were all to get the sack from Mr Big in charge of the growing chain of supermarkets.

Even the media-stereotyped heavies and hards in Notting Hill had a libertarian disposition. Local skinheads objected to being called racist in the pages of the New Musical Express. Bombhead, one of their leaders, in fact usually got VI P treatment when he hit black All Saints Road on a Friday evening to collect his weekend grass. The same goes for the West London Hell's Angels who bevvied in the local Colville and Bevington Arms. In fact one of their members, Mikkelson - and typical of a Notting Hill connected Hell's Angel chapter - a black guy was killed by cops in the south west of London in 1985. For ages the press kept quiet about Mikkelson being black, probably because the last thing they wanted to see was open fraternization everywhere between somewhat racist Hells Angels chapters and rebellious blacks. That particular divide and rule had to be kept intact at any cost.

When the first large scale riot broke out in Notting Hill in 1976 the whites who joined in the fray, apart from the drop-outs, were mainly indigenous working class, particularly those who slung bricks at the cops from the modern ten-storey, council-owned Lowerwood Court, a block of flats at the corner of Ladbroke Grove and Lancaster Road. Portuguese and Spanish youth etc did not join in. Maybe they had been told by their parents to keep well clear. Only later in 1982/'83 did this begin to change, highlighted by a noticeable incident elsewhere in North London. A mixed gang of Portuguese and black youths went on the rampage trashing cars in a large parking space.

Many of these ethnic groups - all more or less working class - in stark, often schizoid contrast with the anti-work undertow of the area, found low-paid employment in the Health Service, local authorities, service industries, hotels, stores, catering and cleaning. A lot of the women worked of course as poorly paid clerical staff in state depts, head offices of corporations and banks etc. The close proximity of the nearby Park Royal Trading Estate meant factory work was also available to some degree. One Spanish anarchist in his early 50' s employed in a Walls sausage factory, once mentioned how he had forlornly looked at the millionth sausage passing by on the assembly line hoping for the day the factory would close forever. Later it did. How does he feel to be too old ever to work again? From forced work to forced redundancy - what a choice!

One gets the impression that while one part of night owl Notting Hill was getting ready for bed, the other half was getting ready for work. It wasn't simply just a deviant middle class/working class split (though that came into it) because the night birds included a lot of blacks and cockney whites. The latter were often from pretty tough families who to reduce the ruinous evils of casualism had in the past, learnt how to exploit the plethora of charities which had sprung up in London in the latter half of the 19th century, later to become institutionalized into the welfare state. To their name they had a long and honourable tradition of "never work" before the couplet had come to signify, post 1968, a more conscious refusal to sell one's labour power, so another could profit from it.

In common with most other inner city areas, Notting Hill has its share of petty thieves, but few make a proper living out of it. Unlike the East End, it's not an area noted for heavy villainy. Even so if you wanted to make a quick visit to the casualty ward, or even worse end up in Kensal Green cemetery you only had to chat up a villains broad in The Pig and Whistle pub next to Latimer Road station. Ironically in Notting Hill valorising/promotion of the image of villainy came from an unexpected quarter: that of a decomposed revolutionary scene around the former Angry Brigade, gone money-mad. (6) The job of subverting capitalist society got mixed up with a fetishization of crime and the proceeds arising from crime, which can be very considerable.

Romantically and mistakenly, crime, Big Crime, tended to be regarded as a left-handed form of human endeavour rather than the foundation of many of the world's business empires. Rubbing shoulders with villains on the Costa Del Crime because the contemporary, moneyed version, of the 19th century adulation of brigandage which, however, did have links with protest movements. When De Sade's, "Crime is the Highest Form of Sensuality" was sprayed up on Portobello Road, it didn't mean three cheers for Ronnie Knight or the Kray Twins.

The splendid French tradition of great criminals, stretching from Lacenaire to Mesrine and its fictionalised representation in Pepe Le Moko or, Touchez pas au Grisbi couldn't be arbitrarily transplanted to the generally vicious and visionless exploits of the typical London villain. In saying this, one must also make a clear distinction between villainy and the gangs of London Jack-the-Lads often with a magnanimous and chivalrous disposition who hold up banks, building societies etc with guns which often aren't loaded. These lads often despise muggings and any form of cheap assault, but want the readies for a wild time.

Footnote (6): Getting hold of a lot of dosh can be very useful at times and no one's making any silly critique of bank robbery here. The trouble comes in spending it. So often those 'subversives' - none too clear theoretically - use it as a short-circuit access, grabbing all the glitz capital has to offer. Or else, deposit it on useless leftist propaganda projects (e.g. funding the now defunct News On Sunday) when dosh for autonomous projects is a crying necessity. Even printing a good leaflet, which attempts to make some practical suggestion, costs a lot.

Then of course there are the buildings - always the buildings - as a steady source of North Kensington employment. Full time, casual or scrounge. Blacks/Irish/Sikhs and Cockneys, in the pub: downing ten pints, moaning about bad paying sub-contractors and hating architects. They chat about how they would draw the line at being recruited to build a cop shop or law court. They are all staggered by the rise in property prices; well aware they could never afford to live in what they are building and sighing about what's to be done. London one big building site and the poor decanted. But alongside them and in sometimes greater numbers, there is always to be found the dumb fuck building worker; the ever potential scab who voted Tory because a stock exchange boom meant work, work and more work and to hell with everything else. It was a joy seeing such narrow self-interest crumble in the face of the stock exchange crash, as subbies raced to finish jobs all over London, knowing that at the top end of the market, every delay meant more knocked off the selling price. Quite suddenly the options market in property was over and London began to breathe a little once more.

October 4th 1972: Building workers throwing out Notting Hill squatters *(Maoist situ Bruce Birchall)*

COMMUNITY POLITICS: THE STILL LIVING DEAD

There was one other important employer in Notting Hill; one which had and has an importance, cachet, kudos - call it what you will - out of all proportion to its size: community politics. Since the 1958 race riot (the subject of Absolute Beginners) when black Americans GI's stationed in England showed their Caribbean brothers how to make molotovs, Notting Hill became a trend setting area for a whole assortment of inner-city initiatives which like all reforms, had to be paid for a thousand times over in that fundamental oppressive currency – social control. Over the years these initiatives have coalesced into what is commonly known as community politics, depressingly familiar all over the UK. The Notting Hill Social Council funded by well-heeled organizations and charities, was set up in November 1960 and it became a forum for all those who had begun to work in the voluntary social agencies in the area after the 1958 riots. Quite quickly the Social Council began to change and expand acquiring a new image, notably through the impact of a 'new' left coming into the area, after the traumas of the Soviet invasion of Hungary in ' 56. In fact there was little that was 'new' in it, though it took years for that to become apparent. It had merely been forced to ditch Stalinism - that's all.

These new groupings developed outside the Labour party. In particular the local Labour party in the 1950s had been overtly racist, calling for an end to immigration. There was a whiff of Puritanism, a fear of miscegenation added to this anti-black stance borrowed from Oswald Moseley's English Fascists who were active in the area at the time prior to being driven off the streets by the blacks and the nascent Trotskyist WRP around Gerry Healey in 1958. The local Labour party in response to shame and outside pressure from those who had outflanked it gradually changed. It took them more than twenty years to recover the ground they had lost. They could only do that by becoming vastly more receptive to the moods of the time.

This face-lift was in retrospect to add up to something far more than a local event. Wedgewood-Benn was to use this local, shell-shocked, rapidly modernizing North Kensington Labour party as a springboard of the parliamentary 'New Left'. In the process what might now be termed a new rainbow alliance was added to familiar Labour left concerns. It was to shine in the skies of Notting Hill well in advance of anywhere else. Only the bucket of gold at the end of this rainbow was not an autonomy of many different hues but a parliamentary seat. 'Extra parliamentary' activity, which Notting Hill played such a key role in pioneering, was usually guided by Parliamentarians and was conceived eventually as an adjunct to Parliament. If you like it was phraseological parliamentary concession to "direct action."

As most of these initiatives ostensibly outside Labour party control were funded by state or charity organizations they were vulnerable to Labour party manipulation in any case. For quite a time, they were able to keep it at arms' length. Behind the libertarian veneer peculiar to the area and which altered the character of local initiatives to some degree, there was hostility to entrenched political structure. As a result the real intentions behind these initiatives, which were never more than capital permitted, became veiled and many a local person hoped to make good their loss with the help of these initiatives. Indeed the Carnival was originally a multi-ethnic invention of a white social worker. (7)

Footnote (7): Wedgewood Benn lives in nearby Holland Park. At the time a lot of these initiatives were in their infancy, Ben - possibly unaware of them - was the highly placed, Minister for Technology, in Harold Wilson's 1964/'70 Labour Government. It was only later and out of such high office that Benn began to take an interest - obviously hoping to use them for a comparable high position at a future date.

It has its funny side too. One labour party councillor became a councillor so that he did not have to work - or so it is laughingly maintained in the area. He thus has a legitimate defense all the way from Unemployment Review Officers to Restart. The allowances he claims for attending meetings is his moonlighting dosh which others had to illegally scrounge for.

After a certain period of time had lapsed, the Labour party was able to spring its trap, relatively unimpeded on groupings as disparate as the local toy Bolshevikhs like the Italian group, Lotta Continua as well as various single issue bodies like the battered Women's Refuge Centre etc. (8)

Footnote (8): Lotta Continua, through the CAC, had an influence on Carnival policy. What the initials CAC stand for doesn't matter. The drift, for some at the time, was that CAC meant cacky (i.e. shite). In Notting Hill, Lotta Continua's group was called "Fight On". But it would have been better described as, "the show must go on". Endless meetings were held, and on demos red flags would be shoved into peoples' hands to 'politicize' them. In 1974, they attempted to stage a glossy evening of militant entertainment. A chic photographer in bright red costume (what else?) recorded the historic occasion on film. A dreadful film they'd produced on N. Ireland was screened. The sending of troops to Ulster was put down to "the deepening contradictions between labour and capital". If it only had been that simple! The only amusing sideshow to this happening of world revolution was the bizarre buffet of free cornflakes and milk. The Lotta Continua elect were the only ones to partake as if needing to guide the people even on this score. Towards the mid 70s, "Fight On" was to be seen hanging around with Labour party types more frequently. It was not apparent at the time that their more explicit Parliamentarism here reflected what was happening in Italy. At the Rimini conference in 1976, Lotta Continua, agreed to dissolve itself as a vanguard organization, not because the strains of autonomy were ripping it to shreds (a view widely held at the time) but because the electoral gains of the Italian Communist party (the moment of the "historic compromise") rendered the need for their separate party, superfluous. It showed yet again, how in advanced countries, Bolshevism always falls back into Parliamentarism.

The often crushing psychologising and bossiness increased the more links with the local Labour party who helped run the centre in an unofficial capacity, were forged. This development caused some local women to criticize the centre on the grounds of common sense. For example, they objected to the case-con psychologizing of refugees, when what they needed most was simply enough space to be left alone, without hassle, until they felt able to pull their shattered lives together. But behind all this was another very real factor. Anti-squatting laws enacted by the 1974-79 Labour government ensured that many squats which Women's Aid had readily snapped up, were closed down. It was at this moment that a cunning Labour racketeering and infiltration could then cheekily shift the blame somewhat on the women victims – mediated of course, through women members of the party. As always psychology became the means of abstracting from concrete social relations.

Throughout Notting Hill the more these para-state initiatives – slowly but then more obviously - began to move within the orbit of the Labour party, the more they started interestingly enough, to be criticized from below. It was a purely spontaneous response however and nothing like a coherent critique of Labourism appeared. Initially though these projects were welcomed and people held their fire as concerns and issues formulating around particular pressure groups began to mushroom all over Notting Hill from 1960 onwards. To give a detailed, historical account of each of these essentially para-state bodies is too boring and rather irrelevant. But to get some idea of how thick on the ground they were, consider the following list:

The Police Group, The North Ken Playspace Group, The Neighbourhood Service, Notting Hill Community Workshop, The May Day Manifesto Group (sociologically-updated nationalisers under workers' control) Colville Gardens Action Committee, The St. Stephens Group, The Housing Group, Powis Playgroup, the Lancaster Neighbourhood Centre, The Mothers Traffic Group, The Group Group etc.

The number and variety does sound limitless and for those too young to remember, it can indeed sound impressive. Living as they do in a period in which civil society is being intensely pulverized, they cannot know what it was like to have lived under an apparently endless proliferation of these bodies amounting sadly to nothing of historic, world-shaking importance. Indeed, although most people living in Notting Hill would vaguely register the fact that these outfits existed, basically 90% of the population took no interest in them. In fact these outfits as they got progressively weaker, related to no one but themselves and in that sense became more remote than trade union hierarchies who are forced, in their topsy-turvy way, to acknowledge to some degree the realities of a workaday world inhabited by alive and kicking people (and not just) the bureaucratically minded and converted.

At one point in the early 1970s, it was even suggested that some of these para-state initiatives, by then emanating from a Peoples Centre, were parallel with the worker/student Action Committees in France in May '68. Whatever the unevenness and inadequacies of the French Committees: they were genuine responses to a genuine situation of intense class conflict. Even if they did not issue organically from the Workers' Occupation movement, nevertheless they remained throughout the French general strike part of the real base of contestation. They were not formed or funded by this official body, or that charity, with all the invisible strings attached. In contrast the para-state committees in Notting Hill were down on any effective direct action or violence signalling out in particular, the activities of an unholy alliance between anarcho pro-situ's and Maoists. However confused and un-worked out these activities as a whole were, they were ever ready to take on the cops and go in for commando-style operations, (e.g. when successfully tearing down fences surrounding private gardens so they could be used for children's play space). Of course some, if not all of these pressure groups arose out of real needs (e.g. children being killed by cars, appalling housing etc) but they all looked forward to the creation of a liberal benign state, ever ready to resource, fund and satisfy an infinity of needs. Inevitably for sincere and naive individuals, who wanted action against the state now, it would bring confusion and even crippling demoralisation. For others more shrewd and cynical, it was the first rung of the ladder to a career in local and central government agencies.

At certain moments, these bodies couldn't help but reflect profounder currents in the air - which is not to say they deepened these currents – merely that they had no resistance to them. For example the 1966 London Free School, set up in Notting Hill, brought together disparate tendencies - most notably - a kind of seemingly disengaging educational, social work and, a seemingly disengaging cultural drift away from institutional frameworks.

The dreadfully naive, non-violent and wimpish, hippy alternative, International Times got some charge here and Peter Jenner, later of Pink Floyd, who was also there, no doubt found some inspiration in this Free School for, Just Another Brick in the Wall - with lines like –"Teacher leave those kids alone" - etc. By the time the LP was produced ten years later, a hip north London headmistress had given permission to use her pupils for the back-up chorus! Some Free School! But then a Free School, like a Free State was always a nonsensical, unrealizable object. (9)

Footnote (9): Equally contradictory, the words from the song, "We Don't Want No Education" were spray-painted on a polystyrene wall as backing for a display of shop window models advertising school uniforms in Top Shop at Brent Cross Shopping Mall in the early 1980s.

Then there was the Notting Hill People's Association, an umbrella body that appeared in the late 1960s, which claimed to draw all separate threads together and give them a focus. In spite of its 'oppositional' stance the capitalist division of labour went largely unchallenged. They just did not feel in the gut the unbearable parcelization capitalism was thrusting on humanity. It was folly to even raise it with them. Culture? Nothing wrong with culture except there's not enough of it and it goes to the wrong people! (As if culture wasn't intrinsically one of the hierarchical methods of judging 'wrong' people from 'right-on' people) However in what participants fondly imagined were grass roots organizations there was some unease about the use of professionals, whether they were 'socialist' lawyers, social workers etc. To these potentially damaging perceptions of roles, quick correctives were suggested to confuse the issue and render the personnel staffing the para-state more impervious to criticism. There were proposals for "partisan community workers and. full time socialist engineers" or "anti-capitalist dambusters" (an appeal for ghostbusters would have been as sensible). What these riddles mean are best left to the imagination of the addled cadres who pretend to believe that all work is the same. But one thing is for sure depending on the local Mr or Ms Fix It, it meant a job, easy money and status. At no point did this bureaucratically latitudinarian passion for organization ever become autonomous. Same of the more gullible participants who read 'quality' newspapers thought it did. Just what is one to make of sophisms like "semi-autonomous"? One community organiser even called for "Anti-Community Disorganization"! Within the orbit of the state it may have represented the ultimate in self-criticism: in relation to sound, practical questions it was gobbledy-gook.

Possessing a half-baked critique of institutions meant these initiatives were vulnerable and easily absorbed by the very institutions they had feebly criticised in the first instance. Since they occupied the same platform as managers of discontent, the bigger, older established institution was more likely to swallow the smaller (e.g. The Housing Action Centre, in no time, moved in with the Council's Information and Aid Centre, when flashy modern premises were built in 1974). But all of it had the look of newly tilled ground, which indeed it was in terms of the recuperation of real needs.

Another first was The Summer Project of Community Action in 1967 where students sporting the first mass-produced 'community action' badges, paid to come and work in the area. What mugs! It was in Notting Hill that the first Law Centre opened in 1970 and from which point was to emanate all the bullshit about radical lawyers being able to defend the proletariat against the ravages of the law. In fact most people who've had any dealings with them are left with a sour taste in their mouths. They've felt they've been given a stern lesson in law. Not only as an objective fact - that is to be expected - but also secretly in the opinion of the 'radical' solicitor. "Whose side are they on" is a complaint often muttered? To practise at the bar a solicitor cannot have a criminal record. Should they be convicted of a criminal offence they are instantly de-frocked by the Law Society, which looks after their interests, (very well). It also polices them. Of course solicitors generally are in private practise a bunch of swindlers but their fiddling goes largely undetected. Radical lawyers disapproving of the stereotyped solicitor (at least to begin with!) frequently come across as insufferably self righteous individuals who will defend a shoplifter for example, but are never able to empathize with them. Tending to substitute a political hierarchy for the more frequently encountered lawyers fascination with criminal hierarchies, they look down on shoplifting and the like as something 'sub-political' and squalid in comparison with terrorist idiocy for example. (Though without apparent contradiction, but reflecting the change from public to private practise, they will follow the former terrorist into big-time racketeering). Nor can radical lawyers encourage people to break the law (e.g. squat, occupy factories or offices etc) though privately they might concede it is right to do so. Radical lawyers can never be the subject of a genuine revolution and are only able to conceive of change within a judicial, statist framework. Perhaps that is why Shakespeare in Henry V111 has Dick the Butcher, one of Jack Cade's Kentish Rebels say, "The first thing we do, let's kill all the lawyers." (10)

ELGIN AVENUE SQUAT: Footnote(10): The best struggle by far in the ear1y 1970s occurred on the boundary of Notting Hill and Maida Vale. This was the massive squat

housing around 1,000 squatters in Elgin Avenue by the GLC. It was to last several years until all the squatters were rehoused in other GLC properties and the Victorian houses demolished, making way for a modern council estate redevelopment which was later privatized. It was an exhilarating squat involving fights with the cops, disruptions of official meetings and the occupation of the LEB showrooms in Notting Hill in January 1974. By the time Elgin Ave ended (it was a 'victory' of sorts) most of the squatters were, in one way or another, exclusively working class (e.g. street cred hippies). Throughout its existence, there were regular "street unity meetings" and a committee answerable to these meetings was elected. Though it was an example of direct democracy, skilled manipulators were able to soft-soap these street assemblies. One spokesperson that became well known was Piers Corbyn. He was a Trotskyist apparatchik belonging to the International Marxist Group (before the IMG dissolved itself into the Labour party). His influence was immense as regards general Elgin Ave policy and the line taken by the squatters newspaper (EASY-Elgin Avenue Squatters? Yes!) This newspaper emphasized getting support from this or that institution (e.g. Young Liberals or, Paddington's then Labour MP) and rubbished the libertarian current which called for "Free Housing for all" instead of the usual "nationalize the land" nonsense. The former demand was put forward by The Diggers who had a few years earlier been based elsewhere in Notting Hill. Later they were to become the backbone of the Rainbow Tribe Tepee people (c/f above photo) and The Peace Convoy. Despite all the mystifications and contradictions surrounding an alternative lifestyle, they nonetheless in Elgin Ave and elsewhere called for a radical approach to housing. Although Corbyn was an adept entryist and able, at times, to push para-state bodies like Student Community Housing (SCH) and the obsessively legalistic, Family Squatting Advisory Service (FSHS) he also kept getting way-laid by the libertarian atmosphere of Notting Hill. He once noted for instance how a guy known as "Shaky Dave" found in building street barricades, more therapeutic help than anything social workers, asylums or drug dependence had to offer. Later - befitting the trajectory of the IMG - Corbyn became a Labour p arty councillor in Southwark (Elgin Ave was rehoused in Camberwell) where from his bureaucratic perch, he defended the Pullens Estate and other Southwark squatters against the more Militant controlled Southwark Council who were evicting them. Many a Southwark squatter has mouthed-off about Corbyn, often saying how his presence spreads the illusion that something can be done by reforming the Council, thus pacifying the necessary direct action. One anarchist even punched him in the face.)

Alternative Social Agencies.

One of the first community printing presses came into existence at about the same time as the Law Centre. We must not forget the innovative alternative social agencies, like BIT information centre catering for the drifters and dropouts which the area attracted in large numbers. In some ways these alternative agencies were less bureaucratic, more responsive to real needs, less at the beck and call of more straight-laced set-ups. Nevertheless, Release (for drugs) based in Notting Dale, to some extent sheltered behind the opportunistic shield provided by the academics of The Sociology of Deviancy whose research into drug taking were in vogue at the time. In their salad days they scoured the area looking for titbits to advance their careers, bringing street cred into the remote world of academia. They were not explaining drug taking, as theirs was a plea to authority to be more sensitive and understanding. In this sense, their later more overt concern with police policy and behaviour in their capacity as shadow advisors to a Kinnockite Labour Party, is of a piece with their earlier work whatever reservations they may now have about "deviancy" (c/f Laurie Taylor on the 1981 riots).

These outfits dealing with a more marginalized drifting population (subscribing now to a hippy ideology, then to punk etc) had charity status like the more orthodox charity-sponsored community work schemes. However their more relaxed atmosphere gave the impression they were more gatecrashed by their freak clientele, than they really were. COPE, the alternative psychiatric set up was 'taken over' by a bunch of libertarian crazies, (grown up kids really) who then spent a lot of their time on their knees waiting for the likes of the traditionally philanthropic Rowntree's etc, to put money in their collecting tins.

The escape clause offered by having charity status also applied to the Ruff Tuff Cream Puff squatter estate agency (the only 'estate agency' for squatters). Despite its ameliorative social function (Harrow Road police station would occasionally send homeless people there), it did nonetheless initiate some audacious squats. Among them, houses in Norfolk belonging to the Royal Family, Mick Jagger's unused country home and the Cambodian Embassy in Notting Hill Gate, which was squatted for several years after being abandoned when Prince Sihanouk was overthrown. Not too mention the brilliant cracking of the huge Palm Court Hotel near Richmond Bridge on the Thames. Ruff Tuffs 'property magazine' containing witty descriptions of potential squats is still a delight to read (e.g. "36, St. Lukes Road. Empty two years. Entry through rear. No roof. Suit astronomer.") Yet many people entering this squatting agency felt immediately ill at ease, overcome by feelings they were unable to put a name to. Was it because it was run by renegade aristos' with hippy names like Mad Dog and Fluke? Was it Heathcote Williams old Etonian manner of barking rather than speaking? Or similarly his references to endless esoteric, occult mysteries which made you feel like a fool for not having a clue as to what he was talking about. The cat's name was "Windsor" and that didn't help either. In occupying Crown Property were they perhaps settling scores with their parents? They were friendly enough all right; never too stuck-up to say hello when they met you in the street. Yet deep down one felt set apart which palaeontologists of the English class system will instantly recognise.

Out of the Ruff Tuff came the mass squats in run down Council property in Freston Road, Notting Dale. But being North Kensington, a mass squat without frills was inconceivable. It was also an act of poetic license, an illusory declaration of UDI. This 'statelet' whose founding father appeared to be no less than William Blake was proclaimed simultaneously as Frestonia (the Marx Bros,"Freedonia"?) and the Albion Free State. Maybe it was tongue in cheek, but such romantic nationalism should have perished as soon as Blake's "Jerusalem" became compulsory singing in English public schools. To accept such notions as a 'Free State' (a contradiction in terms) without quibble is standard Labour party fodder. The term Albion Free State wasn't contested by the squatters but others winced at it.

At about the same time another urban experiment with charity status got under way in Notting Hill. This was Meanwhile Gardens fashioned out of derelict land between the council properties of Golborne Rd and the Grand Union Canal. Intended as a 'visionary' reply to the usual dreary municipal park, its eclectic borrowings from

Japanese landscaping to Celtic Barrows are today yet another mausoleum to institutionalized 'freedom'. Apart from the occasional free, small scale, pop concert or the community bonfire on the 5th of November it is deserted. Shunned by local residents (but not their dogs) who regard it as something of a dump and eyesore, the park has few visitors today. Brooding over this avant-garde cock-up is the concrete and glass monstrosity or Trellick Tower designed by Mars group architect, Erno Goldfinger. Looking at this monument to the failure of the International Style from his "very desirable" residence in Hampstead, Erno Goldfinger fondly thought of it as a veritable modern castle. But to the poor immigrant families who were put there (different floors were given to different races) it was scarcely better than a dungeon suspended in mid-air. On the approaches to Meanwhile Gardens some were to end it once and for all, taking that great leap into space. Though the alternative landscape architects of Meanwhile Gardens detested Trellick Tower, it is fitting that both these avant-garde projects belonging to different eras have been given the bird by the 'philistine' locals.

Perhaps the granddaddy of all this urban experiment is to be found in the Adventure Playground built in 1960 in response to the 1958 race riots. Another Notting Hill 'first' it was initially aimed at pacifying riotous impulses among kids. Way ahead of its time and twenty years before hydra-headed riot was to appear everywhere in the UK, it was the invention, interestingly enough of Lady Allen of Hurlwood together with local residents whom she'd got interested in her pet project. The spirit of courtly, patrician liberalism and noblesse oblige was changing its face changing into the Duchess of the Inner-Cities syndrome.

Adventure Playgrounds were an obviously easy answer to the problems thrown up by an increasingly dehumanised urban environment. The fact too the streets were unsafe for kids to play in and unpromising in terms of the 'imaginative' potential of timber walk-ways and ropes to swing on, merely disguised the fact that every inch of space had its potentially rising price. Though on the economic fact sheet kids were simply a nuisance, lip service had to be paid to Notting Hill's pretence at knowing how to bring up children better. Today it is one of the greatest paradoxes in London (and not just London) as a whole that the more childhood and adolescence is recognised, the greater is the curtailment of kids capacity for expression and play.

It is perhaps the main reason why in London, innocent larking about tends to rapidly drift into explosive confrontation. Fifteen school kids on a bus and everyone expects trouble. As older Londoners will tell you it used to be very different. Post war childhoods were played out on bombsites where property values and rights of ownership were temporarily waived. Only when all this started to go did this idea of an Indian Reservation of play arise. Go north for example and one immediately notices a more relaxed attitude to kids. Industrial dereliction means that in the big cities there are lots of sites to play on. In this respect not much has changed from thirty years ago. It used to be the canals or railways because most of the mills and factories were functioning. Even so, one must be careful of making too much out of the difference. In the North play also develops into confrontation far more than was the case with a post war childhood. (11)

Footnote (11): In the North there is a recognisable continuity between now and a post war experience. Then, fire raising was restricted to that familiar Yorkshire game of setting railway bank sides alight and the occasional platelayers hut, (how those tarry sleepers burnt). But it didn't occur to anyone to torch a mill, even though they were regularly broken into and bales of mungo and shoddy used for the sheer fun of building a fortress, then taking it by storm. Though frequently chased by adults in authority positions, no one really thought they were lawbreakers. Despite the fact that nowadays, play in "the North" has got much more vandalistic, (e.g. mills are burnt down) even a post war response would now end up as youth custody cases. There is in operation today over West Yorkshire, a camouflaged hooligan special train, full of cops to catch and stamp out for good, all that old familiar railway trackside vandalism. In 1987 they spent a long time patrolling the Fitzwilliam/South Kirkby/Frickley mining areas in particular.

Ever since the area began to take on a radical hue, the abandoned Tabernacle on Talbot Road seemed to beckon as the perfect centre, big enough to house all the separate strands of community politics. A place where radical Muslim groups (on a communist prayer mat!) to the local branch of the Spanish Communist party's trade union organization the CC.OO, could feel free (?) to say what they had to say - which was usually sweet FA - or worse. Ironically just as community politics began to fade from the scene, the opening up and use of the Tabernacle had become a reality. Indeed the pot-pourri Tabernacle was the venue in the late 1970s for one of the first foreign conferences of the Anarcho-Syndicalist union, the CNT. However truth to tell it was scarcely more interesting than the usual run-of-the-community-mill meetings, held there. Old films on the Spanish Civil war like the corny "Furia sobre Espana", which casts Durruti as the heroic, benign, great liberator - in presentation at least similar to Chinese films adulating Mao - were shown. It testified to the fact that the revived CNT, sunk in a glorious past, could never break through into a real analysis of modern alienation.

However, there was something refreshing about the first Irish Ceiledh held in the Tabernacle. Even the gabardine mac. brigade felt at liberty to dance with the young gals. It was a fine illustration of the splendid sociability of the Irish. (As a former Dublin based friend said; "there's a lot of sociability in Ireland, but no socialism"). In later years the Ceiledh sociability was pushed aside as the community organizers emphasized all the showy tartanry - the costumes, the kilts, the pipes and all the wearisome stifling tradition. The Tabernacle Ceilidh began to go down like a lead balloon especially among the Guinness drinking Irish pub crowd. If something of greater interest happened (like a radical printer getting planted with forged bank note plates) then more general meetings would take place, though not necessarily in the Tabernacle. At these meetings, accusatory terms like racism or sexism would be thrown around like confetti. It was a hilarious show for those at the back who just went along for the fun and games. It would take too long here to go into all the very many amusing off-the-wall incidents breaking through this elaborate web of fake community involvement, which continually kept running up against the reality of an absent community.

However, one or two incidents were too good to miss. Like the shabby genteel baby sitter, on call from the alternative Co-op/Agency "We People" who, on going to do an evening baby-sitting stint, found a big black guy in diapers and frilly bra waiting on the doorstep to be put to bed with a titty bottle. ...Or the posh woman going bananas in Holland Park on finding her cleaners asleep, fully dressed and snoring in her four poster bed after having drunk all of her liquor cabinet. Scrawled across the wall of the squat above the agency desktop were the words: "I'm sick and tired of waking up feeling tired and sick". Unfortunately it was this sidesplitting oddness of an area like Notting Hill that the left with an obligatory alternative and libertarian image, reserved their most severe frown for. To them it was simply not funny. On hearing about such things barely a trace of a smile would flicker across their faces. Rather it reflected the depth to which humanity had sunk under capitalism. For the socialist priests of authentic communication, salvation was to be found by confessing their sexism or racism or whatever and following their pure example in every walk of life.

The House That Jack 'n' Jill Built

"Don't Trust the Trust" *(1970s wall slogan)*

One of the biggest concerns of the recuperative social agencies in North Kensington was housing. Notting Hill in the late 1950s/early 60s became the main focus of the campaign against Rachmanite slum landlordism. Rents were often extortionate, repairs non-existent and there were cases of families being thrown out to make way for gambling shebeens and organized prostitution. The trouble was condemnation of often appalling housing conditions stopped well short of a thorough going critique of the forced and false scarcity of housing. Outspoken, rebellious tenants courageously fighting these often murderous landlords were, more often than not, vulnerable to manipulation by bodies dedicated to housing reform particularly the Housing Association movements with their links with one of the biggest landowners in the UK, the Church of England. Some were to get jobs in these bodies believing they were furthering 'socialism' whereas they were just another brand of landlordism. Eventually their genuine fury would become bitter and twisted the more they were squeezed by their petty authority position. As a whole however, tenants struggle was channelled towards the elimination at the ruthless private rented sector in favour of Council Housing and particularly Housing Trusts.

In fact the Housing Trust movement goes back to the late 19th century when Octavia Hill started managing property in North Kensington for private landlords. Its illustrious drawing room beginning altered over the years, receiving money from the Housing Corporation and latterly the Council but its patrician style basically remained. Thus tenants were to have no statutory rights and expected to go cap in hand subdued for evermore, by their gracious protectors. Rebellious tenants in run down housing owned by ruthless landlords were flattered by this gracious helping hand, mediated through faithful Trust workers. The fire burning under a tenants' revolt quickly got dampened down by demands for cheap, 'fair' rents administered by them. If not that, they then might suggest approaching the Council for a CPO (Compulsory Purchase Order).

But such was the anger over housing needs, spilling over into a more general anger, that Tory councillors were taken prisoner one night in 1973 and held under lock and key for the duration, to face the anger of the residents. The struggle in Notting Hill was focussed on the elimination of racketeering private landlordism and its substitution by some form of state housing, characteristic of an interventionist capitalist state.

Obviously, because of the degree of controls existing in this sector which favour tenants far more than the private sector, (including Housing Co-op's or Associations), it is hardly surprising that people in housing need are instantly going to call for more cheap, secure, rented Council accommodation. The chorus of approval with few dissenting voices backing their demands was unusual. Even for the post war 'welfare' consensus which then held sway it was simplistic anti-Toryism. Very few had any idea of just how dire the housing built by local Labour authorities could be. Because for some time the North Kensington Labour party had not had its hands on power, it was able to maintain its pristine image more easily. One typical community politico visiting the North East, appalled by the vast housing estates of Felling, Jarrow and Gateshead, thought it would be a good idea to bring the North Kensington Labour party to take a look for themselves at the reality of decades-long Labour party control of local authority. The fact that public housing was much more available in London and the rest of the UK tended to retard in Notting Hill an all round critique of housing. By the time Kensington and Chelsea Council had built a sizable housing portfolio in North Kensington, the rent strikes, in response to Heath's Tory government, Housing Finance Act of the early 1970s were almost over. The area was not to see the binges made possible by council tenants spending their rent money on booze - and having the courage to do so - because solidarity was so high. This infectious merry-making aspect of the rent strikes of the early 70s has never been given the importance it deserves. (12)

Footnote (12): If in the face of the growing housing crisis, we get channelled into a defence of council housing we are merely being manipulated by a facet of State Capitalism. Engel's good pamphlet, The Housing Question that has been regarded for many a decade as a leftist scripture, surprisingly does not call for land nationalization or council housing. This is ironical, coming from a generally banal prophet of "the Workers State". On the contrary, the text has at least something of the aura of a squatter' manual, calling for immediate expropriation of "a part of the luxury dwellings belonging to the propertied class and by compulsory quartering in the remaining part". Its central thesis remains the abolition of the capitalist mode of production, itself inseparable from the supercession of the antithesis between town and country. Despite the pedestrian nature of some of the pamphlet (e.g. paying rent after the revolution) and some wrong facts vis-à-vis recent history, it's still a very necessary text to read for anybody wishing to update the critique of unitary urbanism.

Council housing on a mass level in the UK only really took off as a response by the state (Liberal governed at the time, then followed by the Tories) to the very threatening mass rent strike in Glasgow during the First World War. This mass rent strike was the beginning of revolution in housing. Council housing was the institutionalisation of this tremendous struggle an, basically, an extension of Joseph Chamberlain's municipal liberalism first practised in Birmingham a few years previously. The large-scale extension of council housing was first propagandised through Parliament by an erstwhile member of the revolutionary Clyde Workers' Committee who subsequently joined the Labour party. Hardly surprising too, that council housing in the UK became one of the shibboleths of the Labour party to be furiously defended against all comers, not just Tory Estate Agents, but rent strikers and squatters as well.

THE HIDDEN WORKERS?

Although Notting Hill was predominately working class, off the weirdo streets there was hardly a factory to be found. There were large employers like St Charles and St Mary's Harrow Rd, hospitals, but the area sorely lacked a mass working class visibility. Though workers went on a strike in the area they never stood out as a bunch with the possible exception of the garbage collectors. There was a vast separation between work place and living quarters. They did not seem to tie up at all. What effect this absence has had on the growth of para-state initiatives is anybody's guess. It is doubtful the majority would have ever gotten off the ground if the area had possessed a powerful trade union presence. In fact Notting Hill has never had a strong network of trade union branches, and in spite of the endemic libertarianism of the place, people were generally amazingly laggard when it came to a thorough going critique of such bodies. Attitudes to them would range from an abstract justification, lacking any experience to vague right wing libertarianism, opposed to corporate restrictions on the individual. There were never any unofficial committees in the area, which could have begun to act as a corrective to either extreme, (even though the majority of these committees got caught up again in the union hierarchy) - not to mention the complete absence of any development that might have moved towards genuine base committees.

When links were made over particular struggles they generally seemed somewhat forced and wooden. There was an overlap between squatters and some trade union branches, but inevitably one felt it had been done according to a formula (e.g." to widen the struggle" or to "get the workers involved.") For example, a nearby AEU engineering branch, approached by squatters in the early 1970s put out a statement supporting North Ken squatters, "in their efforts to find and make homes in property that has long been empty". However, it ended with the usual trades' union rhetoric that AEU sponsored Labour MPs had to make certain that rates be paid on empty properties. In fact this kind of resolution-passing and unconvincing show of unity merely covered up often deep antagonisms which were widespread in Notting Hill and elsewhere in London.

It didn't take much - or so it seemed - to whip up building workers employed by housing trusts or even Direct Labour Depts to chuck out dishevelled, work-refusenik squatters, then gut the properties and brick them up. It was easy to demagogically work on anti middle class attitudes amongst the workers because in a good number of cases it happened to be true. But the nasty vengeful acts only served to restore, under the guise of the legitimacy of the council waiting lists; the council as the biggest absentee landlord in the country. (13)

Footnote (13): It's perhaps worth pointing out that there is a difference between the immediate post-war squatting movement (e.g. when Yorkshire miners came out on strike in the mid 1940s in support of mass working class squatting in Sheffield) and the contemporary squatting movement, beginning in the late 1960s. Put very generally, the latter in contrast to post war squatting, was inter-class based more on a recognition of the futility and stupidity of work in an epoch when machines could so easily be directed to carry out most essential tasks. But before the immanent liberation from age - old drudgery, priority was giving to cutting one's personal living costs down to a minimum which included paying rent. For some, not so minded, it was of course, simply a means of saving money to put down for their future mortgage. At the same time, however, squatting was a basic need - not just an ideological refusal to pay rent - and it is this basic need in response to the desperate housing situation, that has come to dominate the squatters' scene in the 1980s.

Fortunately however, it was by no means as clear-cut as this all the time. The same group of workers would vacillate between pro and anti-squatters all depending. A community mediated support for striking garbage collectors' in the early 1970s was reciprocated later when North Kensington garbage collectors were prepared to man (woman?) the barricades to stop an Irish working class woman being evicted from a squat.

Tension between squatters and fully employed working class people is complex in other respects too. The Ruff Tuff squatters got much information about empty properties from sympathetic telephone engineers, postal workers, council office workers as well as a British Gas official! At the same time though LEB and gas workers at the behest of their management – themselves pushed by council top officers - regularly tried to turn off energy supplies to the Elgin Avenue squat. Similarly there was tension between squatters in council property and council tenants, who wanted to see squatting in private property (this was before the Labour Governments Trespass Act of 1975) but were averse to anything they saw as queue jumping the points list and possibly affecting the chances of their sons and daughters being given cheap rented accommodation. It was a division much exploited by the media that neglected to say that a lot of council squatting was in property council tenants would not inhabit anyway. This often bitter internal wrangle was overcome to some degree in Elgin Avenue by the sheer determination of the squatters themselves to fight off the bailiffs with their police back up. Barricades marked a change of relationship as rent-paying tenants became impressed with the squatters resistance. It was a rarity though and tenants' hostility to squatters is still very strong. It's a dialectical problem which - as it were - remains suspended in mid-air. Anti-squatting laws meant the slow peaking over the years of mass mid 1970s squatting and increasing unemployment meant the decline in rent strikes. And with rent paid through housing benefit, this saw off the possibility of a very visible, inescapably concrete, overlap between striking council tenants and squatters. It was nipped in the bud. Unity is however very much there as a low key invisible backdrop in many a bout of London's inner-city rioting. And in late 1986 the rent-striking council tenants and squatters on Pullens Estate in Southwark joined forces to defeat the anti-squatting policies of the Militant dominated Southwark Council: some of them covering the cops and bailiffs with green paint. More recently both squatters and council tenants attacked Hackney's leftist Council, forcing them to flee the council chamber. More generally however, in a concrete way in Notting Hill it was the more mundane, common or garden gesture that proved to be more successful in building links with workers, simply because they were less tendentious. Like simply looking after the kids of striking postal workers, or collecting money for striking hospital workers in 1973 or, giving advice to strikers on how to collect social security. (14)

Footnote14: The area had one of the first Claimants Unions but what marked it off from the majority of other Claimants Unions then, promoting a split within their ranks, was its anti-work bias. Staffed frequently by "crazies" who knew how to play the mental card against the state's work enforcement officers, they were yet able to make sense of the mounds of bureaucratic jargon, setting out claimants rights and turn it to good advantage. Subscribing to a vulgar Situationist ideology with one breath they would, with the next, deliver a peroration on "the starving masses" never suspecting for a moment there was a contradiction here. In fact, they were quite impossible ideologues, humourless and difficult to get along with and easily open to ridicule behind their backs .The area of course still has a Claimants Union but of the routine variety, unable to care to terms with anti-work, even though the abolition of work - with computerized robotniks everywhere - is a more objective possibility than 20 years ago.

In terms of aiding direct action, perhaps the one real practical contact that took place was in the Building Workers' strike of 1972, when the Housing Group of the Peoples Association supplied a list of speculative re-hab schemes in the area to striking building workers who then proceeded by flying pickets to stop all work on them. Some shop stewards who had played a part in that strike were attracted to Notting Hill even though the area had very little trade union presence to it. It was something of a strange contradiction. Drawn by its libertarian impulses, they fell for the trendy radicalism of fledgling community politics. During the strike, building work on play huts, parks, adventure playgrounds - all the infrastructure of the new 'caring' sensitised face of capitalism - were exempt from blacking. What mattered was to nationalize Mowlems/McAlpine's etc and let the state, (a "Workers' State" of course) direct these conglomerates to implementing good works the length and breadth of a red UK! Even today individuals belonging to the builders rank 'n' file group live in Notting Hill. They still persist in promoting the separation between the Lump and on the cards building workers, despite the fact that some of them who support UCATT's founding perspectives (changing somewhat but not necessarily for the better) are on the fiddle or scrounging. Apparently they are quite prepared to gloss over the contradictions between their lives and the moral exhortations of UCATT.

As the tempo of struggle changed on the working class front after the Labour victory of 1974, the image of community politics in Notting Hill lost its shine. So much of its inspiration at its peak had been anti-Tory. It couldn't cope with the reality of a Labour government. There couldn't be a comparable process of subterranean struggle in the sphere of community politics as amongst the working class, which was later to express itself so brilliantly in The Winter of Discontent. Instead what was germinating in the inner cities were the seeds of sporadic but increasing riot. There was a brief minority rallying cry which went unheard, calling for localized general strikes to change the housing situation in North Kensington. It was one of the last calls, but about the best. Despite the activist rhetoric of community politics, there was something untypical about it, almost one might say, beyond their N. Ken.

After 1974 community politics became a much more official and officious affair, dominated more by single issues rather than seeking to establish links with even the official representatives of the Labour movement. Its propensity for hysteria meant it became the butt of ridicule. But at the same time as people took the piss out of it, they did it behind closed doors in the company of trusted friends because it was not something to be taken on lightly. If you did it openly your name was blazoned in neon lights in order to be harried on many a street corner. Being the victim of more than one such campaign of vilification makes one of the writers of this blurb only too aware how nasty such things can be.

So The Winter of Discontent in 1979 passed over a community politics more worried by the fact that it was a strike against a Labour government rather than treating it as an opportunity to forge links. As for the subsequent period of urban riot, on this their terrain, they could only guess at what was happening. Not knowing what to say, they fell silent, using sexism as a shield to criticise "macho-politics", (the macho-politics of rioting!) and later, anything outside the accepted rules of the game including the threat to oppose rate capping! However during the 1984-85 miners' strike the community politicos profile was more visible, feeling on safer ground because the strike, to some degree, was contained by trade unionism. Typically, they were able for instance, to hi-jack tenants' collections in the various Housing Co-op's presenting the money to the miners' wives in a personal capacity, as though they were the donors. (14) Without a hint of embarrassment, they still receive Xmas cards addressed to them personally. This imposture is merely an outcrop of what happens in Housing Co-op's where there is a self-perpetuating, self-elected elite who are periodically re-elected by a show of hands - providing anyone can be bothered to raise them. It is a trick form of democracy for subordinates because the major decisions have already been taken by the Housing Corporation. The job of local management is then to get from local Housing Co-op's a democratic ratification of the undemocratic.

Footnote (14): They weren't the only ones to play this trick: endless political sects up and down the country got away with this con.

Though the weight of these ossified community politicos was considerable, they were far outweighed by the no-goods who were not part of some securely funded, para-state body. At worst the community politics were an irritant but not much more. However, in the late 1970s, the structure of Notting Hill began to change. The former bed-sit land of multi- occupation swiftly became a thing of the past. Squats were closed down becoming single homes and tenants somewhat ghettoised on the huge council estates. The private rented sector virtually disappeared and the number of Housing Co-ops grew. As the former reference point of "the Gate's" popular element declined, the self- importance of institutionalised community politics appeared to increase. In fact these cadres were more and more to acquire the characteristics of a distinct managerial stratum, no longer trying to keep their supposed local constituency sweet but quite openly bent on rubbishing them. For them, the term working class became synonymous with sexism and racism, and with it, contempt, which was only to be outdone by thescant regard they had for the local unemployed and declining number of the casually employed. Any mention of autonomy was thought either right wing or romantic.

The radical veneer to community politico claptrap didn't last long - at most ten years. The change was apparent across the whole spectrum, not least in the rehabilitation of professional roles once thought very dicey. People trained to become architects, planners, proper social workers, lawyers and took up jobs as trade union bureaucrats. Making lots of 'legitimate' money ceased to be frowned on, but the elicit proceeds from scrounging or from failing to declare all income to the Inland Revenue if one happened to be a mere tradesperson were looked on with increasing suspicion by these leftist professionals. In these essentials, standards were reverting back to the conservative nineteen fifties and worse, proclaimed by people whose detestation for Thatcherite Toryism was 'genuine' enough! Generally though, the community politico's critique of this society - going off at half-cock in the first instance - meant that when the harsher reign of Thatcher came along, they could quite easily climb back into the saddle of career roles as laid down by capitalism in a particularly reactionary phase. In many ways Notting Hill has been a kind of training ground for the more up to date, inter-disciplinary professional; one with a more rounded awareness of how to deal with Billy Muggins and missus down below. In the post-Thatcher era there are many mansions and they will patiently sit it out until they get one. But even now we can get some idea from the streets of Notting Hill of the changing face of the modern trade union bureaucrat.

There's the example of the jodhpur wearing NUPE representative; a faded aristocrat in workers' clothing whose nose is stuck up so high in the air, it is in danger of obstructing the Heathrow flight path. Having flirted with dropping out and avant-garde art, he breathes contempt, retrieving his privileges a little as the local representative of hospital workers, although never really working on the hospital floor. He still chips away at his rubbishy sculpture all night - thoughtlessly keeping his neighbours awake. He is in the same mould as his boss, Rodney Bickerstaffe, head of NUPE who rose to power on a qualification from Newcastle Poly. This is only one sordid detail as it affects a particular locality from the never-ending tale of modern separation in a workers bureaucracy that is now being re-vamped. We have not by any means seen the end of all this. For cultivating all this pioneering shit and never defining particular issues/problems in anything like an anti-statist perspective, places like Notting Hill may yet feel the sting of retribution on the eve of the revolution.

However there is a glimmer of hope even for the guinea pigs of Notting Hill, tired of being strapped to a community-dissecting table, without an umbrella or typewriter in sight. Most of the half well-intentioned but essentially bogus community endeavours lacked a real power base anyway because they were situated within the Tory Borough of Kensington and Chelsea. They were pilot schemes that pointed the way - more often than not - to the Labour Boroughs of Hackney, Brent and Islington etc and eventually the Labour controlled GLC becoming the bete noire of the tabloids. There was talk at one point in the early 1970s of forming a breakaway Soviet ("The Golborne Soviet") which, in spite of the colourful rhetoric was nothing other than an attempt to return North Kensington to the safe Labour constituency it once was prior to having its boundaries redrawn by the Boundaries Commission. What has happened in Notting Hill over the years undoubtedly played a pioneering role. But the distortions, half-truths and downright lies are not that important. It is the capacity to see through this that matters and this actually does happen in an individual, almost solipsistic, manner in Notting Hill. More commonly the reaction is one of 'untheorised' cynicism, or a feeling of being let down and fucked over to the point of breakdown. But that might be beginning to change. It has to, because the onslaught now being launched in London is just too ghastly to take lying down.

A tenants committee on the Brunel Estate has been mooted. Labour party councillors are to be banned (which in the UK implies all Trotskyist etc hangers on). Local Labour councillors are annoyed but impotent to do anything about it. The danger is that it is just another of these bodies which from a fine gesture ends up getting sucked up in the orbit of Labourism --- but we shall see what we shall see. One maybe making too much out of it. Tenants committees in Notting Hill, like tenants committees elsewhere, have been ineffectual, dominated by people with close links to local council management and officialdom in general and often run by paid full-time workers who aren't even tenants on the estates for which these associations are meant for. There is a great lack of trust in them. The Brunel proposals could be interesting considering that existing tenants associations in Notting Hill were set up in the first place by housing association management.

THE 1987 CARNIVAL AND THE LIMITS OF AN URBAN PACIFICATION

The Notting Hill Carnival riot of 1987 proved to be the most exciting riot since the great Sunday of Carnival 1976, which lit the fuse on what proved to be the first of many explosions throughout mainland UK. Unlike the 1958 race riots, this was a class riot with blacks and whites fighting the cops together. Considering all the other 'firsts' in Notting Hill, listed in the last few pages, the 1976 riot was, apart from the squats and a few other interventions, the only one to be proud of. In a sense too it marked a watershed in community politics now eclipsed by something that really did open vistas on the urban terrain and beyond. Innovatory community politics were ceasing to inspire illusions, the more it was becoming obvious the rhetoric of community militancy had not changed things for the better. However the corny Notting Hill applecart was upset by black's coming in from the rest of London and elsewhere in the UK. Since then it's largely been this 'outsider' element that has provided all the real trouble in Notting Hill. There is no point in going over again the details of what took place in 1976 because they are reasonably well known.

However in the intervening eleven years many changes have taken place both in Notting Hill and elsewhere - not least in the deployment of an immense variety of counter-insurgency techniques - subtle and brutal at one and the same time. The Carnival is part of this process. It is minutely prepared every year by all contending factions, repressive and cultural, police and the feuding Carnival and Arts Committee. Every danger is examined afresh and a contingency plan is on standby should anything happen. As darkness fell on that warm August Bank Holiday Monday night in 1987, what was to become inspirational about the riot in retrospect, was that it cut through all the years of accumulating modernist recuperation. (Remember Notting Hill is untypical of the UK in this regard.) It took place on a terrain, which has become very hostile to anything significant happening other than the planned-for ritualised Carnival. That was its real victory; exposing the limits of the immense recuperation that has taken place. At the same time however, all the deadweight deployed against the rioters still successfully stopped things getting out of hand.

In 1976, the unexpected happened. The business-oriented Carnival organizers and the police caught unawares were at a complete loss. The battle was intense and furious. Off licences and stores were looted, cars burnt and builders skips overturned, their contents used as ammo. The police protecting themselves with hastily nicked trashcan lids received one helluva hiding. (15) Eleven years later, nothing could be more different. Come Carnival time the shops in the commercial area (particularly Portobello Rd) are boarded up. Builders skips are hauled away and sites covered with corrugated iron sheets. An army of heavies, clubs at the ready guard liquour stores. Above all, the police have been tooled up with an increasingly sophisticated arsenal of riot shields, helmets, batons, gas and guns.

Footnote (15): Suffice to say the best account appeared in a paper with the dull name of Socialist Voice, an ex-Trotskyist group who had gone ultra left after being thrown out of the SWP. After promising beginnings the group just disappeared into thin air by 1980. It's a fate that in particular seems to befall disillusioned Trotskyists in the UK. The pity is, this vanishing act leaves the mainstream Trotskyist heritage, as endemic to the UK as anarchism on a higher level is to Spain, more or less unharmed.

Over the years too, the police have used the Carnival more and more as an experimental testing ground for techniques to be deployed elsewhere in the UK mainland at a later date -ironically, as it turns out - another of the famous Notting Hill 'firsts'. The snatch-squads (originally used in Northern Ireland) were deployed in the Carnival mini-riots of 1981 and 1982. During the UK summer onslaught of 1981, these snatch squads had not existed as a pre-arranged tactical force. In 1987, Carnival was for the police, an experiment in using the new crowd control techniques which one presumes are going to be used in the near future (perhaps against an unfurling strike wave as well as soccer matches?)

As regards the police, it makes sense to concentrate on the big crowd-pulling events which are being torn apart particularly in the UK from within. This crisis in the audience/performer nexus is axiomatic if contemporary spectacular society is to breakdown. The crowds are drawn by the performance in any case but what then ensues is on a scale so devastating as to dwarf the clichés of political upheaval and political activism.

Above: *Notting Hill Carnival 1976*

Above: *Portobello Road. Carnival 1987*

On that August Bank Holiday one needed only to look elsewhere in the UK. Violent confrontations between police and spectators occurred at four other leisure events. A football match between Portsmouth and West Ham broke out into trouble and for the second time within a month soccer hooliganism erupted at Scarborough. Also there was trouble at the long-established Reading pop festival. Finally there was something of an innovation: At the recently devised Californian-style surfing competition at Newquay, Cornwall a beach party erupted as one thousand punters battled cops and fire brigade crews when they moved in to break up the merrymaking. Fresh ground indeed. Such incidents are by no means unusual. They happen most weekends in the UK though not in such a concentrated fashion.

If Carnival is anything to go by these new control techniques do not as the authorities hoped, nip trouble in the bud. On the contrary they seem positively to encourage it. From little incidents eventually came a bigger response at Carnival. In the afternoon and early evening there had been the usual steaming - the not particularly pleasant indiscriminate rip-off of valuables here and there - regardless of social class (although one photographer to a steamer's credit was stripped of £5000 worth of cameras) but it was nothing like 1977 when gangs invaded everywhere including steaming into pubs and making off with the tills. However in 1987 when a gang tried, with dusk falling, to prevent a cop arresting a youth, a carefully rehearsed police plan came into operation within minutes as l000 cops moved in clad in full riot gear. As The Daily Mirror reported a day later (September, 1st) "they were backed up by about 2OOO uniformed officers some of whom only minutes before had been dancing in the streets with the Carnival crowd. In one sudden charge about 200 including women officers in riot clothing charged the crowd in Ladbroke Grove."

In all likelihood though, for the authorities this was the planned scenario in any case: Carnival as a real life extension of the Hounslow riot training centre, a place to try out their new gear and techniques. New protective fireproof clothing complete with CS gas canisters and plastic bullets in the pouches of black waist jackets were issued. A new crack force of some 250-riot cops appeared on the streets, though most of the rest were drawn from the Territorial Support Group. All rather different from the inner cities of late 1985 when the ordinary copper, deployed as a social worker one day was put on riot duty the next! The separate roles were so conflicting as to cause disorientation and much muted anger and protest amongst cops. This drastic and impossible to handle telescoping of functions had not disappeared by August 1987 but it was in the process of being replaced by a more rigid division of police labour. Carnival 87 for the authorities had been a roughly rehearsed over-reaction which did not however, prevent the rioting getting out of hand, spreading farther and wider than before. Notting Hill 1987 saw the first deployment in a UK mainland riot of bullet-proof Land Rovers with gun ports. An armed police detachment equipped with Koch and Necklar automatic sub-machine guns, launched a dramatic swoop on a house in Westbourne Park Rd probably to pick up somebody waving a replica gun. Ever since Broadwater Farm in late1985 where a shotgun was fired, the cops have been nervous about any repetition and this deliberate over-reaction was also a dress rehearsal for what might happen in the future.

In other respects too, Carnival was a means for working on another police idea. An extensive array of video cameras were employed all over the area and connected to banks of TV screens in the usual police HQ, the Issac Newton School at the corner of Lancaster Road and Ladbroke Road. There is nothing particularly new about the use of video cameras. For two years throughout the country they've been increasingly deployed in soccer stands, high above the terraces, not in order to spot the ball but the hooligan. It has been highly effective and the Dawn Knock has sounded for many a guy caught on video. However it is the first time video has been extensively used over an urban area for a particular event. One cannot help but feel this innovation of Carnival 1987 is but one stage in the blanket videoing of entire urban centers. This is almost certainly going to happen in Wolverhampton. Dire though these Big Brother developments are nevertheless one hasn't got to get too paranoid. If hacking is anything to go by, hi-tech re-equip is the most technically vulnerable to sabotage of any prior development in the capitalist mode of production. Moreover the permanent videoing, night and day of All Saints Road in Notting Hill from all sides of the street, over the last five years or so, never once stopped trouble or ever really rumbled clandestine activities on the street. (16)

Footnote 16: Further knock-on effects have become clearer recently. It's been proposed by British Coal that they intend videoing every miner's picket engaged in unlawful, secondary action, with the intention of dismissing those involved. Like the inner-city rioters learnt, balaclavas have become essential.

It is not only overt police control that is tried and tested at Carnival. Counter-insurgency in Notting Hill has been a focus of year in year out strategy. Through different building projects - often encouraged and sometimes funded by the local Kensington and Chelsea Council - various flash points were (or so it seemed) neutralized to prevent any re-occurrence of the 1970s trouble.

Acklam Rd, near the M40 Westway was one of them where in the late 1960s/ early 1970s, local opinion prompted by a fledgling community politics had got rid of a proposed bus garage and a proposed car park wilderness under the Westway flyover. Tenants overlooking this noisy traffic artery were moved elsewhere and the old Victorian houses were taken over by a multitude of local pressure groups under the aegis finally, of the Amenity Trust. In the mind's eye of the latter, concentration may have heralded a new dawn of community experiment. Having got rid of the most gross commodity - the car - expansion moved into alternatives (like turning two bays under the Westway over to "committed theatre"). However in the best-laid plans there are things that escape control. Thus in the late 1970s these buildings became the focus of reggae and dub sound systems during Carnival and with reggae ricochade in its prime, Aclam Rd, became the scene of quite heavy rioting in 1978 and '79. No doubt with these unwelcome incidents in mind shortly afterwards the last remaining dilapidated Victorian houses were demolished. In any case that probably had been part of the plan all along, making way for modern sound-insulated council houses, cunning anti- pedestrian walls and a fashionable paved mall for small traders. Ironically, the alternatives, unable to pay the high rents demanded by the Amenity Trust were finally displaced by up-market fashion shops, boutiques and stores, trading in expensive trinketry and foodstuffs. The complex is now known as Portobello Green Market. The communal waste ground has been turned into an uninviting, nasty little park.

The same was true of other flash points like the bays under the Westway in Portobello Road and Ladbroke Grove. Old brick walls, on or near these flash points walls which were easily pushed over for ammo - were re-built with stylish engineering bricks, costing £1.00 each and with long iron railings firmly embedded in the top. Failing that, walls all over the district were built high and finished off with a top course of bricks each one placed at 45 degrees to the others to prevent anyone from sitting on them, simply to chat and watch the world go by. The first to be built were the walls fronting the council flats on Westbourne Park Road, which faced All Saints Road. People aware of what was taking place at the time were critical of brickies engaged in the tasks of building these walls laying the finishing top course. Most likely they were employed by the council so surely they could have gone on the sick or refused to do it? What was it all about? To stop communication at any cost. Stay off the streets and remain indoors. Loud and clear this was the message being put across.

All these accumulating nasty little urban tricks must be set in a more general context: Notting Hill was slowly throughout the late 1970s becoming a choice area for gentrification. In the1980s the process began to very rapidly accelerate. After clearing out the streets around Powis Square/ Talbot Road during these years, only one real flash point remained: The press/ TV notorious street of All Saints Rd. On July lst 1987 over a couple of weeks after Thatcher's third election victory and her expressed "concern" to do something for the inner cities (i.e. her concern to punish them even more), a police swamp was launched over Notting Hill. Its real aim was to finish off All Saints once and for all. However, more on that later. What is at issue here is urban counter-insurgency and the swamp had been surreptitiously prepared and coordinated with other interested parties, particularly Notting Hill Housing Trust who owned most of the property there.

The black squats largely in abandoned commercial property were closed by the filth, as building contractors moved in on the same day to renovate a number of them. Though in some cases building work did not commence immediately, builders' lean-toos were erected to fence off the properties. Within days a house in MaGregor Road, leading off the Saints, was to fetch £300,000. The very centre of Carnival revolt in the 1980s had finally fallen and the light had gone out on the last remaining shambles of an urban trouble spot. There were minor attacks on the building operations - some windows broken, some skips overturned - but nothing like a mass response.

The Role of Carnival Stewards and Cultural Recuperation.

On top of this, there were other, even worse pernicious forces at work - those coming from within the black community itself. Since 1976, the Carnival and Arts committees had increasingly helped spawn quite an array of black stewards who step in when trouble breaks out at the Carnival. In many respects they were the forerunner for similar structures that have been set up in many inner city areas, where blacks reside in fairly large numbers. During the smaller riots which occurred at Carnival in '1977 ' 78 and '79, the stewards were sometimes heavier than the police and occasionally used iron bars on troublemakers. In 1987 they used baseball bats and even knives. Indeed some of those at the receiving end of the stewards' wisdom were more condemnatory of the stewards than of the to-be-expected police attack. Moreover, it's often impossible to tell the difference between a steward and any other black guy, so you are never sure whether you're amongst people who will be with you if you chuck a bottle or people who'll bottle you if you throw one.

These stewards are more or less complimented - and for all year round vigilance - by a growing array of black social workers (or more accurately "community workers" because generally they are disdainful of social workers) who in spirit have been influenced by such pioneering para-state bodies like the Black People's Information Centre on Portobello Road. However there are differences between black community workers and their white cousins. Black community workers often tend to be heavier, more ready to cut out liberal sentiments and act tough just to get their hands on some readies. All rather different from their guilt stricken white counterparts who, frequently coming from much wealthier backgrounds, couldn't act tough and hypocritically disdain a vulgar interest in money.

In late autumn 1986, a small number of community youth workers attached to the Mangrove restaurant mini-Empire at the end of All Saints Road, were able to stop a midnight explosion of spontaneous anger, when news of a black guy's death in police custody reached the Saints. Critchlow - "the Mangrove boss" - whose credibility rests on the fact that in the 1970s he'd been arrested several times by the cops (including during the 1977 Carnival riot), his restaurant raided, cooled everyone down by saying it would be best to organize a proper big march later thus taking the wind and fire out of the situation. The controlled demos protesting the guys death (his nick name was Crumpet) in the following days orchestrated in tandem with other official bodies by the black community workers, even though they did slip the leash, had none of that raw anger the midnight explosion would have contained. Though by now the rich in the area had really made their presence felt and any flare up couldn't have connected, house-by-house, as in Brixton and Toxteth, nonetheless a spontaneous conflagration of sorts couldn't be entirely ruled out. As it was in the days following the news of the death, Portobello Rd had been boarded up and the market and pubs put under police curfew. Most of the trouble came from invading black gangs from the massive Stonebridge Park Estate two and a half miles away. In the controlled demos, the cops forewarned, kept a low profile. They didn't try arrests despite being attacked with stones outside Notting Dale police station. After some cop cars had their paintwork scratched by missiles, they kept well clear of the All Saints/Portobello Rd area for fear of provoking trouble. Nevertheless, trouble there was: All the windows in Barclays Bank were trashed; a clothes shop, a butchers, Tesco's liquor dept and an Asian supermarket were looted; a chemist run by a guy well-known locally for his insulting, vicious manner (always prosecuting shoplifters etc) was wrecked - in all l5 offices and shops attacked as well as one or two yuppie houses.

How is it these community workers plus stewards have had such a devastating effect on suffocating black (and not only black) anger? The official structure of race relations' community politics - older, long standing and up-standing bodies who regularly meet the local cops for a chit-chat - have been pushed aside and blanked long ago. They have no effect whatsoever and could not successfully calm anything down. They are rightly seen as respectability seeking, money grabbers; salting away for themselves any dough they can get their mittens on. It's these people who climbed aboard Thatcher's pre-election well-funded, inner-city Task Force projects and pilot programs oriented towards, among other thing, the creation of black businesses. There is one such Task Force now in operation for Notting Hill. No, the most effective bodies are those that have sprung up since 1981 and have an unofficial aura to them, although they do receive moneys from various sources including Caribbean states. They are full of anti-cop rhetoric and won't have anything to do with any cop liaison, open or backstairs. At critical moments it's this stance which makes them so effective because being anti-police they are able to protect property all the better for that. How long they can maintain this pure-as-the-driven-slush image remains to be seen and for certain the authorities in the UK now want to repay them for services rendered. Carnival Chairman, Alex Pascall, after the Notting Hill 1987 riot appealed for direct government funding to bring about better stewarding. Bearing in mind growing state authoritarianism, Pascall will probably get what he wants. Moreover, Condon, the Carnival's deputy Police Assistant, praised the stewards alongside his own men. Maybe they had been reflecting on the help stewards had provided elsewhere over the previous couple of months. (17).

Finally in considering the deadly role recuperation plays, one has to look at the increasingly integrative role of Carnival culture. Although the traditional Trinidadian costume/steel band merry go round was despised by the young blacks in the mid 1970s, (c/f A Summer with a Thousand Julys and Socialist Voice) its expansion since has been enormous. A whole local job creation culture has been built around it as Carnival has become more oriented towards business like appeals for increased private spending and less state funding (except where law 'n' order is concerned). In fact it shadowed the era of privatisation. In some ways the organizers would like Carnival to be more like American festivals where for instance Schlitz Beer sponsors a complete Country and Western jamboree in Tennessee.

However, for the insurgent forces present at Carnival the arguments for or against state-funding or private sponsorship are academic and irrelevant. Containment has to be registered at another level outside the contending forces of state versus private enterprise - that of culture itself. Reggae teased with rebellion at the same time as it contained rebellion. But reggae as a forum through which rebellion could be reflected and to some degree pacified, also had an extremely short creative life as it rapidly succumbed to disco programming. In its time however, there were certain musical moments of collective improvisation (e.g. some of Burning Spear/Third World etc), which nearly equalled the best of New York be-bop in the 1950s. In an effort to maintain some kind of authentic street cred, reggae garnished by some dub gave way more to the sound system dub/rap 'poetry' and DJ Poets, around which all the Carnivals mini-riots of the early 1980s took place. The blacks noted the demise of grass roots reggae but were at something of a loss to know what to put in its place.

Footnote 17: The role of the black stewards was no more sadly demonstrated than in Chapeltown Leeds just days after Thatcher's third election victory .Without the services of the community youth workers attached to the local Nelson Mandela Centre - who being only one rung up the hierarchy often seem as close as your mates - Chapeltown could possibly have gone through the roof during the three days of midnight battles with the police. It would have been a much needed whisky and mac in a rather demoralized but nonetheless simmering North and a few miles away trouble brewing once again in the Yorkshire coalfield. What a missed opportunity to make a vital connection! And what a riposte to Thatcher's "concern"! Youth workers, some as young as 13 or 14, (probably flattered to be part of the Mandela Centre and the kudos surrounding the very name rather than the economic rewards} followed their teeny peer group into dark alleys stopping them fire-raising or, luring cops into ambushes. It worked. And the cops must have been laughing all the way to Armley Jail because once the disturbances had died down, they moved in on the local people -smashing down doors at five in the morning -just as if there had been a major riot.

Just after the year long miners' strike in 1985 there was one hilarious incident. Some blacks down All Saints, probably a mite choked by the dull routine of reggae, suddenly began to blast out brass band music. Close your eyes and you could have been in the Riding's shopping mall in Wakefield on a Saturday morning. It pointed to a levelling of all musical style; if brass band (hardly 'rebel music') was a cultural back drop to what was happening in the mining villages and towns, then it was every bit as 'subversive' as Junior Murvin' s Police and Thieves. One might as well listen to anything because capitalism has become a born leveller when it comes to pretending to express rebellion through culture.

As for the sound systems which in the 1970s were glorified jukeboxes and treated as such, they were becoming more expansion minded, more entrepreneurial as business sponsors took them under their wing and the trucks out of which they operated got larger and more costly to hire or buy. The heavily backed three way Instant Edition sound system, of near wall-collapsing reverb on All Saints Road, (whipping up a friendly nationalist sentiment e.g. "anyone here from Tobago, St Lucia, J-A-M-A-I-C-A" - huge cheer) just prior to the mini-riots around All Saints, which would invariably close Carnival was in 1987 completely subdued. They had been told to cool it by Carnival and Art and they obeyed.

On the Saturday night of the 1987 Carnival, the sound systems closed down at 8.30 pm. It was unheard of! The following morning and one of Instant Editions banks of sound had gone. Again it seems Carnival and Arts had been obeyed. By nightfall, it had become all too clear to many revellers what was happening. Most sound systems started to shut up shop one and a half hours before pub closing time. In other years, they had gone on far, far, far longer.

More than anything else, the sudden realization that the sound systems had become a fully integrated part of the system was too much to take and what had been skirmishes here and there broke into hydra-headed, though admitted well-controlled, riot everywhere. (One couple in Portobello Rd showed they didn't need sound systems or any kind of music to have fun: they danced rock 'n' roll style with gleeful faces to the sound of nothing but bottles breaking on riot shields). Some sound systems weren't of course so blatantly on their knees to authority. Continuing to preach peace and love ("no violence") the sound system outside the KPH. - Kensington Park Hotel - (ironically known locally as the GBH) on Ladbroke Grove, carried on for a while longer and was charged by the cops. The charge was unprovoked and the riot police stopped only inches in front of the sound system. It then shut up shop, the police ushering the van through the blocked-off area.

A smaller sound system, backed by the steel framed concrete of the Brunel Estate defiantly stuck it out in the midst of the bottle throwing. But essentially dub had had its day and was, en masse, falling in line behind Lynton Kwesi Johnson's status seeking: resident Caribbean expert at Warwick University and ex-Oxford poet, who contemptuously dismissed the slogan scrawled up in Brixton in 1980 -"Bristol Today, Brixton Tomorrow" -as the silly dreams of white anarchists, which he'd written in that great upholder of mass insurgency, The Observer just a few weeks before Brixton became more exemplary than Bristol. Lately Johnson has become an implicit if not explicit supporter of Chapeltown's stewards in dealing with open insurgency. The collapse of all cultural ranking was complete enough to doubt if there was any real difference between sound system and The Met's Harmony Police Band. Except had the latter ventured down All Saints during the Carnival bluebottle reggae would have received more than a little audience participation.

Although the 1987 riot in Notting Hill could not have had the ferocity or intensity of spontaneous inner-city uprisings, it was inspiring (as stated before) because it took place within an arena of near total containment - or what should have been. It seemed to indicate something: No matter how finely tuned recuperation in pockets becomes in a country like the UK where in the past few years confrontation and outright repression has been more to the fore, it still fails to work.

The old foci of revolt were precisely the spots where the trouble initially flared; the junction of Portobello Road and Aclam Road/Ladbroke Grove and Lancaster Road/All Saints Road and Westbourne Park Road. Interestingly enough, none of the newspapers could agree because truth to tell, the rioting that followed broke out virtually spontaneously in many places around 9 p.m. and lasted sporadically some three and a half hours. Bricks, bottles and thunder flashes were thrown, 70 people were hurt. 13 coppers hospitalised and a W.P.C. was stabbed, ("riot yobs slash girl cop" said a tabloid). Stalls were looted, including one selling hammocks, (what a commodity to sell or nick at Carnival?) By midnight rampaging mobs had broken down police barriers at police HQ although this had been happening intermittently beforehand throughout the district. However describing the riot isn't that important (it was small beer in comparison to Brixton. in 1985 etc). Being so dispersed and more importantly (and it portends better possibilities) it started for the first time to spread to the fringes of the big estates: the Brunel near Qeensway, the Lancaster West Estate towards Shepherds Bush and the estates on upper Ladbroke Grove towards Kensal Rise. Running battles took place down Elgin and Blenheim Crescent, in the very heart of freshly conquered Yuppie territory, where slogans like "Fuck Yuppies" had recently been scrawled on the walls. There was even a ferocious punch-up with cops round the corner from Kensington Park Road where at Rockways, Sting has his business centre.

Though never, as far as one can be certain going on to the estates, the rioting went dangerously close, particularly to the Brunel part of which is now to be sold off by Westminster City Council. However the geographical spread of the rioting reflected the intentions of the Carnival organizers to disperse the Carnival as much as possible. In an effort to defuse central tension, the watchword has been, de-centralize. Carnival chairman, Alex Pascall wants the Carnival in future to become even more spread out, making the task of crowd control easier. Neither the police nor The Economist magazine agrees, because it is likely to make the job even harder. Nearby Harrow Road is one of the streets proposed, but it's the centre of a popular street life and at one point merely one hundred yards from one of the Met's constant fears: the dreaded Mozart Estate! (In the Top three on their list of potential Broadwater Farms).

Carnival however has little choice but to widen out and face the music of all these enjoyable possibilities if only because it gets bigger by the year. Organizers have even commissioned a market research survey to find out exactly how much money is made during the event as Carnival has become more exotically professional and more like Rio de Janeiro; in 1987 there were Columbian, Red Indian and Mexican costume dancers. Following in fact the leisure tendency in modern capitalism towards bigger and better display and given the responses to mass festivities in the UK, bigger and better destruction. Even if very right-wing Tories succeeded in getting Carnival off the streets of Notting Hill (which yuppie colonizers would go along with) by staging it elsewhere, it definitely wouldn't mean an end to the trouble. The proposed open ground around Wormwood Scrubs prison close to Notting Hill is ideal for running battles and incidentally is right next to the modest looking, semi-detached Acton estate, where Mod was spawned in the early 1960s. Roundwood Park in the Willesden / Harlsden area - another proposed venue - isn't that safe either. Right in the heart of Brent, which has the highest percentage black population in London, it was the scene in late spring 1987, just after a small black festival, of a looting/ trashing spree in Harlesden High St.

Lefties claim crudely that the state (or rather they always talk about the government) wants to totally ban Carnival. This is hysterical nonsense and merely gives credence to all oppositional organizers. What the ethos of Thatcherism basically wants is more police control (official or unofficial) and more capitalization. If at all possible an entrance fee to get in would be ideal. Above all, the supposed threat to close down Carnival is intended to push Carnival organizers into making sure there are more stewards and that they get heavier than in 1987.

Moreover, Notting Hill is not now a black area to the same degree as many other parts of London. Its blackness is now almost purely symbolic or nostalgic reminder of the 1950s. However keeping Carnival in Notting Hill does give the two-up to the yuppie attack - now temporarily halted - on all the poor of the area. It was a pleasure seeing them fleeing for the country, on the run-up to August Bank Holiday1987 when their Renault 5s and Volkswagens were conspicuous by their absence.

Mugging and London Pathology

The rioting of that weekend was a fully integrated black and white affair. There was absolutely no racism either way. It's fair to say that this has been the only Carnival occasion since 1976 that the relatively isolated incidents of black racism were totally absent. But what has this to do with breaking the hold of recuperation? Well, after 1976 insurgents were unable to get at stores/clothes/liquor or what have you. And the gangs wired by an atmosphere that tended to artificially heighten though not satisfy expectations, sometimes turned on individual whites and gave them a doing. In 1979, one of the writers of this blurb, was attacked by two members of a black gang during a fierce volley of bricks being thrown at the cops; they were pulled off by other gang mates who apologised for the incident. Broadly speaking all the counter-insurgency techniques unwittingly (though it turned out to be in their interest also) fostered black racism by increasing frustration. 1985 was particularly bad. As dusk fell on a tightly packed All Saints Road, individual white males (though not white women) were often quite savagely beaten up. Obviously if they were prepared to go down that street they were definitely not white racists. However once real things begin to happen, atmospheres also change rapidly and in the mini-riot of that night, the racist flavour evaporated.

No trace of a racist slant was there at all in1987. This was all the more remarkable considering that for many a month previously Notting Hill, particularly around the All Saints area, was plagued with heavy muggings directed at same poor whites. Why this happened is quite complex, but the increasing yuppie presence perhaps helped foster erroneous views amongst some blacks, that all whites around the area were well-off and carried plenty of money on them. Consequently an old woman was done over three times, a male nurse was beaten up and robbed, doors were kicked in and unwary tenants (not householders) opening street doors were roughly pushed inside, robbed and beaten up in the hallways. If you didn't have enough money, you were doubly punished. It was really sickening. Even white women with black husbands and boyfriends were not exempt from this indiscriminate mugging spree. About the only exception not to raise an eyebrow was an Earl's son getting knifed whilst scoring dope.

Just before the Notting Hill crack down (c/f later), and possibly because people were really getting pissed off, the attitudes of some muggers began to change which in turn changed tactics. A gang on the Metropolitan tube line, which runs through north Notting Hill demanded everybody, turn out their pockets. Now, only the wells off were robbed, (i.e. those with plenty of credit cards stashed in their wallets). But it was a gesture that came too late and could do nothing to stop the gentrification of All Saints Road and the repression to follow. The day that indiscriminate mugging becomes social mugging in a situation where it is difficult to distinguish rich from poor any longer with any certainty, will make a big difference; a huge difference. What happened on the Met line that day was a gesture and a good one in that direction. Evidently there were similar incidents like this at the Harnmersmith Concert of the

Bronx-rap messenger, LL Cool Jay in November 1987, although the press only reported the brutal incidents.

To be completely accurate, one has to consider mugging etc within the context of a growing pathology especially in London and which cannot be understood using terms like racism in a simplistic way. A festering atomisation at home, in leisure - growing worse by the minute - aggravated by yuppie colonization and increasing isolation at work is taking a hideous toll subjectively. It's taking place within a class society, which is bent on hunting down the more popular, warmer social aspects, contained and accommodated though they were, by capitalism. Psychopathic behaviour becoming rampant as in the United States mounts up in Notting Hill too. A black guy, something of a religious nutter suddenly murdered his social workery, Communist party girlfriend. He wanted to get "the evil out of her." She was a nasty little operator and through the looking glass of religious mania, he spoke a social truth, but his exorcism is scarcely to be recommended. In fact it's chilling, because there are better, more coherent ways of dealing with such things and which will be more readily understood.

Crumpet, before being arrested by the cops and 'killed', had slashed a woman:('killed' is put in inverted commas because the guy was loaded with coke and given the usual going-over common place at Notting Hill and Dale police stations, a heart attack in these circumstances can result in death). During the first day of the 1987 Carnival there were also more crazed incidents than in previous years. An electrician, Michael Galvin making some pin money trading was knifed to death. He wasn't a professional trader merely somebody who quite stupidly - considering it was Carnival - tried to make a little on the side. Although it seems the guy wasn't a particularly pleasant character, blacks after the Carnival, through the mediation of a black Labour party councillor, organized a few benefits for his family. There were other nasty incidents during Carnival, like when a guy with a broken cider bottle, started plunging it into as many people's faces as possible both black and white. Another guy started laughing hideously at paraplegics and tried to pull a woman's neck-support off. London pathology has a different inflection from its New York parent as the language of a downtrodden class that is twisted out of all recognition, to express a frustration with themselves and everybody else. The examples above are the hideous extremes of this pathology, though more generally it's based on a resentment of literally everything in another person's life. A perverted class antagonism becomes an obscene excuse to spit venom. You are knocked for being privileged no matter what your circumstances are. For having money or not having money ("you're free that way") for having an incurable disease or for being in the best of health, for having the guts to stick a stretch inside ("just who do you think you are for having such guts?" etc) or for having stayed on the outside.

The awesome proportions of international capital and monetarism in London, has brought out a submerged trait that mixes up class antagonism with spiteful deference to the rich. A few drinks and the beast is free, lashing out blindly to the right and left saying and doing the unspeakable with little or no evident remorse. Nasty as these outbursts are, remarkably there is never really a racist side to them in Notting Hill (though obviously this is not true elsewhere in London) (18)

Footnote (18): In comparison, in the heat of the moment in adjacent Kilburn there sometimes is, although resistance to the bosses and all shades of state authority is generally far more consistent. But it's an insult which must be taken with a grain of salt because these "racial" slurs that take the form of, " why don't you get back to where you came from", can be directed at anyone not resident in Kilburn, (as if Kilburn is their property). Sometimes it means nothing more than catching the next 31 bus to the Gate.

This complicated web must be difficult to comprehend people living outside London, though there are other dimensions, like the misunderstandings bordering on hostility between northern and southern blacks, reflecting a more broadly based North/South tension. The Huddersfield steel band in the 1987 Carnival wanted to be withdrawn sickened by the pushy, 'we're the tops' hard drive of its London musical counterparts. In fact there couldn't have been a greater difference between the atmosphere of the June, Huddersfield, largely Grenadian black Carnival and the Notting Hill Carnival in August.

The Huddersfield Carnival literally was a relaxed picnic with a hint of the Labour festivities of the 19th century, keen to project an image of self-improvement. One of the floats carried a lollipop, which read "Huddersfield Caribbean Association self-aid scheme reading and writing." There was no dipping or aggro - it was as calming as a spliff, as Rastas from Pennine villages poured in for a day's outing. Despite the nearby presence of the Sheepridge Estate (renowned locally as Huddersfield's Broadwater Farm) a chief Inspector judged the Carnival floats without so much as a murmur from the participants and assembled onlookers. If anything similar were proposed for Notting Hill, despite (in comparison to Huddersfield) the greater capitalization and brutalisation of the area, the outcry would be instantaneous.

But then comes an August Bank Holiday Monday evening. It was as if racism and pathology had never existed. There was an overpowering feeling of release, a surge of re-awakening friendship and the brief opportunity to make friends. The riot was simply enjoyed as also a brief respite in the great communications breakdown ripping London especially to shreds. It was all the better because there had been in the autumn 1985 uprisings, a certain deterioration in the quality of rioting, (muggings and rape) etc. This was to be off set against the greater fury and destruction of 1985 in comparison to1981 because the overall situation has become a lot nastier. This deterioration was largely confined to London, so perhaps Notting Hill 1987 may herald brighter things to come. In particular this deterioration in London has had one very bad side effect. It has made many women scared of riots just at the moment they were beginning to participate in them more. Rightly their completely understandable horror of rape and mugging - and which they have very little defence against - has to some degree intensified an old conception that rioting is purely a macho act. Such responses however mustn't be placed in the same category as the "macho politics" slur used to rubbish all insurrectionary means spouted by a social democratic mentality anxious to psychologise any struggle that escapes political categories.

One final point: With the stock market collapse and a possible slowing of the invasion of exchange, which has shaped and encouraged pathology, a very subversive characteristic of the London proletariat may well come to the fore: that penchant for taking the piss out of anybody who gets on their high horse, or seeks to instruct in a demagogic manner or has pretension to leadership. It is a characteristic the 19th century anarchist, Emma Goldmann, when heckled for a laugh was quite unable to understand. She considered the London mob "behaved as they would at a country fair, not so much to listen or learn, as to be amused." (My Life). But it is precisely that ever readiness to have a good laugh at all pretensions and foibles that make the London poor so brilliant at times.

Photo left: Notting Hill. 28th September 1985. The night that Brixton blew again there was a disturbance at the bottom end of Cambridge Gardens near the Lancaster West Estate. The photo shows a bid limousine being burnt out. Cars in the UK come under more direct attack and sabotage than else in the world. It's a fairly constant phenomenon (e.g. the recent month's long pyromania in York. When "cars are dead" was sprayed on the walls of Notting Hill in 1968, there was little tangible evidence then of future anti-car assault. When it did come about - as per usual in the UK - it happened without any accompanying explanation by the car destroyers. It's a limitation, which often reduces the vision behind these brilliant acts.

THE SAINTS: AND WHEN THE COPS CAME MARCHING IN

All Saints Rd was (is?) of course, the nerve centre of Notting Hill and has been for many a year. Even in 1958, it was the centre of the race riots and in the late 1960s the scene of attacks by the then famous gob-bolt of speed, PC Pulley (now a gun toting embassy cop). After the 1981 riot, which took place surprisingly at the very end of the July riots, a slow process of attrition began to unfold. Suddenly there was an air of mortality about the place.

The central pub, The Apollo, was closed in the summer of 1981 on police orders because of the grass dealing that went on there. It had been an OK dive despite the many nights of depression in there caused by absent life. And if it has been missed, it was only because pub life in general has gone from bad to worse in the area. Black and whites mixed freely and there was ganja everywhere and the Guv'nor- an ex Irish Guardsman - who had once owned a small pig farm back on the old sod, just let things go though he could be tough at times. Of course the place was full of bollock-aches too: all 57 varieties of lefties, alternative comedians, alternative this, that and the other and dumbo rebel musicians were there in over plus. Befitting strategies of recuperation in Notting Hill, a graffiti board was placed on the bog wall in the gents. There was one memorable comment. Replying to Engels' remark that had been scrawled up: "drink is the quickest way out of Manchester," some wit had written underneath: "suicide is the quickest way out of Birmingham..." But the closure of The Apollo in 1982 marked a moment. Other pubs have been shut down in London by the cops for short periods since so that a clean up could take place, (e.g. the 1987 closure of the Golden Cross on Portobello Road or the refurbishment of The Atlantic in Brixton) but the drastic, complete shut down of The Apollo is probably unique.

Things suddenly began to get very edgy. Houses in the mews running up to All Saints were being really smartened up as the trendy rich started to buy some of them. The siege of rapidly rising property prices was beginning and the place was becoming full of dizzy contradictions. For people with little or no room for manoeuvre, the short fuse they were on got shorter, imploding as much as exploding. A Scottish alchi in a semi-squat and normally a neat quiet guy, flipped and took away part of the head of his best mate – a former Irish building worker- with a broken cider bottle. The reason: his Irish pal wouldn't switch the light off when asked. Instantly sobering up, the Scot who had always been so friendly couldn't believe what he had done. Shell-shocked and walking slowly, he was led away by the cops, who gave him the gentle touch calling him "Jimmy". He received a murder rap and was locked away in a high security mental asylum for twenty years. For the rest of his life Jimmy's dreams will be plagued by that nightmare evening. Mental? What's more maddening than gentrification, which catastrophically erodes the social life of the poor and the necessary warmth of contact. Gentrification proceeded literally through murder in this instance.

But on the other hand, many young Blacks (All Saints was basically a 'black' street) began to resist the invasion and growing police pressure because their small-time, dope-dealing livelihood was threatened. Resistance was not merely resistance to a trade that was under threat. There was also the ideology of Rastafari, while a few doors away the menace of the growing community worker/Afro-Caribbean, black small business scene around the Mangrove restaurant. The Mangrove had been able to keep its radical image throughout the years because of a stupid policy (stupid from the state's point of view) of police harassment of black business in the summer of 1970.

In short, it gave the aura of radicalism to a fledgling black middle class who in their turn in the 1980s, were threatened by something uncontrollable below as they fearfully but patronizingly tried to encompass the lively street scene - even encourage it - whilst also wanting to see it pacified and brought under their control. The Apollo was re-furbished, with the aim of turning it into a black co-operative workshop of various handicrafts and small businesses. It even acquired a post-modernist architectural arcade! Despite all the bullshit connected with Rastafari (return to Ethiopia/ dislike of Lesbians and Gays) it nonetheless had an ideology of community, an ideology of sharing, of the abolition of exchange. For quite a number of Rasta's on All Saints Road, this initially meant going out of their way to keep the rest of the local community sweet, like being nice to the poor whites and those older, straighter blacks who'd never had a joint stuck between their lips. "Where've you bin' all Christmas my man" etc, was a regular greeting after a traditional festivity to someone not part of the street scene but who nevertheless lived there.

There were many truly enjoyable and crazy aspects to life on the street. In terms of the protection it offered it was like a north London Casbah. If you were black you could escape to it and be safe. Simply disappear into the rabbit warren of tunnels connecting cellars. No cops would dare follow. On one memorable occasion, an LBC newsflash reported a stolen car in North London flying through the streets pursued by cop cars, its occupants heading for All Saints. The car made it, crashing into a lamppost. Wild cheering! The occupants dived into the nearest pavement lights trapdoor leading to the cellar warrens and away.

Of course there was an atmosphere of Black Nationalism in these warrens but in practise it did not prove all that strong. White women were allowed in but no other whiteheads. ...Until one night in a basement shebeen in All Saints, some Glaswegians (who else?) not to be excluded from an all hours drinking party barged in, their Clydeside camaraderie quickly breaking the ice. After that they kept coming back, night after night. Indeed at times, All Saints seemed to be like a scene out of a classic Glaswegian slum. Young black guys holding meat cleavers and machetes would regularly square up to each other urged on by their followers. There would then follow a ritual quadrille to and fro across All Saints liberally peppered with the most basic of insults. Generally they were ritual duals and the cleavers rarely sank into flesh. It was really a matter of honour being seen to be satisfied without loss of face.

Then there was the Nigerian woman who sold household groceries. The tins on the shelves were rusty with mildewed labels and the fruit and vegetables were mostly rotten. Even the newspapers were a day or two old. When a customer complained, she replied: "well they are only a day late". In the back of her shop was a big tin bath and every so often she'd collar the Irish and Scots alchis' who lived in the squat above her shop, put them in the tin bath and scrub them. They would emerge from the shop all clean and shiny looking for the next swig of cider. They would return at midnight attempt to break into her shop to pinch the cigarettes. But the big Nigerian woman did not mind too much: a break-in meant an inflated insurance claim. In any case, the groceries were merely a sideline for a small-scale grass trade. The Insurance Companies quickly got very wise to the constant burglaries/ fire raising on All Saints. Plain clothes coppers were always asking locals if they had seen this or that hoist. The locals usually kept schtum. A couple trying to get enough dosh to keep their shop open faked a robbery. The guy knocked the girl around a bit then tied himself up. Because it was so lamentably executed it failed and thus he got banged up for six months.

The street never closed, except possibly for a period from six to nine in the morning; in that sense it had more of a New York than London flavour. Midnight football matches were a regular event. On one occasion a truckload of cows passing by All Saints broke down and the cows escaped, legging it down All Saints. One black guy went up to a cow and said; "want same grass man?"

But throughout, the cops were ever-present and there were literally countless incidents of bottle and brick throwing. The cops generally tended to arrest people in the streets leading to All Saints and they were mainly punters who wouldn't kick up untidy. Only occasionally would the cops attack the main drag directly but when they did, all hell would let loose. The bookmaker, E W Kensington, was a kind of centre and it was often raided as the cops looked for ganja. It would provoke uproar. The bookies cheekily responded by having tee shirts printed sporting the logo "E.W. Kensington, bookmakers to the Ghetto." One daft community copper tried single handed to change the atmosphere by being especially nice. He would say "hello" to everybody, virtually forcing people to say "hello" back. But he ended up getting his truncheon and helmet nicked - sobbing openly in the street. He was never seen again!

During the miners' strike of 1984 and early 1985, though the separate, but connected terrains of urban riot and strike action never came together except in the pit villages clearly the impulse was there. The summer battles of Gascoigne Wood, at the heart of the Selby super pits complex, was shown on T.V. news and all the blacks in Bibs restaurant on The Saints shouted and. whistled for the miners. Other blacks, mainly older, would say to some whites on All Saints "we support the miners". For the young blacks, it was the sheer violence against the police they identified with, rather than the need for some conscious inner-city rioting/ striking miners' unity, (which didn't happen in 1984 partly because the state seemed to have told the cops to cool it in the inner-cities).

However the atmosphere generally was going from worse to desperate. The delightful aspects which also made insurgent outbreaks rich and strange were fading from the scene. The ideology of Rastafari was corning under severe strain and falling apart and reggae was going disco. Yuppie colonization and incoming designer style were taking a heavy toll. The Yardies, the gun toting hard drugs dealing, Mafia-like mob from Jamaica who initially were created to guard Jamaica's ex lefty PM Manley, for a while moved in on the Saints. They frightened the shit out of those 'English' (can one say this?) Blacks who dealt ganja as a means of topping up dole payments. Basically, they just did not want to be a part of a 'mob' network like that. There were unsubstantiated reports that guys, who tried to muscle in on the Yardies scene, were tortured in the basement warrens by applying electric wires to the genitals. Whether the rumour was just rumour, the Yardies, for the moment have left Notting Hill for more lucrative business elsewhere in London. (19)

Footnote (19): If any further evidence were needed this proves yet again, how gun-toting, political heavies always fall into horrible, money-grubbing rackets. The Yardies are the worst, that's all.

It was portent though of the ugly times ahead. A designer style began to take hold of All Saints and the street atmosphere deteriorated as it ate into the heart of the rebel stronghold. Not that designer style in itself was either better or worse than what had gone on before it. After all, working class people to compensate for a life lived on the margin, need to feel good and wearing the latest fashion can give the appearance of having come out on top. The real trouble lay in the putting into practise of what designer style symbolised - aggressive go getting and love of money as the key to all possibilities vacated by the failure to transform life. Designer style advertising was a pressurised hot sell, of a brittle scream to "take me, take me" and on the street it scarcely mattered whether that freedom from restraint meant trashing a store front or nicking from a defenceless kid.

Elsewhere on All Saints Road, black and white artists (particularly the latter) were increasingly moving in being given favourable leasing or letting terms by the Notting Hill Housing Trust. Dixon the junk sculpture furniture maker and cretinus 'inventor' of 'salvage art' (seventy years after Duchamp's readymades) of colour supplement fame, acquired on that basis, a large studio. From this he knocks out at least one chair a day which one can't even sit on, never mind taking any pleasure in looking at and which go for £1,000 a time in plush west-end galleries. During the 1985 Carnival, Dixon as a public relations ploy - even though he is very snooty - opened up his studio for a little party. Carnival stewards were at the door vetting entrants; these latest and for the moment untypical museum attendants were ready at a moment's notice to stop a riot breaking out.

All Saints was becoming a trade street, pure and simple. Trade in art. Trade in dope. Forget the good times! Money was a serious business....just weeks before serious money was to become serious debt for a lot of rich finks. The place seemed to acquire something, somehow, of that pre-crash freneticism and though it was only a shadowy connection because no "serious money" was being made, the war of one against all on the street was at times like a sink version of a futures market-trading floor. People living in the vicinity who used the street daily, were told to get the fuck off the street if they didn't want to buy dope. And this coming from white trash and the white artists were looked up to and left alone. Then the muggings started to increase becoming nastier by the day as heroin and cocaine appeared on the street. (C/f on Carnival1987) Most of this was carried out by designer oriented blacks - those who wanted the flash gear, identifying with the value system that went with it and nothing else.

American style, pass-it-on, that monetarist interjected disregard for 'fair' exchange -wanting to possess everything immediately as commodity - became relatively commonplace as BMX bikes were whisked away from underneath young kids, often from poor families who were playing in the street. However in condemning these forms of muggings, one must recognise that before the great stock market crash - and which may see the end of such a trajectory - money grabbing was on the verge of becoming a kind of social relation/ central axis of society. A polite veneer, getting even thinner, merely disguised the fact that it was also a form of mugging but without the brutal honesty of the street, (e.g. the New York "house slaves" prepared to sell every aspect of themselves including lying proclamations of love in order to move in with a partner while looking out for more lucrative bodies to pillage who owned larger apartments.)

Increasingly cut off from surrounding social basis of support a cornered frenzy on All Saints would leap out half- crazed from doorways. Links with this basis were always somewhat tenuous on All Saints but now it was becoming completely lost. More and more punters had their dope money stolen from them, which just invited retaliation. And sure enough a black guy - who just happened to be there - got savagely knifed by a ripped-off punter in one of the side streets. By early summer 1987 as many as three mini-riots a day were breaking out. At the same time, there were also in Notting Hill, quite a few skirmishes of a far higher quality. On All Saints, it had become largely self-destruct having lost its out-going, laughing, communicative edge. So often it was just ugly as the sun glanced off flashing knives, though to be accurate when rioting broke out, it was purely anti-cop. But by now, the cops were getting heavier too as a particularly nasty crew known as the "Midnight Watch" got down to their dirty work. It was becoming all very contradictory and not a simple, beautiful charge as it had been in 1976 or, on a countrywide level, the heady days of July 1981.

Then came the big clamp down on July lst 1987. The cops descended in droves and they came to stay. Within days it had a name: Operation Trident and it was much bigger than the police curfew after Crumpet's death. Though largely drawn from the southwest and Devon and Cornwall amongst there mass presence could be heard Scottish and Northern accents. The typical divide and rule. Send the Met to Yorkshire when there is trouble and vice versa. Play on regional hostility between North and South! For many locals amongst both the black and white working class though it was a relief. The muggings, the burgling of poor households stopped overnight. The heroin was gone, or rather dealt in a more clandestine fashion.

However when the cops do something or in this case put a stop to something, the truth is left to rot unnoticed. What wasn't revealed in the newspapers/ T V during the following days was that most of these arrested for hard drugs were white and not black. A minority of black street kids who had done the dirty dealing, who had gone cynical with the collapse of Rasta ideology (which was anti hard drugs) were only mug workers for the White big boys. In the weeks to follow (surprisingly, considering cop vindictiveness) most of those arrested for ganja or hash over the Notting Hill area as a whole, were released without charge. The rest, including the whites arrested for dealing smack, were kept inside. The Labour party - even the most dissident - supported the clearing of All Saints and were willing to talk to the cops. Like the locals they wanted rid of mugging and heroin but behind it too, there was the orderly petite bourgeois ideology of the quiet suburban street; of early to bed and early to rise ready for an honest day's wage-slavery. There is a history to such one-sided, killjoy responses in Notting Hill. During the era of Rachmanism, tenants' committees, somewhat commandeered by the Labour party and justly attacking rapacious private sector landlordism, then went on to an indiscriminate taming of the area's wild life. Since the 1950s high on the list of tenants' committees, were the proposals to close down shebeens. Sure a basement shebeen can be a damn nuisance especially when a good night's sleep is essential, just in order to get through alienated work and leisure. But these reproaches were aimed at cutting the top off all highs in favour of a monotonous normality. It does happen to be true there exists a creative dialectic between the 'good' and the 'bad' in areas. Recognition of this does not mean justifying the 'bad' merely in dealing with it one does not impose a stifling watch committee mentality. (20)

Footnote (20): This historically is what happened to Storyville in New Orleans when, a hellfire, lascivious puritanism put an end to all that was creative about the place. In spite of the gangsterism, organized prostitution and scramble to make a buck any-which-way, there was just something unrepeatable and exceptional about those wailing train whistles taking the blue note from the dance halls into the marshalling yards.

On the Saints, the day's work over, the cops continued to stay. One got the impression, they were just so country, that they had been brain-washed during briefings to believe that Notting Hill was jungle-bunny land, inhabited also by crazed white fiends with jacking-irons sticking permanently out of their veins. What a tale to tell back home over a pint of scrumpy with the farm lads in The Barley Mow! On the streets of Notting Hill their country bumpkin eyes were opened wide. They tried to get friendly not because they were told to do so but because of their country manners. One sensed they were beginning to enjoy the place.

It was not just a military-style operation either. The police tried to work on the division between blacks and other locals. Within days, plain-clothes cops (who pretended to be other) went around to every house in the vicinity of All Saints to suggest setting up a Neighbourhood Watch Scheme - the pet project of the new head of the Met, Peter Imbert. Also a huge police mega truck moved in, open to all those in the area who might be interested in beating crime. They got few customers. To top it all, despite the yuppie inroads, the Neighbourhood Watch Scheme failed and not one of the familiar stickers appeared in a window except in the very low-rise flats in Tavistock Crescent. No doubt this still testified to the anti-cop inclination of Notting Hill, although there must have been many punters who didn't subscribe to it out of fear of neighbourly retribution. It was a relief, although it should be pointed out that many Neighbourhood Watch stickers are cynically put in windows because house insurance premiums are cheaper that way. (21)

Footnote (21): Like the Leftists they are, Class War has recently proposed a strategy of entrism into these para-state bodies. They dream of kicking out the cops from these cop-initiated Neighbourhood Watch Schemes, a vangardist fantasy doomed to failure but which may help to boost the image of these schemes amongst the poor and confused. Such entrism is an imagined short-cut, a substitute for the harder task of initiating some anti-mugging, anti-cop, anti-heroin, anti- rapist etc project completely independent of the State. It's about as subversive as the Trots whose delirium leads them to believe the Labour party can be turned into a Bolshevikh party; that the state can be turned into a "Workers' State."

But coppers will be coppers. No matter how washed up and disintegrated they don't change their spots. In the following days and weeks sitting in their riot trucks all over the district (not just All Saints) they began to turn their attention onto the local community who had blinkedly but understandably welcomed them, in the first instance,(rather like the Northern Ireland Catholics who welcomed the British Army in 1969). One agreeable side to Operation Trident. Most of those arrested were yuppies nicked for driving over permitted alcohol levels. But pubs were turned over to. An Irish plasterer had his half finished pint of Guinness snatched out of his hand at closing time and an Irish girl, with a fast food fetish, finishing off her twentieth hamburger of the day, had her feast snatched of her mouth. All over people in pubs were arrested for being drunk even though they weren't.

Divide and Rule and the Media

An Inner-City Big Bang?

There was an ugly twist to the pub raids. Blacks were separated from whites then searched. The tactic was an attempt at a racist divide and rule like had never been known before. Over the years the tabloid press had tried to ferment racial trouble in Notting Hill by scandalously distorted reporting (c/f Mikkelson). Throughout the 1980s it has got horrible and to verify this, just consider two of the worst excesses.

Sometime in 1986, a white guy on crutches died of a heart attack on Golborne Road, on the way to the fish and chip shop. Without checking any facts, The London Standard and LBC picking up on an unsubstantiated rumour, immediately proclaimed he'd been mugged by blacks. A chill went through the area. Was it true? All day fearful blacks everywhere went out of their way to nod and smile at whites whom they only knew as familiar faces. It was a horrendous lie but it took days for the calumny to be exposed and then only as a footnote in the press. It had been the same three years earlier in 1983 when a teenager, the lovely Belinda Greaves was diabolically murdered by a black psycho-killer. From the front page of The London Standard there screamed a headline stating that a black guy had killed a white girl. What it did not say was that Belinda's dad came from the Caribbean although her mother was white. In both incidents, The London Standard's slanted report could have led to revenge attacks, which was probably the intention. That media provocations failed, is down to the on going and long time inter-racial unity built up in Notting Hill (and now elsewhere) over the years that has come about among the oppressed of all race.

If these didn't work, neither did Operation Trident even though Blacks were singled out, as never before by the cops. Black school kids, having a shing-dig the day summer term ended and larking about with foam silly-string, were pushed against the wall and separated from their white mates by the boys in blue. Anti-police hostility grew. Why were they staying? Was it to satisfy the hated yuppies? Maybe the off spring of some top bod in Whitehall was now living in Notting Hill and wanted the place cleaned up to look like Chalfont Latimer? Maybe this mandarin had button-holed Hurd, the Home Secretary, one day in the corridors of power and asked Douglas to do something about it. "After all, old boy we knew each other at Eton."

An inter-racial anti-cop unity, common to Notting Hill came once more into the open. Whites protested at the way blacks were being treated. There was a memorable incident outside The Colville pub on Portobello Rd when some blacks tried to free a white guy shoved in the back of a police transit van. They rocked the van but failed to push it over. As for those blacks who had become cops black street kids called them "black bastards". And as their quisling presence tended to provoke, rather than pacify riot, they had been kept away from All Saints. Fragmented trouble broke out all over Notting Hill but it was all disparate, unconnected and failed to come together into a party.

Black Brothers? *Black Cop & Rasta at the 1987 Carnival*

As for All Saints, opening the door one morning it was staggering to find a black guy, ticking-off share ratings in The Times', financial index. From dope dealing to potential insider dealing, as quickly as it takes for a cop to truncheon a skull! Was this, as it was, 'the dark side' of popular capitalism: a species of born-again mugging, providing the opportunity to get rich quick. It strikingly brought out the combined power of Thatcherism and post big-bang as an international, inter-racial, inter-class force able to suck in broader and broader layers of 'the people', especially in the south east, even able to make inroads into the subterranean depths. (However, "fair shares all round" - the monetarist version of social egalitarianism - was shortly to have its nemesis on Oct 19th 1987, revealing starkly that capitalism had in-built barriers to its popularity)

Then came the expected liberal lefty official protests. Bernie Grant and Paul Boateng, the recently elected black MPs, at a House of Commons press conference criticized the police swamp without of course mentioning the real nitty-gritty, which led up to the swamp in the first instance. What had happened previously on All Saints was largely glossed over, and no one dared speak the truth for fear of being accused of racism. The heroin trade, apart from a few comments by Frank Critchlow - boss of the Mangrove restaurant/ community work scene - was particularly glossed over. He said he would have been able to control it - which he wouldn't .The muggings were passed over in total silence and not surprisingly, because these meetings were basically social workery, guilt-ridden, hand wringing affairs. The Trotskyist SWP in Socialist Worker went along with all this garbage, their account, being so wide of the mark, it made one doubt even the factual veracity of their reports on industrial disputes throughout the UK - the only reason to read the magazine' - even though you have to ignore their ideological slant in any case.

A white middle class, feminist, social worker, whom had quit Notting Hill a long time ago for owner occupation elsewhere in north London, did her do-goody, but very influential bit. In the past to prove how hip she was she'd had a kid by a black guy, though the blacks she'd hung loose with on The Saints, were those on the up. Guys like Jerry Rawlins - the man who was to become the populist army captain and Ghana's head of state. In short, the same old power-as-an-aphrodisiac trip and never a serious relationship with an estate Leroy. It's very different to what happens when working class individuals - with an attraction or love for each other - get together. They don't spectacularise their offspring, which as it were, happen along the way. They don't wear their mixed race children like a race-relations badge as the lefty-professionals do. (22)

Footnote (22): All Saints after all had an image and a past and aspiring, populist, lefty Third World politicians, would in days gone by, pay frequent visits there, before becoming famous elsewhere. For example, Maurice Bishop, the assassinated head of the New Jewel movement in Grenada, decimated by Reagan's paras, used to drink in the Apollo. Amongst all this though, was one truly sad incident vis-à-vis the day-glo desperate life of rebel stars. It was on All Saints, that Jimi Hendrix -perhaps the greatest jazz/rock guitarist of all -on the eve of music entering into total eclipse, either o/d or committed suicide, leaving behind his dying-to-be-loved, final farewell on a piece of paper.

Then suddenly the occupation ceased only three weeks before the 1987 Carnival. But one felt revenge was going to be meted out at Carnival because the word had got out everywhere - what are the police doing in Notting Hill? And just before the Carnival, the cops' presence increased with random searches with arrests in

Basin St and elsewhere. As for All Saints the silence continued and has only been broken since by small disturbances somewhat encircled by the Mangrove scene: Critchlow, in his Maida Vale pad, didn't need to worry too much how to play it. His hands were clean. In the interests of black small businesses he'd opposed the cops. Nonetheless, since the trauma of Operation Trident, disturbances have begun to take place again in Notting Hill in 1988, partly because the cops really want to punish setbacks - and punish hard. (And if it's anything to go by the cops aren't probably going to play it cool like in 1984).

A Council Estate Spillover?

But if the occupation, had ceased in Notting Hill, it has also patchily intensified elsewhere, simply because some of the drug dealing migrated to the danger spots of the Mozart and Lisson Green estates, in the neighbouring Borough of Westminster. Here the police presence had to be low profile. Even so, having cracked down hard in Notting Hill, in the long term, they had only aggravated their problems elsewhere. We can be thankful for police wisdom, in not letting sleeping dogs lie. Irritation at their constant interference can only swell the furore, which is breaking out in Westminster, over the Tory council's ruthless plan to get rid of half the council housing stock there.

So far much of this opposition has been orchestrated, by the very marginalized Westminster Labour party, (which has more than a few members with Bennite leanings, who lived in NottingHill recently.) It hasn't amounted to much beyond disrupting Council meetings, councillors arrested and miserable night time candle-lit processions, protesting the closure of St. Mary's Hospital on the Harrow Road. This hospital has been sold off to property developers with apartments earmarked for sale at an average £200,000 each. With the stock market crash, they won't get anywhere near that price. Such actions provoke a murderous rage, so it's extremely doubtful if the Labour party can in the long term, contain the mounting anger. The last thing they want is a Broadwater type explosion on the Mozart, which they continually predict will happen, and which they're doing everything in their power to prevent happening. The Tory council are stupid enough to think the opposition are trying for another Broadwater Farm, but it is the Tories themselves who will succeed in doing this. Lisson Green is about to be sold off, at cut-price rate. Mortgages won't mean anything there, as most of the tenants are unemployed. Plenty evictions are sure to follow and that could be social dynamite in triggering things off there.

Both the giant Mozart and Lisson Green estates are late 1960s early 1970s Town Planners creations and both have turned out quite differently to what the bureaucrats intended. The systems built deck access Lisson Green, completed in the mid 1970s was more or less earmarked for respectable working class tenancy. Within a few years it rapidly became a sink estate and all who found themselves sinking rather than swimming were re-housed there. Largely tenanted by poor white and black, it recently has received a huge influence of Moroccan families. The Mozart was supposed to be more auspicious than Lisson Green, as it was low-rise and largely brick-built. Many expected it to blow during the rioting Autumn of 1985 and rumours, some probably true, ran wild. Recently however Westminster council has set about demolishing the deck access and it has been mooted (though not confirmed) that the better part could be sold off. Selling off Lisson Green and the Mozart isn't so daft, considering the up-market, American style facelift by Regalion properties (re-named Falcon Towers) on formally, unspeakably awful point blocks in Clapham Junction.

Certainly tenants on the Mozart are very edgy and ever ready to attack the council and anything else that gets in the way. Over the last few years there's been a lot of patchy flare-ups on both the Mozart and Lisson Green estates. The inhabitants of the latter ("the Lisson Green Posse") were blamed for rioting in Praed St Paddington, during the miners' strike in summer '84. There is however a hierarchy of estates, which is pretty effective in stopping inter-estate solidarity. For instance, the brick-built Scott Ellis estate close to Lisson Green, obviously regards itself as being a cut above its neighbour. It is tenanted by people like low paid civil servants, precisely the types who were originally designated for the Lisson Green, Which they keep well of...And would either of these two estates feel solidarity with the squatters on the football terrace like, construction of Rowley Way estate, half a mile away and now being evicted by leftist Camden Council?

All one can say for the moment is this: the situation in London has deteriorated to such an extent that solidarity action, in response to renewed rent strikes, due to cuts in housing benefit or, the new Housing Act, and potential riots, is now more likely, even though unprecedented. Also one must not forget that council workers in London, in response to savage attacks on their conditions of employment, are seething with anger, the likes of which, hasn't been seen for ages. If ever.

The photo of the above graffiti was initiated by Brim Fuentes, a New York subway artist from the South Bronx. It may look like rebel art but in fact was done with the consent of Chelsea and Kensington Council as were other sites in the area. This remedial, halfway house, between the street and the gallery system does not exist in the States to the same degree as the UK. In some cases here the local State and local education authorities (e.g. Wolverhampton) fund such schemes. Actually New York subway graffiti was a response of outcasts to the failure of radical currents in America. It changed appearances not social relations. Looking back, it marked the recovery of the visual, which from clandestine beginnings on subway trains, became ever more neutral as it spread out over and upwards, replacing the aural as the dominant aesthetic of containment. The transition from street artist to gallery is symbolic of this process.

AN ARTISTIC SWAMP: DESIGNING THE EMPEROR'S NEW CLOTHES

In Central London, there was no comparable street anywhere to compare with the low property prices on All Saints Road. Increasingly throughout the 1980s, it became a very desirable residence for chic, artistic business, drawn by cheap rents and the thrill of the place, which did wonders for that precious commodity 'street cred'. With the police occupation, a big push was given to this tendency. The Legal Light Recording Company, a no-nonsense black business opened its doors. Dixon expanded his salvage art mini-empire, acquiring more leased lettings from the Notting Hill Housing Trust, for what seemed at the time, a Warhol-like factory complex. In reality it turned out to be nothing like so grand. But the place was irrevocably changing. A rich and exciting past was coming to an end; its rebellion crushed by art - an old story of modern times.

Backed by the police occupation (completing the pincer movement) a few of the empty properties were developed for working class tenancy by the local Housing Trust who as ever always have an answer as to why there weren't, a lot more. "Straight working class people don't want to live on All Saints, so we're not harming anybody". Whilst this is true, it's not so for the many homeless families and others living in bed and breakfast (the kind of people living around the corner in the Angel Hotel in Tavistock Rd) who would jump at the chance of being housed (however temporarily) on the Saints. But they are not artists are they?

But the bull market in art was coming to an end. Two and a half months later, the world's stock market crashed. It didn't scatter the objet d'art like chaff overnight, but it re-established an old master selectivity where only blue chip taste was safe (i.e. the post- crash world record for 'Van Gogh's Irises) But crucially the index linking of all the top end of the market had come unstuck. It was not that the relationship between art and finance capital was at an end, (Japanese Insurance Companies know better than that) only its 1980s avant-garde phase. Formerly the typical financial entrepreneur, pitifully believing him/herself at the frontiers of creation, would put money in avant-garde stock. With an estimated 5000 jobs for starters to go in the City, many a gallery will close its doors. In fact this retrenchment, in which Bond St. and Cork St, came to loom over pretenders like Notting Hill, reflects on the financial level proper, the drift back to the City of London away from the proposed new site in Docklands.

Ever capricious art (at least the ever renewed farce of "creative" art) must now seek out newly emerging trends, as yet only dimly visible to identify with. Come post-crash dawn and it was obvious, the link between the chic figure of the artist and the estate agent, walking hand in hand, both complimenting and understanding each other perfectly and both speaking each other's language was broken. The estate agent will survive probably by going down-market, where property values are less affected by the crash. Will the artist metaphorically speaking, follow suit? Maybe we can form an idea from observing some of the main tendencies at work in Notting Hill over the last few years extracting those, which an emerging new economic order may muster to serve capital.

Prior to the stock market collapse, one got the impression that capital's hope was to make All Saints a malled, multi-media, multi-ethnic, art ghetto, somewhat like Covent Garden, but far more avant-garde. A place of daring invention and sanitized ghetto living. The very thought of it leaving one feeling sick, even mugging seeming attractive in comparison.

Art all over Notting Hill has been the precursor and aesthetic counterpoint to gentrification. Negatively good in showing clearly which side art is on, it hasn't been combated clearly and confidently. With art galleries opening everywhere and squeezing the number of stores trading in everyday essentials, there's been a lot of muttering and confused anger. Many is the time they've been threatened with fire bombing (particularly the gallery owned by Richard Branson's sister) but alas, only when the drink was flowing. In this artistic deluge though, there's more than meets the eye. To view it as a neo-return to the early 20th century would be very superficial: a reconstructed Montmartre with a replicant Picasso about to break into a replicant cubism or, say, the popular artistic quarter of turn-of-the-century Munich awaiting an equally replicant Expressionism. This is merely the front.

This entire excrescence is really the art junk-bond market, when anything that said it was art, meant an appreciating asset. A time when the miserable pop art sculptures of Claes Oldenburg, twenty years ago, got turned into an even more miserable yuppie prop. Moreover, and more to the point, this art, these art galleries, looking so traditional with all their seen-it-all-fifty- times-before, avant-garde repeats, are, merely service conduits for a very big, up-to-the-minute, media hype: studios for immediate ideas marketing by ad men and women, art galleries as front for advertising agencies in a situation where England (particularly as centered in London) is the temporary capital of world hype. With the telescoping of art and business, all pretence about any gap between art and the commodity has vanished more completely than in the late 1960s. It's now glaringly obvious to a much vaster layer of the population.

Take the seeming repeats of dead end 1960 s artistic happenings, all over Notting Hill, throughout 1986 and since, (e.g. The Mattoids and Big Joe Rush). Basically they're simply dress rehearsals for inventive ads promoting products. Test Dept, with their tin can futuristic music, even bringing in a few Kent miners (forever the populism!) to improvise with them under the M40 Westway, were immediately signed up for a TV Heineken lager ad. The end product was one of the most ingenious promo's ever made. In passing one wonders too, if Test Dept wasn't also a recuperation of those outbursts of a music made by everyone, when an hilarious drunken evening's camaraderie bursts, seemingly from nowhere, into junk tin-panning and everyone starts playing walls, gas fires, chairs and tables.

Take too, the film of Absolute Beginners -was there ever such a build-up? And was there ever such a flop? The greatest movie disappeared overnight without a trace. Absolute Bollocks. But the producer, Julian – "we must create new clichés"- Temple, still holds his court in his local, Notting Hill watering hole, The Duke of Norfolk.

Photo left: The Mondrian visual pun appeared on the cover of Faron Sutaria's estate agency, property magazine, distributed gratis to most flats and houses in the area. It is Notting Hill's most avante-garde property shop. Sutaria is an Anglo-Indian who has risen to prominence during the Thatcher years, his career roughly paralleling the Saatchi Bros who have amassed a 'famous' avante-garde art collection. Where other estate agents may display in their windows their more desirable properties in picture frames concealing a staid interior of oak-desks, inlaid with green beige tops, Sutaria's agency is an art/property experience somewhere between an office and a temple. Giant colour transparencies of properties, illumined like stain glass hang on the back wall while photographs of other properties are framed like the side panels of triptych's. Unlike the typical pinstriped estate agent of a decade ago, Sutaria, immaculately turned-out in various shades of pastel, goes about the business of selling properties as if it were a leisure activity. His self-image is that of a multi-millionaire aesthete entrepreneur, somewhat akin to R. Branson's Virgin Leisure Industries. Simply buying a house to Sutaria is philistine and suburban. As well as an appreciating asset, it is an unfinished symphony in bricks and mortar; a symbiotic meeting of art and property values. And artists, ever more economically minded, respond to this connotation as if they were selling an appreciating asset. ----A friend wittily suggested that one of the newly opened art galleries should hold an exhibition of estate agents boards, comprising perhaps, an early Foxton, a minimalist Ruck and Ruck, a conceptual Sturgis etc......

This blatant market orientation is masked by the appearance of a community of artists, and that's how the erstwhile spirit of community - no matter how bogus - has changed according to circumstances. The Apollo was the communal watering hole of vague libertarianism, which amidst all of its nonsense had something of an anti-competitive, anti-business air to it. Now a similar venue for a more aggressively entrepreneurial time, The Warwick Castle, with more artistic front has come into being. A magazine put together by some of those who work for Rough Trade called The Roughler centres on The Warwick. It is a magazine, which manages to praise Jasper Conran (the ultimate in designer wear at £500 a throw), the cricketer, Bob Willis, and Class War, in almost one and the same breath. Even The London Standard noted favourably it's, "Tatleresque spoofs". In comparison with the Notting Hill underground press of yesteryear, it is abysmal. The, more or less, yippee Ink and Frendz underground newspapers whatever their manifold failings, were brilliant in comparison. Yet Class War seem to be unaware just how contradictory their matey relationship with The Roughler is, especially in view of their professed anti-yuppie stance. The Roughler is not anti-yuppie but pro-yuppie or, more properly, pro the changing face of yuppiedom, which will opportunistically respond to whatever social forces are eventually unleashed by the crash. One of The Warwick Castle's pivotal punters is no less than Johnny Rotten, never able to leave his punk posture of wild-eyed artistic 'daring' behind. When posing for today's glossies, his semi-Thatcherite, Restart radicalism (get off your arse and make yourself a job) combined with a very jumbled appreciation of working class extremism may prove a workable blend in a constitutional transition to a post-Thatcherism still stamped with the impress of the old. In parenthesis, Glen Matlock's status as former Sex Pistol was unable to save him from being threatened with a real Restart interview. One wonders how true this may be of The Warwick Castle clientele -though one would never guess just by looking, because they don't wear their worklessness like a badge, as formerly happened in The Apollo, designer-style being in part a reaction to the stylisation of poverty initiated by punk. (23)

In a sense, The Warwick Castle takeover sums-up what's happened to a lot of the pubs in the area. Gentrified for a new clientele (which somehow never seems to turn up as much as hoped for), the old clientele just won't take the hint and leave. In many other pubs, locals have been barred by trouble shooting 'guvnors' from Yorkshire or Geordieland, (big breweries also using the north/south hostility, just like the police) One of the last Geordie governors of the Duke of Cornwall, even cracked a whip at closing time. It was no joke. He meant it.

Now that the general climate is beginning to change, the scene seems set for a long drawn out battle. The governors, ideologically locked into the past of an eternal bull market, sky-high property prices and inflated city salaries aren't going to change just like that.

What has taken place recently vis-à-vis artistic gentrification in Notting Hill is merely a microcosm of a much wider shift in society, though its effects have been more intense and concentrated, than elsewhere. As a generic phenomena, artists everywhere, are diligently putting to rights, a trail of havoc left by a none-to-precise anti-art scorn, Which 15 years ago, even the most orthodox 'artist' had to make some accommodation with. But behind their newfound reassurance and vicious ways, lies nothing but the most total and utter creative bankruptcy. And any moments of self-doubt are put down) though hesitantly and with a touch of mock seriousness, to the unavoidable sufferings of the artist (viz in this respect the camp parody of 'creative' romantic agony by Gilbert and George.)

During the 1970s it was different. In a belated response to the late 1960s attack on art- an attack that failed to become an onslaught- artists everywhere - altered their image to suit the populist 'art for the people' climate. Because a more coherent critique of art was only grasped by a handful of people at the time, it proved to be an attractive, have one's cake and eat it, alternative. Architects temporarily, forsook their role, to work on building sites. In the space of a decade they had gone from sacking trades people if their work didn't come up to scratch, to seeing what life was like from the other side of the drawing board. The easel was abandoned for collective out of doors painting. Public Pictures group artists in Notting Hill decorated the concrete bays under the M 40 motorway - obviously influenced, (at least in intention more than stylistically) by American WPA projects in the 1930 s plus Siqueiros and Rivera - though lacking even the dubious quality of the American/Mexican originals. A graffiti at the time read "Public Picture: the cosmetic of misery". And such bright cosmetics are still used everywhere to paint over the cracks of a dull street.

Footnote (23): Well over a year before the 1987 general election, Rotten said of Paul Weller and Red Wedge: "Well they can go on tour up north all they like but quite frankly it's not gonna change the kids' point of view. They ain't gonna vote. Period. They just ain't unless it's Newcastle United or Man United they're not gonna vote. They're not, let's face it. The working class are completely, utterly and totally fed up to the fucking eyeballs with the current system and see no hope, and don't want no part of it, which is why they're so bloody violent" (City Limits, 7 12 1986). And as for the rehabilitation of art take the PIL tour of Sept/Oct 1987. "The stage set was a fluorescent, multi-coloured techno-cityscape of tower blocks and bridges. ...The show was modelled on work by the Austrian painter, Friedensreich Hunderstrasse. "We wanted to create somewhere we could have some intelligent fun.(The Guardian 31101'87) Perhaps this is why JR said elsewhere that he preferred the States because the British resent success -i.e. they dislike the rich like him.

A climate of right wing populism developing throughout the 1980s changed the real picture completely. Today's born-again artists are the acknowledged legislators of a romantic monetarism of egotistical greed and faith in their creative mission. And architects, grabbing a bigger percentage of dosh than ever, are becoming once more prima-donna personalities, reflecting the shift from public to private investment in construction with many more, much smaller sites and fewer operatives. In spite of the unspeakable horrors of post-war urban renewal, the local authority architect was to some extent faceless. Now they are to be found poking their noses everywhere, imagining they are constructing an architectural jewel, demanding engineering perfection and a high productivity ratio. They have also become generally much more business-like, employing swine's of sub-contractors whom are bad payers etc. But take heart this renewed positivism at all levels of culture, especially so today, only mirrors economic performance. It cannot survive a slump or severe recession without a jolt. Whether it will shatter this time, is up to the strength of a genuine revolutionary critique and practise.

(However even before the world stock market crash, the yuppie epoch was running on to the rocks. It appeared to peak ideologically even before the economic tumbrels. Now as they begin to fade from the scene we can see them for what they are -a particularly obnoxious form of the middle class spoilt brat, corresponding to an era of global financial deregulation when governments' were foolhardy enough to "risk handing over to stock markets the job of steering the world economy" (The Economist 26th Dec 1987 and Jan 8th 1988). Yuppie was never a term of approbation anywhere in the world. Rather it was sneering, contemptuous, derisory and in the U.K. in particular, few would unashamedly call themselves yuppies. The long hours of sterile work, the unremitting pressure, the sting of never getting a society like the U.K. to submit to a winners and losers division, was for some enough to spark trashy fantasies of the moon and sixpence in preference to a docklands suite and end of the year bonus. Before the nosedive in share values, yuppies were leaving the City to pursue the washed-up muse of art, not as a consumer, but as a creator. Having refused the link between art and finance, they are likely to seek a new creed but one, no less securely tied to the circulation of commodities, because either a Gauguin or a market maker is today a false alternative. Having taken a back seat for so long, perhaps the left yuppies of Marxism Today may provide us with potential clues as to this new creed? (24)

Footnote (24): In spring 1986, artists and staff belonging to the avant-garde Air Gallery in collaboration with Islington's so-called socialist council, set up an open air exhibition of ready-made, junk sculpture on a bit of green space used by the tenants of the council owned, Hartnoll Estate. As they were bringing culture to the plebs, the tenants weren't soft-soaped and asked for their consent. As a result, artists were attacked and on occasion roughed up. These actions brought down upon the tenants the wrath of The Guardian's, hysterical, numbskull art critic, Waldemar Januszcak with the familiar accusations of philistinism. One annoyed Hartnoll Estate resident wrote back to The Guardian's letter page replying to the idiot Januszcak. Though sadly not supporting residents decking artists (it goes without saying that the urge to get your dabs on artists is a creative urge) he clearly pointed out that Marcel Duchamp's ready-mades had made the point much better many moons ago.

This either/or dilemma - banker or artist) is perhaps too archaic formally implying e.g. an exclusive respect for old conventions like easel painting. This will continue to exist (it is surprising the degree to which old artistic forms, like oil painting, sculpture, lithography and etching, no matter that it was all unbelievably bad, were saved from the trash can in the main by the financial revolution) but only as a subordinate cog in a much bigger machine. For instance the number of galleries catering for this latter day resuscitation of the Fine Arts, was far outweighed by the number of print shops opening in malls etc selling 'Art' postcards, film and pop star posters and framed photographs - thirty years ago, a mere handful (but growing steadily in number} would have 'daringly' argued for photography as 'art'. The dominant tendency will be towards a "mediafication" of life replacing the increasingly wearisome conservative surrealism of music promo videos. In this sense the Labour party's slick, TV dominated 1987 election campaign may prove to be something of a forerunner blending message, advertising agencies, copywriters, designers, film makers and ex T V producers. It need not be mind bendingly boring, nor politically tendentious either, because if it is, it won't have an audience. The invasion of the advertisers world by comic artists or, artist comics, already a fait accompli, could also metamorphose, sponsoring a kind of freak consumer protection or, surreal government warnings. Aimed at a broad viewing public, it will be a product requiring much money, team work and professionalism, worlds apart from the amateurness of Public Pictures in the 1970s who survived on meagre local council grants and the like.

Besides, this form of artistic expression was linked to squatting and the tentatives, no matter how faint, to lay hold of the urban environment, repair and shape it (according to human need) irrespective of legal entitlement. With the disappearance of mass squatting the basis for it has, in this respect gone. What is left is a pale resemblance in the opposite direction. The wretched, folksy, decorating of unadorned 19th century engineering structures -like the railway bridges in Chalk Farm and Camden, has been covered up, the girders picked out in alternate primary colours (no return to uniform return to uniform grey here). On the South East rail network, this painterly hype rather than capital renewal means one thing- getting the region ready for privatisation - and includes, everything from the flash South East designer logo of railway stations, to the ornamental coats of paint on aging diesel engines.

And as for the democratic moulding of townscape implicit in squatting, this has been seized on and trivialized beyond measure by the growth of home ownership and the inalienable right in theory of everyone to buy rather than actually having an inalienable right to shelter.

No post-crash scenario, which does not involve total upheaval will fundamentally alter this retreat into the home and design-conscious interior or alter the central place occupied by TV and the video. It is difficult to imagine there could be an explosion of 'radical theatre' without getting wind of it on TV. In the not-too-distant future, reformist rucks could centre on the question of access to the media and attempts to curtail the monopoly of control exercised by programme directors. The media artist could then be placed in the unenviable position of managing this discontent channelling it, so as not to spill over into a general popular recognition of the creative poverty of life as a whole. After all, their monopoly of non-creativity will depend on it when the real creative battle is going to be the subversion of hype and the media. No promo, no 'radical' TV appearance, no gobshite to journalists but how, with the aid of technicians, to destroy media nonsense once and for all!

Also, most importantly a new inflection is needed challenging the boundaries of art and life, differing from the 1980s banking as a money aesthetic. "As capital money is both money and more money" (Paul Mattick) it could lose its enticing glance reflecting visions of 1968 turned inside out, becoming once more a banal instrumentality that puts labour to work, if it is to function as capital. And the rehabilitation of work as a creative experience in banking, (another grim achievement of the 1980's) could undergo change and become 'creative concern' expressed through a sort of voluntary work as living drama.

But enough - this is all speculation and we have no means of knowing and it is too early yet to get any clear indication. Suffice to say, that in Notting Hill, the terrain of community politics now fallen completely into passive consumption, (gigs, cabarets etc) has increasingly been occupied by artists looking for a socially more acceptable future. Going back many moons, community politics used to be pole of attraction and experimental laboratory for sociologists, would be politicians, social workers and the like .Now their mantle seems to have fallen on artists, though without the ideology of grass roots participation which was their originally. The wheel turns full circle, but never quite coming to rest at the same point.

"So ends the Empire of Notting Hill. As it began in blood, so it ended in blood..." G.K. Chesterton: "The Napoleon of Notting Hill" *(1904)*

Is Notting Hill finished? Well that seems unlikely though if it were to lose its special avant-garde position that would be no bad thing. Certainly the area is very tense, but what place isn't in the UK? It can no longer claim to be in the vanguard in this respect and, nor can any other area. In North Kensington, as it was in the beginning, so it is at the end, with the rich still living, cheek by jowl, with the poor. The quickening pace of the area's invasion by the rich, since the late 1970s - amounting to an onslaught – has caused the place to lose most of its free and easy character. Driven mad with each turn of the screw, the poor - still by far the vast majority - slide into deranged frenzy. But hopefully gentrification has now stopped in its tracks though unlikely to go into quick reverse. For Sale notices multiply and buyers are cautious not wanting to be caught out paying a hefty mortgage when the value of property is starting to decline. And to think just weeks ago how overpowering was the pressure to escape, even for a few hours respite to adjacent more conducive areas like Shepherds Bush, Cricklewood, Hammersmith, Willesden and Kilburn where gentrification hadn't made the same inroads.

Basically, it was escaping from a once hallowed refuge to another 'village' - London being a series of urban villages - possessing all the inward, localist, outlook of village life, which one hardly sets foot out of. This is not to say anomie; typical of big cities is absent - in fact, very much the reverse. Generally, unlike Liverpool or Newcastle, London doesn't really possess the atmosphere of a city, although the waves made by the financial Big Bang of October 1986 have to some degree devastated this separate village-like identity. It has in other respects involved a significant degree of change: finance capital in the UK far more than industrial capital, has been the guardian of that complex of manners and ritual recognisable as historical tradition. With the invasion of foreign financial houses, particularly American and Japanese, in the wake of Big Bang, this patrimony has now been broken at its core in the City of London. Finance capital in the UK now approximates more to how Marx described it, in his conclusion to Theories of Surplus Value: "In the capital which produces interest, the automatic fetish is perfected: we have money producing money. Nothing at all is left of the past; the social relation is no longer anything more than the relation of a thing (money or commodity) to itself. ..." From Notting Hill to Nothing Hill.

It's not that in general Londoners are taking this lying down, or crawling defeated into their beds to die, finally suicided by the bankers. On the contrary, as ex-chief of the Met, Newman, on the day he retired in the summer of 1987, strikingly (for a police mind) put it: "London now is in a state of slow riot." Notting Hill is merely one area covering a vast terrain.

Things are so far gone in London that it appears the place needs riot as a human adjustment. The North, on a practical everyday level has a feeling of community, even if it is only a smile or a friendly acknowledgement. After months spent in London, these simple responses, take on an enormous even exaggerated importance. In London and the dense urban/ hi-tech corridor of the M 4 to Bristol, community in all but the most superficial aspects has disappeared. And the Hungerford massacre stands as a warning to what can happen under these conditions. A simple basic need to re-establish human contact must be one of the gut motivating forces behind the sporadic, flash flood mini-rioting, which began to take place all over the southeast corner of the UK during 1987 and the beginning of 1988. One further point: Many people say rioting doesn't change anything. Like today the past was peppered with them and they were just as inconsequential. Looking at the last hundred years it is hard to believe their incidence was anywhere near what it is now. This contestation, breakdown, even mindlessness, must add up to something. To dismiss it out of hand usually says more about the arrogance and complacency of the person who does. A reporter in The Independent (2nd Sept 1987) after the Carnival, said rioting had been "a relatively common event in the 1920s and 1930s." This is overstated. There weren't that many and those that did occur were among unemployed workers, led by the C.P. stalwart, Wal Hannington. Besides these riots were largely defensive and a response to unprovoked police baton charges, when weary marchers would enter unwelcoming towns. There may have others of a different nature, notably the set-to at Harwood Colliery in north Notts in 1938 when the breakaway Spencer Union was thrown out in favour of the National Union. But unlike today, one really has to look very hard to find even the remotest sign of turmoil in the sunset cities of the North and the sunrise cities of the Midlands or London. What's more, a political/trade union framework, like the afore-mentioned examples, does not circumscribe today's rioting. At the antipodes of politics, these riots are spontaneous, unpredictable, unnerving, constantly catching authority on the hop.

It is the sphere of consumption rather than production that has recently tended to prove so explosive in the UK, though with renewed strikes everywhere in 1988, an explosive overlap becomes a possibility again. However spirited the response is to the failure of leisure, it will get nowhere unless ultimately it involves the productive forces. Otherwise it will simply joy ride off into the gloom. Meantime how to do it justice? Autonomy seems too tendentious a word involving theory, consciousness and knowledge of what was best in the revolutionary movement of the past twenty years. If not totally alien these notions just somehow do not entirely suit the uncontrollable lust-for-life, often enough set free by the contents of the bottle and constantly running up against the thin blue line, between us and the good time. It is not class war as the professors of class war understand the term, but there again, few would deny that it had class implications, or that leisure is becoming increasingly valorised (multiplication of theme parks, gentrification of pubs etc) to serve the interests of the leisure moguls. This sort of leisure management is never relaxing; on the contrary, it is stiflingly at odds with spontaneous enjoyment and the enemy of a genuine surprise. It is for instance impossible to get a drink in Alton Towers in Derbyshire, forerunner of many other theme parks, like the Heights of Abraham, Gulliver's Kingdom and the American Experience north of the Trent. Maybe here we have a hidden acknowledgement that drink is doing more to further real destructive rebellion right now in the UK than a traditional, union-shackled, shop steward movement.

Ever since The Winter of Discontent in 1979 and, until recently, the employed working class in the UK has been more and more squeezed back into union led disputes, despite the atmosphere and reality of inner-city rioting - and its knock on effects - making the action, in and around these disputes, exhilarating and volatile (e.g. the miners and printers at Warrington and Wapping.) Now that we're beginning to see as the general rule, the return of wildcat organization, what was missing in the general potlatch is in the process of being re-defined again. But this general movement is also taking place in a dire, up-and-down, manic depressive atmosphere - an atmosphere which is also getting worse by the day and one it's necessary to go into in the following postscript.

It is worth asking to what degree has rioting been a stand-in for the energy that was formally unleashed in wildcat strikes, serving as a rallying point nationally for pent-up frustration and passion. (A major aspect of the British Disease, Thatcher, until recent events, claimed to have cured.) However, one has to be careful about such comments. They can be a form of leftist rubbishing of destructive impulses. An old point forcibly comes to mind when considering the UK's exemplary vandalism: just what is worth preserving of this old world? Nonetheless, there is a risk of falling into an ideology of riot in the UK, like there is an ideology of assembly in Spain, everyday life in America or theory in France.

1987 saw the re-birth of wildcat activity in the UK (West Yorks buses in early spring, Yorkshire pits, civil servants, postal workers, Ford, Austin Rover and bus crews in London and Scotland) and continuing to grow with amazing rapidity in 1988. But they'll have to cohere into something more than a resuscitated rank 'n' fileism. Unfortunately these wildcats are tending to serve as a warning to a lumbering bureaucracy to waste these inspiring initiatives, by calling a secret ballot (required by law), so they can attempt to fuck in action altogether. However, Thatcher's, '"give the union back to the membership" is also double-edged and tending to backfire. It has ironically, tended to take away authority from the union bosses - an authority capital is going to desperately need in the future. It's encouraged workers, in an unexpected way, to handle their own affairs and take matters into their own hands. Finally it's worked-on and stimulated a rare depth of hostility to trade union manipulation that could well break through into something else. But it'll need more than just a spontaneous anti-bureaucratic explosion to get anywhere and for this, frustrated rebels could do worse than look at the planning and self-organization of the French railway workers (Nov 1986 to Jan 1987) or, the Italian base committees, or, the Spanish Dockers Coordinadora for inspiration.

An historical note: In the final years of the First International, Bakunin, got some of his confidence to breakaway from what he rightly perceived as the growing authoritarianism, statist goals of Marx and his followers, from English trade unionists (it is not clear what kind of TU's they were - were they for instance, forerunners of shop stewards?) who were mouthing-off against the Great Teacher. Has it stayed like that: unerring quick-fire responses that suddenly falter and get lost, vacillating between a fatalism and a far from compliant insight into what went wrong? Or, considering those subterranean processes which one can hardly fathom, are things now subjectively very different, more rebelliously sure-footed among the UK proletariat as a whole? Whatever there yawning inconsistencies, we hope so.

Since we are dealing with a past that is still very much alive, we may recall that the origins of anarcho-syndicalism, go back to the insurrectionary notion of a "grand national holiday" (i.e. general strike) advanced by Tyneside workers in the early 19th century. However, the day of classic anarcho-syndicalism has passed ultimately fouling up, just like any other trade union form. What is striking here is the colourful turn-of-phrase and the nascent libertarian tendencies emerging once more at the end of a long drawn-out process of trade union implantation, forever side-stepping the most fundamental question. It may just be the ingredient needed to leap the extremes of contestation, in work and leisure and in so doing, recast both in an autonomous mode.

Photo left: The Time Factory. A new mall and theme park for Los Angeles destined to be the largest in the world. Shopping centres and malls are also foci of trouble.

Though the Gateshead Shopping Centre on Tyneside (with facilities e.g. for men to change babies nappies) is a pioneering example of retail modernity their incidence, though generally on a small scale, is greater in the S. East. This is not the place to go into a comprehensive analysis of the tensions they generate or, to compare Britain with America where the malling retail revolution is far more of a total experience in space and time, creating a parallel 'reality'. However, consider the following from the Guardian (16.9. 1987) - which is something of a departure from its usual bland reportage.... "The urban riots of 1981 and 1983) didn't happen in decaying inner-city areas. Over the past decade most new towns have experienced fairly serious outbreaks of rioting (which often never reached the national press) and these usually occurred in or around the new shopping centres. In many places I visited there was an almost palpable hostility between those spending with credit cards and those with UB 40s and nothing to do but watch. In Oxford earlier this year it was reported that the pedestrian shopping precinct has been the scene of often quite violent clashed." (Part-Time Places). Equally however, we could mention the frequent disturbances in N. London's Brent Cross shopping centre where shoplifters have been pulled away from security men and police. This response does seem to be frequent in Britain's malls.

POSTSCRIPT:

"SOMETIMES WE SEE A CLOUD THAT'S DRAGONISH"

Under the guise of restoration, the last decade or so has witnessed the inversion of the revolution glimpsed so dramatically in 1968. Reaction has in the process laid hold of the revolutionary themes and redefined them for its own ends. The 'idea' whose time has come, has been turned inside out and the language of revolution monopolized for conservative ends, even taking credit for coining the word "revolution", (Thatcher's recent talk of a "cultural revolution") because, what is under attack is some vague 'sixties permissiveness' which substitutes for the spectre of a total soclal revolution, too fearful to be ever openly acknowledged.

It has not, in the UK, been an easy task engulfed during the 1980s from time to time by titanic struggles, threatening to sweep away the slow progress-in-alienation engineered in the opposite direction. But meantime, an ill-thought-through anti-statism is twisted out of recognition to support cut backs in welfare payments and promote privatisation, which parrots the ideology of nationalization (public control) and is also a false critique of bureaucracy at the same time. A wish for genuine liberty is deflected into a resuscitated doctrine of entrepreneurship, the right to exploit others and, most recently of all, the proposed right to scab, protected by the law, even if there is a 99% majority in favour of strike action. And on a subterranean plain, desire has been caught by the tail, on the trading floor of the Stock Exchange promising dreams money can buy. And what adventure could be more fabled than the rise of the Saatchi Brothers advertising firm, in a position, only recently to threaten a take over of one of Britain's top five banks, the Midland? Or Revlon, the cosmetics firm, mounting a table turning bid for Salomon Bros, Wall Street's leading brokerage house! Whilst against a backdrop of mass unemployment and mounting poverty, anti-work combined with a freedom for want - not long ago the hope of millions - is what drove many a city whizz-kid along, looking to retire at thirty, having made a pile. Not forgetting the multiplication of exotic services whose endless variety catering to the tastes of the connoisseur consumer have 'enriched' the meaning of work, changing the spirit of capitalism from a work ethic to a work aesthetic. It may one day be useful to draw up an exhaustive list, but let these items suffice to give some idea of its scope and breadth. Until Black Monday its onrush was so powerful as to render "the work of the negative" almost a spent dream.

What is exciting about the biggest most international stock market crash in history, is that their piece meal ad hoc innovation adding up finally into a total strategy of containment, has been left stranded in mid-air. Particularly in the UK the leading exporter of "popular capitalism" slavishly imitated, even by an emergent super-power like Japan, there is now a gaping hole, a populist vacuum which is exceedingly dangerous for power. The bourgeoisie were the first to build a bridge to 'the people' and in all subsequent phases of its political domination, particularly in the 20th century where the presence of the masses was keenly felt, all government whether Liberal, Social Democratic, Fascist, Bolshevikh, Post Second World War Consensus Politics and latterly Monetarist, had to appear to embody a popular will, for at least some of the time. Once this consensus had broken down irretrievably and could no longer be conjured out of thin air the rulers were in mortal danger.

With the crash a central plank of monetarism in the UK immediately snapped. After the disastrous B.P. share issue the Tories privatisation programme is now in ruins. For the foreseeable future, the small investor (ideologically of supreme importance) will be scared off. Even the marketers of share issues began to have qualms - an indication of just how far and wide and quickly disillusion can spread, because advertising is a leading glamour industry that has flourished like never before under the Tory government. A post BP flop article in The Financial Times (November 12th 1987) remarked -"critical assessment of the creativity of privatisation advertising has been superseded by questions about the morality of it all"- going on to say "City observers are concerned with the increasingly dogmatic tone of advertising - in three years the slogans have moved from "you can share in BTs future" to "If you see Sid tell him" for British Gas to "now it's your turn to say yes" for the Trustees Savings bank, to BP's "Be part of it".

This hectoring tone born of an unshakeable conviction, that if you follow the instruction to the letter, it will be to your great advantage, will now turn into government diktat without even the glimmerings of popular ratification. In a volatile stock market, one cannot command people frightened for their state pensions to buy unit trusts or frightened for their lives, to take out costly medical insurance paid for out of stock market winnings. And what happens if the froth already knocked off the des. res. property markets effects less desirable residences? And the average house owner accustomed to vicariously enjoying their locked-up assets, start to see property values decline wholesale? This could happen both as a result of renewed inflation or lower wage settlement if a recession really starts to bite. But whatever, such people feeling they have been had are going to cast around for a political lifeboat.

No brand of political populism is ever quite the same. And no Chesterfield Conference of Trotskyists, left Labourists and re-nationalizers opportunely held only days after the crash can ever hope to suddenly catch fire in the hearts and minds of the masses, though it did attract a lot of media coverage. (Had there been no crash, it probably would have gone unnoticed). Nor will the rainbow of issue politics (co-ops, radical music, fundamentalist feminism etc) ever be like it was because populism doesn't work like that. It needs time to cohere into something that little bit special temporarily pulling the rug from beneath the feet of the canniest observer. The crash has opened Pandora's Box and pondering the shapes of the future almost in spite of themselves, city commentators were moved to quote Mark Antony: "Sometimes we see a cloud that's dragonish, a vapour like a bear or lion."

This shadowy foreboding may indicate there's a falling rate of populism, a nearing of the bottom line when it comes to drawing up a credible alternative. Nationalization is probably a more durable form of modern capitalist organization than monetary privatisation (the British government is obviously deeply embarrassed by the Kuwait raid on BP shares amounting to a 20% stake) but to acquire 1990s sex appeal it's going to have to work hard on its public image, enough to waylay a workers' onslaught. Perhaps the coming period may only serve to show that all the old options, no matter how glammed up with hi-tac, are worn through and out of Pandora's Box there springs a revolutionary period. But after so many disappointments and outright failures, there is a danger of getting carried away into wishful thinking. (The miners, for all their optimism up to Christmas 1984, were plunged into a year or more of utter gloom after their strike)

The ramifications of the stock market crash are to put it mildly, perplexing. It is the view of most 'experts' with any specialist grasp of the "dismal science" (Ricardo), which again shows how useless specialists are generally when confronted with a threatening event. No one knows for certain what is going to happen, especially as each tentative measure causes more red signals to flash in another quarter.

The politico/banking fraternity had after the initial shock to give the appearance of being on top of things. Liquidity was injected into the system and bank rates reduced eventually, worldwide. Strenuous efforts were made to talk-up business confidence and the message was since 1929 we have learnt a thing or two, meaning there was going to be no return to trade protectionism, higher interest rates and bank failures.

But the system ultimately cannot be manipulated just like that according to the will of powerful individuals armed with the best advice there is. Capital acts behind the backs of people and with the best will in. the world everything points to an interest rate hike in America.

There is the ever-present danger Third World debt will be triggered once more especially if there is a severe recession. And though banks are making a provision against bad debt in the Third World what happens if the threatened debt moratorium becomes a fact? Not only Third World countries become ever more a bad risk to lenders, but also every borrower, large or small (but especially the latter) could take it upon themselves to unilaterally cancel debt. And the impact that could have upon the mechanisms of exchange is nobody's business. So much of 1980s glitz was dependent on borrowing - a banking response to Third World indebtedness going into overdrive – wooing customers like never before, because small ticket credit multiplied a million times was judged sounder than awesome loans to developing countries. 1980's individualism was largely defined by the rediscovery of individual banking. And the consumption aesthetic made more available by the credit card revolution - pretending to be beyond money - concealed the awesome reality of Third World and corporate debt. (25)

What the crash has provoked is a grudging return to economic interventionism on a massive scale, even though at the moment it is largely restricted to the central banks. But it is only that- there is no insistent demand for a new order. However the most farsighted members of the bourgeoisie are thinking along these lines, which, should it ever arise, must be something more than an economic event. It is in this respect instructive to recall that Roosevelt's New Deal was not some predetermined plan but a series of temporary measures largely determined by an increasingly restless American proletariat which eventually turned out to be good for capital as well. (26) No matter how severe the recession, the bourgeoisie will try to develop Latin American countries and certain countries in Africa and Asia, creating a modem consuming proletariat. And depending on the level of the fight back in the highly advanced countries it will need to have a convincing doctrine that what is good for one is also good for the other, possibly expressed through an ideology of internationalism tailored to suit both proletariat and bourgeoisie. There could even be a state directed, more self-interested version of Geldof's Live Aid and this time at developing countries not right-offs like Ethiopia. Capital's control would be just as vice like though appearing more just.

Footnote (25): It is just so hard to imagine Oxford St denuded of commodities -with soup kitchens rather than January sales - but even if it did happen it wouldn't last long. Either a reconstituted bourgeoisie or a revolutionary proletariat doing away with shops would end man impossible state of affairs. The final drop of water being rung from the falling rate of profit is always tendentious. Whatever substance and merit there may be in Bordiga's economic fatalism we cannot really know until the best of his writings on the critique of political economy are published into English.

Footnote(26): It is impossible to condense the welter of legislation produced by the New Deal into a paragraph or go into the opportune nature of some of the acts forced onto a reluctant Roosevelt Administration to divert a workers' revolt in America – even though some of his placebos encouraged that revolt - (the USA was incomparably more strike torn than the UK in the 1930s and 40s) .But through the Industrial Recovery Act of 1933, labour received guarantees on wages and hours and industry permitted to raise prices to get out of a deflationary spiral. To aid the redistribution of income (and hence distribution of commodities produced by industry) corporation tax was raised as were taxes on high earners. However in an apparent about turn in 1937, Roosevelt attempted to cut deficit spending by mainly curtailing Federal funding of the gigantic construction programme. There was an instant economic collapse and unemployment rocketed. In late 1937 the cuts were rescinded and extemporisation gave way to habitual policy.

On a strictly economic plane The Economist is already proposing a world economy that would get rid of altogether the damage caused by fluctuating exchange rates. Maybe this is the next logical step on from the Bretton Woods agreement effectively abandoned by governments in the early 1970s. In this Economist editorial (Jan.9th 1988) their lurks the phantom of World Government ("until real co-operation is feasible - i.e. until governments surrender some economic sovereignty") and a price control mechanism that appears to end capitalism in the form we know it: (The law of one price - that an item should cost the same everywhere, once prices are converted into a single currency - will increasingly assert itself"). Is this Glasnost gone forever because suitably doctored, it could have come from the pen of Joe Stalin himself. Note also the loan words from another epoch: "co-operation", "control", the stress upon unity not free-wheeling division, are words that also could be employed to trip-up a threatening workers' revolt in this coming period.

The UK remains a weak economy despite manufactured illusions stating the contrary. The Treasury is in surplus, but it would have a budget deficit as bad as America's, if it weren't for once and for all sales of state assets. The currency is fundamentally weak, only appearing strong in contrast to a declining dollar. A huge balance of payments problem is postponed only by North Sea Oil (now running dry) and an exceptional imbalance between financial and industrial capital, partially reflects the growing South/North divide. (27) Then there's a pattern of wage drift combined with low productivity (though in some sectors this is no longer true) and a feeble manufacturing base, which has only just begun to reach the levels of the late 1970s again. Any, or all of these chickens will be coming home to roost and then watch out! Of all highly developed capitalist countries the UK is still the diciest. This in large measure explains the ferocity of the Thatcher government, whose chief task has been to try and curb the country's turbulent inhabitants and having to stamp on more bourgeois responses in the process.

Though resting on a re-jigged class alliance, the Thatcher government is likely to become even more of a power state that can only foam at the mouth - almost parodying those of its inhabitants beneath it whom it really has sent mad. It will fight like a cornered rat pressing home its monetarist version of the final solution the more it becomes surrounded so to speak. It has stood firm against wave after wave of miners, print workers, health workers, rioters etc. Any other European country would have sort to placate but the grotesquely unfair political system in Britain which has continental cephologists guessing - means a landslide can be conjured out of less than 40% of parliamentary votes. To more enlightened apologists for bourgeois parliamentarism in W. Germany, Ireland, Italy, Denmark etc it appears an offence against reason. Obviously this must not be taken as a plea for political reform but it does point to, along with many other instances, the basket case characteristics of UK society.

However, all is not doom and gloom. The signs are we could be heading into a period of great social unrest that the disturbances of the last few years may prove finally, to have been the forerunner. The total shutdown of Ford UK, the seafarers strike, the nurses strike action, and, as the tocsin of revolt spreads, the threat of trouble here, there and everywhere. And who knows what marvellous blooms are being nurtured by the determination to avenge past defeats?

The attack upon work conditions, the carnage resulting from ignoring health and safety, the introduction of casualism and contract work over a wide sector of society, the intention to replace the NHS by a system of private health insurance, the phasing out of the dole - all this is creating the conditions of negative unity. And it is important this draconian government is destroyed in inner-city-streets, the offices and the factories and not electorally. If the Iron Lady suffers the same fate as Wilson, Heath and Callaghan – all brought down by a rebellious proletariat - that will be excellent for a morale that has got jaded throughout the 1980s. It destroys the mythological aura that will surround Thatcher's name if she is permitted to retire gracefully at a time of her own choosing. No more heroes, especially not political heroes.

Footnote (27): Celebrating the advent of Big Bang. The Financial Times (29.Oct 1986) wrote. – a year and seven days to Big Crash -"continental centers have hardly been in the picture – the idea of a free wheeling financial centre is not to continental taste .Continental financial markets have been constrained to save industry or finance governments and tight regulations has been part of the framework - the dangers of conflict are seen to be great."

This movement now underway will undoubtedly have its moments, creating a fruitful legacy future movements can draw on. But the weakness of the proletariat vis-à-vis a sound critique of the state will most likely mean an attempted re-creation of a providential state promoted by various oppositional political racketeers. Even so, it means a post-festum state paying lip service to this ideal will have to be more respectful towards the people it governs and 'helps'. In that sense the destruction of a particular government rebounds upon the state as a whole having to use more manipulative methods until it feels safe enough to put the boot in once more. The state will have to do this fairly quickly - after any initial breathing space - because capital's room for manoeuvre in the UK is very limited.

Of course, this very threatening movement now underway is not certain of even limited success. However the indispensable checks and balances provided by the trades unions have (as mentioned previously) been so hamstrung by legal requirements that power is slipping towards the shop-floor in a an amazingly unmediated fashion. It is just so nice, for instance, to hear a boring, legal historian of labour law, Lord Wedderburn bewailing the inability of trade unions to control their members now that finally, trade union law has produced the opposite of what was intended. "And how", he worriedly asked, "do you negotiate with a leaderless mass? It's the law of the jungle". Of course, it's nothing of the kind; rather it is a basis for autonomy. However it is still not as clearly articulated as in Italy for instance where, over the past year or so, base committees (the COBAS) have sprung up in various sectors all, more or less, independent of control by the major trade union confederations. But what movements in the UK lack in consciousness they make up for in elemental power and, a sheer mulish brilliance among a minority of strikers to willingly stay out on strike forever, if necessary.

It does seem with the decline of America, Thatcher is crazily mad, hell-bent on creating a new super-power in the West to match that of Japan. To do this, she wants practically the whole of society on its knees -from the unemployed, to jobs-for-life civil servants, to skilled engineers, and even professionals like hospital consultants. However to be successful in her megalomania, Thatcher would have to go some way towards allaying the fear and insecurity of the base. In fact ignoring the lessons of history she is doing the opposite. Also, she would have to curb the outward expansion of British capitalism and become more of an aggressive economic nationalist, harnessing the mighty financial institutions to an indigenous industrial base. And that is a complete anathema to her. But she will go out for a crushing victory (even though it could take a few years to achieve) and, if she does succeed you can bet your life it will be due to widely held beliefs in trades unions and obeying trade union leaders.

If that happens: WATCH OUT! Because life truly will not be worth living at all. What has been sketched out on a local scale here could be magnified onto a far broader terrain, and a psyche catastrophically damaged by defeat and repression vent itself in hideous acts which wind-up legitimating power. It won't just be dog eats dog. If ever the potential behind hooliganism is driven into a permanent psychotic fit, the urge to kill everyone who just happens to be in the way will be over-riding. Or if not that, mass suicide as a more developed, progressive form of The Final Solution, one offering choice. Before it is too late, let us seek to combat this threatening nightmare with an optimism of the will and a practical and imaginative intelligence.

Paddington Bear, Spring: 1988

APPENDICES:

A Further Note on London Pathology and its possible use by the state

It's not only Notting Hill of course. Elsewhere, an everyday tabloid assault plays on psycho-horror - its grim reality always spiced with suggestive innuendo.

Take one incident. Two little girls were horrendously murdered in Brighton on October l0th 1986. Afterwards, the police wanted to interview a fat man who could perhaps give some lead. But that's not the point here. For some time - and highlighting soccer hooliganism – the cops have been looking for "the fat man" who was ostensibly "the leader" of 30 youths who went on a particularly horrible knife-slashing spree after a Chelsea/Man United game in London on the 29th of December, 1984. Since that day, off and on, the tabloid press has gone on about "the fat man". Finally a guy who was purportedly "the fat man" was arrested and came up for Crown Court trial just days before the Brighton murder. The tabloids, plus radio and TV news - deploying a form of subliminal suggestion - tried to montage these incidents together, even though there was no connection.

A general hypothesis: The UK state, via media suggestion is trying to pathologize (more, much more than reality suggests) all kinds of spontaneous flare-ups. It's something like a warning to each individual; a warning which isn't clearly spelt out (it would lose its effect if it were). It's something like: if you let yourself go you'll only breakthrough into a nether world of dark pathology; of ghastly sexual horrors and sadomasochistic mutilation. Moreover, with an on-going breakdown of traditional patterns sometimes resulting in sad monstrosities, the UK state finds fertile ground for its own psycho-promo assuming the warped and twisted face of a chastising, hideous hell-fire preacher using sexuality as scapegoat. Certainly the strategy works reasonably well in keeping a sizable sector of the oppressed fearful of what lurks inside and outside themselves.

When Protestantism reaches its end it explodes because it is based on the organization of everyday life. These infringements of the repressive order are then condemned as madness and perversion - a point Henri Lefebvre noted in Everyday Life in The Modern World in the 1950s.

Violent response in London runs a gauntlet between what is inspiring and what is sickening. It's more of a complicated thorny problem than one dares to admit. This is true elsewhere but in London violence acquires a special edge closely connected with London's rapidly changing character as almost a pure catchment area for investments related to the City's bankers. In the North it's always been somewhat easier to simply identify exploitation as related to the industrial magnate or the machinations of a distant Whitehall, despite the abstractions inherent in the process of industrial capital accumulation, in comparison to an earlier feudalism when the Lord of the Manor's rip-off was plain for all to see. Finance capital, though one of capital's "antediluvian forms" (Marx) has an almost objectless, unfathomable, mysterious feel to it. In London it's as though money is what makes the world go round and not the exploitation of labour power - something which is nearly impossible to grasp situated within a wealth seemingly flowing in all directions but your own. It's as though everybody is out to con you, slip you a Mickey Finn, and take you for a mug. It individualizes in a bad way as a disturbed economic unit implanted as an alien force in the psyche. Threatened by a commodity bombardment seemingly closing in from all sides, it's hardly surprising that the drifting atomised being (and often cut loose from the family) lashes out in frenzy at these nearly invisible menacing forces. So that old woman walking down the street is the one causing you to feel so fucked-up isn't she? Finance capital encouraging, even implanting a random psychosis, should be looked at more closely.

This frenzy explodes all over London in a fearful way, as it also gets worse month by month. Fortunately there is still plenty of an historical class identity, experience and feeling of simple togetherness in London to mitigate its worst side effects. But it is an identity, which is on the run and almost chaotic in itself, tending to increasingly gel welcomingly with hooligan responses reaching out into insurgency. The media

through its distorting lens tries to grotesquely distort this process of tentative empathy particularly when some psycho-horrific act is perpetrated. It's not inconceivable (though admittedly for the moment far-fetched) and taking into account a declining but general, lascivious Puritanism, used by the media -artificially boosting its legacy -plus, something of a general obsession with the darker Wuthering Heights side of sexuality (in a country where the collected works of the Maquis de Sade are still banned) that riots in London could be increasingly marginalized from the popular support they now enjoy, as the provocations of sex-mad muggers, child rapists, senior citizen murderers and demented sex-crazed, drug fiends. The "increasing aggression of the heart catastrophically sickened by everyday life" (Artaud) must move more lucidly into a clearer social insurgency otherwise the UK state will take up the theme, maim it, cripple it, promote it and turn it (via something like a 24 hour media barrage) into the cost effective counter-revolutionary strategy it has for its own long-term survival plan -a survival plan which apart from some inadequate but fairly predictable, ad-hoc measures - is still in its infancy.

Bolshevism and Monetarism?

The above poster-type illustration appeared on the front of The Financial Times (27.10. 1986) centrefold celebrating Big Bang. The allusion to Bolshevikh modes of propaganda was unmistakeable. It's more than a conceit (e.g. Hungary has a Stock Exchange) but an oblique recognition of the debt owed to a resurgent Bolshevism which played a large part in capsizing all that was best in late 1960s/early 1970s subversion.

Given the obsessional anti-Bolshevism of monetarists world-wide this statement appears absurd. However the presence of subconscious forces has to be guessed at through telltale signs. What Monetarists and Bolshevikhs have in common is a hypostatisation of the state and political party. And all that was new in terms of the revolution of daily life was redefined within these givens. The con having worn thin by the late 1970s.and to head-off the risk of a rediscovery of revolutionary themes - by then a real danger - the revolutionary essence was once more perverted by being appropriated by the right wing of the political spectrum. Bank underground station (taking its name from the Bank of England) was also done-up with Suprematist designs recalling El Lissitsky and Malevich the at times fellow travellers of Bolshevism.

A week before The Crash the City was brimming over with confidence. There was a Big Bang Ball celebrating the "exchange's revolutionary reforms" which financial deregulation had brought in. A financial columnist in The Observer (11 Oct. 1987) described this "brave new world") "The filthy rich are now a classless society. The aristocrats are depleted but still there. The difference is that now they have to share the dance floor with the grammar school boys and worse, the dreaded barrow-boys made good". Big Bang had also been called "The Cockneys Revenge" but this assault on the City was the very opposite of East End mobs pouring down Shoreditch High St to really put paid to the City. Rather it reflected a far broader recruitment basis than hitherto drawing in 'beastly types'. In any case, it was given a prominence out of all proportion to its actual size. This scrum-down iconoclasm would also upset traditional Covent Garden Opera goers when City louts would burst into a chorus of "here we go" when a striker on stage was about to launch into a well known aria.

But there was also a countervailing tendency at work. Well-bred City gents would also affect working class mannerisms. Though a crash course at "the school of street cred" was an advertisers' invention a night at the dogs wasn't. "There is disturbing evidence that some dog meetings are becoming the latest yuppie fad," noted an article in The Independent (11.1. 1988). Now The City cannot hope to preserve its popular 'classless' image, which lasted rather less than a year after Big Bang. It is highly probable City blue bloods will come to dominate financial services at the upper end of the market once more re-establishing the link between top public schools and a job in the City. Popular currents (i.e. not revolutionary) will move in a different direction - perhaps eventually settling for a new-fangled edition of one-nation patriarchs attentive to the voice of discontent as expressed and contained within the trade union.

David Wise: 1988

New Postscript to "Nothing Hill": February 2004

The two of us - the twins - who wrote this text with a little help from friends must admit that of all we've written we rarely re-read, because immediately acute embarrassment kicks-in as we cringe at the failings. Whatever qualities were in the writings - literally often quite arbitrarily pushed together – and not withstanding what we felt at the time are immediately pushed aside. It was initially put together by the now defunct box number, BM BLOB about seven years after A Summer With A Thousand Julys. What makes up this mishmash is a much greater emphasis on the critique of art corresponding to the much greater emphasis the free market was placing on culture generally as distilled in the media and the nascent emphasis on celebrity. Essentially, 'Notting Hill' notes the freezing process inherent in the rise and fall of artistic form which we must firmly embed in the "table turning" of the perhaps open-ended characteristics of the commodity as outlined by Marx in Capital 1. Assisted by the reification process inherent in the attributes of the commodity, essentially the pamphlet on Notting Hill notes this deadly process which must keep alive at all costs the archaic paradigms/paralyses of art which no longer has any intrinsic value. All the commodity now can have is the endless promo-ing of increasing emptiness whilst affirming it is an increase in riches beyond our wildest imaginings. Real life can still only be elsewhere.

It is also much more than that with its insights into the spawning of community ideologies and how the proletarianised/marginalized base of a clued-in Notting Hill got turned into the excreta of Community Politics – that spawning ground of so much 'new' social democratic experiments – through which so much of this 'art' was expressed.

Behind all this lay the libertarian community, its oddness and 'madness'; it's flight pattern for the poor and the welcome maladjusted. Behind all this also lay the welcome Afro-Caribbean community and a subsequent, slowly unfolding on-going riot.

In this text there is undoubtedly a lauding of riot – no matter how brutal everyday life insisted otherwise. To be sure, distinctions are made between lousy and laudable riot when in fact, it was far more of a complicated matter. Loren Goldner in America now always querulously raises this matter: when was it OK and when did it go ape shit? When did the real era of fuckhead culture kick in (let's attack and fuck-up everybody) which it ominously and tentatively forecasts. And then on the terrain of All Saints in Notting Hill, how gentrification and increasing fuckheadism danced, tango-like, to a deadly tune.

However, the times in which 'Notting Hill' was written in the late 1980s meant the insights weren't proclaimed loudly enough. It is an in-detail account of a developing process that goes on far too long and is too far ranging despite the need to constantly keep the concept of totality ever present in the mind when it's still necessary to put forth the even more dire need for total revolution. At the time, individuals belonging to the Here And Now collective in Leeds, West Yorkshire said the text should have been reduced and the section related to the mini-stock market crash of 1987 was a distraction. Well, for sure, as there is a certain desperate clutching at straws – and the hoped for breakthrough never occurred ...and one gets older!

Like A Summer with a Thousand Julys... and other seasons

 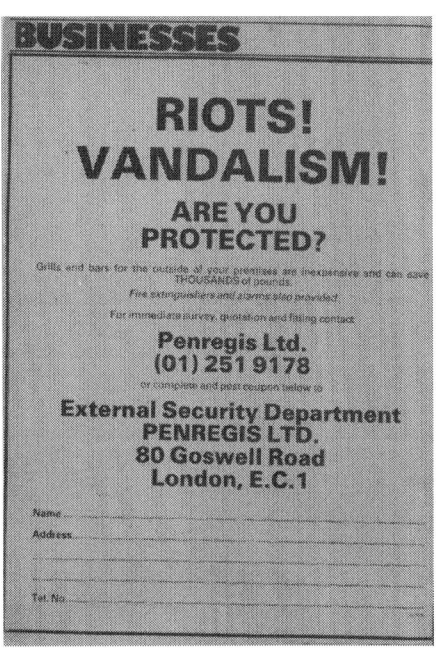
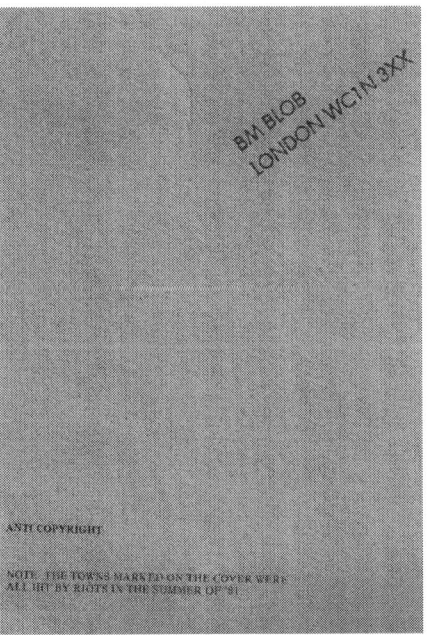 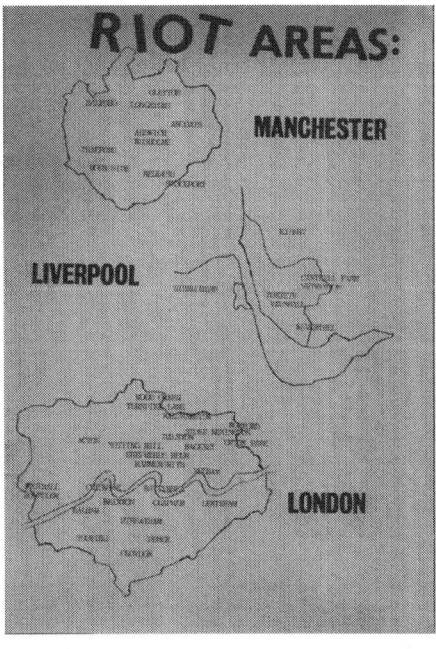

Above: *Front, back and inside covers and original A4 pamphlet*

Photos above: There is an uncanny visual parallel between Mad Martin's (1) apocalyptic vision (left) and (right) this eerie photo of Moss Side burning. Martin's biblical romantic cataclysms once touched off, melodramatic, self-destructive presentiments amongst the Victorian bourgeoisie but his pictures were still given pride of place amid the bric-a-brac. Also many of Martin's images were taken from foundry explosions and pit disasters in which workers lost their lives. Just so long as the workers didn't revolt such disasters were comforts to the bourgeoisie providing a measure of their strength. None of today's rulers will look at Moss Side without shuddering because it represents as plain as day, the beginning of their end.

Photo left: **KNARESBORO' ENGLAND'S DREAMING**. The picture postcard medieval town of Knaresboro' "in its enchanting natural setting", "clothed with deep woods" (Arthur Mee's "Yorkshire W. Riding") was on the evening of July 11th 1981, a picturesque scene of youthful parishioners running through the pear tree shaded wynds of Main Street trashing banks, jewellers, off licenses and shouting "Brixton, Brixton". Photo right: **SHEFFIELD: DARK SATANIC HIGH RISE**. Though only thirty-five miles apart both towns were scenes of riots.

INFANT SORROW: "My mother groaned! My father wept. Into the dangerous world I leapt: Helpless, naked, piping loud: Like a fiend hid in a cloud."

(From reflections of a Moss Side rioter, circa 1981)

Introduction

The rest of the world has long recognised the UK (except N. Ireland) as one of the most liberal countries in the world. This by now reflex view has been slow to die the death.

In spite of the Parliamentary ambivalence intrinsic to declaring several States of Emergency and shortish periods of national government restricted to wartime and the 1930s economic depression, the Mother of Parliaments has adequately served the interests of the ruling class. Since Cromwell's Protectorate following the civil war of 1640-5, it has never resorted to outright dictatorship.

Many illusions have been spawned about Britain's liberal tradition by people who should have known better. The general drift of their pronouncements, if not remembered word for word, have been passed on from one generation to another, inhibiting the emergence of a revolutionary critique.

Marx and Engels (particularly the latter who had many illusions about German social democracy also) went so far as to speculate on the possibilities of legislating social revolution into existence in Britain. In a speech given in Amsterdam in 1872 Marx said, "There are certain countries such as the United States and England in which the workers may hope to secure their ends by peaceful means." This misjudgement, much influenced by English liberalism, has persisted through to the present day. It is the backbone of left parliamentarism and ginger groups from the Socialist Party of Great Britain, the Trotskyists, the revamped ultra-Stalinists of the New Communist Party through to the various still overwhelmingly Parliament-orientated single issue campaigns (e.g. ecology and the increasing professionalism of the women's movement).

But going back to the origins of that other strand of the labour movement eschewing Parliament and politics in general, we find Bakunin's inappropriate judgements on Britain exaggerated the opposite extreme. In Statism and Anarchism (2) Bakunin said, "In England the social revolution is much nearer than is generally thought and nowhere will it assume such a terrible character because in no other country will it meet such desperate and well organized resistance." Marx is naively pragmatic, Bakunin apocalyptic, magnifying out of all proportion the determination of the ruling class to resist at any cost, libertarian revolution. Both are completely wide of the mark - a sure indication of the difficulties encountered in getting to grips with this deeply perplexing society. Analysis tends to get bogged down in a sort of metaphorical swampland and the blood of insurgents dead begins after a while to look like ketchup as the quagmire begins to suck in the partisan. Or maybe you take a leap, expecting to clear the swamp to land on "the other shore." But meanwhile the bank has vanished into thin air like Carroll's Cheshire Cat and you go down, down, down. It is a land of undertones, riddles, top secrets and endless mazes, attracting unsuspecting travellers off the known routes.

Approaching the end of the 20th century, to EEC bureaucrats sitting in Brussels, the UK is the "sick man of Europe." The symptoms that go to make up the "English disease" are many, including a seismic strike record. Unlike the modern technocratic character of French capitalism, Britain's fixed capital is antiquated. Rapid de-industrialization and the acres of reclaimed land, on which only a few years previously stood mighty industrial structures, appears to painlessly blend with a still powerful feudal heritage sold the world over to attract tourists. This medieval tableau appears to stand cheek by schizoid jowl alongside some of the most advanced projections capital is capable of (fashion, pop music, joke packed ads, a sales oriented exploration of the human psyche indebted to the artistic avant-garde of the 1920s and 1930s and surpassing by far the psycho analytical obviousness of The Hidden Persuaders.(3)

Britain is a paradoxically closed yet 'open' society, ruled over by a patrician but condescendingly populist elite, possessing the most remarkable cunning and duplicity, well versed in a token recuperation of everything from below that raises its head in protest. Yet at the same time it unfailingly manages to treat those below as another species being. On almost every side there is also an almost totalitarian repressiveness in daily life at odds with the trajectory of modern capitalism and deriving ultimately from the native strength of the puritan tradition. In The Twilight of the Idols (4) Nietzche said "In England, in response to every little emancipation from theology one has to reassert one's position in a fear-inspiring manner as a moral fanatic." It was a fighting observation only marred by Nietzche's failure to explain why. Much of the historical strength of moral fanaticism in Britain derives from the need to keep the working class pressed down. Particularly in the first half of the 19th century, British capitalism possessed in religious garb a remarkably effective array of penitential ordeals, abject deliverances, a horrifically mutilated sexual imagery, ministering to the whole person, but designed to assure labour discipline and the profane ends of increased profitability.

These religious practices may have disappeared, but the immense Jekyll and Hyde psychic damage they inflicted still lingers on, it tends to generate a sort of unhealthy euphoria springing from being tied down. In fact there was just enough strength left in the beast, its hour come round well over a century and a half ago, reared on hard work and thrift, despising leisure seekers and idlers to ensure Maggie Thatcher a near landslide victory.

At the opposite extreme there is a boll weevil refusal of work, which Thatcherism has only patchily checked. But longer holidays, 'sickness' benefits, absenteesim on the firms time must venture beyond comfy arm chairs, and let the good times roll right on through the capitalist leisure principle. For example the long Xmas break extending into the New Year and still unique to Britain is experienced by many people as a grindingly empty endurance leisure-test.

Leisure in Britain is still organized far more than it need be - even in terms of capitalist alienation - around the maintenance of work discipline. As a moral philosophy, monetarism is the heir to a long line of secular disapprovals of enjoyment forced to intermittently hibernate throughout the long boom of the 1950s and 1960s to the early 1970s. Naturally the workers were not cut out of the shopping spree - that would have made no economic sense. But in revenge they were treated like spoilt wayward kids liable, given half the chance, to put coal in the baths of their new dolls houses. Though the economy held the keys to the toy cupboard, patrician forbearance (e.g. Macmillan) was there to regulate the playroom terrain of consumption in broadly the same manner, as workers could not be left alone to get on with a job at work. (Skilled British émigré workers, particularly in Holland, are genuinely taken aback at the comparative absence of surveillance at work and the adult availability of credit facilities: in contrast British management is hamstrung by attitudes more appropriate to the early stages of capitalism). As a result, leisure time in Britain has a crazed edge, every second is flogged to death as if it were the last. Contrary to myth, Britain is a violent society.

Other than as a means of reviving energies expended at work, leisure has no place in Britain. Latin societies only just manage to maintain a whiff of the good life but wine, good food, relaxed eating and drinking and leisurely naps have long been a mark of class distinction in the UK. This would -be severely utilitarian regulation of social life weighs particularly heavily on the unemployed who are press ganged so often into an a-sexual cell like existence alienated almost beyond alienation. They are left dangling in a void often, without a modicum of social contact. Their isolation is frequently aggravated by a collapsing family structure, excelled only in the States.

Yet over the last decade the UK has lived through profound social turmoil. Mingled with the seemingly never ending hopelessness of drugs, drugs, drugs, drink, drink, drink, the place is alive with an unfocussed rebellion.

There is a path that leads out of this wasteland, and during the summer of 1981 the unemployed started to travel its length unaided. The totality of desperation and misery produced its opposite - The nights were young and though the pubs had called time the firewater was freely circulating. In the space of 10 days in early July 1981, England was transformed. It will never be the same again. Every major city and town was rocked with youth riots. Bored youngsters ranging from 8 to 80 excitedly got ready for an evening's burnin' and lootin'. Even Army recruits on leave joined in. If the grandkid did the hell raising, grandma helped out with the free shopping. In Manchester an 8 year old was arrested for setting fire to a bike shop, and in Bristol a paraplegic pensioner was wheeled obligingly into a supermarket so he could get in on the lootin' too.

Beginning in London, the riots spread north to Liverpool, followed by other big northern and midland cities. Up to now people have been kept in the dark about their actual extent. It was said over and over again that sensational media coverage fanned the riots (the so-called copycat effect). By the end of riot week holidays it was clear; the media were underplaying what was going down in the towns and cities. Clearly things were getting out of hand, and chief cop Oxford had just said few people realized how close the police had been to losing the battle of Liverpool. Scotland and Wales, though less affected were more or less totally blanked by the media. Trouble there would have done for that sociological nonsense which claims all the trouble was caused by black 'unadapted' youth. Apparently there was more to Saturday night aggro in Glasgow than the usual trouble at closing times and Paisley Anarchists got closed down by the police.

Throughout the glorious week, the police received the hammering of their lives. Several police stations came under siege in Bristol, Southall. Birmingham (Handsworth) Manchester (-in Moss Side where youths set fire to 12 vehicles in the police yard), Sheffield (an unmanned station attacked by skinheads) and in Derby where a police traffic office was set on fire. The four corners of England if not yet the whole of the UK were exposed to a force 10 gale of youthful class fury. There will be set backs but in the long run the infectious momentum will hopefully prove unstoppable and roll on through other sectors of alienated society.

What had once been a solitary half mad 1960s vision now grown old with time, of volcanic eruptions affecting vast masses of people in every nook and cranny and backyard, appeared about to come true. Across an incredulous media was flashed the news that sleepy towns - the scented rose gardens of England's dreaming - had suddenly been hit by brief, furious riots: towns like Cirencester, Market Harborough, Dunstable, the fossilizing well spa resort of Knaresboro' and ultra posh Southport where the northern bourgeoisie elect to die on their fat retirement pensions. Old oaken shades and mossy lanes with evocative olde worlde names had lost their immunity from potentially revolutionary turmoil. What happened in the rural Cremlington on the Bumps' was also reflected in Halifax, a quintessential 19th century northern industrial town preserved almost intact. In this living museum of industrial archaeology, silent mills and smokeless chimneys, sand blasted to look a bit like Canterbury, petrol bombs were also to snake through the cleaned up air. Preservation orders may now be organically assimilating the first shocks of industrialization to the more archaic past but the heirs of Robin Hood and his merry men women and children were making doubly sure no such preservation order would be slapped on them. The New Towns descendents of the countrified socialist garden cities, which Lenin loved so much and copied in mother Russia, laid out and policed like old colonial citadels got their dues. Letchworth where Lenin lived for a short while didn't get torched but nearby Harlow did.

The eyes of the world were fixed on the UK and its peoples were for a brief moment to become the latest in the line of oppressed nationals beside those of the Chileans and the Irish. Placard waving demonstrators in Canada supported the heroic struggle of the British People against the fascist Thatcher tyranny!! Applied to Britain this inflated populist rhetoric, which lefties find so irresistible, was inconceivable a mere 8 years ago. Even an Iranian Ayotollah in Qom, accustomed to foaming with anti-imperialist rhetoric, prayed to Allah for the black (but not the white) rioters.

Footnote

1) John Martin (19 July 1789 – 17 February 1854) was an English Romantic painter, engraver and illustrator.

2) Statism and Anarchy – Mikhail Bakunin, Publisher Cambridge University Press, *Published 1873*

3) The Hidden Persuaders – Vance Packard, Publisher Ig Publishing; Reissue Ed edition (10 Oct. 2007), *Originally Published 1957*

4) The Twilight of the Idols - Friedrich Nietzsche, *Published 1889*

PLAY SCHOOL FREEDOM FIGHTERS GO RADICAL WINDOW SHOPPING

It was kids, amazingly who were responsible for most of the heavy shit going down. Teeny boppers dragged weeny boppers along in their wake. Or vice versa - no one was quite sure. It was that sort of 'anybody's guess' time.

Although the rioting was commonly said to be the effect of mass unemployment, top authorities refused to acknowledge unemployment as a cause of the rioting because of the large number of children involved. The authorities were right on the level of facts, but the kids intuitively knew far deeper than any big shot, there was No Future for them in the old world of work. Whitelaw said "Many of the hooligans were aged between 10 and 11, even less, so there can be no question of unemployment being the cause." Children in particular played a prominent part in the battle of Liverpool 8. Out of 67 arrested during rioting on Park Road, 21 were juveniles aged between 8 and 16. The Tories tried to blame the troubles on lax parents and the break-up of the family. Relations within the family are loosening but a growing distance between parents and kids even in tight knit working class families didn't stop parents from being right behind their kids.

...Waiting for night to fall. What was going to happen next? A kid breaking free from school in the late afternoon, shouting loudly to others - was that a signal for a riot to begin? Who could tell? Adults thought so but then they weren't really in the know. "Hey son, where's it going to be tonight?" "Kilburn", came back the answer. And five hours later the police got ready for the battle of Kilburn, which never came. ... a few broken windows, a clothes rack nicked out of a store but Sinn Fein still blinkedly sold their wares in the pubs.

Galvanized awake, many older people, particularly in the northern towns, joined with gusto in the rioting. If caught they could expect no mercy from the courts and several received stiff prison sentences. But it was on a more general, day-to-day, basis that the effects of the rioting, causing people to sit bolt upright and take notice, were the most apparent.

During past proletarian upheavals, the 3-day week, the Winter of Discontent etc, the lives of people not directly involved had been sufficiently disrupted for them to start asking why. Now people were hit in the gut with a sledgehammer blow. Suddenly there was an endless amount to talk about. The baffling uniqueness of the events for a time all but stamped out prejudiced superficial reactions. The battle on the streets opened up closed, frivolous, trendy, desperate minds everywhere. Before peoples' eyes a new level of reality was being unforgettably exposed and a dream of distant Utopias became by fits and starts a real possibility. In pubs there was only one topic of conversation. Trivia: tennis at Wimbledon, the Test Match, the coming Royal Wedding were barely mentioned as talk came to centre on the streets. Did anyone really want to watch escapist films, the lies and half-truths of TV documentaries or listen to music? Rank was going to close 13 cinemas in London because of falling profits. So fucking what!

Eyes and ears were glued to the news media. But the predictably slanted version of events did not signify control over peoples mind. The salient facts were all that counted, and reading between the lines became habitual. At any rate, in spite of the press, TV and radio coverage there was remarkably little animosity, at least in the big cities, shown towards the rioters - excepting the police that is. Bewilderment maybe, amongst sections of the working class and lower middle class, but no thought of ever coming down hard on the rioters crossed their minds. In fact many an onlooker was inspired by their example as buried hopes and expectations were raised. Violence in the streets externalised the violence raging within as the phoney class peace announced by Thatcher came to a dramatic and unanticipated end.

Photo left: "Home Sweet Home". Photo right: The Piece Hall, Halifax, West Yorkshire. Buffing up the 19th century pre-industrial and industrial architecture wasn't enough to preserve the town from rioting.

"WE SHALL OVERCOME" - Maggie Thatcher on the Friday night of riot week hols.

Black youth were the main protagonists but only in the sense that they opened up the gap through which Asians, Anglo-Saxons, Celts, Turks, Greeks, Cypriots, Eskimos - if these categorizations still have any meaning - and others, followed. So sing out if you're glad to be an albino! Truly it meant that the UK was in the throes of becoming one of the first unfolding multi-racial, pre-revolutionary societies. The rioting as press and politicians alike had to frankly admit (Enoch Powell excepted in a BBC radio program on July 7th 1981) was not racial in character. (Here too we exclude fascists like Charles Parker of the New National Front who said, 'the riots are just a rehearsal for full scale war') But elsewhere in the world, accuracy was lacking. A journalist from Corriere Delia Sera, probably hooked on some anti-imperialist ideology of racist Brits, lyingly reported there was fighting between black and white youth in Liverpool. And initially some of the German press (e.g. Frankfurter Allegmeine) reported the riots as racial in character too. They quickly changed their tune in the next few days.

American press, taking their cue from The New York Times which made the mistake of describing the first night of the Brixton riots in April 1981 as racial (again quickly changing its tune the following day), now at least plumped for a semblance of accuracy. Emphasizing class as the prime factor, they rightly noted London had seen nothing like this since the days of the Gordon Riots in 1780 (The International Herald Tribune). Though 400 insurgents were shot by the army in the streets of London in 1780, taking the UK as a whole, it's a fair bet the riots were the most extensive if not the most intensive ever since the Civil War. And Ned and Lady Ludd were weeping with joy in an anonymous grave on some wild Yorkshire moor at the splendid audacity of their successors.

"The Only Race Is The Rat Race" - Graffiti Notting Hill Gate, 1968

Racism exists in the UK all right. But the mixed character of the rioting overcame racial separations, pushing it well into the background. Powerful sections of the State would have liked it to be otherwise, and actually tried to foment racial confrontation. In Derby, police forced mainly white youths running amok in the smart city centre into the ghettoised Normanton Road and Peartree area. Fortunately this tactic came unstuck because a battle ensued involving white, black and Asian youth who more or less fought the police together. Was this an example of overt police racism or were they calculating on disrupting class unity? Certainly as a means of stirring up hostility, the race question in press reports was secondary to the practice of highlighting incidents which, taken out of context, looked like the work of animals.

In the pages and pages of bumph written on the riots, most have stressed racial/ethnic differences rather than class factors. Apart from the gift horse of Southall, everyone has to admit racial confrontation (excepting police of course) hardly figured in the riots. But how come so many writers, who invariably turn out to have secure prestigious, well-paid jobs in Universities, Polys' or in the Race Relations Industry, almost instinctively opt for race rather than class? Is it because race is one of those collective nouns intrinsic to the continual existence of the Nation State? Certainly both trendy academics and race relations' careerists would like to see the status quo changed. But only within the confines of the Nation State, making for instance, the lily-white British state more "a state of the whole people" (positive discrimination etc). At best they will only ameliorate racism, never totally abolish it, which requires nothing less than the international extension of proletarian revolution sweeping away all national territories and Nation States. All their venom and contempt are ultimately held in reserve to counteract this.

Actually there are few things more irritating than the tut-tutting reprimands of the various arms of the race relations industry faced with 'racist' jokes. They are totally unselective in these matters, unaware that 'racial' jokes can actually defuse rather than stir up trouble. They seem not to have any experience of situations where such things have happened. More probably than not, the Race Relations Board will in the future moderate their attitude because on the level of shitty entertainment (Tiswas, OTT), minorities are starting to give as good as they get. This reflects a far more open -ended, and much funnier situation below where there is a stronger desire than ever to escape out of the ethnic, regional, national bolt holds. Being able to laugh at one self is part of this process.

The media on the face of it was unprejudiced. However a current of racist innuendo was apparent, particularly in the press reporting. In the circumstances, its appearance was predictable: the British bourgeoisie when driven into a corner disparage their opponents more through suggestion than out-right calumny. The practise of calling blacks 'immigrants' was especially offensive when applied to districts like Liverpool 8 where a sizable black community has existed for close on 100 years.

During riot week hols, radio and TV were crammed with instant interviews of staid psycho-sociologists in top universities. They would always finalize their homilies (what else?) with the need for more effective police measures. But this was drama! In future what we are likely to see is an 'enlightening' mountain of material, taped on video and in print, interpreting the week's events. It is more than likely Leicester University's Centre of Mass Communications will publish some report examining the influence of the media on the riots, but not the impact of the rioters on the media. They will forever fight shy of raising this upsetting question.

In Brixton rioters attacked photographers from The Daily Star and burnt out ITN film vans, and in Toxteth attacked The Guardian reporter who then pretended he was a dosser to get his copy. However, the sad fact is, the rioters were too negligent about media infiltration, and many poor sods were later picked up by the coppers after being identified in photos. There were unsubstantiated rumours that TV networks had handed footage of the riots over to the police. Failing this the police in any case were taping television coverage on their videos.

TV items, particularly the early evening news, must have had an effect but to accurately assess its influence isn't as easy as it sounds. The British Film Institutes Broadcasting Research Unit, funded jointly by the BBC and the IBA, in a sociological survey to be published later in 1982, claimed the "copy cat" effect was greatly exaggerated. Maybe. Up to a point kids did emulate what they'd seen on TV. For instance youths gathering on Wood Green High Road in north London the morning after the riot there, loudly played back tape recordings of news reports just to goad the police. Chris, a 17-year-old Greek Cypriot said "I hope this gets us in the papers. I hope this counts as a big riot like Liverpool."

On the other hand, the younger generation watch less TV than any other generation since television first became a mass consumer item. Apologists excusing declining literacy point to the effect of TV as decisively influencing this historic change. The relative lack of interest shown by the younger generation in TV suggests there is a basic sea change toward the media in general going on. With luck the media is about to be blown out. Certainly according to The Daily Telegraph, the heads of TV corporations are deeply worried people. The date, July the 13th, 1981, the end of riot week, is telling, showing how convulsions tend to bring out point by point the concentrated fears of the bourgeoisie. Maybe the heads of TV will more than roll. When interest in the box is declining they obviously have more to fear than just being made redundant.

In fact the Police thought the youth grapevine was by far the most effective media for communicating a message, which burst out simultaneously in all parts of the country. It was throughout the entire week, their only promising insight.

DEVIANT SOCIOLOGISTS

The riots at least should prove a lucrative source of income for that symposium of oily rags, The Sociology of Deviancy.

One of their most notable celebrities, the dishonourable Jock Young wrote (together with a certain John Dea) an article on the riots in that lefty rag The Chartist. It is a classic of its kind, ending by condoning what it had just written off as a compromised solution. He knows the Labour Party and trade unions have acted as a drag on the working class, preventing it from ever achieving a revolutionary consciousness. Yet he proposes the trade unions shake themselves out of their torpor and become "channels for the political organization of young people with minimal contact with work." This will only lead to the "compromise solution" he has just panned. But that is what he is secretly after. This example of the purest cynicism shows the pivot around which his life revolves: a sinecure for life and a string of wretched sycophants whom he can wrap around his little finger.

Young does not mention by name "the reconstructed Labour party" but that is what he has in mind when he alludes to "an extension of democracy at a local level" to counteract institutions which have been originated "from above". The sort of mass democracy Young pretends he wants at a local level sporadically appeared once the riots had died down and people spontaneously came together to discuss the events. As will become clear later these meetings were emphatically not political, and the presence of political parties was hotly resented. Though it was never said so clearly, they were, admittedly very much in embryo, a new form of power containing within them the dissolution of state power. It is nonsensical therefore to say "we are witnessing the return of rioting as a form of political expression for those for whom all other channels of political activity have either dried up or are non existent" (ibid).

To further suggest as he does that there are parallels between these riots and those of the late 18th and early 19th century, when a factory based proletariat was in the process of being formed, is stretching it more than a bit. Illusions about the wonders of Parliamentary democracy were then rife. When the mob burnt down Nottingham Castle in the early 19th century, they were protesting against the delay in the passing of The Great Reform Bill in 1832. A good century and a half later and the cup of political reforms is just about drained. If his comments on America in the same article are anything to go by, Young is well aware of this, even though when it comes to assimilating immigrants, Britain has much to learn from America. Yet the sly dog goes through reel after reel of typewriter ribbon saying there are solutions, when deep down he knows as well as anybody, short of revolution there are none. Predictably the article closes with an appeal for the "political de-marginalisation" of inner cities, "more police accountability to local government", and the decriminalization of "soft" drugs - the cause of many a combustible hassle (e.g. Notting Hill April 1982) between the police and young blacks.

All along the frontline, the Sociologists of Deviance have been afraid to say the obvious. They have toyed with revolution in the past, solely to hit the jackpot and the high spots putting on their soluble-in-water war paint of radicality to aid their sexual conquests. Being yesterday's martyrs to the lost cause of Trotskyism is not to their fashionable tastes. Quitting the Socialist Workers Party, they have not sunk below the horizon as the sun finally set on a Bolshevik seizure of state power. They now look to the reconstructed Labour Party as a more realistic option, offering the hope of a glittering prize in place of former mock-heroic dreams of a commissarship.

One of their favourite tricks is to let fly with radical sounding phrases, which are later retrieved for bourgeois democratic ends. In his article on the riots, the fork tongued

Young sounds really enthusiastic. But don't let that fool you. Another of them, Stan Cohen, in an article on prisons he wrote several years earlier, had this to say, "The prison is a small (and not necessarily permanent) terminal point of a much larger process of social change." (New Society, Dec. 1974). Fuck you jack, if you were dumb enough like some of us to think for a sec' that this is an earnest plea for the abolition of prisons. However the remark is strictly remedial in intent, pertaining to the development of non-custodial punishments. Considering the penal obsessions of the English judiciary, it should have done wonders for the deviant sociologists fading lustre of radicality, but the bluff doesn't serve like it once did.

Over the past decade the Sociology of Deviancy has dealt with the social disintegration of modern capitalism. Parcelled up into discreet bundles of essays, books and articles, this has included sabotage, survival in high security prisons, drug taking, pornography, suicide, soccer violence and Weathermen/Women bombing (uncritically clapped on the safer sidelines by that creep Paul Walton).

Originally much influenced by the Chicago school of Sociology, in the aftermath of '68 they looted further afield, lobotomizing more radical theories coming from France, particularly the Situationists. By striking matches under the rigor-mortised toes of state functionaries, the aim of these intelligence spies of the state, then as now, is to promote reforms. Like Grub Street journalists, the depths they are prepared to sink to have yet to be plumbed. The shameless Jock Young for instance, before being scared off by revolutionaries, was about to blow the whistle on the black economy. What did he care if as a result life was made even more insupportable for millions of people?

Finally, just for the record, they are drawn irresistibly to big time villainy (like John McVicar) seeing there a distorted reflection of their own highflying careerism. However much they may protest to the contrary, petty criminality is for nonentities going very much against their success-minded grain.

Having rejected the proletariat they are bound to reject whatever's proletarian in petty criminality. They have, for example, little first hand knowledge of, and indeed sympathy for the conscientious resolve not to pick on the proletariat that lies behind much petty criminality. Jock Young subscribes to the view "most working class crime is directed against working class people" which is hard cheese on shoplifters, scroungers and the like.

Time was not that long ago when Phil Cohen hadn't a good word to say about the Sociology of Deviancy. Now he has cut his losses and teamed up with them. And how? Having rejected the "wageless society" as Utopian dreaming, he must eventually turn on every other revolutionary conviction. The path from revolution to reform is paved with the utmost malice, and we weren't the only ones who were stunned to learn he had been lecturing at Hendon Police College.

As a result of his experiences there, he has proposed a "police education "- composed equally of police with a university training in social science, and academics with a knowledge and understanding of the force' (City Limits) under the control of the GLC Police Committee. These suggestions hardly differ at all from those made by Shirley Williams (SDP) who in a speech (April 6th1982) given at the Police Training Centre in Hutton, Lancashire, stressed the need for police cadets to "learn more about the political social and economic background of the country and of their own areas." She made a point; obviously, of not supporting the 'left' wing dominated police committees, but in all other respects her proposals are the same as Phil Cohen's.

The class rather than racial character of the rioting rules out an American style, purely ethnic educational program in police colleges. Phil Cohen realized this and was only able to rap the knuckles of the police cadets on the race question by first probing the sensitive nerve ends of the class system as reproduced in the police force. This same duality, acknowledging class in order to belittle it from a non-revolutionary middle of the road, middle class standpoint was evident in Knuckle Sandwich, a book he wrote with Dave Robins (former editor of the late 1960s underground newspaper Ink). Published in 1978, the book's interesting empirical details - like the regionally mixed character of Manchester United's football hooligan supporters - are all but swamped by the ludicrous conclusion: "Racism, not revolution is in the air." The riots knocked that on the head good and proper, but for the liberal patriciate, the race issue has the advantage of avoiding the thornier problems posed by a thoroughgoing class war against capitalism. And Cohen doesn't like it when the proletariat becomes too independently minded, neglecting to pay him the respect he so often abuses.

Both Cohen and Robins are experts at tapping charities, but the money is never diverted to revolutionary ends. Rather grants from e.g. the Leverhume Trust go towards setting up yet another social work con (e.g. Street Aid in Soho and Covent Garden). But give credit where credits due, because Cohen had, during the London Street Commune of 1969, displayed qualities the cowardly and parasitic Sociology of Deviancy have always lacked. Regretfully he wished even then to impose a superannuated sub cultural research unit on this audacious squat, interring its radical potential beneath a respectable sounding appeal for money.

Photo left: John McVicar as Roger Daltrey or is it the other way round? Right: On the same day as the skinhead rampage through Sheffield in June 1981, a car was smashed into the local West Bar police station.

Keswick photo: "Upon the Lonely Moor": "His accents mild took up the tale, / He said, "I go my ways, / and when I find a mountain-rill, / I set in a blaze." Lewis Carroll, 1856. A parody of Wordsworth's romantic nature poems. Photo right: Durham police officers mix with pupils in a Newton Aycliffe comprehensive school.....WHEN THE BOOT COMES IN....

ORGANISED RACISM AND INTER-RACIAL RESISTANCE

The one big racial incident which by default preceded riot week resulted from the National Front/British Movement guided skinhead invasion of Southall's Asian community. The battle that followed, as the young Asians cleared the streets of fascists, and torched the Hamborough Tavern venue, was thankfully untypical of what was to come. On the whole racist attacks, in contrast to the orchestrated invasion of Southall, tend to be less well organized and more individualistic.

Undeniably over the last year or so, there has been a series of ugly and horrific acts, carried out by white racists, against blacks and Asians. The most notorious occurred in Deptford on January 1981 when 13 young blacks were burnt to death after an all night party. A coroner returned a verdict of not proven, but collusion between police, fascists and the higher and murkier regions of the State was the real point at issue. Also at the end of the week of fire, after the funeral of Mrs Doreen Khan and her 3 children, a riot of Asian youth broke out in Walthamstow, east London. They died as a result of a petrol bomb attack on their home early in July. On both occasions the police, adding insult to injury, detained for questioning friends and relatives of the victims, repeatedly grilling them hoping to shift the blame for the tragedies on to them. Mr Khan, already a broken man recovering in hospital from his burns, was doubly shattered when he got to learn of this.

These isolated attacks are horrendous, but must not be used to disguise the way blacks and whites have spontaneously come together (outside the reach of lefty contrived orchestration) and fought white racists. There's the memorable battle of Chippenham, Wiltshire on May 30th 1981, where in a supposedly dumb fuck country district, black and white fought white racists after an incident at a nightclub. Also, the example comes to mind of the suicidally depressed black youth who was stabbed to death at a Peckham fish and chip shop on June 20th 1981 by skinheads. Earlier in the evening when attacked by the same skinheads, who were later to kill him, white and black youths had come to his aid. However not all teenage killings are random or racial in character. During riot week, at the Black Uhuru concert in the Rainbow, Finsbury Park a black kid was stabbed to death by another black kid after an argument over dividing spoils. For both black and white, if violence cannot express itself lucidly by destroying commodity relations, then it is going to turn inwards in a whirligig of brutality. Racism finally is part of that whirligig.

'Standing at the corner swinging a chain, Up comes a copper and he takes my name, Takes out my razor and I slit his throat, Blood all down my teddy boy coat." *(1950s psycho billy street Ted song from Co. Durham and W. Yorkshire)*

It's a very complicated whirligig too. There's no clear-cut distinction so far between pathological behaviour and a near revolutionary assault on the old world. Often youths are yenning for a bruise any which way they can. After all, society is organized in a hierarchical fashion, and those at the bottom of the ladder know they are looked down on by almost everyone. They inflect the general values of society by setting up their own pecking order whose values run counter to those of respectable society. Youths who are looked up to are those who have been involved in the most punch ups, those who have been arrested the most times. Their university is the slammer. Youths on the lam try to achieve a status and recognition for themselves, which they cannot achieve in any other way. This made itself felt in the riots and it is pointless denying it at the same time as it merged into a class experience. A youth arrested in Manchester for throwing a petrol bomb into a police van frankly admitted in court. "I did it to make a name for myself."

JOHNNY YOU'RE TOO BAD. WAITING HERE IN LIMBO FOR THE PROLETARIAN TIDE TO TURN

Black youth have the highest levels of unemployment of any section of society. Lacking money to consume, their resentment has often resulted in a form of indiscriminate aggression. Small wonder then that they have turned to mugging. All too often the victims of muggings are poor whites who live in close proximity to them, the people least responsible for their plight.

However being black does not imply immunity. At the 1977 Caribbean Carnival in Notting Hill, blacks were also mugged alongside whites. During a Carnival dance in Hammersmith, a gang of black youths invaded the dance hall mugging and beating people savagely. This incident was mentioned by older blacks who were shocked by it, serving to emphasize just how estranged they had become from their own kith and kin. It said a lot for the myths of racial identity to hear these youths denounced in terms echoing racist police and magistrates.

But having exposed racial solidarity for what it's worth, they then go and put the boot in on class solidarity. Sometimes it does look as though they don't give a piss for anyone. A quite justified pride at having made such an impact during the rioting can so easily be turned into an abuse of power. Drunk with success.

And then there's family complications too. Parents of black youth tend to regard any symbols of rebellion or visible signs of black pride with fear and suspicion. There is a very definite breakdown in relations between younger and older blacks. Aggravation between parents and children is not common (peculiar?) to them but it is much more pronounced in the black community.

This is a legacy of 19th century colonialism. One writer in The Jamaican Gleaner said that the facts about slavery and the obvious ways in which blacks were kept down are well known. "But what is not so generally appreciated is the way in which we are colonized in our minds." The standards of Victorian society were imposed on blacks and these attitudes have persisted among blacks long after they broke down in the Imperial country. Many West Indian and African parents are very authoritarian and take a heavy-handed Victorian attitude when it comes to discipline and orderly behaviour.

Many blacks have fought a losing battle to maintain old-fashioned standards in the face of a permissive society. The kids rebel against this and many run away from home. Some are even thrown out by their parents when they become too defiant. There is an echo here of the phrase from Victorian melodrama, "Never darken my door step again."

In the first year of its existence a hostel for homeless kids in Waltham Forest catered for 64 black kids and 11 whites. This probably gives a fair indication of the breakdown in black families in proportion to whites. In some cases it resulted from social deprivation, which neither the kids nor their parents could do much about. In most cases it springs from a conflict between kids and their parents, arguments about dreadlocks, a father forbidding his 17-year-old son to have a girlfriend etc. The parents of an Islington youth were so frightened he would get into trouble that they forbade him to go out and tried to keep him home every evening. He ran away and became homeless at 14. He was eventually picked up by the police with a gang of other boys and brought to trial for mugging. His parents fear had brought about that which they feared the most. The discipline West Indian parents want to enforce can become excessively harsh and this has been criticized by some black community workers with the unfortunate side effect of lending credence in the eyes of the kids to their function as social controllers. Really they should tell them to sod off double quick. This has on occasion happened. In one local incident we know of a number of homeless blacks who squatted a property in Notting Hill Gate put the frighteners on a local rasta-dandy social worker sent in as the para-state's secret weapon to get them to quit the premises.

Some parents have expressed an antagonism to social security and the social services from an authoritarian family based perspective rather than any revolutionary point of view. One black guy said on TV, "How can I discipline my son when he can leave home whenever he likes and get money from the SS." He also was hostile to social workers because they provided black kids with all the necessary back up when they leave home. Black parents see what they believe to be a too permissive society and the social services as conspiring to undermine the authority of black parents and frustrating their efforts to raise their children in a 'proper' manner. One black woman in a letter to The Times said that parents were blamed for failing to discipline their children and letting them run wild. "Parents are frightened of being too strict for fear of welfare officers coming in. The welfare officers are dying to snatch black kids away and put them with nice white aunties and uncles for love and affection." This condescending bullshit sums up state benevolence: it even produces a sneaking sympathy for the repressive fucked up black parents.

UNEMPLOYMENT...

The Notting Hill Carnival riots from '76 to '79 were almost exclusively a black show. By the summer of 1981, everybody was mucking in. By then unemployment had easily doubled. In spite of the forgoing remarks, unemployment was a contributory factor even if not consistent with a dour 'Right to Work' myth of downtrodden masses hungry for work at any price.

For those in the straight jacket of suburbia, a survey conducted by Liverpool University of 20 year olds living in inner city areas might have produced surprising results. For those accustomed to living in inner city areas, they were as stale as yesterday's news and further evidence of the universities stuck fast in their time machines, waking up to the obvious. The findings were made known in August 1980. The survey showed that not all the youths were unemployed because they had not been able to find work or had been made redundant. Jobs had been given up voluntarily. The principal reason given was boredom. The second, dislike of superiors and inability to get on with work mates and thirdly dissatisfaction with pay. Youngsters would take a low paid menial job and find themselves unable to put up with it and so they would go on the dole. After a period of time the boredom and poverty of life on the dole would become unbearable. So they would try a job again. They cannot stand work and at the same time cannot stand life on the dole. With the recession biting hard, there weren't enough jobs to keep them all in employment all the time but as the kids did not want to be in permanent unemployment, there were enough jobs to fall into when they felt like it. This situation just about kept the lid on the inner cities. However since the survey, the situation has dramatically worsened, although for us, hopes of a new world have dramatically brightened. At the time of the Toxteth riots there were only 12 jobs on offer for school leavers at the Job Centre. There was literally nothing for them to even 'fall' into.

These attitudes outlined above differ markedly from those of their parents and grandparents who, coming from the West Indies in the 1950s, were prepared to take anything available. The young blacks born in the UK expect something 'better'.

Perhaps more so than their white counterparts, they are prone to a brittle image worship falling somewhere between golden-calf idolatry of music, dancing, fashion and theater and easily provoked aggression. Slavery maybe abolished but it remains very much in the minds of young West Indians, and some refuse any job that has the slightest stigma attached to it. One young black girl for instance wanted a job in fashion. After a great deal of difficulty she managed to get fixed up as a receptionist/model with a West End clothing firm. The girl was delighted until she discovered part of her duties was to make tea for staff. She promptly turned the job down.

...AND CRIME

Undeniably the huge increase in unemployment has resulted in an increase in crime. An unemployed white teenager said, "Sure there's robbery - when your dole runs out, which is quick, you have to do something to live. Everybody round here does it." There's even desperation just to get the feel of dole money in your hand too. During riot week, some black youths in Hammersmith post office menaced a long queue of black and white unemployed people waiting to cash their giro's by shoving everyone aside to be served first. Edgy mounted police had been stationed outside the post office in case of trouble and these young blacks, outta their skulls with hope, were looking for any occasion to provoke a riot. But in their understandable eagerness they were well out of line and this silly action only served to put everyone against them in the airless and crammed post office. Even so, the cops were scared of dealing with them.

THE TURBAN ROCKS

What we are beginning to see (the riots were the living proof) is the end of racism. Even a bum liberal like Mr Raj Nayan, a senior officer for Leicester Council for Community Relations appreciated this. "I think we're seeing an embryonic movement of poor working class white kids teaming up with poor black kids." (The Daily Telegraph July 15th1981) and as an unemployed London East End skin said of the middle classes: "They're terrified of the blacks and whites rising together and storming the suburbs. That's where they ought to riot in Finchley and Richmond, not in Moss Side". (The Guardian, July 10th '81)

And the Asians played their part too. Asian kids are breaking away from the traditional values of the Muslim, Hindu, Sikh stranglehold. Elders of the Asian community repeatedly call for youth to remain peaceful and law abiding but their appeals increasingly fall on stony ground. If now you want to see the revolt of Islam, then here it is - the revolt against Islam. The Asian kids have more that's obnoxious to fight against - chaperoned girls, arranged marriages, wives behind locked doors, a culture of passive resignation to one's supposed lot. Now they are making the greatest breaks of all from the nightmare past - actually through a see sawing interaction with black and white kids whose respect for the family is at an all time low. The old Asian values are crumbling fast. Even so, the Sikhs long fighting tradition held them in good stead in Southall. Specially selected racist skins that thought they could easily throw a scare into the predominately Sikh Southall community sure as hell got their ethnography fucked up. They are not submissive East End Bengalis who in any case are beginning to square up to racist provocation. Their standing in the Brick Lane area of East London has gone up by leaps and bounds since they first started to resist racist thugs unaided. At Southall there was an explosion of anger against the police. In the later phase of the rioting, Asians living in other places, particularly Bradford, were to get involved. In Bradford several Asians were later framed and confessions beaten out of them. During the preliminary hearings a high proportion of whites were evident in the pickets surrounding the courthouse.

Although the police do not pick on them to the same extent as young blacks, Asians constantly complain that the police are indifferent to racist attacks and will do nothing to protect them. In spite of the constitutional illusions inherent in this sort of reasoning, it does at least represent a step in the direction of organising one's own defence.

One incident which particularly angered young Asians in Southall was an attack on one of them by three white racists who carved swastikas on his stomach. The police did not believe him and charged him with wasting police time. Many young Asians are angry with their elders who they see as too passive in the face of racist attacks and police indifference. In Southall, in response, militant youth have organised themselves into the Southall Youth Movement in order to defend themselves, preferring not to put their faith in the established Asian organisations dominated by their elders. Many of the Elders are storeowners, supermarket under-managers and restaurant owners - those Asians in fact with a direct interest in protecting capital. The Indian Workers Organisation - a thoroughly misleading title - is dominated by this crew. However worker oriented the ad hoc defense committees also call on Asians to lay down their arms. The Coventry Committee Against Racism for instance made up of councillors and trade union reps is not much more than a lefty talking shop. Its main aim now is dissuading young Asians against self-organisation against police and fascists. Shamelessly the committee call this self-organisation "vigilante" aware doubtless that the term, because of the use made of it in the USA, has a nebulous fascistic implication.

The splits developing in the Asian community reflect to some extent those in the black community. There are uneven features to this and they don't always amount to unequivocal class progress. But much that is reactionary (religion and the status of women amongst Asians in particular) and harmful to class struggle is at the same time being jettisoned.

Attitudes amongst whitey (the chitties) have been changing fast also. Respect for Asian workers has been growing steadily amongst white workers once they began to stand up and fight back. The long battle by a largely Asian workforce at Imperial Typewriters at Leicester in 1973, even though accompanied by trade union lock stock and barrel illusions nevertheless forced admiration out of the local white working class who previously had often voiced ugly racist sentiments. Standing up to the bosses, not allowing yourself to be put down by the police or other authorities, is the surest way of knocking racist attitudes out of those white proletarians in a similar structural position. They then become the best ally in the struggle for libertarian revolution. In the riot at Luton on Saturday July 11th 1981, black, white and Asians went on the rampage together. There was a backlog of racist activity in the town but this act of multi-racial insurgency was a shining example of integrated rioting. Once having gone on the rampage, there was no stopping the crowd and soul brother black and Asian business in Moss Side, Brixton and Liverpool provided no immunity against a more fundamental attack on commodity relations.

Also one must bear in mind that there have been a number of multi-racial strikes. Class as a working category matters more than race in Britain. At work irrespective of colour of skin, black, white, brown and green are treated as equals. Like a piece of shit in other words! As a divide and rule wage cutting operation, the wave of post war immigration blew up in the face of its creators. Whether for sound reasons or not, the unions made certain of that.

However, it is somewhat ironic, considering workers' wages in the UK are now often below those of immigrant workers in the better off parts of the EEC. During the recent British Leyland set-to someone remarked how the predominantly white labour force were having to knuckle under and accept conditions normally reserved for immigrants in other major European car plants. More by luck than good management the British state has not succeeded in creating broadly based privileged categories of white workers who also act as overseers to less privileged 'immigrant' workers. It will therefore encounter considerable obstacles should it ever attempt to intentionally reorganise white workers around the race question.

SKIN COMPLEX. Ne-Ne Na-Na Na-Na Nu-Nu

Standing up changes attitudes before changing reality. Skinheads after the battle of Southall reflecting on that experience began to leave some of their bad old ways behind. In fact many were apologetic later. As one said at an Oi gig in Peckham immediately after Southall: "Why do they think all skinheads is Nazis? Just cos' I'm white and working class doesn't mean I'm racist." Earlier in the year a skin quoted in The Guardian (May 23rd '81) said, teenagers join right wing groups "just for the punch up" and "we hated the police too." Unfortunately the guy was exchanging one set of 'extreme' capitalist values, for a nicer but finally no less insidious opposite: the Anti-Nazi League. The skins are like souped up versions of the Cossack hordes, wanting activity and life above all else, but always, or nearly always, through the aggro stakes. During riot week, skinheads joined with blacks on many occasions. Brixton, Croydon and Upton Park in London. Further north, in Leeds, a large skinhead contingent coming from all over the city joined in with mainly black youth in Chapeltown. Finally there is the odd Jewish skinhead who goes round rassing out reactionary Hassidyn Jews.

In some areas there is a more permanent tie up between skinheads and blacks. Not for nothing are the London Notting Hill skinheads called "commie skins" by others belonging to the hell fire fraternity. This does not mean they have been infiltrated by the local CP or Trot group, or even felled by the general liberal/left ambience of the area. Something of the sort has brushed off but chiefly they are pretty unique amongst skins when it comes to articulately defending their point of view. They were, for instance maligned, as an NF contingent in 1979 when members were denied entrance to a Rock Against Racism gig at Acklam Hall. They hit back fiercely wrecking amongst other things a couple of sound system transit vans. A RAR rep described them as racist thugs. But outside Acklam Hall there was no such clear-cut racial demarcation. As skins, punks, rude boys and Rasta's slugged it out, most of the older and heavier blacks collected on the steps outside of the garage/ sound system repair shop stood impassively by watching the fun and games and expressing no preference for either side. The Gate skins were so incensed by the coverage in the musical press that they wrote a collective letter of protest to The New Musical Express denying any involvement in racist groups. To no avail. The liberal/ left anti skinhead consensus meant they were cast as NF boot boys in an attack on (presumably) Acklam Hall in the film Breaking Glass starring the nauseating Hazel O'Connor whose street credibility consisted in knowing how to use show biz connections to cast herself as a rebel punk superstar.

The skins possess all the quality and defects of modern day barbarians and vandals. In one week in May1981 they firebombed Indian and Commonwealth clubs and a Hare Krishna temple in Coventry. What did they have in mind? The transcendence of religion? Well, even though such acts are unnecessarily barbaric, it comes into it. They have after all been caught ransacking Methodist chapels, though they never receive anything like the same publicity for wrecking such home-grown articles. Inversely, during the riots in Derby a group of Asians were seen carrying a large cross through the streets. The cross was later recovered but Our Saviour had been nicked.

But this was no Islamic anti-image jag, more probably it was a protest against a band of young Catholics who marched with all the sensitivity of an elephant through Derby's semi ghettoised district singing "We Shall Overcome."

Nonetheless the attacks on religious symbols in Coventry were interpreted by Asians as racist and it's an accusation that cannot be lightly dismissed. Skins often do hit the right enemy but random cruelty (hitting old age pensioners etc) provides perfect material to the word smithies of sensational news copy. Screaming headlines are tied up with circulation wars but the 'news' they help in this respect to convey is one of psychotic lawlessness everywhere. This has the added advantage of keeping the proletariat locked away day and night in fearful little boxes of routinised existence. At one moment skins can drag the filthy rich out of their deluxe cars in Chelsea, hand out a fistful of fives to ex-PM Sir Alex Douglas Home and split into the night. At other moments they succumb to a maimed psychotic rage lacking any class content whatsoever.

THE SHEFFIELD STOMP

There was a few weeks before the mass rioting, a vivid example of class-conscious skin activity. One Saturday, skins and a handful of blacks and punks (already a break thru') organised a demonstration themselves in Sheffield to protest against police harassment. Standing on the steps of Sheffield Town Hall, skins hollered out impromptu agit verbals to the rest of the assembled mob before proceeding to rampage through the city centre. En route, they caused thousands of pounds worth of damage to the Crucible Theatre, which with its £100,000 grant from Sheffield City Council had been invaded five times in the past 18 months by mods, football fans, as well as skinheads. These guys and gals really have taste because the Crucible Theatre is a showpiece of 'enlightened' leftist theatre/music which in the past played host to every conceivable shade of dramatised bad conscience, including the Sadista Sisters and Red Ladder (or, as it has come to be known locally "Gets Sadder"). But the one thing a skin sees red at is that mixture of inexhaustible guilt and superiority typical of audiences likely to attend the Crucible Theatre. A skin and his girlfriend find it offensive because in every case they are written out of the script as barbarians, picked on and pilloried as an example of everything that's bad. Guilt likewise is a luxury they can ill afford. By negating this aspect of culture, they were making a class protest. How did Bruce Burchall a regional cultural organizer feel about all this? It's a fair bet he conveniently forgot how he once called for something like a total assault on culture.

Two Sheffield social workers had planted the idea of a demonstration in the skinheads collective minds when they had suggested calling a protest meeting. The local Sheffield Labour Party had then participated in the event. So did the local Euro' MP looking even more ludicrously out of place. As per usual, a Labour Party councillor David Morgan blamed the trouble on a minority of vandals. But as the editorial in The Sheffield Telegraph more accurately pointed out on June 22nd 1981... "The element that raided the Crucible was estimated by staff at 150, the march itself numbered only 200."

Though the local Labour party was held to be guilty by association, the main culprits according, to the Regional Chief Constable, Brownlow were the youth workers. Like so many in the ultra repressive State Apparatus, Brownlow counts the soft cops amongst his pet hates. For some inscrutable reason, mutual acknowledgement that they are performing equivalent repressive functions is scant. The social workers didn't after all justify the wrecking of the Crucible Theatre. In some senses, the wrecking by the white youth was often more 'aimless' than the often selected targets of the blacks (c/f later in the account of the battle of Liverpool.) After riot week in the great mod battle of Keswick, a travelling theatre was again torched and on August 1981 bank hols, the model railway station at Brighton was molotoved by white youths.

What happened in Sheffield was skinhead energy and destruction at its best. During riot week, 2,500 coppers in Sheffield were put on full alert for use against rampaging skins, more in fact than were on standby during the steel strike of Jan/March 1980, when steel workers and miners tried to close down Hadfields for scabbing.

HULL AND HELL AND ....

50 miles to the northeast lies Hull. During, riot week a different saga unfolded in Hull, epitomizing some of the worst aspects of skin activity. In addition to wrecking the city centre, rival gangs of skins, punks etc set upon each other. Symbols of wealth like the Leeds Building Society plus a number of large stores, including Binns, were trashed. But excepting anti police verbals (one guy was jailed for shouting "kill the pigs") class-consciousness generally rose no higher than the Humber riverbed.

Shouting football slogans, some rioters nutted ordinary people standing in bus queues. One youth threw a concrete block through a bus window while passengers were still inside.

This chaotic response not surprisingly created amongst some Hull transport workers a passing sympathy for the police. The local TGWU official, with the backing of the rank and file, made preparations in concert with the police and the transport management to close down the Ferensway bus station at the centre of the riots. The Hull Daily Mail rubbed its hands in glee as workers, management and police clasped hands throughout this mid summer week of countryside proletarian insurgency.

Over the past ten years the Hull working class have exhibited a notable radicality, even as recently as the Winter of Discontent, which makes this understandable reaction doubly sad. They are not by nature hostile to class violence and sabotage. For instance during the 1972 dock strike, some Hull dockers cut ships, moored at the disputed container wharves up river, adrift. But they didn't then go on to root out innocent crewmembers to give them a thrashing as local skins might have done if their performance throughout riot week is anything to go by.

No one knows in advance whether skins will take a left turn or a right turn, or drive straight on into a brick wall.

Some skins could in future be recruited by para-military organisations like Column 88, Leaderguard and the League of St. George. The latter is reputed to lead right into the heart of this most secretive of states. Throughout the world, state manipulated terrorism is growing in importance (e.g. Italy - the Red Brigades, Spain - GRAPO - plus authenticated examples in France, Brazil and to a lesser extent in Chile) and there's no reason to think it couldn't form part of a counter revolutionary strategy here.

The colonial armies of the British Raj utilised terrorist atrocities, and as recently as the Heath Government, agent provocateurs (the Littlejohn Brothers) were employed to infiltrate the IRA and carry out bank raids in the Irish Republic. The names of their employers reads like something out of Burke's Peerage: Lord Carrington, the Defence Secretary, Geoffrey Johnson Smith and finally the Littlejohn's friend Lady Pamela Onslow, an ex social worker. They have never denied the charge levelled at them by the Littlejohn bros. There is a real possibility the Birmingham pub bombings atrocities of 1974 were not carried out by the IRA. The six convicted men have always protested their innocence, claiming confessions were beaten out of them. The IRA has never admitted responsibility for the pub bombings, which is unusual. Forensic evidence used to convict two of the men has been discounted. A swab test revealed traces of ammonia and iron nitrates on their hands, a compound substance left by either gelignite or smoking! Both men were smokers. Like the bomb in the Piazza Fontana detonated by the Italian Secret Services ending Italy's "Hot Autumn" in 1969, the Birmingham pub bombs were in all probability planted by an arm of the state. To achieve what ? To disorientate Brummy's militant proletariat? During the now famous miners' strike, engineering workers from Birmingham's extensive industrial belt had joined with the miners and picketed Saltley Power Station. Together they had inflicted a memorable defeat on the British Government. However the bombs did nothing to dampen class struggle, but they did achieve the immediate aim of the Special Branch; preparing opinion for the passing of the Anti Terrorist Act, which was implemented immediately after the outrages. In future the act could be more fully used than at present for detaining subversives.

And what of later episodes of class struggle? If the bomb planted on the Canvey Island gas and oil terminal during The Winter of Discontent had not mercifully been defused in lime, a fireball would have ripped through Canvey Island, leaving maybe thousands dead. It would have in addition cremated a strike wave, which included hospital ancillary workers. The bomb was said to have been planted by the IRA but a nagging doubt remains like a toothache, which won't go away. Just supposing...? Pro republican sentiments in the Republic (e.g. The Irish Times), though not wholeheartedly for the strikes (Ireland was itself about to be plunged into a big strike wave) never the less took pleasure in seeing the British Government squirm. The IRA is respectful of moderate republican opinion and whenever possible would prefer not to antagonise it unnecessarily - so it is highly unlikely that the Canvey Island bomb was the work of the IRA.

 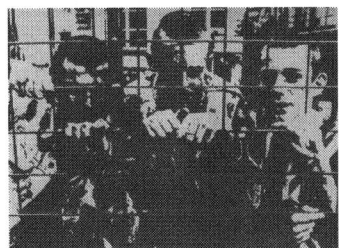

Photo left: Canvey Island bomb on oil refinery and terminal. Photo right: Skinheads behind the bars of a railway trolley on Brighton station.

Fascist groups inevitably gained members during and after the rioting, but the media was obsessed with uncovering evidence of left wing and IRA infiltration. The hidden face of protest was invariably one or the other. The News of the World (July 19th 1981) hysterically reported that black power leaders had made their first contact with two Provisional IRA leaders in Chapeltown, Leeds. Wearing balaclavas was to the press evidence enough of IRA involvement, and the daily tabloids carried photos of youths wearing them. In fact balaclavas were only worn to protect the hidden face of protest from vampirish press photographers.

Finally, Special Branch, clutching at straws, unearthed a couple of terrorist suspects. Jean Weir along with an Italian girlfriend was arrested for allegedly throwing a molotov during the Brixton riots in April 1981. Bratach Dubh which Weir belongs to had critically praised the Red Brigade in a pamphlet entitled 'Armed Struggle in Italy'. When it came to suggesting that the violence on the street was manipulated by unseen hands, a refusal to condemn state manipulated terrorism outright made the job of the press that little bit easier.

The Sigh Of The Oppressed Oppressor

YOUTH/SOCIAL WORKERS

Those 12 nights in early July 1981 marked a watershed. Revolutionary potential remains both a real and distant possibility. The youth valiantly fought the coppers but when it comes to subverting intermediary bodies of the state - youth work/culture/alternatives etc are easily thrown off course. Though the special pleadings of social workers in riot situations goes largely unheeded, the youth clubs have yet to be consciously attacked. Though sly kicks are frequently aimed at them, only in one notable incident has a youth club come under attack. This was during a small riot in Leicester in the summer of 1980 when a mainly black youth club was attacked. The incident was not reported in the national press.

In these hard times, youth clubs must find room for the growing numbers of young unemployed. They are consequently stretched to breaking point, and youth workers are being sent loopy with even heavier workloads. As they cannot recruit more staff enabling them to do their job 'properly', preacher man pep talks become a victim of the cuts and static manning levels. With the result kids minds are just that extra bit liberated from the paralysing effect of youth work.

Physically, youth workers are often lightweights having to contend with real heavies. They are extremely reluctant to call the cops, yet are often in need of protection themselves, nervously selecting keys from loaded key rings, dutifully locking doors behind them to keep youth club property safe from 'never-miss-a-chance' snaffling fingers. In their heart of hearts, how many yearn to be a strong-arm Cagney, outsmarting the not-so-angelic upstarts at their own game?

Ever since the state systematizing of social work first took off in a big way during the 1880s, social work in the name of more spiritual capitalist values has thumbed its nose at the 'cheap thrills' on offer in the market place. Nowadays the private market in youth entertainment, more expert at grabbing kids attention, is a source of competitive annoyance to youth workers. They dislike the rampant commercialism of amusement arcades and space invader emporiums where the only source of authority is the dubious money-changing bouncer. Confronted with this racketeering magnet, either the youth club makes concessions or risks losing all custom. But swimming with the current is also an admission of defeat, and there is an unhallowed something in the spectacle of youth workers attempting to become as slick as the next kid at playing space invaders on one of the clubs two machines. The market induced drift into backsliding ends the day the youth worker quits.

Having become more mechanised (videos, sound systems, music rooms, recording studios) youth clubs find themselves having to hire technically minded youth workers, fix-its. Employed in a less ideological capacity, they tend to poke fun at their harassed colleagues who obediently read and swear by The Guardian, New Society etc just like they've been trained to do. As pure cynicism, this dismissive gesture takes some beating in a scene which is noted for its close professional naiveté. Only time will tell if it is at all capable of progressing beyond mere cynicism.

There are other pressures leading the youth worker astray. Some gain the respect of kids by infringing the law in rather minor ways and generally making out they are tougher than they really are. Holding high their self-esteem and the esteem of others, they are easily nagged into continually proving themselves. However, there shortly may come a day when on account of former braggardly actions, they get pressured into throwing petrol bombs just for the sake of keeping up appearances. If caught they will quickly find out they have thrown away their job - and probably the keys to the jail.

In Britain the time has long gone when there was a manifest relationship between the owners of large-scale property and social work. There are echoes amongst today's social workers of Beatrice Webb's "new consciousness of sin amongst men of intellect and property", but the 19th century combination of guilt and fear of personally being expropriated, has greatly diminished. The moralizing function of social work has become progressively detached from defending individual property, being more a question of protecting the state as the collective capitalist. Social workers today dread the onset of role crisis more than they fear expropriation of their property, which in any case is rather petty. But low rates of pay, long hours, being on call, add their weight to a significant number correctly gauging their role as merely compounding misery.

Come this potential major turning point and the greatest danger comes from honey tongued Marxist ideologists of "social welfare work". They step in to save the social worker from social crises of deep personal significance. Arguing the state is not a monolith built to safeguard bourgeois class rule enables the social worker to pick up the pieces and cheerily soldier on convinced, having made the switch from liberal or Christian values to a Marxist approach, they are now helping the proletariat. When have social workers ever believed they were doing otherwise?

Social workers cannot initiate any authentic activity themselves, while the activity of those they police gets out of hand. Yet social workers can, all of a schizoid sudden, flip in with the insurgents. For example, a social worker was arrested for throwing a petrol bomb in Brixton in April 1981. Exactly a year later he was sentenced to 3 years in nick. At the trial the judge made it clear if he had not been of previous "good character" and a social worker the sentence would have been much stiffer. Obviously in some eyes social work still counts for something. Amongst those arrested and present at the scene of rioting were a number of teachers and professional sports people. Class pressures from below, the strains of the job etc, also cause them, like the social worker, to act in this explosive, definitely 'unprofessional' manner.

THE TEACHER AS INFORMER

The tensions of social work corresponding to the era of mass youth unemployment are analogous to those of teaching: increased workloads (but usually as a result of cutbacks rather than having to cope with more pupils) and more, much more police involvement. Moreover there has been over the past 8 years or so a slow but sure process of weeding out the more liberal and 'rebellious' teachers, leaving behind a core of either frightened or avowedly conservative teachers. Sir Keith Joseph's pronouncement (Jan 6th 1982) to local authorities to find 'better ways of getting rid of ineffective teachers' is the latest in a long line of similar strictures.

The strain of the job contributes to teachers' hardening of attitudes, and a defensive posture bordering on hysteria. To typify education nowadays as compulsory mis-education is, if secondary school teachers are present, tantamount to a declaration of war. Assembling the nitty gritty of details, enabling one to form some kind of accurate picture of what is happening in schools, is then halted by abusive, crass apologetics. Necessarily, an analysis of the changing role of secondary teaching is fragmentary, because details are lacking. Teachers keep mum about the shocking reality they are a witness to.

But the kind of policing activities teachers are progressively involved in was revealed with refreshing and chilling clarity in Toxteth. The Times reported "during the weekend riots, school teachers had reported seeing not just children from their own schools in Liverpool amongst the rioters, but those from schools outside the city." That just about says it all.

Though schoolteachers needn't in private uphold the views of e.g. education committees, they are virtually constrained in practise to follow suit or risk disciplinary proceedings and the sack. In Liverpool for instance, there was a striking concurrence between Councillor Michael Storey's (Chairman of Liverpool education committee and head teacher of a school outside the city education area) opinions and those of the Home Secretary, Willie Whitelaw. "Parental responsibility" he said "has gone out of the window. Not knowing where 8, 9 or 10 year olds are is disgraceful. The position is quite clear. Parents are responsible for their children." (The Times July 9th).

Councillor Storey refrained at least publicly from endorsing Whitelaw's proposals to punish parents (never incidentally enforced by fining parents directly) but he did call a special meeting of education officers, inspectors, welfare officers and school attendance officers (once known more appropriately as kiddy-catchers). Teachers were conspicuous by their absence from the meeting, which had the merit of laying bare the power structure in which teachers either rest content playing second fiddle, or get out. But with the rising incidence of arson in schools (c/f the wave of arson that engulfed school after school in Tyneside during the early 1970s) truancy and general hooliganism, a schoolteacher cannot distance him/herself from the job. A take it or leave it approach was always a luxury in the teaching counter-insurgency front line, ever since the beginnings of so called mass education. Today it is non-existent.

Education cuts have also caused a resurgence of powerless liberalism in 'educational' matters, particularly among concerned middle class parents. The pressure exerted by this body of people is wrapped up usually with the preservation of the local state. In so far as they view education as a positive good it is diversionary, inhibiting, in a perhaps rather minor way, the emergence of revolutionary theory, which must never be confused with state education. It is also idealistic and severely elitist because it tends to equate 'information' with survival chances: to reformulate Francis Bacon: knowledge is employment. On this reckoning the unemployed are condemned to remain claimants for the rest of their inferior lives because they lack 'knowledge'. It is nothing short of scandalous how the shining truths of clear as mud liberalism stand revealed as raving reaction.

However it is true that the kind of person who holds these views recoil if pushed, before this sort of inexorable logic. The same goes for their public utterances (letters to newspapers etc) on the riots, which were chosen with a snobby view to sounding respectable rather than from inner conviction. Judged from this privileged vantage point, education should have provided the tools for the full enjoyment of leisure (failing which kids rioted for lack of adequate preparation) rehearsing once more themes that started to become familiar from the mid 1950s onwards. Mass unemployment has knocked this nonsense for six and it is only naive dreamers, not Ministers of State, who continue to believe in this. A final word - ironically many liberal teachers who profess to hold these opinions dear spend much of their 'educated' leisure time getting rotten drunk or stoned! (There's nothing wrong with getting continually drunk or stoned in this alienated day and age. It is the holier than thou facade which is inexcusable).

It is possible to locate one major drawback in the crisis of mass secondary education. (Higher education is of no consequence here because struggle, since the qualitatively different ones of the late 1960s, has centered on restoring grants, extending facilities and not on the outright rejection of courses, the destruction of the university and an end to the student role.) Quite simply the runaway subversion is seemingly happening without any theoretical elaboration. It should come from the kids themselves. (We looked in vain for even the merest glimmer of a message that however fleetingly might have explained the arson in Tyneside schools. Resistance to corporal punishment in one school unaffected by arson is all we could come up with).

The inconsistency of school rebellions was also brought out in the riots. The mass truancy in Liverpool schools wasn't accompanied by a single recorded incident of a school coming under attack. Since the riots however, Liverpool schools have experienced an upsurge in destruction. At the now notorious St Saviours Church of England School in Toxteth, pupils "have wrecked class rooms by fire and vandalism and turned fire extinguishers on any teacher who dared to remonstrate." (The Daily Telegraph Feb 23rd, 1982). To begin to put together an absent critique even in the midst of so much destructive activity is not easy. The educational system in Britain has certain specific features that set it apart from most other highly advanced capitalist countries. It is perhaps less closely integrated with vocational training than any other major industrial country. Excepting maybe, pure science and basic literacy, the main function of mass education here is unobtrusively ideological and 'cultural', unrelated at first glance to the need to reproduce certain work skills necessary for the capitalist labour market. If this is the case then the revolt in secondary education contains within it the seeds of a critique, which is far more complex than a straightforward resistance to being force fed for a particular job at the end of it all. Where does it lead? To what beauty?

THEY HURT YOU AT HOME, THEY HIT YOU AT SKOOL CRISIS OF THE SCHOOL - FAMILY COUPLE: THE LOOMING INTO VIEW OF OTHER HORIZONS

The declining importance of school and the family, the two main institutional covers for kids almost inevitably brings the law more prominently into children's lives. With children especially in mind, extra police powers had been projected a good while before the riots by the Royal Commission for criminal procedure (Jack Jones the former 'radical' General Secretary of the TGWU had sat on this commission). Its recommendations to finger print children of 10 and over were enough to freeze the blood, marking something of a watershed in the criminalization of children. If the Chief Constables get their way the recommendations will become law.

The relevance to capital and the state in putting children under the police microscope has now become of pressing importance. The massed presence of children in the riots made public to astonished onlookers what the state had been maintaining all along; children were being progressively lost to view. It couldn't add - for their own good. Over night kids became strangers filled with new powers and parents and other adults peered quizzically at them as if they'd just hatched out. Yet this - one of the most advanced affirmations children have ever made - had not gone unheralded and parents had cause to wonder at their past casualness at not setting a time when children should be back and only occasionally asking them where they were going. Even going to skool is, because of rising levels of truancy, no longer the safe bet it once was.

Aries in 'Centuries of Childhood' linked the rise of school education to a "desire on the part of the parents to watch more closely over their children." It is this dual surveillance process which is now in such crises. Once it presaged the rise of the bourgeois family, just as loosening opaque family bonds, moving out onto a new terrain with no known reference point in the past, now signals its disappearance. Under the growing sway of police surveillance an eye as sharp as Fourier's is needed to see the potential.

Responding to the failing authority of parents, the Tories drastic solution is to first isolate the family unit before proceeding to give back its former powers. Like "the magic of the market" this is deemed to occur spontaneously. But what really happens is this: their redrawing of the boundaries of the state, like other instances, is more a question of substituting existing bodies for other ones. What is actually taking place is a realigning of extra parental authority rather than a return to base, replacing family guidance councils more with the courts and the police. The two in any case have never been totally separate, but shit social workers are more likely in the future, irrespective of changes at Government level, to be drawn into co-operating more closely with the police. Almost certainly the greater encroachment of statutory police authority is bound to put a severe strain on their woolly liberalism.

Thus parents, particularly working class parents, are not expected to assimilate the witchcraft of the 'experts' but instead hand out clouts around the ear hole like there's no tomorrow. The onus of the blame still falls on the parents but the terms have changed. (The findings of a survey commissioned by The News of the World on rioting kids was headlined "It's our fault children go wrong.") They are not now accused so much of a lack of sympathy and understanding but of a failure to act with brutal promptness.

At the time of the riots there was much talk of coercing parents into acting 'responsibly'. But the idea had been in the wind for some time. Only three weeks before, a research project was forwarded to the Home Office Research Unit proposing a study of the effectiveness of fines on parents for controlling their children. If the amount of doggerel now piling up is anything to go by, the ruling class are clearly very preoccupied with "lax parents."

Not all lax parents of course, only those belonging to the working class. For once, the inherent bias of sociological studies is there for all to see because it all depends on which side of the class fence you happen to be on. Laxity amongst working class parents becomes acceptable permissiveness amongst middle class parents. The Times (July 11th1981) was sympathetically frank about this in an article titled, "Why so many children take to the streets" summarizing these views as follows: "permissiveness in child rearing during the past 10/20 years, while perhaps all well and good for the educated middle classes in leafy suburbs - is counter productive for the families of manual workers living in inner city housing estates."

(By quoting from this newspaper article we are not entering a plea on behalf of permissiveness. Whatever the differences, both contending approaches are essentially about how best to bring up that pain-in-the-arse, a model citizen).

Particularly in child rearing methods, the bourgeoisie has liked to think of itself as a vanguard, confident that what it has pioneered today will benefit the proletariat tomorrow. But dual standards like these means its crusading days are over because it implies one method for the rich and the other for the poor. Using children as scapegoats (and anyone else in the family who gets in the way), easily provoked working class violence is, in this way, cynically whipped up.

But this controlled experiment in a punishing society hadn't banked on the effects of a rapidly rising unemployment surpassing that of the 1930s. When an unemployed parent lashes out from frustration it nullifies the rationale behind this narrow-minded dogmatism. Differences in brawn aside (which matters) beater and beaten are alike in at least one respect. Both are the trapped victims of an indivisible system, losing the power to divide and rule to its own satisfaction. As more and more tales come to light of wife, baby, child and granny bashing linked to rising unemployment, state manipulated violence rebounds to the detriments of its strategists.

INNER CITIES AS INWARDNESS

The riots do not presage an era of novel concern with the particular 'problems' of inner city areas. They come at the end of a dozen or so years of official anxiety.

The first efforts at isolating inner city areas date back to 1968 and the Labour

Government's Urban Aid Programme. The future PM Callaghan warned of the "deadly quagmire of need and apathy."

By confining problems geographically the program had a clearly divisive intent, isolating locality from workplace and the rest of society. Callaghan's statement needs to be set beside Harold Wilson's, made in the same year, warning of an assertion of power on the shop floor which Governments have yet to find an answer to - and never will be able to. The immediate backgrounds to these parallel and complimentary statements were the riots sweeping American cities and revolutionary struggles in France and Italy. The great fear was that the consensus in workplace and locality, which had bound the proletariat to social democratic reformism, was cracking apart. To repair the consensus was given henceforth top priority.

At the level of the factory, much more emphasis was placed by the TUC and management on the training of shop stewards. Courses set up to addle the minds of shop stewards included company finance, management, industrial law, labour relations etc. Since Harold Wilson first made his remark, the role of the shop steward has undergone a conservative reversal. The only point in history that the shop stewards movement has posed a revolutionary threat was during and just after World War One. They have ever after periodically marked time in a drift into rank and file 'chaos' they weren't able to control. Neither the state nor management can allow their activities to go unchecked, even given that their shop floor werewolf prestige has irreversibly declined.

At the level of the older industrial cities which had once formed Britain's industrial heartland, a series of 'community' measures were planned outside the more orthodox channels of political enfranchisement (e.g. the local Labour Party.)

This apparently ambiguous function was attractive to 1968 radicals who were none too clear about the state's sophistication in these areas of policymaking. Without doing much damage to itself, the state was able to use the catchwords of '68. Robbed of any precision, "alienation" was bent to merely signify "unneighbourliness". In this way contradictions inherent to capitalist society were pushed to one side and the go ahead given to redefining inner cities in pathological terms suited to remedial treatment (delinquency, crime, deprivation, children at risk, problem families, etc.)

The range of these 'unorthodox' bodies was astonishingly varied, covering health, education, urban planning, housing and social services. The approach was as near total as possible: political reintegration accompanying economic regeneration.

For this purpose, organizations like the Community Development Project were founded in 1969 to pioneer unconventional approaches to unemployment. As often as not, CDP activities were viewed with suspicion as 'communist' by chain bearing Labour mayors and local councillors. They need not have worried: the state has long known how to dress up over-due modernization with feigned subversion. But they did and these ossified responses only enhanced the allure of the CDP.

"Community strategies" accorded well with the historicizing tendency of the times. Potted histories of selected areas and localities were prepared. All depending, state sponsorship was either direct or more discreet. Sometimes it was a bewildering combination of both. But having shaped the overall retrospective spirit of the 1970s decade, the state had little to fear from quasi-independent initiatives. For example, the Hackney Writers Workshop formed with the intention of encouraging old timers to write about the neighbourhood as it once was. There was more to this venture and others like it than recollection of things past.

Looking Back at Bristol - a Bristol Broadsides publication, revealingly the central St. Paul's area, the scene of the riot in 1980, was the subject of the first transcribed interview given by a woman who had been rehoused on the Hartcliffe estate four miles from the city centre. Memoirs like Coronation Cups and Jam Jars (1976) evoke an unfailing neighbourly good humour and stability circumscribed by the Labour party and the trade unions, able to take on the chin the very worst blows capitalism could deliver. The riots of 1981 vividly brought home the near total absence of comparable punch-drunk safety valves today.

Local histories and the unbearable image of harmony they conveyed was a preparatory vector of communication to the local state. But they were only able to properly act as an emotionally charged stimulus to the political economy of the area if shuffled with 'alien' cultures now flooding the inner cities. That is why local community centres like Centreprize in Hackney trade on the paradoxical affinity of a pre war white working class and politically stable post war images of ethnicity both about as relevant to the present as pit ponies and dug out canoes.

The principles of political economy rarely in the 19th century included the principal of getting to know one's own work force, their past histories, neighbourhoods etc. Or if it did it was a comparative rarity. The political enfranchisement of the masses, more an achievement of the 20th century than the 19th, changed all that. In so far as they constitute the majority of the electorate, working class history is important to the bourgeoisie just so long as it doesn't threaten its interests. It is an indispensable part of the representative apparatus of government. When consensus breaks down, the historian is called on to secure the present for the past. What passed for radical local history coming straight from the horses mouth with a moral in it for today's generation, was not meant to form part of an eventual digest of international capitalism. The whole aim of the project was to encourage an introverted 'community pride' covering identity, self-help schemes, individual and co-operative ownership all tied in with the resumption of the voting game. The net effect sometimes is so claustrophobic it's like going around with a feather pillow strapped to one's face.

Photo left: Wall mural in a Glasgae' tenement slum. Public Pictures as the cosmetic of misery.

Photo left: N.U.R. (National Union of Railwaymen) training centre. Trades Unions to the Manor Born. Photo right: This pastiche of naive art was painted by a youth worker and secretary of Bethnal Green and Stepney Trades Council after a visit to the Grunwick picket line in 1977. Throughout the 1970s the local State has patronised efforts extolled as "peoples' art", self-consciously imitated and drummed into serving a cause, they lost their innocence. Like in the patronising example above it is about supporting a struggle for trade union recognition (NB at the height of TU power in 1977) this politically calculating genre would like nothing better than to permanently tie the explosive inner cities to the stake of parliamentarism.

Autonomy And The Seasons

"Three things, all of the same sort, are merciless when they get the upper hand, a water flood, a wasting fire and the common multitude of small folk. For these will never be checked by reason or discipline and therefore, to speak in brief, the present world is so troubled by them that it is well to set a remedy thereto. Ha! Age of ours, wither turnest thou?"

John Gower, landlord and lawyer, writing just before the Peasants Revolt of 1381

Undoubtedly the outbreaks of rioting in 1981 put the long overdue social revolution back on the agenda once more. The industrial revolt of 1970-74 and The Winter of Discontent of 1979, pale in comparison. None of those out on the streets called for leftist inspired parliamentary alternatives to the capitalist system, which were a tacit ideological rider to the industrial revolts of 1970-74. Contrary to Cajo Brendel's opinion in Autonomous Class Struggle in Britain 1945-77 the actual amount of autonomy in these essentially industrial revolts was rather less than he imagined. Making allowances for the hyperbole, it must be admitted 'Echange et Mouvement' have consistently expressed the view Britain was heading towards a crises of revolutionary proportions. In this respect most others have been less optimistic.

But even the strikes of 1979, during The Winter of Discontent, never really transcended a rank and file shop steward/local bureaucrat unionism - like the ringing of Hull City by striking lorry drivers who exercised a considerable degree of control over the administration of the city. Still, they were highly significant strikes. A friend estimated that well over 30 categories of workers with no previous history of conflict went on strike that winter. This served to set it apart from the more industrial conflicts of the early 1970s. Careerists now visibly rising on the back of 1970-74 struggles maintained a judicious silence throughout those ice bound weeks when nothing much moved - including the stiffs piling up in a Liverpool warehouse requisitioned especially to accommodate the overflow from the city's morgues. Compared with the 1970-74 strike wave it was rich in unusual incidents, making play with the fact Britain was experiencing its worst winter for 20 years. The elements of unattended fire, ice and deep snow became during that winter tactical weapons from striking firemen to road gutters. An eerie silence spread over snowbound city streets, deserted railway sidings and the empty porticoes of railway stations where the snow was allowed to whirl.

In the Winter of Discontent the working class used bad weather conditions to press home their advantage. But in the winter of 1981-82 the tables had been turned. The snow and floods only added to the crushing weight of the bourgeoisie's counter offensive. There was no defiant pleasure to be gained out of the chaos. Streets were piled high with drifting snow not because of striking council workers, but on account of Government cuts. Spirits slumped unresistingly like the laden branches. The fact that steel plants in Wales were snow bound were used as an excuse by BSC to close them permanently. Unlike the winter of 1978-79, the gleam of a new order never once shone through the blocked roads, the overflowing riverbanks and iced over floodwater lakes stretching far and wide.

Back to the summer heat and bonfires of 1981. Where did the real difference lay? Those early July days were the clearest expression yet of the proletariat becoming a "class for itself" in the UK. The youth, unencumbered by trade unionism, naked and abandoned in a 'social void' that is exceedingly dangerous to capitalism, went straight for the jugular, unhampered by the sabotage of 'their' absent 'worker' representatives ensconced in the state apparatus. And that's why those in power were so disturbed by the riots. 'Left wing' Labour councillors just looked perplexed. At the other end of the scale, the Queen on the eve of the Royal Wedding was all bust up inside. The Queen and other Royals were reported as far more disturbed by what was happening than ever during the miners' strike of 1972, the 3-day week or The Winter of Discontent!

Photo right: A snowman in Putney, London during The Winter of Discontent.

Photo top left: The Winter of Discontent trash aesthetic engulfs the bust of Sir Joshua Reynolds in 'Fester' (Leicester) Square. Photo bottom left: Empty sidings, Winter 1979. The journey to really get into touch. Photo right: Telephone kiosk. Winter 1982. An absence of communication.

Leftist Vanguards And The Labour Party

THE VIEW FROM THE FRONT ROW SEATS IN THE REAR

Leftist parties attempting to use the insurgent youth for their own ends were rapidly exposed for what they were. The newspapers also tried hard to link the Leninist/Trotskyist groups with the rioting. The truth is they had no influence whatsoever and were only tail ending the movement, appearing with pamphlets and trying to organize meetings after the riots had occurred. They were met by open hostility or a wall of indifference. They were seen as outsiders muscling in, in a manipulatory fashion, which is exactly what they were doing. Each Leninist group believed it alone had the correct political analysis and program of action. Tony Cliff of the SWP said at a meeting in Liverpool, "The young have provided the steam and now we must provide the engine for the steam to drive." In the age of high tech and the microchip, these weary clapped out metaphors probably deriving from Lenin are more ludicrous than ever. Besides he obviously can't tell the difference between steam and fire. He went on in his usual florid way, which he mistakenly believes is gripping the absent masses: "Because they have not been organized the kids have been attacking shops when they should have been attacking factories. We must teach them to take the bakery and not just the bread". (One apocalyptic sympathiser wished they had "kicked the factories to bit.") The arrogance and insensitivity of these people is such that they cannot see why these attitudes should be resented.

The Labour Party Young Socialists held a meeting in Southall after the riots and got a rough ride from the Southall Youth Movement. Balig Sing Purewal said: "These people come here to exploit us. We do not want anything to do with them, the Socialist Workers Party, the Workers Revolutionary Party or any Marxist group. We are fed up with these lefties telling us what to do." When the LYPS held a meeting in Liverpool the reaction was the same. Claire Doyle who works for the Trotskyist Militant tendency was constantly heckled by the youth of Brixton and Toxteth when she tried to hustle in on their action by calling for the setting up of a Labour Committee (euphemism for the Labour party) for both neighbourhoods. She was rightly accused of trying to make political capital out of the riots. When she told a Brixton meeting, "You have to organize to defend yourselves", the reply came back: "We will do all our organizing ourselves." At another meeting three members of the Revolutionary Communist Tendency got up to speak and were booed. One kid said "We are fed up with them hanging around since it started."

Black people are particularly sensitive with regard to left groups. The 1981 pre-Carnival issue of Socialist Worker bemoaned the fact the black 'leaders' were telling black youth not to have anything to do with the white left. Because of their position, the 'leaders' reasoning would in all probability be highly suspect, but their conclusion is certainly right. The groups are funded by and dominated by the white middle class left. If it is true that people in positions of power in capitalist society will fight to maintain their positions, why is this not true across the board? Everything about them serves to maintain their position; they abuse the white working class so there is no reason to suppose they will behave differently to black people. These groups do not present any opportunities for black and white proletarians to organize themselves to achieve their own liberation. The reality is accepting leadership from the white middle class in what is supposed to be their own best interest. Despite their anti-capitalist and anti-racist rhetoric these groups do not present any alternative to society as it stands. Rather they present a fairly accurate reflection of it in their structure and organization.

The so-called practical help of the lefties through the Labour Committees was ostensibly to ensure that arrested youth were represented by solicitors in court. As it stood, it boiled down to little less than para-statist law centre work with 'politicizing' implications coming later. As for the rest of their comment, it was bullshit. The International Marxist's Socialist Challenge and the Socialist Worker's weakly paper achieved the ultimate in hypocrisy by defending looters, then condemning looting as 'unsocialist'. The Workers Revolutionary Party's Newsline (July 18th) was pedigree basket case splutterings, which was hardly surprising considering its long history of chronically blocked mental collapse. Breakdown for them is certainly not breakthrough. They claimed the riots were at the behest of the state, "police and army provoked", because "the Tory counter revolution is gearing itself to make a violent pre-emptive strike against the working class", concluding "the main war is still in front - against the trade unions." What drivel! But at least they didn't flinch from showing their true colours, unequivocally condemning all looting and vandalism as the acts of "gullible youth" falling for "police provocation". The WIRP's have the merit of being just too crude to manipulate. Groups like the Communist Workers Organization (CWO) stemming from the old German and Italian ultra left were also only capable of writing nonsense. Having an ideology to realize they simply failed to grasp what was unique about the riots. They sounded for all the world like Trotskyists.

The CWO, for example, in the Platform of Unemployed Workers Group, predicted "the unemployed, discarded by capitalism today, will be dragooned into the factories to produce armaments under military discipline. This (their italics) is the only future which capitalism offers."

But increased automation and the higher technological composition of capital required in today's armaments industry, combined with a reduced need for conventional armed forces, makes today's situation utterly different from the 1930s. (The source of all their cock-eyed theorizing).

Today's unemployed are not likely therefore to be dragooned into the war machine. Apart from staging bread and circuses, capital is at its wits end to know what to do with them. Obstinately ignoring these very elementary facts, how can the CWO even begin to create an effective unemployed workers group? Like diehard Trotskyists they even condemn looting as "a gift to the ruling class since it leads nowhere." (Platform of the Unemployed Workers Group).

But Solidarity's (June/July 1981) coverage of the Brixton riots didn't amount to much, unable to see that it has become a victim of views and attitudes that left parliamentarians increasingly tend to encompass. For instance Solidarity objected to those rioters who smashed the windows of small shopkeepers "who did not deserve it". Let's face it; small shopkeepers have a well-deserved notoriety. Not only do they often charge more than supermarkets because they cannot purchase in bulk and don't own an agri-business, but are far from averse to short changing inattentive customers. Moreover working all hours, small shopkeepers are often classic canaries. So often their deceptive chattiness is simply earwigging which ends up down at the local cop shop.

In a similar vein, Solidarity went on to condemn all those who trashed "The Community Action Office whose work" they said "is appreciated by local people". But is it that simple? Who hasn't heard people, drunk or otherwise, sounding off against these para-statist bodies? And what they say often makes a lot of sense. In Solidarity's case they probably haven't because their membership is overwhelmingly drawn from the professional strata, and some are involved in the 'community' racket themselves. To crown it all, there is more than a suspicious hint the police are absolved from acting like they do because they are simply doing their job protecting the commodity and the state. In inner city areas such views are a luxury, and points to the fact Solidarity members tend to live in easier parts of the city, where cops breathing constantly down the back of your neck is not an everyday experience, and which makes an enlightening observation of role structure, without frothing at the mouth, a bit difficult. Let's wait and see, but in future, it is possible Solidarity members could opt for the soft cop/community policing line.

Solidarity never got down to the real nitty-gritty of analysis. It cannot be stressed too often the extent to which urban dereliction was a major contributing factor to the trashing then burning of small shops in poor neighbourhoods. It crystallised the worst fears of urban reformers who, following the lead first suggested by urbanist Jane Jacobs, began to dread the consequences of high-rise estates, desolate spaces, barren streets and alleyways, and planning blight generally. These conditions, they believed, destroyed the informal network of vigilance and surveillance, which, including authority figures such as teachers, parents, shopkeepers, local businessmen, publicans etc, together made the job of the police almost unnecessary. By one handle or another, people were always 'known' to each other but increasing anonymity has meant the local shop could be done in without much risk of anyone being made to pay the cost.

Concealed behind a veil of good intentions there always was an inherent class bias in which small business interests came first and foremost into their apparently damning indictments of urban redevelopment. These urban reformers want ultimately to approximately recreate the conditions which they assume once bound otherwise class divided communities together. To achieve this they tend to highlight and sensationalize indiscriminate street crime. But what they fear the most is an explosion of class war, which has no compunction about attacking small business. This is exactly what happened on the streets of Britain's inner cities between July 4th and 13th 1981.

Of course one can criticize the rioters, but it has to be more imaginative than the run of the mill lefty criticism .... Like the following.

RIOTING IN ST PAUL'S BRISTOL, APRIL 1980. SOME SHORTCOMINGS

The rioters, unable to consciously get to grips with the more 'ghostly' aspects of the commodity economy, were easily pulled up before institutions whose brutality and nakedly system-serving function all must have experienced at some time or other. While shops were looted and a bank burnt in the St Paul's riot in Bristol 1980, the rioters shopped short of getting the Labour Exchange. They were held back by a black ex-civil servant who had recently been employed at the local St Paul's Labour Exchange. He warned insurgents - within seconds of torching the building - that if they did so they only stood to lose their weekly giro. Old ways, even in insurrectionary moments, can still exert a fearful grip on events.

At the very worst, the unemployed of St Paul's would have only had to wait a few days longer for their giro's - no senior civil servant would have dared leave St Paul's without any welfare support in the days following the riot. The real effect would have been felt in other Labour Exchanges, and Social Security offices throughout the country. The petty bureaucrats would have got the jitters, and more importantly, the hideous fraud squads who harass all claimants (particularly women in single parent families) would have received a well-deserved slap in the mouth. (Union backed blacking of the 'scrounge' squads outlined for use in 1982 would not have the same impact, even in the unlikely event of it ever happening.) The final irony came a year later when striking civil servants, without the aid of incendiaries, in some inner city areas, cut off cash aid to the unemployed. Courageous people, they preferred to do this rather than snarl up NATO defences or the Whitehall administration.

THE UNACCEPTABLE FOOT OF BRITISH CAPITALISM

As for the central core of Labourism - the Labour party - perplexity reigned. They couldn't even muster one call to kick out the Tories, which on past, tho' hardly comparable occasions, had been the thing to do. Did wor' great leader, Michael Foot see in those July days the lion's claw he had prophesied would smite the land? What a joke. Scarcely six months previously, he had called on the unemployed during a speech on Liverpool's Pier Head, some 3/4 of a mile from Toxteth, to "rise like lions". Being a fustian ditherer, he later reversed his position on the use of CS gas and water cannon secure in the knowledge that he lived in a world where the only projectiles thrown are made of paper. (That, or the less immediate and more respectable repudiation of nuclear weapons). In the midst of proletarian anger boiling over in the streets, all the unacceptable Foot of British capitalism could do was call the government's decision to axe 20.000 university places "an act of barbarism." (July 9th19'81)............. And what of Wedgewood Benn, the ace lefty manipulator of the party machine, confined as luck would have it, to a hospital bed. Not a word, not even the hint of a whisper. Sister called for "Silence" and got it. When peace was restored, he broke his silence to say Britain was heading for a police state. ....

But best of all were the antics of the Parliamentary extremist Eric Heffer, author of the book Class Struggle in Parliament acclaimed by the SWP. Pressed to make a statement on TV the panicked Right Hon MP for Walton, Liverpool said rioters and looters must be punished with all due severity.

..........AND THE LABOUR PARTY THAT CANNOT CHANGE ITS SPOTS

The UK may be tripping headlong down the primrose path to social revolution, but a word of caution. Political parties are unlikely to give up that easily. The left in particular can still do much to slip-slide the movement awry. Ken Livingstone, leader of the Greater London Council, quick off the bureaucratic mark as usual, called for the immediate release of Asians arrested in Southall. He was applauded for saying it, then barracked by other Asians who bluntly asked him why hadn't he been on the streets the previous night. Later on in the week, Livingstone was to address the moribund Anti-Nazi league in Brixton when rioting was literally going on only 100 yards away! This prince of media, deadlines arranges, Council meetings timed to suit the press and approves of the Communist Council of Bologna in Italy; never once mentioning that these Stalinists thrashed the Bolognese insurgents in 1977. He has also gone on record as saying in an editorial in London Labour Briefing (late May1981) that the street fighting in Brixton during April was "excellent." (Later he denied he'd ever said such a thing).

The Labour party is nothing if not chameleon like. The new or reconstructed Labour party is just as prepared as the old to cut its coat according to its cloth. There have been several media scare stories of mobs stirred up by the "new left" in Parliament. Not, however, to demolish it, but simply in order to bring more effective pressure to bear on MP's. This is what the media in general fatuously calls "extra parliamentary activity".

Livingstone's intentionally vacillating behaviour during the riots was repeated when the Law Lords ruled against London's "cheap" transport policy. Hiding behind a smokescreen of radicalism, he had no intention of defying the ruling himself. And sure enough on the day London's fares became the most expensive in the world, dear Ken paid his full whack. Even a reformist 'rebel' had been tamed by office and the media exulted. He even went so far as to say breaking the law was "not part of the British tradition", urging Londoners to pressure 'their' 92 MP's to get the Law Lord's ruling overturned in the House of Commons (New Standard March 22nd '82). A week or so later, having recovered from ticket collector jitters, he was to be heard sounding off against the Met's prospective top pig Sir Kenneth Newman, the former RUC police chief from N. Ireland. This time everyone knew it was to save face.

Livingstone's duplicity is important because he is the first of the characteristically issue-conscious "new left" to drop his mask. Respect for legality may still hold good, but otherwise there is little love lost between the old and the 'new' Labour party. Throughout Britain, the old hulk of consensus politics is breaking up and the classes are drifting away from the traditional parties. It behoves in the long run a profound social crises, but meanwhile new political re-alignments are being launched daily.

The rhinoceros hide of Labourism provides no lasting immunity against this frantic political experimentation. The old sub-Orwellian band of Tribunite intellectuals defending a non-conformist heterodoxy, standards in art and garlanding the image of the cloth-capped worker, are no match for the fledging alliance proposed by the reconstructed Labour party. This still tentative consensus includes workers drawn from traditional sectors like coal and steel plus ethnic minorities, gays, women, ecologists, peace movement activists, paraplegics, pensioners, 'rebel' musicians, community workers, you name it Tony Benn in his report (12th Dec1981) to the London Labour Briefing said as much..."We should welcome radical liberals, community activists and those from the woman's movement, the ethnic groups, the peace movement and the pensioners, along with the young, into our party now."

It is a striking testimony to the power of issue politics. On the other hand Benn is also exploiting an endemic weakness for politics, happy in the knowledge that the task of winning over an issue to the reconstructed Labour party has been smoothened from the start by a statist orientation. Broadening an initial exclusivity then carries a heavy political penalty, as single issues are refracted through the Labour party/Communist party "Alternative Strategy" for capitalism.

Many of the new recruits were student 'radicals' in the late 1960s who, without a moment's hesitation, had joined moribund Trotskyist parties. From the mid 1970s onwards, most have begun to wake up to the utter irrelevance of vanguard parties derived from Lenin. There was even a hint of profounder insights: that working class lack of interest in 'socialism' was more intelligent and egalitarian than the repentant vanguardist had previously given credit for. But to continue in this vein may well have had disastrous (finally liberating) personal consequences, raising searching questions about the state, power, the sort of job one was doing. As they had craftily slid around these thorny questions in the late 1960s, they were not likely to confront them in the mid to late 1970s, when the next instalment of the mortgage was due. So they plumped for an 'independent' line which was neither one thing nor the other, uniting so to speak 'extra parliamentarism' with parliamentarism. Hilary Wainwright (joint author of Beyond the Fragments) has said as much in the ludicrously acclaimed "political debate of the decade" when she and others from the 'far' left had got together with the Labour party to thrash out their scant differences. "The Labour party" she said – "lays too much emphasis on the State and on Parliament, and is unable to develop extra parliamentary organizations." (The Times March 1980).

Their notion of what constitutes 'extra parliamentary' is intentionally vague. It can signify 'unorthodox' parliamentary methods. On the other hand, the reconstructed Labour party will lift a precious word like 'assembly', knowing full well it has a certain autonomous resonance, to promote a form of corporate assembly, fudging capital and class (e.g. The London Assembly convened to discuss London's "social problems", fare increases etc). To keep pace with growing political disaffection, the Labour party's new auxiliaries must maintain a hygienic distance from political parties, appearing to merge with the struggles of the underdog. The moment these struggles get out of hand, the reconstructed Labour party is nowhere to be seen, reappearing with Labour Committee's etc once the all clear is given. The new auxiliaries of Labourism were the authors in the late1960s of a counter revolution of dirty little tricks when obviously bogus libertarians, anarchists etc all of a sudden put in at the safe harbours of vanguard Leninist/Trotskyist parties even then OK with career stakes. But at least these parties did not flinch from using the term revolutionary, albeit in a hopelessly deformed way. The Labour party always has. These seasoned rookies of the reconstructed Labour party are now faced with the unenviable and contradictory task of pretending to support more clear-headed autonomous actions than anything seen in Britain in the late 1960s, whilst sanctioning the shabbiest parliamentary voting reflex.

Meanwhile these new recruits to Labourism ranks tend not to blurt out comments they could have cause to regret later. During and after riot week, they maintained a judicious silence, which was neither whole-heartedly approving or disapproving. The reconstructed New Statesman limited itself to exposing a very biased press report on the second Brixton riot which appeared in The Daily Mirror and in a detailed but ultimately light weight article, to criticising the behaviour of the police in Toxteth.

Photo left: The 1001 faces of Wedgewood Benn. Photo right: Painting the demagogic finger. Arthur Scargill before a social realist portrait of himself

KING ARTHUR AND THE KNIGHTS OF WAGE LABOUR

But what of the new breed of militant trade unionist who shall henceforth provide the muscle in the reconstructed Labour Party? Men like Arthur Scargill, former leader of the Yorkshire miners and now President of the NUM (National Union of Miners). He could from his bureaucratic throne threaten strike action if such things as pensions and the low pay for YOP schemes aren't immediately upped. During the Grunwick strike of 1977 and the steel strike of 1980, King Arthur, chirpy as a cock sparer, led well drilled battalions of miners into the picketing foray. There was, however, method to his anti-sectional conceit. He was getting miners accustomed to the idea of one big union cutting across much basic industry. When the pathetic Bill Sirs of ISTC (Iron and Steel Trades Confederation) said he was retiring, the King announced he already had eyes for merging the two unions.

As an adjunct to the expansionist game, the King is to be heard cockily airing his views on a number of subjects, including racism. He simply cannot resist invites to appear on TV chat shows, putting in a plug for the forthcoming NUM presidential election, and pleased as puff to be rubbing shoulders with show biz celebrities. Could it be that the BBC wanted this formerly brilliant strategist of the blockade of Saltley Depot in 1972 to be the new boss man of the NUM?

Just after the riots, the King seated in his Barnsley Camelot in South Yorkshire could gloat he'd prophetically predicted at the end of that artistic charade The Peoples March for Jobs, that violence on the scale of Bristol and Brixton "will erupt the length and breadth of Britain" unless (always unless) "the Government changed its policies." But for King Arthur, rioting is not the stuff of 'socialism'. He believes all anger should be directed at the Tories and at the "Tory policies" of all the other political parties emerging, like the SDP, into the light of day.

However even before his elections, Scargill had come to mellow his simplistic anti-Tory stance. The awesome power of the miners having brought him to power could just as easily sweep him away. He is better placed than anyone to know it. Raising the temperature must in future be carried out with due regard for the King's safety. Long live the King! Many miners, particularly from S. Wales and Kent had harsh words to say about Scargill when he steadfastly refused to encourage Yorkshire miners to strike during the lightening pit strikes against threatened closures in the spring of 1981. And on TV, the knucklehead half suggested the Yorkshire miners had stayed on their knees, solemnly hewing coal like painted black National Coal Board manikins during the miners' strikes of the early 1970s. But the basis of Scargill's reserve goes back to 1979 and the Winter of Discontent, and the strike wave sparked off by the Labour Government's 5% pay freeze. During these critical weeks he was neither seen nor heard. Except, that is, one evening when he put in a TV appearance, quietly, deliberately and agreeing with top management about the lack of investment in British industry. Lack of investment in industry, lack of investment in the inner cities. Lack of investment, lack of investment, lack of investment! Like an annoying jingle that won't go away, these bureaucrats drone on in the same old key. What about a world without money? Is it so difficult to envisage?

Got any Money?

The Tory Government had by the end of Oct 1981 nominated a hit squad of 25 "socially concerned capitalists" (!) drawn from the banks, building societies, insurance companies and funds (including Barclays Bank, the Woolwich Building Society and the British Petroleum Pension Fund) and charged them with producing a series of reports on private/public sector cooperation. Since then, they have visited several American cities including Detroit, Philadelphia and Atlanta. (All in the line of duty, £2000 smackers apiece was provided by the Government as pocket money when they visited the States). This sham fact-finding mission is sure to underline Thatcher's determination to reduce the economic role of the state still further. The reconstruction of American cities following the long hot summers of the 1960s will be used as a pretext to fundamentally alter, in theory at least, the pattern of state financing which has overwhelmingly dominated urban renewal in post-war Britain.

However the clocks are unlikely to go that far back. Heseltine (Minister for Environment) has wisely kept his options open while pretending not to. In a carefully worded speech to the Tory Party Conference last year, he accepted the inevitability of central government spending if all else fails. The Thatcherite Tory faithful gave him a standing ovation, but the joke was on them. They had moronically assumed Heseltine's bussing of 30 odd bankers and financiers through the devastated areas of Liverpool to be, in strict accordance with principle, the Tory Government's final word on the subject. When Heseltine eventually repudiated this error, their ears were too clogged to hear properly.

Heseltine's strategic retreat does not mean the Tories are any nearer to understanding the special position of finance capital in Britain. Going to America won't help in this respect either. Though the dollar is still the world's major trading currency, finance capital has never, in contrast to Britain, occupied the same pre-eminent place in America. There are, for example, Federal regulations restricting inter-state savings and loans. To believe for one moment that those remote banking leviathans that straddle the City of London are now going to sponsor, in partnership with the state, a localist 'community bank' ideology is the height of absurdity. On the contrary, they have long since consigned everything in the UK outside St Paul's, Blackfriars Bridge and a very select mythology of British gentility, to oblivion.

Shortly after the Brixton riots, a wealthy Nigerian businessman, Chief Francis Nyeribe came up with a pet project for stimulating private enterprise in Brixton. He has not been heard of since, but at the time it made the Front Page. This hoax, clutched at like a last straw by the media, was also highlighted because it set a mock-serious example for other businesses to follow. Not only the moneylenders, but also industry was expected to make due atonement to the inner cities and regions it had plundered with such 'insensitivity' in the past. Significantly, after the Financiers had reported back from the States, an organization called BIC (Business in the Community) made its appearance on the British scene, subjectivizing political economy still further. Again it does seem to be influenced by American examples. For instance after the Watts riot in Los Angeles in 1965, a group of wealthy capitalists got together and formed The Community Committee to see what could be done to save their worthless hides. They did this spontaneously, but British business has to be cajoled. Sir Monty Finniston and Lord Melchett, former heads of British Steel, may readily put their names to ace deviant sociologist asshole Laurie Taylor's 'Keep Out' campaign, aimed at "reducing the use of custody for young people". But British management is generally characterized by a suicidal introversion, making them their own worst enemies.

Bradford cotton manufacturers, formerly the vulgar butt of T.S. Eliot's derision, are pawning their silk top hats by the dozen in the local Oxfam shops as mill after mill closes. Instead of becoming more capital intensive or moving overseas in the 1950s and 1960s, they preferred to rely on round the clock working, decades old machinery and cheap docile, mainly Asian immigrant labour. Confronted as they were by the summer riots of 1981, with an insurrection of Asian youth who number over a third of the school population, Bradford's depleted Chamber of Commerce will, going on past behaviour, react with all the speed of a tortoise on crutches to inner city rescue operations to save capitalism.

What little dough the banks have coughed up - a mere £70 million: the Bradford Interchange alone in the early 1970s cost £18 million and a packet of crisps to construct - is based on the Urban Development Action grants which were used in the US, so apologists would have us believe, to attract six dollars of private money for every one dollar of public money spent. In fact these urban aid grants will still be funnelled through the government. Only now bankers will in theory assess the viability of the competitive tenders put in by local authorities, business or community groups pushing to one side wasteful tribunals of civil servants accustomed to thinking money grows on trees.

To even begin to apply lessons learnt from the American experience is to whistle in the wind. When it comes to palming off the view that peace in the American ghettoes during the 1970s was traceable to the success of these joint ventures (e.g. the still flourishing Watts Labour Community Action Committee) the British government is a major shareholder. Differences in economic climate limp along in second place as an explanation. The 'reconstruction' of the ghettoes is looked upon too as a shining example of American free enterprise. In fact whatever change has come about is more than likely due to profligate Federal expenditure which convincingly donned the mask of American style independent entrepreneurship. Only days after the riots had subsided in the UK, some reporter managed to sniff out a Watts rioter who picturesquely recalled how in the mid 1960s he had only to stick his hat out of the window to hook the greenbacks whizzing past. No one living in English cities in the months after the riots can possibly match this welfare yarn. A year later the charred rubble is still there setting fire to the imagination..............

The British government, as part of the 'riot package', is pedalling for all it's worth the appearance of social peace which has swept across American society since the late 1960s. There is little doubt it is banking on cool short summers in American cities this year and the next and the next. (Some hope!!) By singling out the importance of derivative political strategies, they can play down the much-changed economic situation, which will weaken their likely impact. To hope for a respite like America has enjoyed over the last 10 years or so is to hope in vain.

Twist and turn as it may, the choices open to capitalism are quite narrow. But the sheer scale of its present difficulties has led to this undeniable foreboding of the imminent suspension of the laws governing capitalist accumulation. It strikes like lightening in day-to-day contracts, positioned somewhere between liberation and the funny farm. An 8 year old kid in Brixton's April 1981 riot exchanged a ripped-off gold bracelet for a can of coke just because he was thirsty. Strictly speaking it wasn't even barter because there's nothing commensurate about this form of exchange. Even the bourgeoisie pale before their calculations. Their once superior econometric models, 'understood' by the select few, and always managing to end in some obscure but comforting note, have been almost levelled. It's as if the 'continent' of higher mathematics had been reduced to a few intelligible ciphers scratched in the sand. 2 million unemployed, then 4 million, finally even 10 million. To even admit to this statistical probability is for economists equivalent to playing Russian roulette with an adding machine. Losing their nerve, they reach for the bottle and the abacus in the playpen. The Cambridge Econometrics Unit recently suffixed one of its predictions with the staggering claim that unemployment will only begin to fall by the year 2000. Privately they must know as well as anyone, high tech and developing automation ("capital's self contradiction in motion" - Marx's Grundrisse) makes this impossible.

But even the most advanced extrapolation possible from the Grundrisse quote, that can, in a highly schematic way, be applied to the general drift of capitalism, have no immediate relevance to Britain piled high amid the scrap metal of industrial dereliction. British monetarists may have had before all else an industrial and social plan, one that appealed to the foulest instinct of the bourgeoisie and the proletariat, but this has now foundered. Those who stood to really gain have been the financiers in the City of London - as always. Sir Keith Joseph, former Tory Minister for Industry, said on June 19th 1981, barely three weeks before the riots, "there has never been so much money available in this country" locked away in banks, pension funds and insurance companies. He went on to speak colourfully of banks with "money running out of their ears."

This is just the sort of loose talk that gets the labour left hopping mad. Consequently they have once again undertaken to nationalize the banks and the pension funds, which has always been good for a rousing cheer at Labour Party Conferences. How they are going to prevent a flight of capital in the face of such a threat is not clear. But it's a good gambit, able still to reign in some of the proletariat behind an imagined 'red' nationalism. For this reason the industrial bourgeoisie aren't over enthusiastic about such schemes. They know that in the unlikely event of such a thing happening, the proletariat, in the interests of social peace, will pre-empt money that would otherwise have been available for capitalist investment.

MONETARISM. BRITAIN v AMERICA: A MULTITUDE OF SINS OR JUST BAD HOUSE-KEEPING?

Monetarism as practised by Thatcher and Reagan may have eaten out of the same Friedmanite trough, but comparisons all but end right there. In Britain monetarism is not a cultural movement to the degree it is in America. It is brutally economistic, unadorned by born-again Christians, moral majorities and creationists.

Top ranking Tories may in private be sympathetic to regressive sexual codes, and there are backwoods murmurings amongst constituency parties favouring their restoration. But such things as high street chastity centres, successfully sponsored by a Republican Senator from Alabama, will never open in the UK. The Tories lack the money, the will and even the pretence to a "moral majority".

Having a woman as PM has made it harder to convincingly argue that the proper place for women is in the home. Even in America where an unliberated first lady, affecting to not miss wearing a tiara, obediently hosts for the Big White Chief, plans to repeal the Equal Rights Amendment are loaded with contradictions. How come Mrs Schlafly, the sweetheart of this monetarist kinder, kirche and kuchen movement found time to write so many books and be so active in the Republican Women's Federation? In between house cleaning, changing nappies, cooking and ironing for six kids? Or was it all done with a brace or two of black maids?

Irrespective of legislation, either way, mass unemployment does mean women are likely to be more house bound. But by the same token so are men. In fact all the pressures of unemployment ties everyone more to the home, which then becomes as tense as an over crowded prison cell. This is not restoring the family unit, on the contrary straining it to breaking point. Things have come to a sorry pass when eagerly seized on evidence (Mary Whitehouse) of a teen revival in happy families rests on such shaky foundations.

A major political realignment of the drivel that generated The Festival of Light is also unlikely. Campaigns against abortion, porn, and sex n' violence on TV have in the past attracted individuals known for their continuing or former support of the Labour party. Moral conservatism in Britain is in comparison to America a free-floating commodity belonging as much to the establishment left as the right. It is neither militantly for capitalism or implacably hostile towards 'communism' (i.e. totally nationalization or state capitalism) still bearing the imprint of its birth - in particular Thomas Carlyle. There is talk of 'communist' infiltration into the media from time to time, but in Britain the typically rightist muddling of liberalism with 'communism' is a comparative rarity. Media vigilantism in the UK, parting company with its American cousin, is obsessively preoccupied with the great bawd sex, and to a lesser degree by violence.

Homespun virtues combined with a cracker-barrel religious faith in laissez faire capitalism has traditionally been the bedrock of the American right. The obverse is true in Britain: on the hot-tin-roof fleshpots of the unregulated market place, sexual lewdness is the ultimate profiteer. Moreover, in the century or so which has elapsed since the left was first cast as defilers of children etc, it has never been in this country a serious rival to Vanity Fair.

Getting party political backing is not the style of moral rearming politics in Britain. Even if there was such a thing as a plebiscite in Britain when it comes to legislating on morals, a private members bill is preferable because it is unencumbered by the bourgeois voting rights responsible for leading the flock astray in the first place. Fundamentalist movements in the States are obliged to drum up some sort of 'majority' no matter how wildly exaggerated the sums turn out to be. But in the UK the custodianship of public morals is the business of the select few, harking back yet again to the elite quasi-feudal anti-capitalism of its beginnings. Not surprisingly, it shrinks from laying hold of the machinery of publicity, treating radio and television especially as the devil's own handiwork. Lastly, behind the prim and proper demeanour there is no rich ministering angel ready to payroll (or bilk, all depending) every squawk of moral indignation.

And what of creationism in a country where On the Origin of the Species first saw the light of day? The Museum of Natural History in Kensington, London, issued a pamphlet for the public that included the phrase, "If the theory of evolution is true" and was immediately pounced on by the Nature journal. However it was far from being a popularising concession to creationism. It was simply a way of stating if fitness to survive determines the selection of the species, primitive organisms are "excellent solutions". So why the change in complexity? It is a scientific question reflecting the difficulties some dissident biologists now have with Darwin's theory. Not remotely is it likely to herald a rash of court cases or government lobbying as in America.

Only in a couple of instances are extra-economic monetarist comparisons between Britain and America permissible. Both Governments have got the backs up of environmentalists. However, ironically Heseltine (Minister for the Environment) while on the one hand failing to stop farmers from ploughing up National Parks, destroying Sites of Special Scientific Interest and turning the countryside generally into prairie has, in response to the riots, proposed plans to bring back nature into the cities by changing industrial grey belts into green areas. Even here Heseltine trod warily. There has been no hearty slaps on the backs pace the United States Interior Secretary Watt, for farmers preparing to plough up Exmoor. Instead a 'code of conduct' has been got up that panders to traditional folklore by charging capital intensive, agri-business Tesco-type farmers with the custodianship of the hills and dales and trees and flowers. Fat chance.

Finally, turning scrounger/welfare bums into devils incarnate has been endemic to both election campaigns. As a vote catcher, it more than helped swing the election in Thatcher's favour. But she lived to rue the day. Rapidly mounting unemployment was lessening tension between the unemployed and employed who, well before the riots, were beginning to turn a blind eye on a crumbling black economy.

Culture And The TUC.

FRAMING THE PROLETARIAT

The TUC, moving with the times has started to grant full bureaucratic status to ethnic minorities, conning a few into becoming brokers of wage labour. As black equal rights charter chairman Ken Gill said, "the structure of the union should be examined to ensure the removal of barriers which can prevent black workers from reaching union office and decision making bodies (e.g. shop stewards, branch officials, regional and national committees, national officials etc" (The Morning Star, June 17th1981). Dressing itself up as progress, this is the essence of counter-revolution, because respect for trade unionism and other forms of external authority is declining. Ethnic minorities are being sold the lie of democratic integration into the trade union superstructure at the moment of its worldwide demise. Consider the fate of the infamous TUC led Day of Action (May 14th 1980). In a desultory way, the TUC's call to strike was obeyed by 100's of thousands of workers. But the millions of workers who instead went to work that day had not opted to kiss the guvnors arse. The clearest example, the one that best sums up the situation, was provided by that semi-insurrectionary City of Liverpool. Disobeying union instructions, some factory workers toddled off to work as usual that morning only to down tools an hour later after a flair up with management. A wildcat stoppage on, of all days, the TUC's Day of Action! What a paradox, and one so disheartening to both unions and management. As a friend put it, the decision to work or not to work was about quits in its essential ambiguity.

The TUC can't hope to carry on manipulating proletarian anger indefinitely. All they seem able to do successfully is eulogise moments from the historic past of their failed Labour movement, endlessly commemorating the Tolpuddle Martyrs, Peterloo, a watered down version of The Peasants Revolt. Never once have they commemorated the excellent excesses of the Luddites, Captain Swing, and the

Ranters, because they don't conform to the TUC's rulebook of do's and don'ts.

Having become soap opera historians (wait for next year's instalments) with a flair for pageantry, they have learnt to consign the immediate past to the labour museums in the fond hope that class struggle will remain showcase material. The historically patented People's March for Job' was instantly turned into stone when Ken Livingstone, even before the march was officially over, unveiled a commemorative plaque at County Hall. That day County Hall was even thrown open to skinheads who, put off their stride, bemusedly wandered the miles of corridor.

A further wonderfully ludicrous example was provided a few years previously by the Upper Clyde Shipbuilders occupation/work in: the Formica negotiating table around which the shop stewards and management had sat was put on permanent show in a newly created Labour History Museum in Limehouse, London.

The TUC has not lagged in acquiring some knowledge of avant-garde art. They can thank ex '68ers for aiding them to move on from evening classes in oil painting. Their economic committee for the autumn of 1981 ran a special "jobs express" of "gaily decorated" chartered trains stopping at specially arranged meeting places throughout the country. Comparison with Russian Agit prop trains inevitably spring to mind. Even before the carriages started to roll down the track, it meant sweet fuck all.

THE THEATRE OF UNEMPLOYMENT

There can scarcely be a more telling example in recent history of the fragile veneer of organized protest. Four weeks before the Toxteth uprising, a mass demonstration attracting well over 100,000 was held in Trafalgar Square at the end of the People's March for Jobs. All the TUC bigwigs and labour left-wingers were there. The weather-tanned marchers were given pride of place. Applause followed them everywhere. The marchers politely returned the applause. This vast demonstration passed off in an orderly manner. There were no arrests. Not one even reasonable leaflet was to be found. A man with performing budgies brought up the rear. A month later Liverpool 8 was a burning cauldron.

The People's March for Jobs set off from the Pierhead on May the 1st 1981 - Labour Day. The original banner carried by the Jarrow Crusaders in the 1930s hunger march was gingerly unfurled. Insured for £25,000, It was a labour antique and was to be used again in the autumn in another Labour sponsored march in Jarrow itself. On Pierhead, the young unemployed marchers had all been kitted out in green anorak uniforms and natty backpacks. A snappy graphic symbol bearing the legend Peoples March for Jobs had been designed especially. One might as well have sported an I Love New York badge.

In fact design aptitudes had played a major part in the creation of this theatre of protest. When drawing up plans for the March, the organizers had been struck by the visual impact, as refracted through photos of the original crusaders. (Cameras were waiting to record the moment when the march passed through the village of Lavendon in Bucks, sight of the most well known photo of the Jarrow march). Then the impact came mainly through the newspapers, now there was colour telly to think of. So the advice of design teams reflected the depth of change since the 1930s in trade union responses. The original TU sponsored march from Tyneside was got together on a budget of £300. Now the bill exceeded £50,000.

FESTIVAL OF FORGETFULNESS. TRADE UNION RESOLUTIONS AND THE ORGANIZATION OF DEFEAT

Amongst militant Labour party activists and fellow trade unionists, a conscious amnesia is a handy tool. Other than a few days madness on the streets, the summer riots are forgotten, consigned uneasily to oblivion. The official view of the unemployed has hesitantly come back to prevail once more: the unemployed are weak, downtrodden, declasse creatures who shall remain so until the TU's or para-statist bodies shall come to their aid. This conception of powerlessness is institutional. Really they are safeguarding their own jobs and self-importance. Ruth Lister, director of the Child Poverty Action Group (Sept 27th '81) said ... "The unemployed seem to be cowed and don't know what's happening. The TU's and Labour MP's aren't protesting anywhere near enough." This idiot must have closed her eyes to the clamour on the streets.

HISTORY REPEATS ITSELF "THE FIRST TIME AS TRAGEDY – THE SECOND AS A B MOVIE STUNT." (JAMES JOYCE).

The Peoples' March for Jobs in early 1980 stopped at the same point as the famous photo of the 1930s Jarrow Crusade march to London!

The Lingering Death Of Rock 'n' Roll

"They say it's gonna die. But baby let's face it, We just don't know what's gonna replace it" *("Move It" Cliff Richard)*

Ever since punk first came on the scene, more musicians in the UK than ever have been quick to join in supporting a very ill defined socialist cause perceived as coming about, in spite of the anarchist labels, through a political transformation of society. Groups like The Specials, The Jam, Gang of Four, Tom Robinson etc have tagged along behind diffuse campaigns (e.g. racism, unemployment, nuclear disarmament) mounted by Trotskyists, Labour party left and centre, and the trade unions. Without exception, they have been dead to profounder, negative and moreover, broadly based, currents that have prevented these political bodies even at the height of

Thatcher's blitz from recovering their former prestige. Somewhat resembling Bianca Jagger's black sobranie dress-conscious (Marxist Leninist) appeals on behalf of the poor of Central America, groups in the UK have been manoeuvred into passing around the begging bowl with one hand while laying out for a country mansion with the other.

There has been in the UK for some time a fairly general, if not necessarily revolutionary, insistence that music and protest have terminally parted ways. It goes from lefty rags like The Leveller right into the headquarters of the music press. Take for instance one recent issue of The New Musical Express. No post punk, quietly aspiring pop star stared out at passers-by from the newsstand cover. Instead, the wary, slightly paranoiac faces of unemployed teenagers headed towards the annual Tory conference in Blackpool. On page 4 the usual Lowry cartoon. A music executive of Redundant Records Ltd is demanding to know where the voices of the younger generation are, the new Dylan, the Stones - where? A fawning blood sucking music scout is making excuses. The executive cannot hear him. Outside there's a riot going on: the voices of a generation with no credible musical accompaniment.

Cartoonists who make a living from their cartoons are invariably deeply compromised people. Lowry, for instance, usually prefers to fool around with the fascistoid mummery of the music biz. It says much for the state of the industry as a whole to admit the crisis is leagues deeper than faint hearted censuring of Fuhrer like manipulation, compromising pop star cults, lebensraum record companies and dazed audiences. It is often difficult for people from other countries to appreciate just how widespread this view is in the UK. Added to which a resolve to sing in languages other than English is a way of saying, "I'm not in the business to make money."

Around Xmas 1981-82 there was broadcast on radio a program listing "alternative charts" hits of 1981. The Specials, Ghost Town recorded on the commercially successful 2 Tone label got a few bars airing which was ironic considering it shot to No 1 on the British Market Research Bureau's chart during the July days. The BMBR chart is very important to the music industry and to DJ's, especially on Radio 1, when compiling their play lists. But it is far from being the whole story, otherwise the spectacular intrusion of small labels into the major charts would never have been possible. In part the Beeb's traditionally watchful relative autonomy from the grip of big business is responsible for this.

A fair amount of air time on this particular program was taken up playing American singles, enough to make one suspect the credibility of an alternative chart depended here on much tighter controls elsewhere. Telephone conversations with punk groups in the States had been recorded for the program. Replying to criticisms that bands there were "politically feeble" in comparison to the UK, the American musicians could barely contain their anger. "Goddam Limies" hadn't the foggiest notion what the power of the "corporate media" was like in America. The wide difference that now exists between Britain and America suggests that the Anglo/American near monopoly of rock music is riven down the middle. But strong reactions reflecting the different realities are also inevitable whenever Brits and Yanks get together and the subject of music crops up. With Yanks, music is still reckoned to have a modicum of subversive potential, with Limies that response goes right out of the window.

MUSIC AND NOSTALGIA: THE REPRESSION OF A REVOLUTIONARY MEMORY

As a popular music, rock was in real trouble once the promise of a good life for all had elapsed into Cayman Isles bank accounts and bulletproof sanctuaries on Malibu Beach for the successful few. So long as the money was rolling in, this was OK by the giants of the music biz. But it was contrary to the popular traditions of rock n' roll, and not likely to remain that way for long. The music biz may have always wanted to make entertainers out of rock musicians, but it then had to contend with the disaffection of the audience. Come the early 1970s and it was apparent rock music had hit an all time low. The tons and tons of good stuff from the 1950s and 1960s had suddenly given way to the occasional one off. There was no escaping it: rock music was deader than a Dodo and just about the best on offer was Gary Glitter's tongue in cheek fakes, which became even more hilarious as the teen and pre-teen market rose to the bait.

The once important but problematical overlap between music and protest had come to a full stop. It was an unreal time. The world seemed to be settling back into its old ways and the global watershed of 1968-69 had been turned into a trauma of world history. People en-masse were flung into reminiscing, which somehow always stopped short of vital reflections on the revolutionary events of the late '60s. It was a lead up to nowhere and to this historicizing vein there corresponded a much-commented upon nostalgic revival of early1960s hits.

But no matter how hard memory of the world-shaking events of the late1960s was repressed, a still unfolding class struggle was bound to effect this essentially conservative reminiscing. And in the UK, it took the form of constantly mulling over class origins; a search for roots which in the restricted sense implied here, safe guarded the class system. The main culprits were union bureaucrats, shop stewards, teachers, part-time lecturers and social workers etc coming from working class backgrounds, whose structural position finally pitted them against the cause they were espousing. This contradiction some years later was eventually to work through into the punk explosion, which also played on this extraordinarily long lasting demagogic response to class divided society in the UK.

The class struggles of the early 1970s in Britain barely affected the music biz. It was a period of consolidation for the musical majors, a time to follow up the consequences of the quite superficial rapport that existed between superstardom and the largely working class audience. To restructure for any length of time the audience/performer nexus in favour of the new pantheon of Hollywood royalty was desperately out of tune with the changing economic climate that eventually would push the proletariat in a different direction. Only for a time could stage door Johnny's be expected to look on the latter day Rod Stewart - a working class lad made good - without starting to get angry with the mother. Later, Sid Vicious of the Sex Pistols was to invert this relationship by pretending to shoot passive onlookers. It was simply a variation on the same old scene, but for the big companies it was unsettling.

Big capital in private hands is rarely sympathetic to popular movements and when the punk/independent label explosion occurred, the big companies at first reacted to it with a mixture of fear and loathing. Then scenting a profit they began to give chase. It cannot be stressed too often that punk (as a musical experience) was a popular rather than class movement, in which the interests of musician and small capital were kept in a state of precarious equilibrium. It brought together 'creativity' and venture capital in a way the musical majors, their attention riveted on declining profit margins, zooming production/ admin costs and increasing expenditure on aggressive marketing, were no longer capable of pulling off. Fortunately some independent labels like Tony Wilson of Factory Records have been honest enough to admit "you make money and something special by investing and believing in talent, not by marketing crap."

Throughout the 1970's, popular music, from bloated corporate rock to new wave, has been in a situation of constant crisis. In spite of repeated transfusions, music has not been able to recover its former powers. Punk began as an avowed attempt to destroy rock n' roll, and the architect of this musical situationism (one of the by now familiar recuperations of Situationist theory), Malcolm Mclaren, called his company Glitter Best, emphasizing the continuity between hoax and the guilty pretence of new wave.

Malcolm was able to mint "cash from chaos" just so long as publicity conscious notoriety overran more radical perspectives. He was the last buccaneer of the music biz, but ironically he was unmasked and music's claim to even a pseudo reality crashed. Punk had wavered as it dipped in and out of the music scene between genuine working class aggression and show case pretence. Attempting to live up to yet another concocted scandal for the sake of a few sensational headlines eventually drove Sid Vicious to murder and suicide. A sticker read "Mclaren - wanted for vicious murder". However as an ideology of radical art, punk was lethal to all who got involved in it. Never before in the history of rock music had so much emphasis been placed on not 'selling out', which implied a critique of capitalism was taking root. So far so good. At the same time Punk's original mentors have sold out with indecent haste, forfeiting all open house claims to being a mass based egalitarian movement, as individuals and groups rose into the super tax bracket and stardom.

It took time to sink in, but those who had meant at least some of it, felt ever so badly let down. This bewildering mixture of image and reality, astounding hypocrisy and honesty even impacted on some of the recording artists whose heads had been turned by fat cheque books. Poly Styrene, not happy as The Police were making "giant steps, walking on the moon" fancies she has made several trips to Mars and is only now beginning to comedown.............................

When rock music borrowed from more authentic R. and B. sources, essential details that place the music firmly in the context of everyday living would frequently be omitted. Punk did the same, only this time by recuperating revolutionary critiques. Take for instance the flysheet promoting the Sex Pistols, Holidays in the Sun. The only reasonable bubble speak is the last line... "A cheap holiday in other people's misery." Otherwise it is a nonsensical mosaic of deservedly throwaway lines. "Wanna see some history cos I got a reasonable economy." (?????) "I don't want a holiday in the sun, I wanna go to the new Belsen." (huh, you what?????) The Clash also at a recent concert in Paris refused to publicise the plight of libertarian prisoners in Spain jailed on raps ranging from 10 to 40 years. Yet they were prepared to devote an entire album of 3 LPs to the Leninist/Guevarist Sandanistas in Nicaragua whom in comparison haven't an ounce of revolutionary potential.

Fashionable recuperation: Situationist theory as performance! (The wimmin punk group merely plagiarised the jacket of Fredy Perlman's first-to-be-published English translation of Debord's The Society of the Spectacle as record cover promo).

"GET BACK, GET BACK, GET BACK TO WHERE YOU ONCE BELONGED..."

Like most populist movements the proletariat was important to the new wave just so long as it never had the final say. It was amazing the speed at which the relationship between punters and groups began to turn sour once a number of punk musicians began to make it. We can recall talking in 1978 to a couple of unemployed brush hands in their late teens that only a year ago had been squatting with The Police. The group had really started to make it and rake in the dough and one of the youths in particular was full of contempt referring to The Police as "cunts" (a kind of obligatory sexist put-on). His dismissal of the group was damningly retrospective because he could find nothing nice to say about them, even when they were just squatters who liked to play music.

This attitude reflects some of the savagery and complexity of the social apartheid. Those who make it can never be washed 'clean', because it stems almost from an accident of birth. This subjectivity has been the basis of a workable paradox, which UK capitalism has effectively applied to keep the working class in its place. Because origin is primary and structure secondary within these topsy-turvy scales of class identification, it is feasible for a PM to say, "I'm working class mate" - and to a point get away with it.

The independent labels have manipulated this subjectivity to their own advantage. Once it was clear the Sex Pistols, The Clash, The Stranglers were not destined to a life on the dole, it made nonsense to sing of survival drudgery. On the maintenance of this paradox depends the survival of the music industry because the consumer is continually breaking away from their unfaithful representations in search of ever more accurate expressions that catch both the intensity of their desires and the reality of everyday miseries. To a previously unprecedented degree, pop music in the 1970s has played on class and roots. Because of its associations with reggae, "Roots" has something of a racial connotation but as will be seen, class and roots, as a concept of identity was, for both black and white, interchangeable, forming a part of the corporatist strategies of independent labels.

When the televised version of Alex Haley's Roots was first screened on British TV, New Musical Express devoted a front cover of the magazine and a centre page spread to the book. To a black living in America and the Caribbean to know your ancestors arrived there bound hand and foot in a slave ship matters, but what overriding interest can that serve in a largely white music industry in the UK? In fact the industry had just lent over backwards to acknowledge the UK's particular form of 'rootism', which by a sort of infinite regress allows a Lord (Tony Benn for example - the former Lord Stansgate) to lay claim to working classness on the basis of some long dead ancestor!!

This typically British duplicity was also present in Punk. It came as a surprise to learn later how many musicians had come from high up backgrounds, been to posh schools etc. One would think from The Clash's first LP that the entire group had looked out on was the Westway flyover in London W10 from the top of some tower block. It later turned out Uncle Joe Strummer had been to a public school and Dad was a diplomat. Lack of honesty in these matters in the UK is astonishing and Americans for one find this ability to successfully cover all traces very puzzling. It tended to confirm their impression Britain is a nation of born double agents.

The ideal of the independent labels is a music business made up of small independent producers. If they could ever get a political act together it would undoubtedly include the disbanding of the centralised monopolies of the music business. As a fraction of the bourgeoisie they do engage in struggle against their far more powerful brethren. For example, Branson of Virgin Records in a statement damaging to the interests of the big companies, drew attention to the way they hyped charts. Exposures like these are welcomed by the majority of musicians because more of them are likely to be represented in the record market if the practise of chart hyping is stopped. But it does not automatically mean musicians will therefore speak kindly of the independents because they are when all is said and done into the business of making money out of musicians.

It is frequently overlooked how the meteoric rise to fame and fortune of mid 1950s rock musicians was helped along in the early stages by independent labels who hoped they could shift maybe 100,000 copies of a record. Pretty soon they found they could sell a million - even more - and the likes of Atlantic began to enter the big league with a monthly turnover of millions of dollars. Some of these labels began almost as a spare time hobby, which in view of today's developments has a familiar ring about it.

LEFTIES AND MUSIC

Though today's independents form part of a growth dynamic endemic to capitalism, the changed political and social climate prodded the independent labels,, particularly in the UK into supporting radical sounding proposals stemming originally from trade union and Labour party left wingers and Trotskyist militants. Branson, for instance, closed some of his record shops on the TUC Day of Action in February 1980.

The unique rapprochement between the union biz and the music apparatus is further advanced by their common involvement with mass youth unemployment. There is a certain inevitability in the way trade unions are drawn into making clumsy pronouncements on the music scene, unthinkable even 5 years ago. This recognition is gratefully acknowledged by the music press, and they in turn, particularly the New Musical Express, reciprocate by continuing to propagate hoary clichés left parliamentarians are anxious to keep alive. These points are highlighted in incidents which occurred in the Peoples' March for Jobs in May/June 1980 and in the NME response to the riots. When the March reached Manchester on May 8th 1981 (two months later almost to the day Moss Side erupted) amongst the scores of union present to welcome the marchers were a band of drummers from Moss Side who had been prevented from performing through loudspeakers by the police. A regional organiser of UCATT (the building workers union) had immediately sprung to their defence. "It's disgraceful" he said, "the police are coming down on their own class."

This stupid view, which fortunately the people of Moss Side disregarded, is also echoed by the 'politically aware' music press. In a pitiful article on the riots, in NME journalist Chris Salewicz came out with the following asinine remark: "the government is playing a dangerous game with people's lives, the kid's lives and the policeman's lives - working class lives". Frivolous word-smithing was unable this time to dress up the poverty of music journalism. Waving aside Foot's doddering, Salewicz said the only constructive 'political' moves he had heard of came from the Labour party Young Socialists who proposed "the idea of collective action through a socialist transformation of the Labour party, as the only way through and out of our problems. For sure we can't dance our way out of them. End of sermon."

End of Chris Salewicz. There is not the merest hint of ridding the planet of commodities, the state, wage labour and what have you, and it was from the same conservative vantage point that The Specials judged the riots. Their record Ghost Town as an advance warning "'No job to be had in this country/ can't go on no more, people gettin' angry") called for further comment. "I wish" said Lynval Golding, "the government would listen to our song. We're able to communicate with the kids at their own level. We talk to them in pubs, we know what their problems are." The song's success in the charts had been undone in the streets. Had Ghost Town had the government's ear, then things might have been set to rights by courtesy of the state and the riots stopped before they ever started. A depressing prospect.

Some six months later and another ex-Specials member Terry Hall (now the Fun Boy Three) was still harping on the same old tune. "Ghost Town was number 1 in the charts and there was still riots and fights long after that, so it didn't achieve anything so far as stopping it."

Short of social revolution, stopping the riots isn't an achievement to be proud of, and Terry Hall because the record never went even half way to doing this, was let off the hook. But if wishes were omnipotent, Ghost Town should have capped its success in the Hit Parade by clearing the streets. (Ghost Towns?) Whether he knows it or not Terry Hall is siding with all the obstacles that prevented the riots from heralding in a full-scale social revolution.

NEWS FROM JAMAICA: What 'appen?

The present wave of politicized rock and journalistic comment provides a mandate that a 'left' leaning party political structure might conceivably use to far greater effect in counteracting, particularly amongst the young, a tendency towards chronic abstentions. But it is to Jamaica we must turn to find the most perfected example in modern times of state patronage of contemporary music. Under Michael Manley's populist social democratic regime (1972/80) reggae, though sustained totally by private capital, became a focus of political patronage. Manley made it his duty to put in appearances at special reggae concerts, gaining political benefit from his overtures to Rastafarianism and recourse to patois. In the One Love Peace Concert held in 1978, accompanying the riddims' were huge placards exhorting the people to "Build Jamaica with Discipline" – "Work Together for Self-Reliance" – "Forward With the People's Constitution".

These concerts may still prove to have been a politico/aesthetic experimental prototype, giving a renewed lease of life through the glitter wax of art to this 'battle for production', analogous to Stalinism. Needless to say the revolutionary contents of these festivals are nil.

But the ease with which Manley and the PNP (People's National Party) manipulated reggae musicians meant forfeiting some of their radical claims. The rush to patronise reggae by Manley and the PNP more or less coincided with a draconian IMF loan leading quickly to a further fall in working class living standards (during the 8 years of 'democratic socialism', the cost of living increased 320%), which lost Manley a lot of support. Manley had tried hard to manipulate the more corporate aspects of "black consciousness" in Jamaica (including calling himself "Joshua") but in the last analysis religious and racial mystification were unable to make good rising working class discord.

Behind the tough exterior, reggae has a party political soft core- Manley's premiership proceeds from reggae musicians performing at these politically inspired concerts went towards social work and job creation schemes. In fact the politics of reggae has for a long time been taken up with the management of the unemployed - and its special message for the unemployed has always been to "simmer down" (the title of Marley's first record a tranquilliser for Kingston's rude boys).

Without seriously affecting reggae's doctrinal credibility, Jamaican fault finding has on the whole been far more of an open secret on the UK scene. There is in Jamaica an organised interface between unemployment and political gangsterisms (prior to the election in 1980 as many as 700 people, the majority of them poor, were killed by armed gangs of JLP - Jamaican Labour party - and the PNP) which provided a platform from which reggae musicians without losing face can call for peace.

In contrast, the experience of unemployment in Britain is altogether far more social and let's hope it stays that way. Black Uhuru, appalled at the speed at which youth in Eglington (Canada) Utica Avenue (New York) and Kingston (Jamaica) reach for the holster are compelled to recognise Brixton youth "leave their 45 Smith and Wesson pistol". For the present, the absence of guns and gun toting political partisanship on the streets of Britain means it is less easy to manipulate violence, and social questions can come more out into the open. Enough finally to make nonsense of Black Uhuru's concluding line: all the kids want to do is "go to school"!!! Besides the unique varieties of social breakthrough now being chanced in Britain, such lyrics fade into sermonizing nothingness - and what remains is the unsatisfying aesthetic of the music qua music.

Photo left: The above sleeve cover is an example of dingbat recuperation of the riots put out by Scottish Oi group, The Exploited. This directionless mess of quasi fascism and anti fascism, thrown together with a visceral yen for violence for its own sake, gets nowhere fast on 45 rpm. Reasonable lucidity, "I'm filled with aggression / Want to smash your television / Saturday night you watch TV / Saturday night does nothing for me." Gets mixed up with Storm Trooper allusions, a celluloid Hitler, memories of Mclaren's "Belsen was a gas" and just in case you're completely lost by now, ends with a final clarion call for "CLASS WAR".

Photo left: One Love Peace Concert, Spring 1978. Bob Marley with the Jamaican PM and leader of the Peoples' National Party, Michael Manley and the future PM and leader of the Jamaican Labour Party, Edward Seaga.

A ROCKING BLACK ECONOMY: A MODICUM OF RESPECTABILITY

Like no other phase of rock music, new wave drew on the experience of unemployment and a refusal to even contemplate doing the few wretched badly paid jobs still available. Within days it was known as "dole queue rock", providing a shop-window on unemployment. It spot-lighted in particular unemployed school leavers, giving them a measure of incorporation into the circus not achievable to older, often chronically unemployed and unemployable people, who had 'settled in' to a lifetime on the dole. Being unemployed and a musician represented, between signing on, a sort of vagrant populism awaiting valorisation into a gob soaked star. When new wave broke, it was in government circles beginning to sink in that mass unemployment was here to stay. Means had in the long term to be found to alleviate the stigma of unemployment. But with the Tories election victory in the short term, the unemployed were to be harassed and made a scapegoat for all of society's ills.

Choosing to stir things up like this meant the Tories were unable to apply the lessons that could be learnt from this freelance experimental sound lab into how best to manage the unemployed. Even so, the odd shoestring recording studio can now be found at the back of youth clubs. And social workers any day are a more durable creation of capitalism than Thatcherism. Monetarists in the UK had no stated artistic preferences, but they were bound to doubly dislike new wave because of its past association with the black economy. Records were being pressed and financed from out of the black economy, even if signing on and doing the bizo in the seediest job imaginable on the side was an exaggerated creation of punk mythology. Unemployed punks constantly ran the risk of being caught by the fraud squads at gigs. There was one particularly mad example when a group were busted playing at the local labour exchange Xmas hop.

Up to approximately this point, the Labour party and the trade union apparatus had despised the black economy, regarding it as a cesspool for scabs. Now they had cause to change their mind. Bad taste aside, the ideology of punk could, with a few exceptions, be fitted into a leftist framework, and with every RAR (Rock against Racism) carnival and gig, new wave gained in respectability. This unprecedented contact with a mass 'socially conscious' art was a vital stepping stone in trade union tolerance of the black economy - or shadow economy as it was politely rechristened. Having to stretch a point or two does not mean the TU apparatus and Labour party dominated local state in the major towns and cities are prepared to let the black economy run riot. But they would like to keep it in political reserve by progressively linking it up with subsidised community-based industries, co-ops and training initiatives geared to solving local unemployment. They hope against hope all will become eventually self-supporting - perhaps on the day the TUC's Programme for Recovery is implemented and begins to take effect.

This eventual objective is not intrinsically alien to the present Tory government. The focal point of the bitter wrangling is the amount of government expenditure needed to save capitalism. In fact the Tories have granted to the black economy a de facto legality if it can be shown a person is drawing benefit for as long as it takes to get a viable business off the ground. Self-help must be paid for and a pop group that makes it from the dole queues to needing the services of an accountant is part of that mould.

"YOU DON'T KNOW HOW LUCKY YOU ARE - BACK IN THE USSR"

State regulation of the conditions of small business is a product of centralised management that has grown immeasurably since World War II. But it is still a far cry from the economic and ideological constraints that the state capitalist regimes of the East bring to bear on the activities of small-scale business.

The Eastern bloc has not so far effectively co-opted rock music, unemployment and the refusal to work with anything like the West's success (though the refusal to work in its essence can never be recuperated). There it is a much more explosive combination where riots at rock concerts, unless dealt with promptly, can easily spill over into a more general rebellion (e.g. East Berlin 1978). Moreover pop groups don't possess the economic and ideological freedoms their counterparts take for granted in the west. Short of a major shake up, it is virtually impossible for rebel musicians to double-deal the proletariat by flaunting, as they take their leave of it, all the insulting trappings of success.

WHEN THE MUSICAL MODE OF PRODUCTION CHANGES..........?

A thorough going critique of music, one that doesn't skirt around the difficulties, is hard to get going. To dismiss everything that has happened since the mid 1950s as the diabolical work of musical conglomerates out to ensnare the proletariat just won't do. Rock music has possessed, from the mid 1950s onwards, a mass following which no other art form has ever achieved. Yet rock is inescapably caught up in capitalism's heady distancing mirror system of representation and contradiction, which its largely proletarian audience reacts to in a relevant manner.

But so far there have been few attempts to analyse rock music as a specific branch of capitalist production. The music and the rock artists hogged the limelight while managers, record producers, recording engineers, financiers have gone about their business unobserved. The few existing examples are at best ambivalent and undermined by a failure to hit hard. Charlie Gillett in his book on Atlantic Records rightly says the "book is about songs and money", but he then goes on to pussy foot around praising Atlantic as a "record company with character - not a faceless corporation" extending even into Atlantic's New York office which is "lively and efficient - compared to any other bureaucratic office I have ever seen."

Perhaps this is what is meant by the soulful corporation? Gillett's book can quite legitimately be read as a plea addressed to other music corporations like RCA, Capitol, EMI etc. imploring them to mend their ways. There is not one even telltale hint in Gillett's book Making Tracks that musical companies, with the rest of capitalism, must be abolished.

MUSIC'S SUPERCESSION......................

More than any other art form, music gives off a sense of life bringing into play, sex, love and body rhythms. To even contemplate severing Hendrix - that music equal of Charlie Parker - from currents tearing America apart in the late 1960s is unthinkable.

Musical venues rarely provide a cathartic release of energy, and when the clubs close the real business of the evening commences where the music has left off. Beside, what happened outside the Dalston discos in May/June 1981 and the club 200 in Balham in July 1981, the notorious gig by the 4 Skins at the Hamborough Tavern is a nasty irrelevance.

In the first of a series of urban riots to hit Britain, the Notting Hill Carnival riots of 1976/77 frustrated expectations of fulfilment, and the provocative presence of the police contrived to produce an explosion. They made as great an impact on the 'black community' as on 'white society' because it was at once apparent to many people that West Indian youth born in this country despised the traditional Trinidadian merry go round in the streets of Notting Hill. Appeals from the organisers to stop "wrecking carnival" went unheeded and crestfallen steel band floats and nerve shattering sound systems called it a day and went home, sorry they were prevented from playing through to the early hours as they had done on previous years.

Unlike the police and the plate glass shop windows, there was never any question of the music machine being directly in the line of fire (tho' rumour has it, on occasion it nearly was). But for the bands and owners of sound systems the gnawing realisation they had been unceremoniously pushed aside was hard to stomach. Even if it was still pitched at a pretty low level, they had been made the object of a critique that almost by default included music.

There is an even chance that at least some of the young blacks taking part in the Carnival riots also belonged to mobile sound systems. Some use it as a means of topping up dole payments and often are remarkably unassuming people. Though they are involved in music, the artistic ego is not for them, having acquired a take it or leave it attitude to music.

This casualness is amongst other things a product of technical factors relating to the increased mechanisation of music eroding the status of manual dexterity on an instrument. Co-incidentally, the greatest impetus to this development has come through the evolution of reggae in Jamaica where the part played by electronic processes in the recording studio has pushed live performances more into the background. Dub grew from the mobile discos and sound systems. King Tubby, one of the first innovators, was originally by trade an electrical engineer. Shot through with massive voltages of reverb and echo, the essentials of bass, drum, keyboard and vocals were dropped in and out of the mix in random sequence. Small wonder then that black kids in the UK lean more towards sound systems than to becoming themselves performing artists. In contradictory ways they are already leaving behind the concept of the artistic individual.

There are now so many inter-related technical and subjective factors pressing towards the supercession of the musician and the music industry. The making of music is becoming available to all. And for many years, like few other 'folk' traditions, rock has reserved a special place for the 3 chord wizard. But the 'cult of genius' and sales combining as never before, lifted the chosen few to a higher, much more well off plane, where they alone were the music masters.

It was an inevitable sequel to the gross capitalisation of music, involving something approaching a signing away of common property rights. This conveyance was made possible through the connivance of professional musicians set on making a superlative career out of music. Professional musicians who in no time at all like to regard themselves as such goddamn important people with special privileges, already are the targets of derisive comments, but it still needs to be made much more explicit. For the moment the pro's main line of defence is to pull the populist wool, something all professionals do once their role is in jeopardy. Hence a critique of music is organically connected to recovering other functions which capitalism has withheld from the proletariat. There must be a huge demolition job on music. Only when the planet is rid of commodities will music cease to fall well short of our desires but then can we be sure it will be called music? Until that beautiful dawn down with musicians! And while we are at it, down with all art and artists. It has been said before but its comeback is long overdue.

Race not class. An anti Nazi League tableau from 1978. A liberal campaign for liberal minded professionals, the ANL was set up in 1977 by a detestably middle class crew after the success of the national front in the GLC elections. The founding statement was drawn up by Ernie Roberts, ex-CND campaigner and former Gen. Sec. of the AUEW, Peter Hain, then a Post Office Workers' Union research officer, and organizer of 'Stop the 1970 Tour' opposing the South African cricket tour and Paul Holborrow, former teacher, freelance journalist and member of the SWP. Taking it to the limit even one time could not be more alien to this lot. A year earlier RAR (Rock Against Racism) had set up shop in response to David Bowie's camp fascism and Eric Clapton's bad mouthing of black musicians. RAR was founded by Larry Lensman a designer (NB) and the two organizations started to work hand in hand as finger wagging anti fascist, but not anti capitalist, musical tents were pitched next to the likes of Brian Clough (the real manager of the NF – Notts Forest) and Arthur Scargill. The flogging of anti fascism – the badges, the posters, the instantly recognizable ANL lollipop with the red arrow symbol, deeply affected more TUC backed campaigns like The People's March for Jobs.

Crime And Punishment

"Modern prisoners are imperfectable since they are perfect. There is nothing left to do but to destroy them'. *Victor Serge: Men in Prison. (1914)*

IN THE SLAMMER AND THE KEYS THROWN AWAY

The sum total of those arrested and imprisoned at the end of the riot week reached over 2,500. Initially they were going to be accommodated in overflow army camps like Rolleston, which had been used to house prisoners during the recent prison officers pay dispute. Though not exactly "veritable concentration camps" as Tass (Russian News Agency, July 14th 1981) would have it, if the prison officers had still been in dispute the camps would have been run by the army. The Act (The

Imprisonment Temporary Provisions Act) was passed 12 months before in 1980. It looks suspiciously like a step in the direction of a military state, even though prison officers' disputes are likely in future to break out once more. In December 1981 for example, the screws, because of overcrowding, refused to take any more short term prisoners sentenced by the courts. Pressure had softened up the hard-boiled screws who, casting about, decided the arguments of the formerly hated prison reformers best suited their 'industrial' action. However the quality of this mercy is measured in droplets ready, as the screws are to send prisoners to army camps to serve their porridge.

WHITELAW, THE BEAKS AND MOB RULE

As was only to be expected, pressure on the Tory government to introduce special riot packages during and after riot week was particularly intense. They had after all been elected on a law 'n' order ticket. However the Home Secretary, Willie Whitelaw had been forewarned many weeks prior to the rioting that the prisons were fit to burst, and that a further influx of short term prisoners could prove catastrophic. Even before the first stone was thrown, Whitelaw had got ready the 'overflow' army camps which he then proceeded to pass off as the Tory government's response to the clamour coming mainly from the media for new measures to deal with the rioting. There was much talk for instance of reviving the Riot Act, which had been on the statute book ever since the days of the rampaging London mobs in the 17th century and repealed, incredibly, only in 1967. Under the terms of this Act anyone arrested on the scene of a riot was presumed guilty and access to a jury denied automatically. Tories with ministerial posts have for the moment backed away in haste from introducing such draconian measures but this should not blind us to the existence of powerful ministerial currents favouring increased sentencing powers for magistrates (responsibility for administering the Riot Act was left mainly to magistrates) and squashing the right to opt for trial by jury in a higher court for a whole number of offences. (Since this was written a modified Riot Act of sorts has been proposed by the Law Commission. The three new statutory offences of riot, affray and unlawful association can be bent for as much as it takes to get a conviction. For example if three people should heartily agree on the need for determined resistance to some injustice and attempt to convince others they could wind up doing five years. These proposals are not as arbitrary as the original Riot Act but they're getting warmer.) It might be said of Thatcherite Toryism that reform and the blackest judicial reaction chop and change repeatedly in the same pickled brain cells.

However, even for Thatcherism, pragmatic considerations have had their sway. Solely because of conditions in UK prisons, Whitelaw alone had to perform a penal 'U' turn even for short-term prisoners who had served one third of their sentences. The plan was thwarted by judges and magistrates who warned Whitelaw they would increase sentences to compensate if ever the proposals because law.

Faced with the might of the judiciary, Whitelaw's retreat back to square one only served to underpin the instantly recognisable 'independence' of the British judiciary which is altogether such an anomalous feature of the legal system in the UK.

The ease with which individuals can end up in stir in Britain is for many a continual nightmare. Hence features on prison life put together by liberal minded prison reformers are read and watched by masses of people with a fascinated horror, (e.g. The BBC TV documentary inside Manchester's Strangeways nick regularly drew audiences of 8 million. The programme obviously did not call for any unconditional, revolutionary demand for the abolition of prisons). Add to the scales the fact that Britain has a prison population in excess of any European country and we are faced with the most notorious example in modern bourgeois democracy of judicial insularity, pigheaded obstinacy and ignorance.

In truth the Tories promise of stern measures to deal with the rioters was all piss in the wind. That was left to the care of the judiciary holed-up in their jealously guarded territory, which is as the Tories would have wanted it originally, as they were set on restoring a hypothetical 'civil'/'political' division associated with laissez faire capitalism. It is the greatest irony of Tory rule that they have been steam-rollered into attempting to wring changes out of a sector of society they revered among the most.

The sentences meted out are frightened. 8 years here, 5 years there and just for trashing or torching with molotovs. Truly if The Angry Brigade - despite their terrorist illusions - had been active in the 19 80s they'd have got 50 years each. Those that have been consigned to the slammer have received little publicity apart from snippets in the more 'concerned' newspapers. A high proportion of the rioters coming up in court were unemployed, significantly increasing their chances of facing jaundiced magistrates and judges. It is commonplace now to link the work ethic to the rise of industrial capitalism, but the relentless persecution of the workless, especially among the judiciary, has far older roots in Britain.

Marx devoted a chapter in Capital entitled "'Bloody legislation against the expropriated" which still makes harrowing reading. In it he describes how from Tudor times beggars expropriated from any means of subsistence were branded, striped, lashed and imprisoned. The backdrop to this torture was the genesis of ground rent in the countryside. Various statutes belonging to a recognisably capitalist legal system set out in grisly detail what the local judiciary was empowered to cut. It would be silly to suggest that statutes passed in 1530 had a direct bearing on vengeful judges sitting in session during the summer of1981. But equally, old habits die hard (especially in long lived institutions like the British judiciary) and the judicial frame of mind lingers on. Any explanation of the atrocious prison sentences must, in part at least, be traced back far into the venerable past. To the day the first ear was chopped off to be exact.

In modern day Britain workers, in comparison, possess a far greater immunity from prosecution, and haywire rulings affecting powerful groups of workers (Denning and Co.) tend to be over-ruled double quick in more realistic courts of appeal (usually the House of Lords.) The bourgeoisie have been scared shitless of introducing legislation to curb industrial disputes (e.g. the Heath's government ill fated Industrial Relations Act) ever since the traumatic weekend in July 1972 when five dockers were bundled off to Pentonville nick. On the Monday morning, following a breathless example of 'judicial' fiat, they were released under a legal loophole. We might be wrong in accrediting this piece of legal pie in the sky to an attempt to storm Pentonville prison and a wildcat general strike beginning to sweep like a prairie fire through the UK.

Even though the unemployed cannot use the industrial weapons of strikes and occupations of plants, more could have been done to save arrested rioters from the wrath of the judiciary. In order to publicise the plight of those imprisoned and awaiting trial, public buildings could have been occupied. But no inner city neighbourhood assembly with some degree of permanence arose from the ashes and any proposals along these lines were hemmed in by lack of a public forum. When for instance, in a very different setting, striking workers at the Ascon company in Vigo (c.f. The Poverty of Unionism in Wildcat Spain Encounters Democracy) rioted, trashed banks, stores, torched cars, built barricades etc. they did so under the cover of an assembly led strike where in spite of manipulation by the strike committee and unions, the shortcomings and successes of the actions undertaken were openly discussed.

When a society is ravaged by recurrent crises like Britain, the judiciary and penal system will be among the first of the state's guardians to feel the strains. That is why to defer to tradition and hope for the best as Whitelaw did when confronting the judiciary is unhistorical. They are a different breed from what they were in the 19th century because the underlying situation has dramatically worsened and Britain is likely over the coming years to be faced with a revolutionary upheaval.

Once this happens, the law loses its pretence to equity (necessary for its continued legitimation) and becomes increasingly arbitrary. Violent hiccups appear within the normal framework of bourgeois judicial rule. Combined with a growing police licence (even to kill and be excused on the grounds of "justifiable force" in the case of the school teacher Blair Peach, not to mention the much publicised dubious deaths of Jimmy Kelly, Liddle Towers, Barry Prosser and others while in custody) the system of 'civil liberties,' once the proud boast of the British ruling class and which many political refugees like Anarchist Johann Most to his cost, took for granted, is now lurching crazily sideways.

Though the punishments handed out to the rioters were exemplary and constitute a break with the traditions of 'fair play' normally deferred to by the British legal system, they still form a continuum with the system. British law is notoriously based on precedent, having the demeanour of a higher political power able to undermine statute law passed in Parliament if it should offend the judiciary's anachronistic code of right and wrong. The recent Law Lords ruling abolishing London's cheap fares policy dusted off as legal justification a quaint 19th century law requiring public transit systems to pay their way as part of their "fiduciary duty". In the rest of the world it is accepted that all major city transit systems run at a loss.

There have of course traditionally been safeguards in its procedures simply as law, to check that the inherent wilfulness of British law does not get out of hand (special judges conferences for examples where notes are compared). Failing that in the case of sentencing 'aberrations', the Lord Chief Justice might have responded, as on other occasions, to declarations of conscience-smitten outrage, provided they came from respected pillars of the establishment. But none of it was brought into play over the sentencing of rioters. It marks a watershed in law as practised in the UK and a sickening foretaste of things to come. Behind the robes, wigs, baronial manners and legal pedanticism of this idiosyncratic cabal of geriatric bigots, eccentric mystics, and truncheon fetishists a weakness for sadism has finally slipped the leash.

THE PEOPLE'S DISPENSARIES FOR SICK JUSTICE

There are plenty of countervailing forces around trying their level best to check that the Big J(ustice) doesn't run amok. The bottom rung, if you like, of the alternating judicial ladder, though it includes influential bodies like the Parliamentary All Party Penal Affairs Group. Actually a report by this group (Young Offenders - A Strategy for the Future) was published, on the dot (July 7th 1981) during riot week. The report called for a reversal of the trend towards locking up more and more "young offenders".

The report's appearance was at the time all but drowned beneath disciplinarian howls of outrage, but it isn't true either to say the gates were flung wide to an absent welcome. The same can be said of similar groups (e.g. The Howard Group for Penal Reform). Briefly their main aims are reform of the legal system, community policing, and continuing to preach the gospel of non-custodial sentences, in order to reduce the prison population. It is all done with an eye to circumventing "random law enforcement" before it is too late.

Fortunately the normally deceptive radicalism of their congruent statements was shown up by events to be quite explicitly not revolutionary. A case in point. The General Secretary of the National Council for Civil Liberties, Patricia Hewitt, was moved to write to The Times (July 16th 1981) condemning just about every injustice in sight - C.S. gas, mass screening of the population in N. Ireland, rubber bullets, water cannon, riot acts, curfews. But trouble in the streets for once made it clear which side of the fence the NCCL was on. "It is appalling" the Gen. Sec. of the NCCL wrote, "that police officers should now be facing petrol bombs."

The illusions of these pressure groups flow from their conception of law as inherently able to 'fairly' manage profound social crises'. A national body of lawyers, the Legal Action Group, condemned for instance proposals to introduce a new riot act. A new riot act it said would "have serious implications for the criminal justice system which needs to be more not less fair at times of political and social unrest."

All historical experience points way to the contrary, and what happened in the courts recently in Britain ain't no miscarriage of justice. 'Fairness' is the property of stable bourgeois regimes because there comes a stage when class conflict reaches a point of no return, and the bourgeoisie is left to restore the rule of capital with every means at its disposal. At these moments getting the consent of the proletariat becomes an unattainable luxury.

The ultra legalistic statements (re the above) that radical lawyers have a tendency to come out with are historically blind for other reasons. Radical lawyers are a product of the tensions between the two basic classes of society. Depending on the degree to which the neutrality of law is accepted as common currency, they stand or fall. They operate between the two main classes, having a firm anchor in neither. Their concept of the law as neutral to some degree must inhibit genuinely revolutionary class struggle. The judicial apparatus is after all a state apparatus. To insist on the increased vigilance of the law ('more fair not less fair') is merely a way of sensitising the state, not a prelude to its abolition. When laws are broken en masse and authority openly defied in every nook and cranny, the state is disintegrating. When it gets to this stage, law is pushed to the brink of annihilation, being replaced with the developing momentum of proletarian social justice. Caught in the crossfire. the radical lawyers are only likely to dither, raising an ineffectual finger of rebuke at the excesses of contending sides, as they become daily more tragic figures.

There was one outstanding example of this in the days following the Brixton riot in April 1981. Several papers mentioned that Rudi Narayan, the black lawyer who had helped defend the Bristol rioters was given a rough reception in Brixton when he attempted to capitalise on the events there. According to the Anarchist twice yearly 'eXtra', the Brixton Defence Committee dropped the demand for a general amnesty of all arrested and fearing trouble, called off a demonstration. Narayan never once made it clear in public whether he was opposed to the proposals or not. The law was, it seems, the law. The severity of the law against blacks helped make Narayan. The severity of their response is exposing him for what he is.

TRIBAL WAR. LAW AND THE SURVIVAL OF THE STATE

The Bristol riot in April 1980 broke like an unexpected thunderclap on the British scene. It came from out of the blue on the weekend the steel strike, the longest in post-war history, was fizzling out. Because it looked at the time an isolated incident and not the first of many, the bourgeoisie could afford certain luxuries. They searched their consciences for an explanation, which largely helped sheath the avenging sword of Justice. All the defendants who elected to go for trial by jury were acquitted. It took nearly a year for all the cases to be heard.

Come the nationwide rioting of the following summer and it was obvious the boot would go in on some of these 'luxuries'. They were strictly a one-off affair, a mere drop - not never-ending tap water. Now a sort of summary justice was inevitable otherwise, at the very least, the courts would get choked up.

As The Times admitted, Ministers were anxious that the courts provide "early deterrent examples" as a warning to others. On the other hand an unreservedly indiscriminate policy would likely do more harm than good. So PM Thatcher used the sentencing quandary as a means of dividing the so-called copycat rioters from those in Toxteth and Moss Side. The Times (July 13th) put it like this. "Her main conviction appears to have been that the hooliganism of the past 3 or 4 days does not require a search for deep-lying causes as do the major riots in Toxteth and Greater Manchester." By sanctioning the courts to act in a particular way Thatcher was throwing a garland to the copycat rioters. It was a hidden acknowledgement that post war Britain's very well known outbreaks of hooliganism had reached a new stage. Hooliganism was at last beginning to merge into a lived experience of class unity, elevating copycat rioting above the many blind alleys of Saturday afternoon football hooliganism and bank holiday punch ups at seaside resorts. Beyond the question of doubt. The rioting pulled in youths likely to be involved in both, but there was little evidence of either inter-sub-cultural aggro or the psycho-slob frenzy (including racism) associated with football hooliganism.

In the event, no enabling legislation was passed to set up special courts. The clamour subsided but make no mistake, the thought lingers on. The type of special courts that were set up were familiar enough because they were the same as those convened after a Celtic v. Rangers match or following August Bank Holiday in Brighton. But when and if (depending on the tempo of class struggle and not just random acts of violence) a riot package resembling the original riot act does appear, post war hooliganism, so closely related to the moment the working class becomes important to capitalism as a consumer, will have played its part.

The last major sub-cultural disturbance had occurred over a year previously on Easter weekend 1980. Bristol was just days away and the steel strike was still on.

It had certain unique features that set it apart from other outbreaks in the 1960s. Stylistically, discounting punk, it was a repeat except that there was a far greater stew of outfits than ever in the 1960s. More importantly it flashed all over Britain (Ayr in Scotland, Great Yarmouth, Cardiff and Bangor in Wales as well as Margate and Brighton) thus displacing the dominance of the south-eastern corner of England. (A Mod convention was held in Scarborough - of all places.)

At the time, one felt there was something auspicious about these weekend events. The new factor of countrywide mobility was more apparent than ever during the riots when gangs of youth travelled from one trouble spot to another.

In the courts, though heavy fines totalling £650 were levied, the maximum prison sentences were only 3 months. Only!! - but they were trivial compared to the full fury of the courts some 15 months later. This was because it was no longer 'tribal warfare': the difference between the seed and the fruit.

The immaturity of class conflict causes the minutiae of style to matter. It was by no means sure that the sub-cultural styles of the1970s, borrowed though they were, reflected the same class realities, to quite the degree they did in the1960s. For a start the great leveller of unemployment had brooded over the 1970s. But style nowadays is saying more about the tailor's dummy than the person. A youth with fluorescent orange hair and a white painted face with a broad red and blue lightening flash over the right eye was interviewed following the Easter disturbances in 1980. It turned out he worked as a driller and blaster in a quarry in Colne, Lancs and his idol was David Bowie. He went on to say, "Bowie fans are totally against violence". 10 years previously he would have been a dead ringer for a skinhead.

Once May Day was made into a Bank Holiday all remaining pretence to it being workers' day disappeared in Britain. It always was a ritualized Labour party, trade union do and demonstrations were as mild as the spring weather. But by legalizing it even that speck of defiance in choosing not to turn up for work that day was taken away. However, even gently sitting on class struggle in one place causes it to pop up in another. Meagre looking 1970s hairdryer customizing aside, May Day, as the poster hints at, is becoming a focus of less institutionalized festivities leading to regular skirmishing at seaside resorts. Hand in hand with the 'de-politicisation' of May Day is the rise of May Day festivals, which aspire to revive long dead customs and fertility rituals reaching aeons back into the pre-capitalist past. However deadly these state financed rites of Spring are (the Labour controlled Greater London Council put up £130,000 for 1982's new look Maypole and visit the country fayre at the back of the high rise council estate. Falling as it did more or less on the anniversary of the first Brixton riot, last year's fire raising had to be confronted in a business-like manner. Under the guise of democratic 'consultation and participation' and ethnic pluralism all the available firewood in the London boroughs of Tower Hamlets and Hackney was figuratively speaking collected by an 18 strong team of 'community artists' (grrr) then made into "huge images of things they (who else but 'the people')" most want to burn. The East End - Best End festival ended with the best available substitute for a fire extinguisher: an arty-community-fartsy 'Carnival of Fire'.

As this and the sequel showed, it was neither a relapse nor unambiguous progress. Each successive revival wheeled out from the 1960s was messing up the cramped stylistic hall marks of competing class fractions: contrary to the 1960s they were consumed not 'created', and to many a survivor from that decade it did look a forlorn, deracinated sight. Had it not been for the underlying class reality which was far worse (better for us) than anything experienced in the 1960s, things were well on their way to becoming a narrowed-down battle of the styles.

But finally, when the big day did arrive, this medley was also a factor in lessening tension. As style did not reflect the minute particularities of class division as it once had done, this typically British obsession and obstruction could not act as a fatal drag on the first flowerings of united class action among the unemployed.

Over Easter weekend 1980, a "blazing missile" was thrown among the crowd at Tottenham Hotspur's ground during the game with Arsenal. It was a sickening incident but moralistic censure is no substitute for analysis. The same hand that threw the missile could a year later have lobbed it on the right target.

Many peaceable and fanatical supporters of soccer have for some time been aware that a hard core of soccer hooligans aren't much interested in the game. What happens on the terraces and outside the ground comes first and foremost. For some reason these supporters, because it really does expose a crisis at the centre of this highly capitalised game, are shocked. People are actually turning up who would far rather riot than watch the game! This is just the kind of problem the Polish military was presented with when they imposed a ban on all sports. They knew that sporting fixtures would be used for ends other than sport. Class-consciousness had reached, it goes without saying, a far higher level amongst the Poles than amongst UK soccer hooligans and there is not the remotest chance of the game being banned in Britain in the foreseeable future. (Bans on soccer fans are, however, become more frequent.)

But because soccer spills over into so many areas of Britain's strife-torn society, it is too important to be left to private market forces as it formerly was. It has, stage by stage (or game by game) become a focus for political initiatives. The state, for instance, regularly profits from nationalist frenzy whenever the proletariat gives in to the fool's paradise of support for the home side in international matches. To date the Argentinean world cup victory in 1978 is easily the most imposing example of this.

But in Britain, because soccer crowds are so unruly the game has become a testing ground for crowd control techniques, which include learning how to deal promptly and effectively with riots. It is also a centre of punitive experiments combining the soft and hard approach ranging from 10 year prison stretches to 'lenient' community service orders for arrested hooligans. Soccer chairmen now find they having to square up to problems like crime and the community and how not to land up with a situation, which makes "hooligans out of decent people". Now this has a familiar ring! No, it isn't said by liberal Chief Cop, Alderson, but by the Chairman of Sheffield Wednesday FC in a letter to The Times (Sept. 8th, 1980). There is more to come. Like a 17th century Philosophe reflecting on founding Political Principles he adds, "Good Government in this country or any other, requires bread and circuses". Believe it or not this is an FC Chairman fearing in as many words that on the fate of the game hangs the survival of the state!

ABOLISHING THE POLICE OR POLICING THE ABOLITIONISTS?

It is a great rarity to meet anyone in the UK who has a clear notion of what the police are there for. This lack of consciousness could possibly even deliver the proletariat into the arms of the police once more - even after having smashed their power. Because the question of police power is posed in an atemporal way - law 'n' order - common so far to every society that has ever existed, the specificity of what this really means in capitalist society is ignored.

For instance when asked point blank in areas of Merseyside where relations with the police are particularly tense people said they supported in principle the issue of law and order. Put like this the police are safely distanced from the economic system they are protecting. However when questioned in detail about the practices of the police in their own particular neighbourhood this brought total condemnation - a view shared by adolescents and parents alike.

But for those who are still into the belief that the Labour party (reconstructed or otherwise) is out to demolish the police let's get rid of this myth once and for all because it's getting late and frightening shadows are drawing in. The Labour party is anti the police as they are presently constituted but they certainly aren't out for the abolition of the police. This demand is inseparable from the abolition of the commodity economy, wage labour and the state, which the Labour party would never agree to. Instead they prefer to prattle on about community policing. As that King of reforming zealots, Tony Benn said: " ...in the regions and in the localities the police are insulated from any real control by the elected representatives of the people who live in the areas." (In fact all community control of the police amounts to is, party political control of the police under a reconstituted Labour party.)

By definition, no police force is ever socially neutral: all that can be altered is political allegiances. The Tory party has traditionally been the party of law 'n' order and long before the election of 1979 they made certain the police were with them promising to improve wages and fringe benefits and to increase the numbers of police. However it wasn't merely a campaign of economic inducements. The Tories undertook to back the police to the hilt reinforcing the simple-minded bigotry and prejudices of the force by promising greater immunity from criticism. (However, police unilateralism is by no means party political; it has been growing 'unchecked' for years.) The Labour left wants to reverse the tide while the Tories are hell-bent on leaving the centralised apparatus of repression alone while dismantling as far as possible centralised economic control. But both parties are in their differing ways for a centralised state as is their 'new' offspring the Social Democrat/Liberal alliance. The Labour left intends to nationalise (i.e. centralise) all leading industries and banks while devolving as much as possible the task of political legitimisation, which includes the issue of community policing.

At the moment, the Tories are wilfully ignoring these indispensable safeguards. If property handled they might save Britain from social revolution. By pigheadedly trampling them underfoot the Tories are reaping a whirlwind. The Labour Lefts are out to undermine the power of the regional Chief Constable and the Police Commissioner in London, seeking to veto the ultimate accountability to the Home Secretary, which reduce the locally elected police committees to an empty charade. Wow! Heaven must be within our grasp to dare such things.

Just after Brixton, Ted Knight, the 'notorious' leader of London's Lambeth Council in April 1981 said that he wanted to see the entire Metropolitan force disbanded and "replaced with an organisation answerable to the working people." Sounds radical, don't it just!

Labour politicians in the UK have a history of revolutionary statements made on great proletarian occasions. Ramsey McDonald called for the setting up of Soldiers and Workers Councils in the wake of the Russian Revolution. Red Ted's statement is of the same order. It is a tongue-in-cheek response to a popular mood. If Red Ted was at all logical he should also call for the 'disbanding' of the local state. As the highly placed boss of Lambeth Council, he is unlikely to do this. In fact he, alongside all other Labour councillors is struggling to extend the local state against the unprecedented onslaught of centralised government.

His comments on the police must be judged in this light. What he wants to see is the restoration of 'civil' hegemony in policing matters exercised through a liquorice allsorts of various committees. As he has his own 'leftwing' axe to grind these must include shop stewards committees, local union branches, works councils etc. - in short, workerist bodies which get in the way of the proletariat abolishing itself as a class.

Shifty characters like Ted Knight won't flinch from using rioters as cannon fodder to achieve their ends. Lady Smiley did just that in Liverpool on the day before the detestable Royal Wedding. This life peer with the unfortunate title of Lady Simey of Toxteth seemed about to gamble her job as Chair of the Merseyside Police Committee on a fire risk. People in Toxteth she said, "ought to riot" and sure enough, police sources reported a "large-scale disturbance" within hours of her statement. It was the desperate act of a bourgeois democrat, not a specimen sample of an eminent Lady about to chuck it all in. She made plain in an interview that she was "worried about policing methods but I can't take the matter up with our Chief Constable. This is the flaw in our society."

Much has happened since Lady Slimey made this statement. The Scarman report came and went but his recommendations did have some effect. Statutory control by police committees has been thrown out but increased consultation and a variant of community policing is now the name of the game. Shortly after Xmas 1981, foot patrols were back on the beat in Toxteth and the first to enter the district since the summer of 1981.

So Lady Simey has after all got something of what she wanted. But her gain has been, in the eyes of the people of Toxteth especially, loss of notoriety for her, because it is an open secret she has fought a behind-the-scenes campaign to protect Chief Cop, Ken Oxford. As a member of the police authority said, "She could have had his head on a platter. She has actually tried to keep him on. She didn't want the mob to think they could get a reward like that for rioting."

Disband the Special Patrol Group? There has been no end of demands for just that, especially since Operation Swamp in April 1981 has been much publicised as the final straw that lit the camel in Brixton. But what's to stop these elite police thug brigades from merely pretending to shut up shop? A lot of police work is after all cloaked in impenetrable secrecy. Moreover if the Labour party once in power cannot check the rioting it's unlikely Police Chiefs will consult the brothers and sisters before going in for the kill and "please, comrade chairperson, may we be allowed to gas them."

This type of aforementioned rhetoric is a preparatory noise. The louder the noise the more any incoming Labour government (if there's ever to be another) will feel it incumbent to alter the Police Act of 1964 creating (who knows?) in its stead a more overtly party political police.

Sketches as to what form this could take have been drawn up by the fledgling GLC Police Committee chaired (typically) by Paul Boeteng, a middle-class, black barrister. Boeteng, in addition to monitoring police behaviour, has other empty- headed political ambitions. Like his arch rival and comrade in arms Rudi Narayan (who, attempting to parachute in over the heads of the Brixton rioters, got a fully deserved mauling) he thirsts to be a black Labour MP.

As against the near fascistic proposals of Manchester's Chief Cop, Anderton, these bureaucrats look more towards the liberal, sociologically loved example of John Alderson, Chief Constable of Devon and Cornwall. Alderson is retiring to take up a Cambridge fellowship but that may only be temporary. His ideas have received enormous publicity and Alderson and Scarman regularly pat each other on the back. Cornwall's top copper is firm-set on conjuring from the upturned policeman's helmet an illusion of poetically liberal bucolic gentility, which appears to carry such authoritative weight in Britain. When he got protestors to peacefully quit the proposed site of a nuclear power station in his constituency he did so with all the charm of a country gentleman dressed in checks and tweed shooting hat, a model of propriety and politeness. At the same time Alderson lets it be known that he was brought up amongst Yorkshire miners and fancying himself (!) much influenced by their egalitarianism. If this 'revolt' emphasising locality against the growing centralisation of the police force (reduced in geographic area from 117 to 43 between 1969-74) is even temporarily to succeed it will need to muster more than a tradition bound deference, even in policing matters, to a small is beautiful village bobby ideology.

As for the TUC they are pressing for more coloured coppers. Significantly at the same time, they are also demanding more coloured teachers for inner city areas.

The greatest challenge for the philosophers of community policing (the Devon and Cornwall constabulary actually does employ philosophers) is stemming the drift into random law enforcement, which rapidly escalates into widespread uncooperative hostility to the police. By putting coppers back on the beat intent on getting to know 'their' manor, they help roll back a process, which changes a mugger into an unapologetic social being. Community police, by being selective in their approach isolate the mugger or burglar lessening in this way the chances of a generalised explosion brought on by indiscriminate policing. With the escape route to transcendence cut off more effectively either a mugger (say) reforms or stays a mugger caught up in an escalating spiral of crime and violence in between lengthening spells in the nick.

The fate of revolutionaries' vis-à-vis community policing is pertinent to the above scenario. The support community policing receives from social workers, community workers, radical lawyers and guardians of civil liberties etc, also isolates genuinely revolutionary critiques against which they then pit the combined strength of their dislike.

This is not as far fetched as it sounds. The headlining John Alderson to loud acclaim has made a show of weeding out Special Branch files in his constituency. Files on anti-blood sports campaigns, anti-apartheid activists and political undesirables who were seen having a jar with Benn have been thrown into the dustbin. An intelligent move because what's left behind is a hardcore of files certain to include the names of more consistent enemies of the state and capitalism. Not only is the state educated as to who its real enemies are but veering off to take down the names and details of anyone caught raising a finger is stopped.

On present form the Special Branch is trawling its nets so wide and deep that only a few sprats are lucky enough to escape. But screening the population like this also tends to be much more trouble than it's worth, devaluing its importance as a policing technique and creating amongst the people at large a healthy antipathy to the police. One further point. The subliminal effect of community policing is to internalise the violence engendered by capitalist social relations. Allowing little scope for real expression violence turns psychotic. In sum community policing makes social despair more unpalatable by allowing flowers to adorn intolerable prisons. Do your nice local copper a favour please. BEAT YOURSELF UP.

HANDSWORTH

Handsworth, Birmingham, with a large black and Asian population is the one spot where community policing has so far made the most strides. During the early 1970s the cop shop regularly came under siege and if it hadn't been for the pioneering hip pacification treatment the explosion would have equalled Liverpool. Chief Cop David Webb, like Alderson, is now quitting the force in utter disillusionment with its cod-eyed outlook, to become hopefully the local MP (most likely Liberal/SDP). On the day Toxteth erupted a festival was held in Handsworth attended by 8,000 people. According to The Times reporter (July 1st 1981): "The spirit was as amiable and peaceful as a village fete." It was jointly sponsored by police and community groups and the chairman was none other than the superintendent of the local nick. Programmed 'roots' festivals are part of the conciliatory baggage inseparable from the soft cop approach and many locals and reggae musicians boycotted the Handsworth festival. Yet five days later, Handsworth blew and the police station came under siege. Though the kids yelled for the head of David Webb, the outbreak lacked the ferocity of either Toxteth or Moss Side.

Community policing is now the in thing to advocate. A glib panacea for all our troubles in all probability, it will only be a marginal addition to strong-arm methods. Once rioting starts up community policing is of no avail. Six months after the first bout of rioting, European style riot squads equipped with CS gas and plastic bullets and estimated at 11,000 strong evolved out of the police support units set up originally to deal with civil defence in time of war. No matter how much they might borrow from America's experience and Mitterand's reform in France, only when things have calmed down will the paraplegic Dixon of Dock Green scarecrow be wheeled out once more.

TORTURE AND SAND CASTLES

Even a strained combination of the two is possible if the appointment of Sir Kenneth Newman to the post of Commissioner of the Metropolitan police in London is anything to go by. This difficult to swallow cocktail was first mixed in Northern Ireland when Newman as Head of the Royal Ulster Constabulary from 1976 to 1980 reorganised the force into the best equipped, most sophisticated police force in Britain. During this time he presided over the notorious Castlereagh interrogation center where terrorist suspects were tortured. For light relief in between these scenes of medieval barbarity, Blue Lamp discos were also organised attended by tens of thousands of Catholic and Protestant kids, and hand-picked coppers especially trained in social work took slum children away on outings to the seaside...

It is finally being rammed home the extent to which N. Ireland has been a training ground. Newman admitted as much when he first took over the job as head of the RUC: "I did have it very much in mind that British police forces might well be faced with similar problems in the years ahead." Newman has conveniently reduced the problem to one of policing minorities and he has obviously not got the size of the class question in Britain. He was appalled that the RUC could do nothing to police the Ulster Workers strike of 1974 and the lessons he learnt in N. Ireland may turn out to be damn all use. Still tactics developed in Northern Ireland were deployed in the first major incident of 1982 in Notting Hill Gate London. It looked for a brief ten minutes as if the police had withdrawn killing the momentary rush of blood with boredom. Then in they came - the heavy mob - the first real engagement of the 'immediate response units' modelled on similar units in N. Ireland. Within minutes it was all over bar the cleaning up.

However, the authorities weren't suddenly in the summer of 1981 prepared to throw away the last remaining distinctly British approaches to policing. Assistant Commissioner, Pat Kavanagh (New Standard, July 20,1981) said: "It is the public and the press who have been ahead of us in demanding things like water cannon and better shields" and McNee, the then London Police Commissioner declared he was opposed to a French-style riot police. It was left, perhaps inevitably to Jim Jardine, chairman of the Police Federation (the coppers' union) to get really heavy, sinking £30,000 in an advertising campaign calling for the restoration of capital punishment.

However with the exception of the police murder of David Mower in Liverpool, run over repeatedly by a land rover both sides tacitly drew the line at killing. It was fit and right to bash each other's skulls in and set coppers alight. But when it came to actually killing each other, a deep-rooted 'civic' respect for human life was intangibly present in the fiery street air.

LAUGHING POLICEMEN?

During riot week the police force was stretched to breaking point. On the first night of rioting in Moss Side, Manchester's Chief Cop didn't favour, as he claimed, the cool approach. He literally didn't have enough police to deal with the rioters because many had been called away to the battle for Liverpool. Sir Robert Mark had to admit, "in all but the biggest forces some hours will inevitably elapse before a reserve force can be concentrated to deal with an unforeseen emergency." (The Observer July 12th 1981).

Although the riot movement spent itself within ten days, at the end of that time the police were knackered. Constantly on duty or on immediate recall, many collapsed in tears with the strain, some even falling asleep on their riot shields. As a factor contributing to yet further demoralisation this will in future have to be born in mind. It is for instance already claimed that police turnover in the UK on account of crack up is higher than in any other profession. Why? Surely it's because they're constantly deployed against demonstrations, mass pickets and flying pickets and this deeply troubles those cops who still have some shreds of humanity left. In fact during the riots, strains within the force were beginning to show. On the one hand carpet slippered Inspectors and Chief Constables safely tucked away in their plush bunkers, on the other, the ordinary copper dead on his feet, the target of endless flack.

To keep up their spirits, the cops in Liverpool joked about this. One cop had finally snapped and taking to his heels had collapsed in a doorway. "On your feet lad" he heard a voice saying. "Sorry Sarge" he replied, "I just couldn't take it any more." "You mean Inspector" came the reply. The huddled figure looked up. "Blimey", he said, "I didn't know I'd run this far back." That beery, red-faced old time British institution the laughing policeman never had to joke like this before.

The Strangled Embrace

The rioters caused the pound sterling to fall something only powerful sectors of the working class have succeeded in doing. But there was no instance of rioters directly calling on the employed working class to join in. bringing the strike weapon into play. The bridge must somehow be made and employed and unemployed must be prepared to meet each other over a pint of home brew, maybe a box of matches and a cement mixer. Although the riots were more destructive and extensive than those in France in May1968, they lacked the clarity of the French insurgents and when the smoke cleared there were no occupied factories to be seen.

In the nights of rioting, a spontaneous coming together, particularly in the Northern cities was definitely a distinct, if distant possibility. Rioting took place next to industrial complexes in cities like Manchester and Hull. Moss Side isn't that far from the wound down industrial estate of Trafford Park (still amazingly the biggest in Europe) and tactically it might have been better to go there than suggest moving on to loot the Arndale centre situated in Manchester's city centre.

In Leeds, a fatigued police force could have been pushed back over a mile or so of industrial old bones and planning blight separating the city centre from Chapeltown. However Leeds is the commercial and financial capital of the region, insulated even in the 1930s from the surrounding catastrophic levels of unemployment, so it is unlikely the rioters would have met with a ready response. (Incidentally in Chapeltown a sex shop was torched and flaming rubber dollies floated into the warm night air - although it wasn't quite women's lib because many other commodities were coming in for the same treatment.)

In the south the action in towns like High Wycombe and the Medway towns in Kent wasn't really big enough to make any immediate impact on industrial workers. And London is so vast and disparate and so unlike any other English city that comparisons are futile.

THE MERSEY BEAT 20 YEARS ON: LIVERPOOL 8. COPPERS 0.

If the Old Bill were petrified in London, in Liverpool the scuffers got the hiding of their lives. Friction with the police is not new in Liverpool. Some 20 years ago, it was said the police were more like an army of occupation. It was said that the three worst police forces in Britain were Belfast, Birmingham and Liverpool.

The Scuffers conventionally refer to Liverpool youth as "the bucks". This does not necessarily refer to anyone who has reputation for violence. It means common. In its widest sense it refers to accent, dress and general life style. It is a term of pure class contempt and most likely to be used by people from the upper working class and lower middle from whom most police recruits are drawn. They are the people most anxious to disassociate themselves from those elements in the working class they see as not respectable. Thus justifies a permanent open season on them. This applies to young whites but blacks are treated with even greater contempt. Here racism compounds class contempt. Because of the high level of petty crime in Liverpool 8, the police follow the usual pattern and regard all youth as criminal elements and because they regard them as a lower form of life any sort of brutality and harassment is justified. As one kid put it: "we hate them and they hate us, it's as simple as that."

Conditions in Liverpool "the Bermuda Triangle of British Capitalism" and the particular nature of the Liverpool police have combined to produce the most intense urban violence on mainland Britain since the 18th century. Many youths involved in the riots had been involved in mugging anybody from old age pensioners to Liverpool dockers with the Thursday night wages packets in their pockets. There's no point in pretending otherwise. Attacking any business is commendable but unfortunately people living above the row of shops in Lodge Lane were also burnt out. They deserved better than this. However neither in Liverpool or Brixton did people whose places had been burnt down show any animosity to the rioters. They seemed to sense the rioters were merely poking the fire. One member of the Liverpool 8 Defense Committee accused top cop Ken Oxford of incompetence in not having police at hand to prevent "the burning of our Lodge Lane." Our feeling is that this person was pretty ashamed of what happened in Lodge Lane but preferring not to grasp the nettle tried to shift the blame.

This negative emphasis was all The Guardian could see bemoaning a lack of class-consciousness which would have stamped on that paper if it had been fully matured. "Surveying the scene, counting the costs, the saddest thing is that the victims of much of the destruction were ordinary citizens of the area. Though a couple of chain stores were attacked most of the shops destroyed or looted were owned by local people living on the premises and struggling to make a living. If the riots had had a political character one might have expected a more direct attack on the symbols of capitalism. Capitalism has destroyed the social order in the inner cities but no real class identity has emerged."

Traditional, smug, self satisfied, such is The Guardian and contrary to their opinion (which was later corrected by a concerned academic) some of the targets were consciously selected and for good reasons. The Racquets Club was torched because as one black youth said, "My father used to tell me it was where the judges went to dine after they had sent black people to prison. It is like a hotel for the people who run Liverpool." An antique furniture warehouse was burnt out owned by Swainback a former Tory councillor who had shown hostility to black youth in the area. One youth questioned by a radio reporter while the riot was in progress said, there was no reason for anyone to be frightened. "We do not hit family homes." "What about the garage on the corner, people work there" – "Yeah but they don't own the place, it's owned by Shell."

And Liverpool 8 has a strong and close family structure and as any Liverpudlian knows "Me Mam" is a much loved and respected figure. A Daily Star journalist said a child hurling bricks stopped to ask the time. "Eh! - I'll have to get home soon. Me mam will kill me if I'm late." Parents also tend to stay solid with their children whatever they do. A Sunday Times report on Kirkby a few years ago mentioned a youth who had been arrested a number of times for vandalism. When asked what his parents thought about it, he simply shrugged his shoulders and said "me Mam loves me". One of us spoke to a middle-aged woman in Sefton Park at the start of the anti-Ken Oxford march. She was not going on the march herself but said: "I've got a gerl who's terrible militant. I've brought her cardy down, case she catches cold." A good example of family disintegration as feared by the Tories if ever there was one. These comments are not intended as a defense of the family; it is simple the case of Liverpool 8 that the family does not conform to the nice respectable middle class ideals of Jill Knight, Tory MP for Edgbaston who was much moved at the time of the riots to say: "The family has been derided, debased and weakened by trendy permissiveness but it is the cornerstone on which a nation's strength rests. In a good and loving family a child learns unselfishness, responsibility and respect for other people's property. He loves his parents, cares about making them proud of him and is strongly deterred from behaviour which will distress or disgrace them."

Above and beyond all the issues and separations, in Liverpool there's the irrepressible Scouse humour, which adds real spice to all proletarian revolt there. After the riots a scuffer stopped and searched a kid and found a brick in his pocket. The kid came back..."That's not a brick officer but a deposit to put down on a telly." Although this joke was born in the Liverpool riot, it rapidly found its way into northern club-land humour and finally wound up as a TV crack on a fairly sentimental

Alan Bleasdale TV documentary on Liverpool a few months later. Ripped off from its source, only to improve the image of Bleasdale's hip populism as smart alec playwright.

A MERSEYBEAT SOVIET?

What happened in Liverpool during the early hours on Monday July 4th amounted to the greatest missed opportunity industrial Britain has probably known. The police were clearly losing the battle. The rioters were moving towards the main arteries of communications. (Lime Street, Pierhead, the Mersey Tunnel) used by 1,000's and 1,000's of workers. If the police in terror of their lives hadn't fired CS gas around dawn contact would undoubtedly have been established between the rioters and early morning shift workers. Camaraderie between employed and unemployed is more out in the open in Liverpool than in any other English city and the explosive ingredient of an aroused working class might well have proved near lethal. To then go on to loot, even arm in arm, the shopping precinct on the site of the old St John's Market would have been a diversion. With the police utterly beaten and disarmed, the entire city would have lain at their feet. A local 'soviet' unique in the history of soviets might well have materialised. It would have thrown into the public forum in no uncertain manner issues like the break-up of the family, the right of kids and tiny tots to self-determination, the refusal and growing irrelevance of work - all issues, which were hardly present in the past experience of soviets. Considering the galvanic effect of the riot on the rest of Britain this example could easily have been followed elsewhere. The day this happens (or something like it) revolt is turning into revolution.

During the riots there had been limited examples of working class intervention. The fire brigade in Liverpool refused to intervene "against the community" and allow their hoses to be used by the police. Like fire brigades elsewhere, the rioters had stoned them. It says something for their class-consciousness that local fire brigades refused to become, under intense provocation, an arm of the police force. Also even in the thick of the fiercest rioting on Upper Parliament St rioters talked to ambulance men and made a truce with the police so that old people could be evacuated from the Princess Park geriatric hospital next door to the burning Racquets Club. (Later it was discovered that some of the old people's lockers had been looted. This inexcusable and pathetic incident was not in the least typical of the riots and a saddening reminder of just how maimed people have become under the necro weight of capitalist dominated daily life.

In the months prior to July 1981, strikes in Liverpool had been at an unusually low ebb. Still Liverpool dockers would have been returning to working on that glorious Monday morning after a ritualised 24 hours union strike over manning levels. The warehouses adjacent to Toxteth where they once worked are now empty awaiting conversion into a museum, leisure center or luxury flats (no doubt on Man Power Services Commission grants). The majority of dockers are now employed in the container port of Seaforth down the Mersey estuary but they still meet in the stadium in the city centre.

Later in the week, Thatcher had the cheek to foist the blame for the high levels of local unemployment oh the Liverpool working class. This lady really is for burning.

It wasn't the coolest thing to say and for the second time in a week the Liverpool working class didn't respond in a fitting manner even though they are quite steadfast in their belief that capitalism is running Merseyslide into the ground.

"ALL THE PEACE MAKERS TURNED LAW OFFICERS"

On the Monday night social workers finished what CS gas had started the night before. The Merseyside Community Relations Council toured the riot areas in vans with loudhailers lent by the police asking the crowds to go home. Home to what? At best telly, a spliff, a few cans of ale, at worst to desperation, tranquillisers and endless numbing bed. This mockery of what real community relations could be was no different from the united appeal of Liverpool church leaders. Considering that social work arose out of church relief in exchange for humbling penitence it is hardly surprising. As for the Anglican Bishop of Liverpool, the Rev D. Sheppard, that oh so understanding liberal, ex England cricketer, he would do well to ruminate on the rioters transcendence of cricket outlined in Brixton later in the week when cricket bats looted from sports stores were used to spar with police batons.

STREET FIGHTING MAN......

The rioters were very well organised. Within the space of a few hours, the rioters became skilled and tactical street fighters inventing techniques as they went along. In Liverpool, they covered the road with oil between barricades, which could then be covered with petrol and torched once the police had made a successful assault in the first barricade. At the same time people made petrol bombs in the back of vans as they travelled around the cities. In Nottingham, Inspector Colin Sheppard was moved in awe to say..."There was no end to the imagination of the mob used to vent their feelings on the police." (The Daily Telegraph July 14th 1981) adding, they were "Nottingham's blackest ever days."

...............PLUS RADIO AND CB

The use of radio as a guerrilla medium has been a new and all but unprecedented speciality of insurrectionary revolts over the last few years - in particular Italy 1977 and Britain 1981. In both countries come the moment of revolt radio broadcasts In Italy and CB intercom in Britain were snapped back into focus. Trouble in the streets halted the drift into merely being exotic, ear-catching supplements to the established news media and run of the mill telephone conversations.

The Mao-Dadaist, Radio Alice in Bologna had any number of taped 'subversive' cultural infils combining music, poetry and comment that were used as sandwiching between phone-in programmes. It is a well-known fact more commercial radio stations play top 10 hits during peak hours to harness listeners. But during the Bolognese events the cultural bullshit (a mixture of commedia dell'arte, cultish 'artistic' parallels drawn from the Russian Revolution and mind blowing illusions about multi-millionaire pop musicians) was laid aside and the radio station used to inform insurgents of police manoeuvres.

Technically CB has more democratic potential. It is also a transmitter as well as a receiver. With radio programmes there is a greater editorial control. A flick of a switch and a caller is cut off mid sentence. And it is never possible to instantly canvas listeners for their opinion on the matter. The use of CB during the riots must also be linked to the mobility of the rioters. They came in from miles around to the riot hot spots even utilising car hire firms. In London homemade transmitters needing only a modicum of electronics know-how to construct interrupted Capital Radio and LBC with messages like. "This is a warning: there's going to be a riot on the Kings Road." As a spokesman for the Independent Broadcasting Authority said. "There is absolutely nothing we can do about it." This development does seem to suggest infinite possibilities. Like jamming broadcasts with material transmitted from the back of moving vans making it doubly difficult for Home Office radio spies to pin them down.

This dismantling of the state monopoly of the airwaves carries its own penalties. Assuming CB does become accessible to everyone what's to stop police and other authorities listening in and becoming as proficient as anyone else in CB jive? As a consequence of the riots and many related incidents the police are now being told to learn the 'language'. This is why CB glossaries and dictionaries are self-defeating because CB must constantly be on the move if it is to retain its subversive potential. But always being one step ahead could easily result in the total privatisation of the language. In this event opposite extremes meet because CB was fast becoming anyway a 'safe' one up exchange of unfathomable secret codes. As one enthusiast put it "If I'm talking to someone on CB and he's using the slang words I don't know he might as well be talking Serbo Croat for the good it will do our conversation" (letter to CB magazine).

To overcome this, close networks of friends who have been told beforehand of changes in handles could become important. On a Warwickshire council estate recently a rent collector had failed time after time to gain admission to households owing back rent. Eventually someone snitched. Rigs had been installed in flats to warn tenants of his approach. Now the rent collector has been equipped with his own CB so he can also pick up any advance warning. Next time he won't be put off by people pretending not to answer the door. But it's possible to get even. By inventing a secret code known only to trusted tenants the rent collector will be thrown off the scent.

Though now legal there are well over 1/4 million illegal CB radios in the UK broadcasting on forbidden wave bands. The government has outlawed them claiming they block vital messages which for instance hamper ambulances from functioning properly. This may on occasion have happened but the converse is also true that in the event of an accident, heart failure etc help might arrive sooner.

No - behind concern for the 'public good' there was a real fear that CB freaks might block police radios. This happened when police recently were unable for some time to alert the fire brigade to save a factory from burning down. Their radios had been blocked by a breaker calling himself Yankee Bucket Mouth. Later it was discovered that the fire had been caused by an arsonist. Yankee Bucket Mouth? Police weren't sure but 'YBM' had better sign off double quick.

There's plenty new under the sun but CB lingo when used for subversive ends renews in London a much older tradition recapturing the forgotten essence of cockney rhyming slang. In the days of the much-feared London mob in the 17th and 18th century, government spies were sent into proletarian quarters to earwig. The quick-witted cockneys improvised a constantly amended parallel language to avoid unwelcome eavesdropping.

Photo top: Alderson's country swamp operation? Photo bottom: Hastily got up riot gear? Spring 1980. The photo appeared in The Times next to an article on the number of police held down by the Hadfield picket in Sheffield during the 1980 steel strike. Montaged with it - further hastily got up riot gear? Riot week July 1981.

All Quiet On The Frontline?

Above: **SPEAKS FOR ITSELF**

Photo left: An incident in the early 1970s as cop nicks demonstrators' drum!

An uneasy calm has settled on the streets. But the press will have it only minor rumbles continue in the major battle zones of the inner cities. It's more - much more. The inner cities fizz like never ending firecrackers. Despite all the talk of community policing and liaison committees the cops are as heavy as ever resembling an army of occupation. Sirens blare continually, lights flash and cars race past at top speed while down some darkened mews or alley a van load of police wait menacingly. Is another polymorphous urban explosion in the offing? One thing's for certain the cops are not likely to be caught by surprise like they were in the summer of 1981. At the slightest sign of danger a better-trained police force equipped with all the necessary riot gear moves in immediately to seal off the potential trouble spot.

SSH - THERE'S A RIOT GOING ON

The police are also giving a hush hush policy of their own devising a twirl. A local cop shop in Bedford, a town 30 miles north of London came under siege in late March '82 but the police suppressed all news of the event for a couple of weeks. As far as we know Bedford was free from trouble last year. The same also happened on two occasions in Notting Hill in London once over Xmas and the other in early April. But when on the third occasion when barricades were erected across several road the incident was too big to be ignored and was immediately reported on the radio and in the press next day.

However Scotland Yard's Press Office have been keeping their lips buttoned up for a long time. Either that or the media didn't want to know or more plausibly didn't want others to know, electing to report only the 'good news'. To corroborate what we stated much earlier on it has just (April 1982) come out in the press that firebombs were hurled in the Welsh mining valleys during riot week. This astonishing piece of news has been kept in the information lock-up all that time! Just how close is Britain coming to revolution?

But is a Toxteth of the factories laying waste to all the horrors of capitalism likely in the immediate future? The workers have taken note of the riots all right, slotting them alongside their own struggles. During a recent occupation of the British aluminium smelter factory at Invergordon in the Highlands of Scotland a laid off worker suddenly interrupted a T.V. programme to say Brixton and Toxteth had shown the way forward. No one within earshot protested. The workers terrain is however warrened from end to end by trade union power ever ready to drag breaking-away workers back to the negotiating table and the last century. Most of those living in the inner cities are free from this encumbrance and therefore still able to go straight for capital's jugular without getting sidetracked along the way by kiss-my-arse representation.

The employed working class must respond to the 'new' situation brought into relief by the riots. As a block the Liverpool working class has again been the first to recognise this. But before they can blow at all radically they must first blow out the unions and procedure laid down by the unions. It must be done definitively. Over the past few years at very crucial moments when literally minutes and hours mattered, the workers time upon time have handed controls over to union delegate conferences - usually through the mediation of the stewards. Psychologically they have just not been ready to act on golden opportunities. Thus undischarged anger becomes two days later mute, pent-up desperation.

During the union led steel strike of Spring 1980, steelworkers in South Wales instead of going directly to the local pit heads to extend the strike, postponed their action until ratified at a later date by local union meetings. A week later might as well have been a century. The atmosphere of tense expectancy passed and solidarity melted into thin air. The miners (actually against the wishes of the Welsh NUM. The Welsh NUM might appear in this instance to be in advance of the workers. However workers increasingly resent being told what to do. At a Northants Weetabix factory earlier this year the workforce were told to come out on strike by 'their' union. The workers steamed up as fuck by this high handed decision immediately called a mass meeting to discuss themselves whether or not to go out on strike didn't come out as expected. One passionate plea by striking steelmen addressed unswervingly to pit head coal miners might have saved the day. Discouraged the dockers then lifted their ban on imported coal, not wanting to be left out the headlong retreat.]

A revealing postscript to this mess was provided by the rugby match played between England and Wales at Twickenham. Commentators and spectators described it as easily the most brutal match they had ever watched with serious injuries occurring even in the first minute.

Again at British Leyland in late October 1981, the initiative was lost in what promised to be the most important strike for years. So many intangibles were posed by the threatened 'strike' taking it well beyond the run of the mill dispute. The manager of BL Michael Edwardes for instance may well have implemented his threat to sell off the plant. And pressure had reached bursting point from the shop floor.

CRISES MANAGEMENT

As the name implies crises management has involved drastic changes in management methods, as the last vestiges of gentlemanly protocol, which had helped keep the lid on industrial relations, were brushed aside. (Maybe it needed a ruthless South African to do this. British managers have been noticeably slower in following suit). As one worker in Leyland put it "Call it the need to keep our dignity if you like - But we think our very rights as free men are at stake in B.L. now."

The utter insensitivity and tough guy take it or leave it approach which had been such a winner in the last three wage settlements finally rebounded - as it must. When foremen went up and down the line at Longbridge threatening to sack those who failed to clock in the following day there was nearly a mass walkout. John Barker the local transport union official in Birmingham admitted union officials had to "use some restraint" to stop workers walking off the job there and then.

This incident happened nearly two weeks after the Chief Executioner had sent a crude letter to any workers threatening to sack anyone who went on strike. But as always faced with a cataclysm, the final bulwark supporting capitalism are the damn unions who were able to delay the workforce long enough for management to recapture the initiative. During the three weeks run up to the union appointed deadline, Longbridge management upped bonus payments to record levels to divide Longbridge from the other smaller plants scattered around the U.K.

Heraclitus said '"Those who submit are governed by blows." After B.L. workers in late October 1981 had agreed to a wage rise paid in buttons a S.A.S. (Special Air Services) inspired militaristic operation was immediately mounted against the workers of Lawrence Scott in Manchester. Helicopters were flown in over the heads of the pickets to collect machinery destined for use in Polaris submarine pens. The cops had been forewarned. Locked outside the gates all the pickets could do was look on as imitation S.A.S. Action Men ran all over the factory - and Britain took one further step towards a banana monarchy. Immediately after the Moss Side riots while the embers were still smouldering workers occupying the factory had been evicted by bailiffs wielding pickaxe handles and hammers. Who dares doesn't always win because had this dawn raid been carried out against the inhabitants of Moss Side the reaction would have been swift and terrible. The response of the employed working class could be more lethal but they must overcome their present, lack lustre showing. Their destructive power at the moment only resides as a threatened memory.

Lawrence Scott is a subsidiary of Mining Supplies in Doncaster. Once flying pickets from the Manchester factory installed themselves outside the factory gates in Doncaster after the swashbuckling raid the manager just crumpled up. He could right there and then have easily used the law on the pickets. But something had happened in the meantime to really put the wind up him. If he dared as much as lift a finger against the pickets the local miners had promised to come to their help.

But back in Manchester outside of the immediate reach of South Yorkshire miners, the manager in February 1982 supported by a fleet of lorries and scabs smashed through the pickets once and for all. The rest of Manchester's engineering workers turned to look away - perhaps to watch Coronation Street instead. 10 years ago thousands of them were occupying in and around the Manchester conurbation.

Determined now to show who was t'gaffer once and for all, Lawrence Scott sent the bailiffs mammoth bill for breaking and entering to the workers.

But north of the border the fist of fury thought it judicious to wear mittens. Shortly after New Year 1982 two factories belonging to British Leyland and the Plessey electronic multinational were occupied in the small town of Bathgate. Though the BL workers abandoned their sit-in, the Plessey workforce composed largely of women stayed put ignoring the interdict to vacate the premises. The occupation was a popular one in a town where unemployment was heading for over 30%. Local people were constantly dropping in, leaving behind them bags of groceries etc without saying a word. As the workers of central Scotland were putting their money where Manchester's mouth was, the Court of Sessions in Edinburgh thought better of it and declared the occupation legal. But not before helicopters had circled overhead leading to fears of an SAS-style raid to seize the £650,000 worth of capacitators held in the factory.

There have been a number of factory occupations since then - just as the bourgeoisie feared. The biggest has been in Coventry where a subsidiary of Massey Ferguson was occupied twice in two weeks until ordered to vacate. A noticeably quickening tempo of class struggle amongst the employed working class is apparent since last summer. Nurses, operating theatre technicians and hospital ancillary staff are threatening to strike together for the first time. Let's hope they are the first leaves of a proletarian spring, summer, autumn and winter because something big is getting ready to push through the permafrost of capitalist accumulation.

Even if when these words are published there has been a major reversal, since 1979 the working class has by and large been frightened into survival sickness.

EVERYTHING STOPS FOR TEA 10 YEARS ON

The situation is overall far more fraught than in the early 1970s. The details of class struggle, worth fighting over, must be inserted into this changed perspective.

In 1972 ten workers in Coventry cheekily downed tools and went out on strike all because they had asked for, and been refused, bigger mugs of tea. They looked as if they didn't have a care in the world, but in fact many of the struggles dating from this period were hard fought.

The significance of such details was determined less by the logic of capitalism than by the workers' lively, infectious resistance. (The idea caught on and strikes spread to other factories.) Going on for ten years later, the situation is much altered. The tea break strike at BL in December 1981 was a last ditch stand by workers forced onto their knees by a management determined to wring from them every last ounce of productivity. This is not to say that workers have during that time become the passive objects of capital's counter attack. Rather it means high spirits have been progressively abandoned to a grim war of position in which every inch of ground is bitterly fought over.

As a reminder of the bourgeoisie's longevity, immemorial details are, more than in every other comparable country, paraded fetishistically at the level of the state in Britain. Once these emblematic tokens are either discarded or drawn into class struggle they become further reminders of the gravity of the crises. In 1979 during the Winter of Discontent the unthinkable happened: Beefeaters at the Tower of London downed pikestaffs and went on strike. Early in 1982 as part of the Government's cuts the navy's time-honoured rum ration was withdrawn...

Strapped down like in Madame's dungeon, very occasionally the workers break free in a fury of destruction that compares well with the riots. In December '80 BL workers at Longbridge went on the rampage wrecking cars on the assembly line, and surrounded the management block known locally as The Kremlin. The same thing happened with John Knott (Trade Secretary) when visiting Portsmouth dockyards in the late summer of 1981: he risked being stoned to death. This was not jeers and rotten eggs but the shape of things to come.

Losing your cool like this is the flip side of crisis management. The bosses are no longer satisfied with a lockout instantly threatening to wind up business once and for all. But is it a wind-up, a calculated gamble, or do they really mean 'business', or more correctly none at all? During the ASLEF stoppages recently there was talk of tearing up the railway lines and covering them up with macadam and concrete. By sharing lifts in cars people were getting to work OK and it was argued to do this would be a chastising lesson in self-reliance to BR's workers. But the train drivers called British Rail's bluff and the board backed down. However in every other case it has not been put to the test. Would Sir Michael Edwardes have auctioned off British Leyland if the workers had not done his bidding? Around 10,000 tons of machinery is being sold to buyers from abroad each week. Some of it, like the looms from the Courtauld factory, is the most modern plant available anywhere. The dominant impression is of a fire sale to beat all, but this may only be the wrapping to divert attention away from the de-nationalisation of British industry. Of the 50 or so major firms in Britain 40% of production is now located abroad.

Given this situation it is important workers, when combating free ranging multinational enterprises, aren't split along nationalist lines. If struggle is to reach even greater heights of lucidity the multinationalism of the rioters must be honoured in the factories. Equally if the proletariat is to combat the drift into the gotterdammerung twilight of the bourgeoisie the stakes must be just as high, positing right from the start a nonnegotiable new world beyond the one that now belongs to capitalism.

At the moment the hardest conflict to live with is that between worker and worker. However the whys and wherefores of this almost unique situation must be placed in their proper context.

Strike meetings like the recent ones in Ford's or British Leyland are ending in uproar and bitter recriminations. With the vote almost evenly split down the middle a display of hands can quickly turn nasty. The clenched fist then usually signifies a readiness to knock the shit out of your opposite number on the shop floor.

This ferocity of conflicting tendencies, and not merely the last swipes - as the Tories like to pretend - of a dying trade unionism forced like a rat back into the corner. For example, the recent assaults on shop stewards in Dagenham (Ford's) must have caused unease in government circles because they were carried out by workers who were pissed off with the stewards for recommending acceptance of Ford's pay offer. The Tories are victims of their own propaganda. They had cast the unions as the real villains of the piece responsible for "shop floor anarchy." At the last election it had proved a powerful vote catcher and when, to take just one example, Derrick Red Robbo Robinson, the Communist party convenor had been sacked from British Leyland without even a skirmish in November 1981 the Tories hailed it as a milestone and a victory for the new "mood of realism" allegedly sweeping through industry.

BL management had estimated - fuck knows how - that Robbo had been responsible for £200,000,000 worth of lost production. They omitted to mention that Robbo had probably saved the company that amount when throughout the Labour government's last term in office he had spoken out against strikes (in particular the tool-makers' strike) in British Leyland.

In view of the contradictory stances Robbo had adopted over the years his dismissal should have given rise to misgivings in anyone less mule headed than the Tories. Even the crudely reactionary tabloid The Daily Mail had to acknowledge shop stewards had "proved useful lightning conductors defusing issues on the shop floor before they got out of hand". What's more, employers had "turned more and more to shop stewards for communication with their workforces" because the "small numbers of full time union officials simply could not cope" (November 4th1981). Yet the Tories have pressed on regardless with their plans to minimalise trade union hierarchies by making a show of wresting power from the head offices and shop stewards and placing it in the hands of the members.

The Tories blinded by ideology haven't got wise to the fact the lunatics were only able to take over the asylum in an interregnum. Shop floor tranquillity over the past two years had, in addition to the high levels of unemployment, depended on a complex admixture of reaction and radicalism in which the main ingredient is a shared dislike of unions. Anti-capitalist/anti-union hostility has still to attain a decisive level of coherence and maturity. In particular it must disassociate itself completely from the present wave of capitalist intolerance of trade unionism in some countries. Following the Winter of Discontent when the community of interest between big business, the state, the nationalised sector and the trade unions fell apart the Tories had been quick to exploit the situation by shabbily laying the blame for it squarely on the trade unions.

However, many a worker who had been in the thick of the struggles that had suddenly swept Britain between 1970 and 1974 knew differently. They had suddenly after the mid-1970s woken up to the fact the unions and shop stewards apparatus we're playing by far the major role in the suppression of class struggle (the moment of the "social contract" con trick). The effect was shattering - some junked being stewards and convenors altogether, taking to drink, or perhaps unenthusiastically attending pottery classes and generally mechanically going through the motions of living. However as a rule the pseudo conservative disillusionment with the representative apparatus was in the absence of more pertinent conclusions unable to go even part of the way towards accepting a conservative political identity. Equivalent reaction at the level of issue politics and community politics were also apparent though not necessarily at the same moment in time.

It is against this background that the aforementioned violence must be judged. Misdirected fury by creating needless enemies and hardening attitudes can be counter-productive. However the violence that has recently broken out in strike meetings may serve as an apprenticeship to direct action which rejecting intermediaries and representatives instead of stopping at the factory gates goes on to envelop the whole of society.

These barely controllable outbursts of anger are an accurate measure of the urgency of the situation. They are an inevitable response to the tearing, grinding, heart stopping psychological climate of crisis management leaving the workers with no choice other than to accept or take giant steps of their own leading to a decisive showdown. Starved of alternative options the unions have no stomach for such end games.

Weakening and discrediting the trade union representatives apparatus has met with little working class disapproval. This has lulled the Tories and considerable sections of British management into a false sense of their own security because they haven't been able to create anything like a durable proletarian bodyguard organised everlastingly around government and managerial dictates. Much depends on the ability to sustain the friction between the employed and unemployed, allied to which is the fear of unemployment itself. But when and if a breakthrough comes the Tory loonies along with the rest of the capitalist asylum are likely to pay a terrible price for having dared to cure workers further of the habit of looking to unions to represent their interests.

But for all that Tebbit's (Secretary of State for Employment) Employment Bill is not as green as it's cabbage looking. Unlike Heath's club-footed Industrial Relations Act of 1969-74 it proposes to make unions liable for actions taken by shop floor trade unionists unless the "corporate leadership" repudiates them. The unions are not likely to do this because of the serious risk of unofficial action. As for the fining of unions, Heath's original act showed it left the workers cold. No matter what, a version of this act will eventually come into force.

AS YOU WERE: THE CHANGING FACE OF TRADES UNIONS

Photo right: This ad issued by HM government was used to sell the Social Contract in the period of the 1974-9 Labour government. On the left, Len Murray, Director General of the Confederation of British Industry, on the right, Sir Campbell Adamson,

Gen Sec. of the Trades Union Congess. Photo left: All because of the conflict between craft and industrial unionism Sid Weighell of the NUR and Ray Buckton of ASLEF are usually bitter enemies. They are seen here riding on a rinky dink train at a toy fair in Harrogate, Yorks. Once anti union proletarian assemblies' spring into being on the railways flinging switches on toy train sets will be the only contrivance left to the bureaucrats of British Rail.

As in most other countries high levels of unemployment have meant a decline in union membership. This provides union leaders like Alan Fisher (NUPE) with a handy excuse when asked to explain why unions are unable to exert much influence on Government policy. After having knocked frantically at the door of No.10 the previous Tory Prime Minister Heath in 1972-73 had finally invited the unions in for consultations. And boy, did he need them! But if it's the last thing she does Mrs Thatcher is determined not to do the same. Granted she is a tougher nut any day than Heath, but the unusual docility of the working class has postponed the day of reckoning when a subdued Mrs Thatcher could have well begged the unions for assistance.

The unions make a virtue of weakness. The truth is they are still immensely strong but unwilling to exercise their power other than through legal parliamentary means. They are mightily afraid of stirring up their members to implement the TUC's frankly capitalist Programme for Recovery, preferring to wait on a Labour government to do it. The TUC knows full well the working class once aroused is not going to stop at the TUC alternative policies to save capitalism. But if aroused, again these arseholes will have to attempt to lead an essentially leaderless movement in order to try and divert developing autonomous energy away from its real goals.

The memory of the early 1970s and the 1978-79 Winter of Discontent is still fresh in the mind of union bureaucrats. During the intervening years an ethical universalism (the TUC's 'moral policeman' of1976-78) supplanting what on the continent would pass for the equally bourgeois 'general interest' had served as the antidote to class struggle. Different 'interest groups', i.e. contending classes, were encouraged not to act selfishly but to think of others instead. This difficult balancing act appealing more to feelings of right and wrong than mystified calculations on the continental model was master-minded by the joint Labour government/TUC Chief of Staffs with the latter playing the role of supreme commander.

Then along came the Winter of Discontent. The TUC tight rope snapped. The ethics of public service including ambulance staffs and gravediggers were henceforth no guarantee against mass strike action. The various unions involved were unable to disown the strikers for fear of the consequences but knowing as a result Labour would lose the election.

But then under Thatcher a strange thing happened. The trade unions took up the plea-bargaining puppy-begging approach so recently overthrown. It meant in the short term deferring to Thatcher but in the long term it was a defence against their members' real interests; a preparation for the day they will be called on to police a re-edition of the 'social contract'. Appearing to shame the nation's conscience is good practice for when they have to try and put the workers to shame.

Before being reprieved in 1975 the Shelton Steelworks in Stoke on Trent had been threatened with the chop for four years. During this time a career minded local theatre director bull shitter, Peter Cheesman of the Victoria Theatre in Stoke, the General Manager of the plant and members of the action committee got together to save the plant. Cheesman is seen here (picture in original pamphlet) taping interviews for a local documentary on the plant called "Fight for Shelton Bar" which was duly staged before TV cameras and the chair of BSC, Sir Monty Finniston. The one person in other words that really counted in this 'living theatre' of duped steel workers. In the play, workers, blast furnaces and local management were stuck together as if with superglue and all past battles belong to war-time not to class

struggle. The difference between what the theatre director said in justification and what the general manager said can be just about tucked under a finger nail: "Above all Shelton Bar is its people, a deep rooted, living and richly successful human community. That is one of the reasons it makes a profit." (Peter Cheesman, theatre director) – "The occasion produces the man. It is a great lesson if you can engender team spirit and loyalty to the job in hand, and these men (i.e. action committee) can be incredibly good at grass roots level. In many respects they made the job of management easier. Our aims were exactly similar." *(Derek Field, General Manager)*

This ethical universalism tailored to fit the TUC corresponds to an advanced degree of integration in the state only temporarily held up by Thatcher and her cronies. However it also arises from the growing importance of white-collar workers as opposed to the declining importance, relatively speaking, of industrial workers in the TUC make-up.

Following the mainly industrial revolt of the early 1970s recruitment of white collar grades including low ranking bureaucrats gained in leaps and bounds greatly changing the TUC public image. The main unions involved (the GMWU, ASTMS, the civil service unions) turned to account the reputedly more comprehensive views of bureaucrats/white collar strata eclipsing the narrow sectionalism of industrial workers.

Hegel in his theory of the state had placed great store by low ranking bureaucrats, believing every citizen could become an official: as long as this lasted the bond between state and society was secure. So was the pan logical Idea enshrined in the state. There are an infinitely greater number of low-grade civil servants and the like around today than in Hegel's time and mechanisation and humdrum routine has destroyed its former status. But equally they are under pressure to set a progressive 'intelligent' example proving there are still plenty of 'frills' attached to the job. They are both the hammer and the anvil. The trade union movement has capitalised on this split personality (cultural pretensions included) to extend its sphere of operations.

Formerly it had been in the interests of both unions and management to ferment a reactionary willingly-put-upon self reliance amongst industrial workers in particular.

As a heroic myth, ascribing supernatural powers to labour, it had merged up to a point the identity of worker and capitalist around sacrificial slogans like "Britain's bread hangs be' Lancashire's thread". As an outlook it was too trade conscious, censorious, 'uneducated' and introverted to enable it to cope with the newer concerns pouring in upon the trade union movement (music, racism, the women's movement, unemployment etc.) and inadequate to its recently acquired universality as 'a second parliament'.

"WE SHALL NEVER WORK OH SEAS OF FIRE" – RIMBAUD. YOPs: SOCIAL AND LIFE SKILLS AND JOKE/JOB CREATION

The TUC has not as it did in the 1930s turned its back on the unemployed, opening for example centres and organizing marches. NUPE (National Union of Public Employees) has made efforts to recruit the young unemployed on government YOP (Youth Opportunities Programmes), schemes stoking up the fire only to throw water on it. At around the time of the riots young people were brought out in ineffectual strikes in the northeast and northwest while those who played with matches eventually found the light.

Through the mediation of Further Education Colleges, many unemployed teenagers pass through YOP courses designed to teach the euphemism of "social and life skills" (SLS). These courses represent a clear break with school and if anything points to the failure of schools to provide the 'right attitudes' to work. In an interview given to the NATFHE Journal (National Association of Teachers in Further and Higher Education) June/July '80, Frank Ward, Head of General Studies at South Shields Marine and Technical College said… "We tried to create an atmosphere that was patently not school - while maintaining some of the constraints of the normal working situation."

The rapid extension of YOP/SLS courses provides the most blatant example of the intrusion of behaviourist principles (so in favour with the real owners of capital) into education the UK has seen. Unsurprisingly it is unaccompanied by fanfares to Eysenck and Skinner because debate for or against is conceived as belonging to the remote and authorized world of the university which FE (Further Education) colleges more responsive to the whims of the bosses regard as only for the 'clever'.

The basis of this philosophy which in the confines of FE Colleges must pass for incontrovertible realism can be summed up in a nutshell: the bosses are always right. Even so learning how to kiss arse is done with flair and subtlety, which disguises the crude authoritarianism at work.

The curriculum is constantly changing and each group of youngsters chooses its own topics over and above the core. Teaching methods are non traditional; the teachers say they never use the word 'teach'!!!!!! In particular students are encouraged to criticize each other, video taping for instance mock jobs (or joke) interviews that are then played back to the whole class. The communication skills workshops which includes the video equipment contains, if the truth be told, the hardware of detection through which the all-seeing eye of the boss is able to monitor conduct by winning the early collaboration of future employees.

At the South Shields College, the staff dealing with the SLS part of the YOP programme come from a variety of backgrounds including youth and social work, careers counselling and industry. Unlike colleges in the southeast their class of origin tends to be more exclusively working class. Proud at having landed a teaching job in an FE College, tutors especially in the north may, every so often, look up to a regular Times reader as an earthly divinity. But that closeness with the youth they teach born of different levels of feelings of inferiority has its limitations. It has been found necessary to lift adults with requisite skills out of the dole queues and appoint them as group leaders in YOP schemes. They then become a key figure in the government's wage cutting operation. Because they understand enough of what life is on the dole, shared experiences are used as a leaven to ram home the Government's intentions. ("Group leaders have, been recruited from the unemployment register, and this practise has brought in men and women who understand and sympathize with the young people, and can talk to them in their own language" op cit).

THE UNEMPLOYED PROFESSIONAL

Unemployment especially in Britain is unevenly hitting sections of society brought up to think such things could never happen to them. With the Official Receiver working overtime, the skids under whole tiers of middle management, droves of skilled workers out of work and the numbers of graduates looking for non existent professional employment at an all time high, things are not looking up for that great leveller, the dole. To counteract this tendency the MSC (Manpower Services Commission - a post OPEC State sponsored unemployment body) tries its unlevelling best to drive a wedge between the mass of the unskilled and semi-skilled and the numbers of unemployed professional and skilled workers. Hence for some the dole gin-trap is carefully sprung, staggering over a period of time the shock of proletarianization.

Failing to find permanent employment in their particular field, professionals are given a chance to branch out. Thanks (but no thanks!) to the MSC there are a growing number of short term contractual jobs on offer which in one way or another involve overseeing unemployed youth especially in the performing 'arts' (ugh), sport, archaeological digs etc. "Appropriate qualifications" are not waived so much as bent and when applying for these jobs being unemployed is a stipulated condition. The unemployed pro can only hold out against these inducements for so long before he or she is unceremoniously picked up by the scruff of the neck and whisked through the deskilling process. This far from pleasant but necessary experience generally takes place behind closed doors in the presence of a URO (Unemployment Review Officer) at the local SS Office. Once this happens the unemployed pro can expect henceforth to be continually harassed by the state because their claim to special consideration has just been brusquely torn up.

The MSC looks to unemployed professionals to provide a lead in other ways. In 1980 a pamphlet commissioned by the MSC from the National Council of Voluntary Service appeared. The pamphlet entitled Work and the Community looked as though it might be in praise of idleness but a second glance showed this to be totally untrue. Banishing the stigma of unemployment forever, the report argued, was long overdue but chronic unemployment is no excuse for not sharing "Beveridge's view of the evil of unwanted idleness."

The report's distinction "between the term 'unemployment' and 'work'" is really a cryptic way of saying unemployment benefit should be earned. Through the optic of this perspective, Beveridge's cold as charity distinction (and it is not by chance that Beveridge's name - the architect of the post war welfare state - crops up) between deserving and undeserving poor is used to prejudge the unemployed. To qualify, in so many words, for 'deserving status' the unemployed must, the report hints, be willing to do voluntary unpaid labour.

The report has something other in mind than giving the front door a lick of paint. It means to lay hands on the free labour of the unemployed for "neighbourhood services co-operatives, community producer and consumer co-operatives and other community originated work and employment activities" as a substitute for cuts in "social services". The only trouble being "in inner city areas - a tradition of voluntary effort is often absent". It is just possible that at this sticking point the unemployed professional can be relied on to fill the gap, providing an example for others to follow.

The report became the basis for the MSC Community Enterprise programme set up in April 1981 to deal with the numbers of long term unemployed nearing half a million. Now under Tebbit the programme is being dragged kicking and screaming into realizing its philosophy of unpaid community work. Why protest so much? Tebbit is after all only sticking closely to the letter of the report.

The ex-professional can with some effort become other. They are in any case, depending on the length of time unemployed, shoved in this direction by the state. Under these conditions an ethic of public service cannot linger on indefinitely. Providing he or she remains on negative ground the ex-professional is well placed without being able to pull any punches, to expose and clarify the pernicious games of capital and the state.

QUIET FLOWS THE TYNE?

Some of the most comprehensive YOP innovations started life on Tyneside. It was one of the first areas to introduce "21 hour benefits" enabling unemployed youths to attend up to 21 hours of FE (Further Education) without forfeiting their social security. The quantity of experiment particularly to self-interested empire builders connected with the unemployment industry savours amid the theatrical plenitude, of human fulfilment. The area has for Jack Grassby, trade union NATFHE Liaison Secretary at South M and T College "learned to use unemployment creatively" (!!) But the MSC's Regional Representative for Special Programmes expressed a more disillusioned and accurate view. When asked what was the point of an extensive programme when so many kids will only wind up back on the dole, he answered that, at the least, it prevents violence on the streets.

The YOP strikes in the Tyneside and Consett region experienced during the summer of 1981 helped defuse an anger that could have been as intense as Liverpool. The extensive YOP programmes must have had some impact on minimizing the rioting in the region. In fact the blanket YOP schemes pioneered by these seemingly impregnable Godfather-like Labour party citadels where every unemployed school leaver even in 1980 was within six weeks "offered" a place on a YOP course, must now appear as a prototype that the Thatcher government, in response to the riots, applied to the rest of the country. Even the newspapers were frank enough to admit that unemployed school leavers would now be "under considerable pressure" to take up YOP places by Unemployment Review Officers. The same could have been said of Tyneside, which anticipated under the auspices of the Labour party dominated local state, the national trend by at least one to one and a half years.

Photo left: Is everyone really as happy as Sam on the Social and Life Skills course at the South Shields Marine and Technical College? Photo middle: ....These secretaries employed by GEC have nothing to smile about. At £25pw and £31pw respectively this apology for a wage is only fractionally better than YOP or the Dole.... Photo right: Photos like this appear continually in the press to emphasise the working class popularity of legislation to curb flying/secondary picketing. Odds on bets the lorry driver seen here attempting to black jack a miners' picket in the early 1970s was himself an unpaid administrator of supplies determining what moved and what didn't during the lorry drivers' strike in the Winter of Discontent.

JOB TRAINING IN THE 1980s: THE SORCERER'S APPRENTICE

The Tebbit Plan is another example of knock-kneed foot dragging centralization thrust upon a Government caught unawares by the summer riots. Looked at from a distance, government strategies form a schizoid mixture of subservience to dogma followed by hesitant backsliding, rescue operations requiring more state centralization, not less. When Tebbit announced that 16 Industrial Training Boards were to be abolished he was placing the responsibility for industrial training more firmly in the lap of industry. At the same time he has created the space for the MSC (Manpower Services Commission) to assume responsibility for apprenticeships when he guaranteed from September 1983 a year's training to all school leavers who fail to find a job.

It is timed when fully operational to just about suit an incoming Labour or SDP/Tory party coalition government. This is good news for us because all parties will have a hell of a job attempting to convince the masses of unemployed school leavers that the cheap labour 'abuses' will stop. When YOP schemes were few in number it was possible for the MSC and especially the trade unions to clamp down on firms with "suspect teenage employment schemes", which used "trainee"' as cheap labour substitutes for older workers whilst claiming MSC subsidies.

Monitoring went against the grain of government policy but once the schemes were extended following the summer riots, the unions openly relinquished responsibility for monitoring the schemes while continuing to prominently sit on the MSC board. Now that YOP is to be replaced by a desultory, generalized "training package", which looks set to continue the "misuses" of YOP programmes, the unions will be placed squarely in the firing line. "Misuse": it's such a nice neutral term chosen carefully by MSC and trade union apologists to hide the horrible truth. In the 12 months to June 1980 5 school leavers were killed on job training schemes, 25 had limbs or fingers amputated (government cuts?) while a further 2,000 were victims of industrial injuries. Most were not entitled to compensation because they had, out of ignorance, disregarded safety regulations. And not one of them received a penny in sickness benefit!

On present calculations the training part of the Tebbit plan covers some 3 months with the rest of the time taken up with "work experience" on employers premises. Even bearing in mind the large scale deskilling sweeping through industry, it is not even a speeded-up apprenticeship so much as at best a preparation for an apprenticeship. Really it is a mass exercise to slash wages primarily, but by no means exclusively, in unskilled occupations. School leavers are to be paid the measly sum of £16 per week - a drop of £7 from the £23 received on YOP schemes. It is also considerably less than the dole and Tebbit's plan intends withdrawing the right to supplementary benefit from school leavers who refuse 'training' schemes. The tender hearted Economist finds "these are actually two of the best features of the scheme (making) youths less expensive to employ"(19th/25th December '81). Tebbit's White Paper A New Training Initiative: Programme for Action is bluntly open about wanting to "bring about a change in attitude of young people to the value of training and acceptance of relatively lower wages for trainees." This may appear to be directed solely at bringing down apprentices' wages, the highest in Europe, but its real purpose is to help bring down the general level of wages. This scheme, like Thatcher's series of unemployment measures hastily got up in response to the riots, really comprise at one remove a very drastic statutory incomes policy from a government pledged to keep the law out of wage bargaining. Because these apologies for training schemes are being applied to the mass of school leavers it seems fireworks will shortly be used to back up verbal resistance to this super exploitation. Hopefully it will this time involve more directly the employed working class. It will mean vaulting a few hurdles because the pressure of gully-low paid youths performing work or even attempting to perform work normally reserved for much higher paid adult workers acts as a barrier to unity.

Just what the Government ordered, only this time the unions because of their participation in the MSC, have been manoeuvred into overseeing the process. How unfortunate. About to lose a lot of control over entry to particular trades they must try and placate the fears of time serving workers while preserving the two-tier wage structure neatly dividing teenagers from adult workers. An unenviable position and one, which will strain to the limits trade union jiggery pokery. They must be looking back nostalgically to the good old days when at the slightest sign of danger they had the option of withdrawing into their tortoise-like carapace.

The Tebbit Plan, unlike the earlier Finniston Report on Industry. (The Finniston Report was more or less suppressed by the Thatcher Government because among other things it was an implicit challenge to the notion that the British worker Johnny is bone idle and responsible consequently for the "crisis of profitability". Finniston with the interest of industrial capitalism at heart, placed the emphasis on much greater investment - getting government and banks to stake a lot more in UK Inc, - stepping up training to hi-tech sectors and re-evaluating the class status of engineers in the UK, where, like in France they would be classed alongside managerial functions. It showed in other words that Britain does not reflect the requirements of modern day industrial capitalism and that it was about time it did so because "real economic decline now stares Britain in the face." Although Finniston's arguments are those of an intelligent technocrat a failure to update Britain, will also undoubtedly be a factor in precipitating a revolutionary crisis one that has already well transcended the perspective of a technocratic state capitalism.), was not conceived as an answer to skill shortages which afflicts British capitalism even with massive unemployment. The Institute of Mechanical Engineers in August 1981 on anecdotal evidence (just how primitive can UK Inc get?) found that skill shortages were developing in its sector. At the same time 68,000 jobs in mechanical engineering were hanging by a thread supported by a short time working compensation scheme. Rather than attempt to rectify this situation in the interests of capitalist regeneration, Tebbit's plan represents a continuation of the good old-fashioned principal "the devil finds work for idle hands". What the hands should be doing in relation to the training needs of capital was never really at issue. No one pointed to the riotous apprentices in Zurich and Berlin. The entire hullabaloo in Parliament following the riots about lack of training was more a requiem on the failures of social engineering to keep the young off the streets than a belated fanfare to capitalist technocracy.

GRAY POWER AND YELLOW UNIONS

If the young have to be kept off the streets, the old have to be encouraged to die.

The growing number of elderly people living on pensions has also begun to attract the TUC's attention. It might look as if the unions are lending their industrial muscle to help the aged wring more benefits from the state. But the real motive lies elsewhere. In the past few years pensioners have started to flex their own muscles evolving informal self-help schemes which could easily tip over into using more aggressive tactics against e.g. the worm eaten bully boys from the Gas and Electricity Boards who can condemn pensioners to death by shutting off supplies of heat. By demanding greater allowances from the government, the TUC is pre-empting moves in this direction, which might easily have unforeseeable consequences like the refusal to pay and the local Derby and Joan club with exploding pension books.

As the TUC extends its range, it starts to infringe on areas traditionally dealt with by voluntary organizations. TUC demands are beginning to sound like appeals on behalf of charities choosing to sting the conscience rather than threaten force. At the same time newer organizations relying a lot on volunteers (Task Force etc) refer constantly to 'workers organizations'. In the not-so-distant past most voluntary organizations would have preferred to break their teeth than say this.

Taking a more overall view of the situation, these developments within the TUC are linked to the growing unproductive sector of the proletariat whose wages, pensions, dole money are exchanged against revenue. A majority of the 'working' class now resides outside of productive industry that is why unions cannot continue to act in a negligent fashion. Left to themselves these sectors are too dangerous as the inspiring example of the riots demonstrate.

AFTER RIOTS BLUES...PRESSURE... PRESSURE...PRESSURE...PRESSURE

Finally what happened to the kids after the July days? A change has been noticed by a number of people. There definitely are more teenage nutcases to be seen wandering the streets wild eyed, brows furrowed perhaps performing some mysterious hand mime or just talking gibberish. Sure, they were there before but the sound and fury and expectation left many more looking all washed-up. Hopefully not for long. Conditions generally are just too bad for cynical careerism and a killing nihilism to even temporarily appear to get the upper hand. Anyone who lived through 1968 and the decade or so of reflux afterwards knows how deadly that can be driving the more sincere to despair and suicide.

But the signs meanwhile are good.

The brief experience of solidarity has survived defeat. The influence of events like these is incalculable. They never are over and done with just like that. Two unemployed teenagers Sean and Raffy, topped themselves in Widnes on the banks of the Mersey. Condemned on telly as hooligans by their ex-headmaster they were avenged by their mates who torched part of the Head's shitty school.

Some youths are individually taking it upon themselves to avenge others. There is something pitiful and sorely troubled about these incidents, which in other respects bring to mind the filial reprisals of 19th century anarchists. A youth was given 8 years detention at Her Majesty's Pleasure after attempting to shoot her with blanks during the trooping of the colour. Several weeks later a youth was picked up outside the gates of Buck Palace with a "loaded" airgun. Both had given ample warnings of their intentions and it subsequently proved difficult to unravel class-consciousness from crackbrained cries for help as details of their case histories emerged.

Bollocks To Theory?

How worried should we be about the absence of theory in Britain? It is doubtful if any other country has advanced so close to the brink without ever affirming a need for theory. Nor is it easy to say why this should retard a proletarian movement, which is in all other respects so advanced. Yet this uneasy feeling something is not quite as it should be just won't go away. As it turned out the rioters were more served by 'instinct' than reason. Like the Italian insurgents of 1977 they gave as never before short shrift to the 'left'. Unlike the Italians, they seemed unable to go beyond very angry though near sighted denunciations of manipulative practises. No real effort was ever made to generalize the struggle but most everyone, particularly in Liverpool, in a quite casual easy-going way, was free to join in. Deeds substituted for choruses of "class unity".

Altogether there was a near total absence of graffiti. Nowhere on the smoke blackened gable ends could graffiti be found remotely approaching the penetrating, retrospective yet highly topical refrains of the Italian spring, ("Let's retake life", "Rest assured I shall not suicide, Italy 77", and "We are realizing culture suppressing it" etc). There wasn't much either in the way of flyers and agitational broadsheets. The best pamphlet to appear in England was "A Second Blast of the Trumpet Against the Capitalist Nightmare". In France a similar uprising would have produced a deluge of leaflets - never mind the near inevitability of wall-to-wall graffiti. In spite of a much-changed situation a direct line of descent from May 1968 would be instantly apparent to most people there.

In Britain nation-wide upheavals glance only fleetingly across the oceans and national frontiers. Localized fury never aspires, even if in name only, to a genuine internationalism. Yet home grown class struggle in the UK attracts a lot of attention elsewhere. The wave of strikes that engulfed the UK between 1970-74 was commented on the world over but the UK proletariat remained indifferent to the impact abroad. In 1981 a few weeks after the July days placards were fixed to the backs of lorries in Berlin proclaiming "Manchester, Liverpool, London, Berlin", while graffiti appeared on walls in Spain demanding a Toxteth and Brixton there. And one of the best leaflets to come out on the UK explosion was produced in New York under the name of "Barbarians for Socialism". It is highly insulting to say the UK proletariat cannot see farther than the end of its nose, yet the quality of comment coming from outside Britain continues to mount up putting to shame most theoretical efforts to get to grips with class struggle here.

A troubling, maybe far-fetched image sometimes flickers across the mind's eye. The UK in the not-so-distant future has been turned upside down from one end to the other. Young, old, black and white, employed and unemployed have by stages become involved yet not even a muted call for its international extension can be heard above the din of multicoloured little Englanders.

Naval watching in the UK is however very distinct from US isolationism. Historically both have been ill at ease with the Pax Britannica and Pax Americana electing to let the rest of the world go to hell if needs be. However in Britain, it has traditionally taken root as much amongst the centre/left as the outside right (the left Labour party MP Dennis Skinner prides himself in the age of mass travel on not possessing a passport). And it is not in the main aggressively racialist like some extreme isolationist movements in America, which tend to fear New York and Washington more than they do the world outside. Hence immigrants softened up by exposure to this condescending but sympathetic ear attuned to their plight, are more likely in turn to be vulnerable to the narrowing influence of left wing little Englanders.

Once upon a time it might generally have been supposed God was an Englishman but not one speck of this pompous self esteem has brushed off on proletarians living in the UK who dares attempt a searching analysis of class struggle in the UK or elsewhere. An utter lack of confidence in these matters easily tips over into a do-nothing paralysis born of inferiority. Which is a shame but before branding it as cowardice we need to know why. Part of the trouble arises from popularly held misconceptions, which automatically confuses theory with academia and paid-up intellectuals. Because the latter have such a high standing in Britain, higher even than businessmen in the pseudo-bourgeois scale of value so typical of the UK, they tend to be bracketed (and rightly too) alongside "them". Now "them" has a special inflection in Britain. It implies a sort of archetypal snobbery against which the exaggerated extreme is alone safe from contamination. The trouble is all theorizing is consequently suspect though the one-sided reaction hasn't seriously handicapped the proletariat yet. But it could well do so in the future and prizing theory away from past attempts to pull the wool might save lives and prevent disaster.

STRANGER THAN FICTION:

Hours before 3 days rioting in Derby word had gone out a library was to be the center of attack. Over the last year or so libraries all over the UK have been invaded as unemployment shot over 3 million. The generally snotty-nosed staff are determined to prevent libraries being turned into informal community centers where the unemployed can gather. Tending to treat everyone who uses the library as unemployed their superiority and condescension knows no bounds arousing the hostility of every library user. It's a bit like the arguments for community policing all over again. Rather than risk a Toxteth of the bookshelves libraries for instance in Gateshead-on-Tyne, are becoming part of the institutionalized strategy for the management of the unemployed. Punk groups for example are allowed to perform on the premises during opening hours. Meanwhile another local library in Gateshead is popularly known as Colditz.

At the moment to step beyond a quite narrowly demarcated territory criss-crossed with razor sharp but fragmentary observations, defiant witticisms and knockabout fun is to risk exclusion. Gentle ridicule and less frequently a mockery bordering on plain viciousness clouds any attempt at revolutionary theory, which is only allowed to go so far before, it trails off into embarrassed silence. Britain's immobile but also moving class-in-itself social apartheid oscillating from one moment to the next between self reliance and lack of confidence hinges on this increasingly precarious balance. But for the time being there's simply no getting away from it: in comparison to France, Spain, Portugal and Italy, the UK is theoretically underdeveloped though it remains on the practical plain quite extraordinarily rich. It is also true that here and there workers in the UK are becoming theoreticians and excellent ones at that. Let's hope that tendency gets bigger and wider until theory in action becomes an unstoppable force.

The most hectic periods of class struggle always leaves time for reflection but it is far from immediately obvious that lessons have been learnt in the UK. But learnt they must be otherwise class struggle in the absence of any mechanistic providence may not keep to such an unswerving course for much longer. There is for example not one instance of a genuinely collective theoretical creation that can stand comparison with the assembly statutes of the Barcelona dockers in their strike of 1980-81.

And because it was an assembly, others from outside (including foreigners) were given the right to speak and enter. (There have, in parenthesis, recently been joint assemblies of the employed and unemployed in Spain). What finally emerged was a revolutionary tract subsuming trade demarcations (the basis of trade unionism) with the wider realities of class. In the UK the only comparable examples were the occupations of Plessey's in South West Scotland and the Fisher Bendix factory in Liverpool in 1972. Following the example of Plessey's, the workers of Fisher Bendix created an open assembly ("our struggle is your struggle") where wives, children, brothers, sisters, aunts, uncles, dogs, cats and lovers could come along and have their say. But it also remained something of a Liverpool family affair and it is doubtful if for example foreigners disseminating revolutionary material and opinions would have been made all that welcome. Still Liverpool has repeatedly defied all expectation.

When comparing the riots in the UK with those in Berlin parallel deficiencies are again apparent in a shared movement whose centre lies outside the point of production. In the aforementioned riot in Berlin, loudspeaker vans reeling off the names and other business interests of real estate speculators (including incidentally, the German trade unions) could be heard urging demonstrators from one swank apartment to the next. The apartments were systematically being stoned. In the UK, this extra dimension of clarity was sadly missing. The riots in Britain were, to be sure, more exclusively proletarian than those in Berlin and far more deadly. But after having made due allowance an antipathy to all theory did seem to cramp horizons. It cannot be said too often: Britain and the rest of the English-speaking world desperately needs to set up a radical publishing venture. The need is especially urgent in Britain considering how close the country is to a gigantic explosion, or, catastrophe if things don't turn out right.

If the employed working class doesn't in the near future respond in a revolutionary manner, a death's head psychosis could lie in wait on every street corner. If fresh headway is not continually being made the floodtide of rioting could get jammed up and start to flow in the other way. And if this happens it's no use the workers blaming the bourgeoisie when their own passive toleration of the circulation of commodities and the state is just as much to blame. There are no eternal truths that make the success of the social revolution certain in advance. The goal of an everyday life liberated from capitalism has to be fought for at every stage. Lack of clarity could mean "the common ruin of the contending classes" (Marx). And that today amounts to trillions bending down and kissing their ass goodbye forever.

"WE ARE WITNESSING THE SPECTACULAR REARMING OF OUR GREAT ENEMY. THE STATE, SOMETHING THE WORLD'S RULING CLASSES DO WHEN THEY WANT TO GIVE AN APPEARANCE OF SOLIDITY TO THE DECOMPOSITION OF ITS FOUNDATIONS" (Poster on gaoled Spanish Libertarians, 1981)

No amount of window dressing - and there wasn't much of that - can alter the fact that the state in the UK is now making long-term preparations for an insurrection. There have recently been two disturbing developments related to the growing power of the para-military. The first consists in offering to young employed from inner cities the chance to get in some army experience. The second involves a revival of the Home Guard (called now the Home Service Force) to guard key installations such as telephone exchanges, electricity transformers, oil pipelines etc, "against Russian wartime saboteurs"! In short, using the threat of a Third World War fomented by the super-powers as a front to put down indigenous insurrection. The army stresses it is not really looking for teenagers (no doubt they are too unreliable) preferring ideally to take on ex-servicemen and ex-coppers. Defence officials emphasised there was absolutely no intention of calling out the new Home Guard to cope with" civil disturbances" but it would be the height of stupidity to think otherwise.

The lessons of the riots have begun to unevenly sink in all quarters. The state, quick off the mark, is making preparations for its defence well in advance of a potential proletarian onslaught. The proletariat has to take note of this and anticipate some of the problems in advance. Poland has been a testing ground for some of these problems and a clear warning you can fuck around with the system just for so long. Out comes the big stick eventually. The Polish telephone operators for instance, were caught napping by the coup. So the telephone communication system was easily immobilised by the military. Have telephone operators in the UK thought what the consequences might be if telephone exchanges are ringed by armed thugs? Unable to make physical contact with the outside they will be exposed to the most frightening forms of intimidation from 'their' armed guards.

Lastly the advertised holiday with the army for the young jobless marks a turning point in the Armed Forces' involvement with unemployed youth. Ever since the Boy Scouts, the army has settled for making its influence felt in an off duty capacity. The volunteer recruits won't (for the moment at any rate) receive weapons training but they will be subject to army discipline and salutes and more likely therefore to respond positively to an army takeover if it should ever come to pass. It is too early to say what sort of youth is likely to be attracted to this cut-price offer. But it could well appeal to repressed, still tentative authoritarian undertones in some of today's youth sub-cultures.

"MALVINAS PARA LOS PINGUINOS" – "VICTORY TO THE SHEEP" *(Anti war slogans)*

In the exceptionally severe winter of 1886 unemployed building workers and others rioted in central London. Engels condemned the "opportunism" of William Morris and sundry that saw in these unemployed battles "the first skirmish of the revolution". They were, according to Engels, the work of desperate riff-raff on "the borderland between the working class and lumpenproletariat - ready for any 'lark' up to a wild riot apropos de rien." Drifting back into the East End the unemployed numbering some 20,000 rattled off a chorus or two of Rule Britannia.

This other sea borne 'national anthem' has once again been heard wishing the fleet well as it sailed for the Falklands/Malvinas or rather the Penguin Isles. On a London bus a graffiti read "Skinheads fight for your country, go to the Falklands" and the number of applicants applying to the naval recruiting office in High Holborn zoomed up. When asked on a radio programme if these included unemployed skool leavers, a spokesman with a kilo of plums in his mouth answered, "We are not a recruiting office for unemployables."

This cold-water reply sets limits to the hot-blooded nationalism of the phantom spray can writer. Together they reflect the potency and limitations of this ad hoc response to the conflict in the south Atlantic, which the state has used to the utmost, tapping both popular imperial residues and the legacy of anti fascism deriving from World War Two. Set beside other memories retrieved from the historical deeps, Maggie Thatcher on the even of the Mark No 1 Task Force setting sail opportunely quoted Queen Victoria. "Failure? The possibility does not exist." However against memories of Drake and other expeditionary forces sent to sort out some corner of a far-flung empire, were mingled allusions to the Dover Patrol of the Second World War and an anti fascist resistance.

Behind the irrelevant and anachronistic facade of territorial imperialism or righteous anti fascism, the hidden purpose of the war is to disorientate the proletariat. Never at any time in the past has the fleet so explicitly put to sea to prevent the proletariat from setting sail in its own drunken boat. To the aft of the unexpected show of strength mounted by the Task Force lies the fear of riots, strikes and a dissident youth whose aggressive energy needs to be nailed with official blessing to the mast of hooligan patriotism. The unrelenting media swamp operation has drowned any mention (until June) of three days of heavy rioting in Liverpool, and has only partially succeeded in jamming the trouble in the health service, the support striking miners have already given nurses, and the promise of more aid to come from steel workers and water workers. A national dock strike was narrowly averted and massive trouble on the railways threatens. Apart from the hospitals these struggles are-not about higher pay, raising questions of class solidarity, unemployment and the erosion of working conditions (e.g. the Wandsworth refuse collectors strike against competitive tendering). Counteracting the drift to class unity is the British Bulldog divisiveness created by the south Atlantic war. Suddenly racial, regional/national differences have taken on an importance once more. Military success has mesmerised many a skinhead. A year ago they ached to trash rich suburbs and were putting out feelers to young blacks who look on the Penguin Isles as just another piece of land. Irish proletarians who over the last few years have never made a big thing out of being Irish, lowered their voices, wary lest anyone think them unpatriotic and northerners became somewhat 'suspect' as 'socialist' by the 'loyalist' south. All this old divide and rule crap has reared its head again but now without any substance to sustain it for any length of time.

The war in the south Atlantic had from the British Government's point of view to be sold as a just war. This is the key to the anti fascist rhetoric, references to D-Day landings, The Longest Day, Poland 1939 etc. But the real effect of this propaganda will be felt in Latin America, not in the UK. At a stroke Thatcher ruined the US/Argentinean axis. As the former US Assistant Secretary of State William Rogers said: "We face the erosion if not the dismantlement of the entire inter-American system." Thatcher however is supremely unaware that she might actually be fomenting revolution in Latin America. Formerly, British expeditionary forces were often as not despatched to put down popular rebellion. Now it is the reverse: success for the British military means fanning the flames of social revolution abroad. Lacking a worldview of likely causes and effects, the business in the south Atlantic is a parochial throw of the dice. It has in the UK been a spectator's war, conveying an impression of effortless conflict meant to overawe the proletariat and restore the confidence of the British nation state accustomed to falling flat on its face. This was the pearl behind the successful storming of the penguins massed on South Georgia and the ludicrous despatch sent out by the Commander of the Fleet to Queen Liz. The only concession to anti fascist sentiment - excepting the rhetoric - has been the capture and bringing back of Capitano Alfredo Astiz, the notorious Argentinian torturer. All in all there are built-in limitations to the manipulation of the anti fascist heritage in the UK, which the state seems to recognise by not making much of. A tradition of armed guerrilla resistance to an indigenous fascist regime lending itself to manipulation by Secret Services through acts of terrorism is lacking. This rules out any slavish imitation of the Italian-style "strategy of tension" though the British state has not been averse to using terrorism when it saw fit. The British state has to extemporise ever anew, unable to hit on the right formula for containment. Penguin Islands were a gift horse all right, but how much more mileage can be got out of these remote islands? Interest wanes with victory and mass attention is beamed back from the south Atlantic to the social war within.

Insistent prodding shall keep alive the memory of these events. Threats, real or imagined, of a renewed invasion and bombing raids are going to mean the garrisoning of British troops on the Islands for some considerable time to come. A flotilla of boats large and small are likely to be kept on the ready in the south Atlantic. Cuts in naval expenditure shall be temporarily postponed and the rundown of naval dockyards in Chatham and Portsmouth (scenes of rioting in 1981) leading to the loss of 40,000 jobs deferred for a while. One third of the navy, prior to the conflict, was due to be scrapped and some 40 of the jolly jack tars who put to sea were clutching redundancy papers. 1000 professional soldiers were also, due to be laid off. No future but signing on the rock 'n' roll.

The navy was however going to bear the brunt of the cuts. Naval high commands threatened with imminent eclipse (minus subs) are staking their survival on this nostalgic Senior Service fag packet Armada silhouetted against westering guns more evocative of World War One than the nuclear/missile age. The rebuilding of the lost ships, the maintenance of an 8,000-mile supply line and the enormous cost of the war nearing two billion pounds will be paid for out of increased taxation and a further reduction in the social wage as money available for health care is snapped up by the armed forces. This is bound eventually to exacerbate still more the social crises, which just goes to show what a one-off adventure this has been. In the not so distant past, jingoism and gunboat diplomacy had to be paid for with increased welfare expenditure and domestic reform - the reverse of what is happening now.

The subversive process within has gone too far and bread and water phrases like "peace with honour" will do little to set back for any length of time the beginnings of a revolutionary unity and totality, the like of which the British proletariat has never experienced before.

The summer riots of 1981 were the foretaste of the future for us. One day sooner or later the roof is going to blow off the UK. Faced with an assertion like this most people in pubs, streets, supermarkets or at work tend to nod their heads. The old phlegmatic reassurances that "it can't happen here" has finally gone - let it be forever.

By: Wolfie Smith, Speed, Tucker and June *(1982)* ....

When will King Coal and the Old King Coal burn merrily together?

(Old King Coal was rhyming slang for the dole)

For Vicki on Ralph Rumney: Hidden connections, ruminations and rambling parentheses

(For those who don't know and to all the victims of the dumbing down engineered by the media class, Ralph Rumney was a co-founder of the International Situationists in 1957. Originally from the north of England he was an artist who tried to move beyond the boundaries of art; one encompassing a profounder social vision helping initiate psychogeography and the practise of the derive. Failing in his quest he fell back on prior artistic paradigms venturing into the circles of a cultural high society forever tending to give him short shrift.)

Let's first consider Ralph Rumney's excellent points: In his mid teens in the early 1950s he tried to get hold of copies of De Sade's books creating violent contra-temps with his parson father. He then courageously refused the compulsory National Service stint in the army. Going on the run he was forced to appear in a Bristol court where he gave a spirited, existential, even Camus-like defence of his refusal when it would have been much easier to have fallen back on a more conservative, 'thou shalt not kill' religious plea-bargaining. Not too afraid of the consequences he had the courage to face penury with equanimity: 'I discovered material poverty at the same time as intellectual wealth'. His undoubted lust for life meant he could take on board a more or less youthful street existence for a while in London and Paris; an experience which obviously helped enormously in opening up his mind. Rumney's lifestyle was thus inseparable from developing concepts, which later were to produce the more fully worked out derive. It meant too he came slap bang up against the modernisers, the city developers and planners and he had the guts to confront them head on. Rumney hated Colin Buchanan, the chief architect responsible for the 1950s London clearances and had the honour of being excluded from the so-called radical Independents Group for condemning the architects in their midst. (No doubt this was the Smithsons and others belonging to the school of brutalism). Against the 'flattened universe' of modernism, Rumney's alternatives for London, though hardly fleshed-out weren't bad at all, envisaging a psychogeography of pedestrian zones (down with the car) bringing out the ambiences of the different huddled together villages that make up London.

Unfortunately we must now consider the down side; the soft underbelly. Despite all the excellent contrariness, Rumney, no matter what, was always an artist even in his most rebellious early days. By 1953 and only twenty years old, he had landed a paid-up contract with London's Redfern Gallery and over 25 years later, not having moved on, he was teaching art at Canterbury School of Art. Throughout the years from the early 50s onwards, exhibition after exhibition of his works followed in England, Italy and Belgium etc. Sorry to keep repeating this but Rumney was essentially a gallery artist and the vast majority of his writings and interviews are concerned with this central fact, endlessly name dropping about all the artists - with all their bullshit works - he met and met and met. It's all pretty pointless, even sickening because real critique was marginalised and when he attempted to get to the heart of the matter it was always through a deflection. Thus totality - which for people like us implies the attempted praxis of total revolution - became for Ralph Rumney 'the total praxis of art' in a re-vamped Renaissance, Italian city state sense where the artist strutting his/her stuff on the stage overshadows and overawes the paymaster: The Modern Prince. Concepts like detournement were deployed in the narrow, artistic sense of collage and montage and Rumney's substitute attack on art was against 'artism', that endless repetition of marketable themes. It became a get-out clause; a means whereby the guy didn't have to confront his artistic role. Half measures were it seems enough! All these foibles are today entirely familiar and in fits and starts deployed by all the rag-tag post-modernists far, far, far more mediocre than Rumney. We need only think of Tracy Emin, the Chapman Bros and Banksy.....

So much for a brief historical, critical context: What follows are some thoughts on Ralph Rumney I've mulled over in my head for many a year. He's a guy who wasn't to be one thing or another, who searched but hardly found who fell back on past historical roles (the bohemian artist) but was unable to really cut through into anything like a fully-fledged revolutionary critique - one that superseded art - and thus offering hope for the future of human kind. He seemed unsure of what he did find like the outcome of certain derives he initiated, the best concerning east London (Limehouse) and the worst concerning Italy, (Venice). Hesitating, unable to complete and to make ruthless but necessary jumps, Ralph fell backwards only to then many years later update himself, revisiting somewhat his lapsed past - the explosions of the late 1960s largely I think passed over him - and alas, for this update to lack substantial cutting edge. It was at this late hour and getting on in years a mode whereby he merely mimicked original situationist anger as the done thing to do, a substitute anger he hoped would give him some historical presence the more he realised he was acquiring fame seeing much younger people were seeking him out. There was however nothing original on offer having quickly acquired a second hand knowledge of what had happened in the interim since he'd been evicted (rightly) from the early moments of the Situationist International. This may sound harsh but there's no way Ralph Rumney achieved the clarity, audacity and heights of a Patrick Cheval, a Sebastiani or a Rene Riesel and all those largely unknown others who proved to be so effective in the late 1960s...and having started like this does not mean the following is a paean of praise for the Situationist International.

For me Ralph Rumney is personal, perhaps too personal. He came from the same neck of the woods as my twin brother and myself and where we spent a big part of our childhood and early teens, only to return - even closer to where Rumney was born - a few decades later but without leaving London wholesale, the city we'd been forced more or less into exile and, because the place is so big, we could find ways of rudimentary survival where our infamous names meant little.

One huge and shattering difference between Rumney and ourselves: Ralph didn't really like the north of England; we loved it and still do. For us The North is also a passion, for Rumney it was almost as nought. Maybe this points to the essential class difference between us? Having been forced out of the Bradford/Halifax arena in the mid 1950s Rumney was never to return spending the rest of his life in either Italy (Venice) or southern France with a few lateish interludes in the most supine, traditional enclaves of a time past, typical southern English rural retreat. Rumney had called Halifax: 'A town without culture' meaning a philistine place in a pejorative sense, and try as I might to see this description indicating the beyond of culture, I obviously cannot! None the less the town that had forced him into exile put on an exhibition of their rehabilitated son in 2002. Moreover, Rumney had been born in Newcastle just like ourselves.

Yet in a way Rumney's experience of Halifax/Bradford was the real crux of the guy's intervention in the historical becoming of the modern (or rather anti-modern) revolution. Though not so much a child of the manse - the Wesleyan thread that courses these gaunt, shorn hills - but a Church of England's parson's son, his was first and foremost a revolt against the puritanism, perhaps even the somewhat hell-fire puritanical denial and death obsession of the area, which made us so coldly shudder as children imagining we were seeing haggard looking ghouls lurking behind high, overgrown privet hedges with sealed gates fronting the then blackened Victorian Yorkshire stone of modest mini-mansions where it seemed all life was forbidden always fearful putrid green arms covered in sores would reach out from an ever-welcoming grave as we hurried on by! It was an atmosphere so unlike the more seemingly libertarian face of the northeast coalfield we'd originally hailed from. We initially hated it and as if symbolising the essence of this hatred, at the bottom of the Calderdale escarpment beneath where we lived in soot-strewn Horbury Jct, that most horrible of horrible Methodist hymns 'Onward Christian Soldiers' had been coined in a hovel of a dwelling.

Rumney as a teenager of 17 must also have felt this ambience acutely as ourselves, though much younger, and only a few miles away in Ossett, we certainly did. Our escape even at the age of 9 or 10 was New Orleans jazz and the Mississippi blues especially Pinetop Smith with his brutal but practical lyrics like: 'I want a woman who'll help me rob and steal' etc though obviously hardly knowing what this meant, the passion of Pinetop's spare boogie piano and equally spare voice were enough to keep you going. (Jazz had yet to reach the era of its potential becoming in the greatness of be bop where it sounded like the search for a new world and another life leading to a break it failed to make simply because it would have meant a 'recovery through transfer' (Marx) i.e. revolutionary praxis, though the signs were there in Pinetop). Within this West Yorkshire context, at the time, Rumney cut through to the very essence of such vague longings managing to get hold of a copy of some of De Sade's writings via a naive, clueless local librarian simply doing his job providing books from all over the country to an earnest young man in Halifax. At the same time Rumney refused army National Service. All hell broke loose and Rumney was scandalous news. The guy went on the lam. Escaping the wrath of his father and giving a forefinger up to the family and church, he escaped '- for the time - into 'revolutionary' Halifax asking the innovative but then largely unknown social historian EP Thompson to give him a bed for more than a few nights. Malcolm Imrie said in Rumney's Guardian obituary (March 8th 2002) that staying with EP 'deepened his understanding of Marxism' though finally I've got my doubts about that.

How did Rumney know about EP Thompson, was it through the Communist party and its youth league which he was a member of? Rumney had helped picket the army-recruiting centre in Bradford demonstrating against National Service and did he casually meet Thompson at one of these events, or what? That we'll never know! But let's imagine: Thompson at the time was revaluating the history of the English working classes, though his classic book on the subject was yet to be published. His research though was gradually becoming remarkable greatly assisted by on-the-spot evening class tuition via the Workers' Educational League, itself product of a form of social democratic inclusiveness. In a way Thompson was a well-meaning toff - one of the very best of them - his students, lowly, mainly manual workers who wanted to broaden their minds. The times though were opening up and things weren't what they used to be. The workers were talking back! Thompson was telling the workers their history through his assiduous, remarkable and painstaking researches. For sure his worker students would listen but then they'd query and query and query. Thompson responded, acutely listening in turn and a dialectical process unfolded, just as it should. Perspectives morphed getting subtler, getting profound.

Thus I fondly imagine, Thompson quickly realised these workers weren't stupid people: they had their own kind of often profound learning and sometimes a relevant memory passed on from generation to generation few of the more superficially literate middle classes had ever grasped. Perhaps this helped EP see - or at least bring out - the realisation the Luddite movement of this region during the early 19th century could also grasp broad, general theories; theories largely emanating from 'revolutionary' France, illiterate as these handloom weavers were supposed to be. Thompson was able to incorporate all of this into dawning new perspectives. He was right! He was then able to imaginatively reconstruct for instance and for the first time moulding it into an exciting, readable account, the battle of Rawfolds Mill, just around the corner from Halifax where a son of the Wesleyan manse joined with the armed weavers taking on the army (Sharpe's army!) in a magnificent battle where many died, and which still resonates to this day in the hidden history of this still benighted area. (Indeed only nineteen years ago or so, the development agenda in Rawfolds oriented mainly around big warehousing and being as bland as warehousing is everywhere, refused to countenance the suggestion that the new road through this consumer estate be called 'Luddite Way' recommending 'Mandela Way' instead simply because the latter name was less divisive and inflammatory. Seeing the first suggestion provoked furious letters in local papers, in the event the much more business-like 'Rawfolds Way' was chosen).

What did these two talk about in the evening? Perhaps Rumney was listening to all of this? Perhaps he began to realise the area had something remarkable about it, or, at least a certain train of thought was beginning to penetrate suggesting there was something joyous and unrepressed about it where men could dress as women in a subversive way like Lady Ludd holding Enoch's hammer smashing up the machines (& madness) of capitalist industrialisation? Where industrialised manufacture was negating the Luddite lifestyle of a pleasant and fairly minimal working week of independent cottage employment, their revolt pointing skew whiff to the abolition of pointless overwork which capitalism, more than ever, depends on.

Perhaps EP Thompson was listening to Rumney also? The agonised Rumney must have been wringing his hands at the misery he'd caused his father but also cursing the repressive character of Halifax knowing he had no choice but to ship out. No doubt Thompson asked him about De Sade - for after all the guy was virtually banned in Britain - and no doubt Rumney was able to elaborate somewhat about sexual transgression of all varieties whether leading to a kind of death-in-life or a wonderful fulfilment. Though this is speculation none the less, I cannot help feeling this must have had an impression on EP. How could they have not discussed De Sade seeing, along with military desertion, it was the main reason Rumney had arrived on Thompson's doorstep in the first instance? Moreover, for his sexual transgression and anti-militarism Rumney had immediately been thrown out of the Young Communist League but wasn't Thompson also on the brink of leaving the CP? The East German workers uprising of 1953 wasn't far off leading to the even greater ferment of the Hungarian revolution of 1956? All this uncertainty surely must have been mulled over in some way.

Later, much later, in fact just before he died, EP Thompson wrote a book on William Blake, which I initially thought was meant to be oriented around Blake's fiery, and it seems, transgressive manuscript/notebooks with the lid off on sex and liberation that may even have been as profound as De Sade though that is probably doubtful. Different maybe. As we've sadly heard (but from where?) on Blake's death the manuscript it seems was instantaneously burnt and so typical of philistine England which regularly was to frequently resort to the same procedure throughout the next 200 hundred years. (My twin brother and myself have felt its scorching presence as our elder brothers and their wives put some of our subversive statements from the late 1960s to the flames). Evidently Blake's manuscript was amazing but we'll never know what it contained. Expecting something of a lascivious thriller, in the event the book by EP Thompson, 'Witness Against the Beast' was nothing of the sort and Blake's transgressions are hardly mentioned. Though Thompson brilliantly explains Blake in terms of a lost history of antinomianism which among other exhortations emphasising social injustice, proclaimed villages based on free love and sexual orgies in place of religious services, through which one experiences God or, experiences the God within oneself, had had its real focus initially among the Ranters in and after the English revolution of 1640-9. Open expression had been followed by Restoration persecution 'disappearing' underground and reappearing decades later in 'irregular' Methodism and others cults as well as in Blake around the time of the build up to the French revolution of 1789. Tepidly even pruriently stated, EP Thompson's book apart from this history is so monumentally dull yawning quickly kicks in, though I like to think, perhaps behind these concepts lies something of the shadow of Ralph Rumney and those forgotten conversations?

It also took an occasional student of Thompson's, Peter Linebaugh to fully explain much later something else that's extremely telling: Blake was to the forefront of the rioters that swept through London in 1780 in what was to become the massive conflagration of the Gordon Riots, ending up at Newgate prison which was burnt to the ground. On the walls an emblazoned mark was left: 'His Majesty King Mob'.

One of the antinomian sects that Thompson describes was the Muggletonians. In 1968 Thompson gave a lecture on William Blake at Columbia University in New York.

At the time the place was in uproar with on-going strikes and occupations and going with the flow Thompson proclaimed himself to be 'A Muggletonian Marxist'. It went down well. Yet again the shadow of those early years in Halifax and passing acquaintance with Rumney was to the fore though by then, EP was blissfully unaware of its consequences. The occupation at Columbia University was heavily influenced by the New York Motherfuckers who used the freshly opened up terrain to promulgate some of the hippest notions of subversion many of them hot foot from the French situationists, ranging from radical sexuality, to the bankruptcy of culture via the destruction of the university with its propensity for a pointless, pedagogic learning completely removed from daily life, to even putting some of the Rector's prized artefacts on the makeshift barricades preventing full-scale police assault.

Back, though, to the 1950s. Though Thompson must have gone on to Rumney about his illuminating researches vis-a-vis the exploited, were the workers (to put it crudely) of any real interest to Ralph? Did EP soften him up on this level revealing a wider vision? Interestingly, work, workers, proletarianisation - call it what you will - never seemed to have any foci in anything Rumney wrote or said. Again was this down to our different backgrounds with RR a public school product (and thus so typical of the original English situationist milieu) we secondary modern school cannon fodder thrown together in gangs comprising weavers and miners off-spring with the occasional petty businessman's son thrown in for good measure? Some of this experience took years to sort out never mind sink in. On reflection years later, the elaborate, even bizarre oaths we all had to undergo to become members of a particular gang were more than reminiscent of the 'twisting in' pledges demanded of new Luddite recruits, perhaps meaning really explosive, historical moments die hard, if ever and we have EP Thompson's revelations to thank for being able to even begin to make such possible connections!

For Rumney enforced, alienated labour wasn't something that was to figure in his life. In fact it seems he had only one typical humdrum job in his life and that was as in telephone operator in 1968 when destitute in London having escaped from Peggy Guggenheim's private security agents in Italy and France who were trying to pin on him the blame for her daughter's suicide (Pegeen Guggenheim was Rumney's wife) he had little other choice. Well, that's usually the case for all of us who have no dosh. Yet later and interestingly Rumney never wrote or recalled these experiences; it seemed it was something to be forgotten, something to be quickly buried as soon as he was able to resume the serious business of the artist's role. Yet in a way that should have been his renewed starting point if he'd really wanted to make a belated, concrete contribution to the fallout from the situationist critique as it was then generally encountering a much more proletarianised space after the late 1960s. (Writing on say a telephone operator's scams and/or how you push the power structure off your back in an office context would have most likely fascinated Guy Debord at that moment in time). Instead after 1970, Rumney was to become a broadcaster on the French radio station ORTF, a cadre role and the type of bullshit Rumney felt more at home with.

That down over direction was sadly not to be as his old ways of existence were too ingrained in him to make such a break. After all, as befitted a product of the English public school, Rumney always knew how to turn on the charm and con the system, how to play the enfant terrible as a form of entre and cache into a well-heeled, cultural coterie that the powers that be are acutely dependent on in soft selling their rapacious reality. He was therefore easily able to hob-knob with a kind of late 1950s, La Dolce Vita jet set in Italy and France, which with its entire early tabloid limelight, celebrity promoting tittle-tattle, was just coming on stream. This type of banal media expose was the type of thing that was bound to get the early adherents of the Situationist International, especially Debord, particularly uptight and Rumney was to pay the price: He was expelled. (Well, this together with a weakening cultural critique as he cultivated the likes of William Burroughs and other American Beats in Venice. In fact the two seemingly distinct scenes weren't that inseparable. As an aside to this, for me such drastic action was necessary as along similar lines in the late 1960s some individuals belonging to the King Mob milieu made a big banner for a London demonstration on which was emblazoned Burroughs' words: 'Storm the Reality Studios. Re-Take the Universe'. Even though these were perhaps the best lines Burroughs ever wrote it none the less sent out wrong, cultural signals).

In fact no matter how Rumney fell out of grace and favour with this cultural coterie he was forever to hang on to its coattails like the aforementioned ORTF job. It ruined him. All he could forever do was ceaselessly proclaim himself as 'a situationist artist' - an obvious contradiction in terms - hanging out producing more and more lamentable artistic offerings, mainly twee paintings and collages reminiscent of 50s and 60s vinyl LP covers. They were completely worthless as far as any genuine creativity was concerned. This evaluation isn't meant as any particular critical weakness inherent in Rumney's oeuvre rather it should be taken as a statement concerning the general creative bankruptcy of all art in this era and even more so since when nothingness can only be the essence of anything officially, or even unofficially, deemed part of the arts. In the age of the aesthetic economy the common thread is the redundancy of artistic form coupled with the redundancy of all the tons of empty prattle related to it and Rumney really did believe in art. In 'Le Consul', the interview-like book about certain aspects of his life, he says: 'Art once played a real role in society, and I thought it might be possible to reproduce that situation. In 1962, Debord didn't believe that at all. He was wrong I think'. No, Debord was utterly right.

Money though is quite a different matter and that's what the prattle essentially relates to; the massive wall of fictive capital, which imperiously must find an outlet in order to further enrich its self consuming cancerous growth. The more Ralph got older gaining a reputation that grew daily because of his previous association with the Situationist International, the more his 'artistic' abominations were churned out, ever increasing in value dollar-wise thus occasioning the following very telling but nasty tale.

In the mid to late 1970s we collaborated somewhat with Infantile Disorders, a kind of student pro-situationist group in Leeds. There was something above the ordinary, run-of-the mill about the group though you could well see their limitations as none of them had really ever set foot into the big, brutish - and getting more brutish - outside world and which makes all the difference to genuine revolutionary critique. Its erstwhile 'leader' Dave Dunbar hailed from Newcastle and had been enormously influenced by the post-Icteric fall-out there. We kind of got friendly engaging in a few critiques and more especially he helped in the production of the book, 'Wildcat Spain Encounters Democracy' under the auspices of the now defunct BM Bis. Imagine our horror when we found out Dunbar had stolen all the money accruing from the sale of the book, money which was needed to fund a publication on subversion in Italy in the 1970s. (You can see the remnants of that project on the Revolt Against Plenty web). Threatening the guy with violence he immediately coughed up. It was thoroughly underhand and very unpleasant though he then went on to cross swords with Michel Prigent and Nick Brandt both rapidly finding him an unsavoury character.

Although a lot of us at the time extolled shoplifting, not paying fares, withholding rent and could manufacture gizmos allowing massive auto-reductions in telephone, gas/electric utilities and the like that didn't mean anybody and everybody were fair game to be taken to the cleaners, even more especially where it concerned close friends. Dunbar pretended friendship the more to create a vulnerability he could then exploit economically. An emphasis on crime without specifying precisely what was meant by acceptable crime thus fostered pathological character traits. These unpleasant incidents sharpened our critique of crime and its limitations. It was a sad lesson and we rightly fell back on a more popular, time-honoured Robin Hood example - robbing the rich to give to the poor - as anything else was more or less counterproductive in terms of the necessity of fostering compelling up-front and open vibrant personal relationships so necessary for over-turning this ever viler old world.

Then the toe rag Dunbar seemed to disappear. Imagine our amazement when he turned up again ten years later having in the meantime cultivated Ralph Rumney even organising an exhibition in London with Dunbar himself hosting lectures at the Tate & Lyle (as Michel Prigent tellingly renamed it). Naturally Michel picketed these performances handing out his usual amusing, often trenchant leaflets. Then, ah hah, we learnt Dunbar was up to his old tricks as he attempted to steal some of Ralph's pretty dire exhibits so he could make more dosh on the side. There it was again that horrible duplicity that simply broke people in two and finally executed in such an amateurish way you simply couldn't get you head round it! Moreover, as Geoff S, a friend said, with his trademark, brutally ironical guffaw: 'I hate incompetent dippers'! Rumney however was so hurt he never again spoke to Dunbar.

It wasn't long before we realised we'd inadvertently set Dave Dunbar on the track of Ralph Rumney. One night sometime in the mid to late 1970s a few of us were having a drink. Dunbar began to elaborate on some of his recent ideas on a new subversive human urbanism in relation to the atmospheric backgrounds in De Chirico's paintings. It had been a question that had fascinated others including the surrealists who'd asked individuals to point out where the sea was in specific De Chirico paintings. Dunbar further ruminated saying it was impossible to translate any of this haunting presence, this 'new melancholy' (as De Chirico had described it) into 3D human interactive space, or rather what were the problems involved and just how delicate? This was really fascinating stuff obviously set to encounter the fringes of the derive, then, as if it was an entrance cue, he asked me: 'Whatever happened to Ralph Rumney'? I hadn't a clue though I thought he was still in Venice venturing to suggest - without any foundation - that perhaps he'd got involved in something to do with urban restoration like saving the Doge's Palace from sinking into the surrounding lagoon. This in itself provoked an argument for or against urban restoration though the outcome was that Dunbar seemed quite determined to follow up the mystery of Rumney's present whereabouts and activity. And from Dunbar's initial quest others followed like Tom Vague, Stewart Home, Alan Woods, Malcolm Imrie and Andrew

Hussey. (The truth is; it's doubtful if any of them would have shown any interest in Rumney if he hadn't been a proper artist/writer connected to the Situationist International. Can you imagine any of them doing the same to Patrick Cheval or Ben Trueman?)

Interestingly enough whilst googling through the Internet coverage on Ralph Rumney I expected Dunbar's contribution to be prominent. It seems cyberspace does not acknowledge it though the very absence was also very telling. Was it too contentious in the sense it provoked the memories of Michel's caustic disruptions? Never the less I was forced into trying to remember the gist of Dave Dunbar's arguments but couldn't. Then in a flash it came back to me: Even way back then I couldn't understand the argument because the language was so dense and opaque peppered with long, incomprehensible words placed on the page, I suspect, for the sole purpose of obscurantism. Memorable it wasn't. As for Dunbar he later retrained as an IT software engineer joining the dwindling band of English surrealists and two friends of ours who lived in Leeds - we called them the Armley Surrealists - in the mid 1990s told us they found him 'a creepy guy'.

The problem with Ralph Rumney was that he couldn't make any clear break between the artistic past and the more visionary side of himself. He allowed the old world in its dead duck forms to smother all that was tantalisingly pointing to something that was a sweet wind blowing from the future in the best of his derives especially the investigation of London's Limehouse. It is a sad comment on modern times when comparing the situation say with a century and more earlier when De Quincey and Hazlitt who initially tried to write to poetry in the style of the earlier romantics like Wordworth, Coleridge or even Southey, when finding they were making a mess of things, quickly realised something ineluctable was unfolding within the spirit of the age. They took full heed of this new, beckoning spirit painfully realising in their different ways, the arts were dying and thus set off on the road of profound exploration never repeating, or returning to their early fumbling beginnings and inevitable mistakes. Sad to say Ralph Rumney could never get away from his mistakes; indeed he constantly returned to them pointing to that profoundly blocked dialectic strangling our times. Even his excellent, borrowed insight: 'the map in not the territory' was constantly revisited as art in the studio rather than a signpost on the hopcd for road leading to a passionate, vibrant, renewed daily life.

Ah yes, De Quincey! By the time Rumney hit early to mid 1950s London, De Quincey's central London rookeries around Tottenham Court Rd and Clerkenwell etc had all been well and truly cleared out, not to say completely neutered, replaced with a dull respectability. You had to go east to find anything that remotely approximated and Limehouse beckoned still retaining something of its 19th century character, though obviously far removed from the ambiences De Quincey had experienced. Limehouse was lined with terraced housing for those streets that had been lucky enough not to have been bombed by the Luftwaffe even though the houses were often cold and damp with wet cellars prey to the effects of the river and its constant fogs. (Rumney reckons he coined the 1950s phrase: 'London destroyed more by developers than the Luftwaffe'). A Chinese community existed there with more than the occasional opium den still hanging on though by then an emerging consumer market meant opening a Chinese restaurant offered a more lucrative future. Some quickly acquired chic status serving a growing number of artistic bohemians having chosen the area for its charm plus a nascent gay community then still criminalised. Both were attracted by cheap rents. The area also became a magnet for the changing face of London's gangland also fascinated by its informal atmosphere and the pub, the Prospect of Whitby became a hang-out as emerging Carry On film stars like Barbara Windsor (later governess of EastEnders, Queen Vic) hooked up with that vicious sadist Ronnie Knight (later exiled to the Costa del Crime in southern Spain) who started to glamourise the pub's name as Royalty in the name of Princess Margaret and Lord Snowdon tarried with rough trade roles that Knight's crew obligingly deferred to. The coal cats that gave the Prospect of Whitby its original name were truly now serviced by a new - the original media-savvy clientele - meant glamour had arrived giving a new inflection to 'taking the piss'. (Originally the coal cats did the return journey to Newcastle-upon-Tyne laden with urine, denoted by the local east end population for a few precious pennies, hence 'taking the piss', bound for the alum quarries on the coast a mile north of Whitby and used to cure the alum important for among other things, pharmaceutical products which later were to form the basis of ICI on Teesside. There were often so many coal cats immaculately jammed together in Whitby's two harbours that there wasn't 'enough room to swing a cat'). It was indeed all this ambience, its changing tempo between the old and incoming febrile modernity that obviously so captivated Ralph Rumney; an entrancing embrace he enthusiastically communicated to his new European cohorts of the early Situationist International whom, no doubt instantly felt the same attraction when they visited the area.

Alas, like the derive it so inspired it was not to retain its 50s character simply because the dynamics of capitalism cannot let anything remain within its own organic propensity for whatever innovation might be needed and to prove the point, there's no need here to quote apposite lines from Marx as they as they are so plentiful in the pages of the Communist Manifesto to the Grundrisse to Theories of Surplus Value. Almost immediately Limehouse was torn apart as an ugly, pared down, cost-cutting pastiche of reductive modernist, square block urbanism did away with all the damp cellars and twisted alleyways. No more would there be the ghosts of Shadwell Stairs Wilfred Owen hauntingly invoked only a few decades previously. The destruction was carried out c/o the LCC (London County Council) precursor of the GLG (Greater London Council) and if former 'Red' Ken Livingdeath had been boss way back then he would have done exactly the same as today as he proceeds to viciously humiliate, trouncing all that's leftover of a decent and different, though still penniless, east London for the sake of some poxy Olympic Games!This appalling arsehole!

The derive, despite the fact that its precursors are still startlingly prescient in the history of the long, drawn out, demise of art searching for its limitless but ever more beautiful transcendence from the romantics through to Baudelaire, passed on to Rimbaud and so on is marked today by its absence; its final, forced exit. The Surrealist communal walks of the 1930s were to prove the beginning of the derives last, greatest and essentially most clearly conceptualised moment in the late 1950s within the orbit of the Lettrist International and what was to follow. It was of course an impulse wider than that coterie acting behind one's back as it were and there for the taking for anyone who cared to test the real temperature and smell of the urban terrain. It could be said that Jack Common's breathtaking book about Newcastle-upon-Tyne in the 1930s, 'The Freedom of the Streets' is in a way, a contribution to the derive though also a record of the most remarkable pub crawl ever recorded. And if we need to find more historical pedigrees, why shouldn't Engels's incredible book 'The Conditions of the Working Class in England in 1844' be considered here because regarding analysis of the ambiences of Manchester and central London urbanism and the cleverly discreet separation of the rich from the poor, it is incomparable?

Over the last decade I've felt something else about Ralph Rumney when considering derives and drifts. They concern another drift; the drift mines that once surrounded well over half of Halifax up to the 1850s. Here on these gaunt hillsides past the village of Mountain that connects Bradford to Halifax, I increasingly felt I was inhabiting an awesome place that once was something of a nightmare of child labour and brutal, back-breaking work that has evolved into a lonesome but ever-increasing paradise of biodiversity packed with now estranged industrial leftovers of abandoned, overgrown, often half-buried machinery whose original use you can only guess at, coming up against steep shale faces no doubt leading to subterranean passages where miners sweated and died knowing there was nothing in life but revenge and death. And where you can still find long, cool, very dark stone built tunnels built into the hillsides leading where? To a long gone quarry or a walk back to a hovel of a home? It is a massive area stretching through Shibden Dale to Holly Bank Bluff to the newish wind farm cresting Ovenden Moor overlooking Wuthering Heights, scene of the greatest anti-novel/novel ever written (well until James Joyce really did destroy the form of the novel) in that all sense of time and narrative is deliberately telescoped and stretched almost to the point of incoherence and where if God ever existed he was threatened with being dug up and destroyed. (No Russian Dostoyevskian sentimentality about religion here).

Yet this supreme, wild moorland site of industrial dereliction also harboured another more recent secret one also profoundly related to the disintegration and transcendence of art. It was here in the early 1970s the Angry Brigade were able to get up to some wild antics, even one might say some playful guerrilla training if that isn't today an over-loaded term and too misleading considering the stupid terrorist provocations of Islamic fascism. 'Ben' Trueman, the guy who'd doffed the Santa Claus outfit for the invasion of Selfridges' store on Oxford St, Xmas 1968, had become the tenant of an old Yorkshire stone cottage outside the village of Wainstalls above Halifax and high on the edge of Ovenden Moor where Ben worked for a local 'libertarian' farmer, a Mr Scholes who'd was a lapsed member of the Communist party. This lonely though sizable cottage was in the following years to become a wild scene of all kinds of seemingly insane activity and merry making and many is the time over the last few years around the table in Jim Greenfield's kitchen as the wine and dope flowed, story after story spilled out relating to these episodes that still had us falling on the floor with laughter.

This place and others including some of the old 19th century urban terrain of higgledy-piggledy landscape sometimes sets my teeth on edge because it is so remarkable. Yet did Ralph Rumney experience any of this and wouldn't he in any case have found it awful rather than aweful? Better Limehouse, better the left bank of Paris, and better Venice than this thankfully God-forsaken place. Yet when walking through these overgrown hillsides, hearing the cries of buzzards, observing green hairstreak butterflies or suddenly stumbling across rare plants that must have been blown here, who are you kidding? (These hillsides continually remind me of that delightful photograph of Breton and Peret trawling a butterfly net on a surrealist walk; a walk specifically organised as an insect discovery expedition). And if you meet anybody chances are a growing passionate conversation ensues that can cut to the bone of things (and their price) very quickly. I know, simply know that Ralph never talked to anyone at the sharp end in Halifax or Bradford, never mind showing any ecological interests, though he evinced an interest in natural history as a child. He didn't know, or rather didn't really know how to talk to those that finally really can overthrow the capitalist mode of production despite the fact his parson father was the son of a miner! And believe me when walking these forsaken transcendental hillsides, wrestling with its memories, I often think of Ralph Rumney, and what would he have made of the Angry Brigade and would he have been able to make the connection. I think it's fair to say RR wasn't interested in strikes or any kind of general insurgency. There's no way he could have discussed these things with any kind of depth never mind make any relation between these acts and a possible fertile ground for fruitfully evolving 'the map is not the territory'.

What I've said about these hillsides isn't really a prelude to an area deserving of a new derive, though it can relate perhaps to say, the Surrealist walks a la Earnshaw's and Thacker's English surrealist walks in and around West Yorkshire a few decades ago. We must face the fact the historical moment of the derive is long dead and gone. Essentially the fully conceptualised derive came about product of the lacunae between older, mainly 19th century areas tacked on to previous dwellings and the rise of mid 20th century town planning carried out with the assistance of quasi-architects with their cost-cutting audits, themselves pitiful reflections of what architects had been even 50 years previously. Any repeat of such experimentation rapidly becomes meaningless; either empty like Stewart Home's and Fabian Thompsett's attempt to recreate Rumney's, London Psychogeographical Society or, empty via some barren media stunt. Even in the late 1980s, Guillaume formerly of the French revolutionary grouping, Os Cangerceiros and more lately of 'the Happy Unemployed' in Germany said you could just to say consider an experimental derive in Latin American or south east Asian countries like Vietnam, countries sufficiently under-developed. Alas since then all this perspective has gone - and so speedily - as just-in-time prefabricated cities geared towards a push-fit, bolted together legoland are thrown up virtually overnight. Cities where, if the inhabitants did but know it, anything remotely approximating the passion of a derive is out of the question. What we have here are replicant cities where replicants replicate going hand in hand with the 'home' as the pivot of the aesthetic economy and realisation of all 'must-have' Bleak House commodities. None the less, Guillaume was for a while to play on derive fallout choosing odd and evocative places like old wartime, underground Berlin bunkers to host Happy Unemployed parties more, most likely, to keep the group together than create an aura of urban possibility.

Ralph Rumney was a handsome man. He had a passion for Michele Bernstein, the erstwhile, married companion of Guy Debord. The couple had an open relationship though as far as I know nothing in the early days of the Situationist International ever happened between Ralph and Michele in a sexual sense. Not that such tittle-tattle matters but deeper impulses do.

Guy and Michele broke up around 1970. Hardly surprising as everybody's did including my own; a break up, may it be said, I never got over and I've thought about my beloved Anne Ryder every day of my life since. Basically these break-ups weren't about sexual difficulties or inadequacies nor about not being able to relate or even love but finally about history and how the most profound revolt ever experienced, failed so utterly, and the essential by-product of such failure was a psychosomatic pain so desperate it seemed in need of therapeutic treatment; a treatment simple warm cuddling and quiet affection couldn't match. We stormed and smashed open the gates of paradise to let in every exploited nutter who cared to join in. We really did and yet on the brink of utopia were refused entry and where, just where could you go from such a point of no return? We didn't go far enough that's true but how, how, Howlin' Wolf, how?

Passions usually don't subside but go ape-shit forced into a hardly manageable sublimation, never to be fulfilled in the way they should have been. All that remain are tokens of the past, distorted memories sending you crazy. Coherence goes out of the window and the mind three sheets to the wind penetrating to the very essence of mores, irresistible in its growing perception of horrors you instantly knew were stacking up for the future.

I was no exception to such madness. One cold night so many years ago and out of my brains with misery and general erotic loss; a loss essentially around the growing eclipse of passionate love, I stood on the corner of Gt Titchfield St and Oxford St where De Quincey once stood waiting to meet with his beloved Annie, the kindly, destitute teenage prostitute he'd fallen in with. It was an arrangement he made a few days earlier having suddenly being called away on a courier's errand. She never turned up and although De Quincey searched and searched these then uncontrollable teeming streets for days on end, he was never to see his beloved Annie again and her absence was to forever haunt his life. For me I was also longing and searching for my own Anne, also from Manchester the city De Quincey originally hailed from. Completely insane, the two women had become collaged together in my fevered mind. Sometime later, much later, in a Grasmere churchyard in The Lake District where De Quincey vividly describes an astonishing laudanum fuelled dream where again he sees his beloved Annie sitting on a tombstone I too had another moment (though by then somewhat saner) when I hoped to see, to conjure up like a hologram, the two women sitting together; De Quincey's opium, wish-fulfilment of a dream having proved to be far more potent than banal reality.

Then there was another night sometimes in the early 1980s and I was talking with Michel Prigent and Lucy Forsyth about Guy Debord. Michel back then worshipped the guy (excuse the pun); a worship no matter whom or what it concerned, I've always found impossible to understand, seeing I'd never worshipped anybody or anything though profoundly respectful of those deserving of respect. Michel was talking about Rumney and Ms Bernstein. Debord had just told Michel how he'd thrown both of them out and what he had to say was rather different - and I think more accurate - than what has subsequently appeared in books e.g. Andrew Hussey's, "The Game of War". It seems Ralph Rumney had suggested to Guy he must be in the pay of the police in order to live out his the subversive lifestyle, and if he was paying them off could he help get him some official residents documents? Debord rightly went berserk and had shown them the door. By then it seems Rumney had decided to 'return' to revolution after a long, long absence. He thus re-invented himself donning a somewhat militant image proclaiming he was under threat from the police for being a dangerous man with dangerous views. Nothing could have been further from the truth and Ralph's dangerous phase was well and truly in the past. As we well know, he ventured to say: 'The police know who the real revolutionaries are, obviously they have to, it's their job'. But do they? Anybody who's been in any kind of trouble with the police relating to revolutionary theory and action knows Plod is pretty slow, even dumb regarding these matters.

Though I nodded, this tale was passed over with mild interest but then, almost as an afterthought, Michel laconically said - as if it was of little importance - that Michele Bernstein just before they broke up, asked Guy to whip her. Michel looked mildly perplexed and said Debord couldn't do it and that was that. It was mentioned as a casual fact; a comment without theory as to the whys and wherefores and yes, maybe it wasn't worthy of further elaboration.

None the less my mind raced. Why? To me it was now symptomatic of a maimed, imperious, genitalised impulse having tipped over from the essence of the expected beautiful social liberation, inseparable from the totality of liberation having utterly lost its way, even capsizing. The walls of the late 1960s were full of transcendental longings like: 'You say you love me. Oh say it with paving stones' or Vaneigem's: 'I love my love so much I wish to give her the magnificent bed of a revolution'. (My own somewhat Eng Lit biased King Lear reference was: 'Love comes empty handed like Cordelia bringing nothing' and that had been culled from Norman O' Brown's book, Love's Body). Failure to achieve any of this as vital years rolled by finally produced a cry of agony expressive of a new depression that had never figured in the clinicians' books on the subject; a new ugly concoction indicative of profound misery, darker mirror image of an earlier light-hearted erotic liberation and bringing with it the bottom line of a much greater emphasis on consumption. The backdrop to all this was an ever more invasive capitalisation as sex and 'love' went bizarre. Nor could it be satisfactorily described in the categories of traditional kinky responses, more to the realisation sex was entering the arena of something like a spectator sport and/or a form of commodified shopping compulsion endlessly repeated pointing to erotic absence, bringing no satisfaction; sex inseparable from an aberrant form of commodity fetishism which all relationships are forced to succumb to simply because there's no internal escape from capitalism and no place to hide. It does mean though we cannot blame couples or individuals succumbing to its invisible might mangling relationships everywhere in its deadly embrace and, least of all, paragons of revolution like Guy Debord and Michele Bernstein.

Behind the scenes such darkness reflected the movement of capital from relative openness to a growing ultra-repression; from Eros to Thanatos; from the making of capital to the consuming of capital concentrated especially in America alongside a more subordinate Europe. It has culminated in an immense success for capitalism the like of which history has never seen at the same time as it is rapidly proving to be the most pyrrhic of pyrrhic victories one bringing on the extinction of most life on this planet. In 1968 I painted on a London wall: 'The Sky Has Died' and little did I realise at the time how telling such observation was to become as I see my clumsy, spray painted handwriting reproduced over and over again. Perhaps too, seeing the times are so dire, the definitive moment of loser wins is again returning.

All old, pre-'68 relationships abandoned, a little later Guy was to take up - and marry - a much younger woman, Alice Becker-Ho which came about most likely as by-product of his growing fame which was reaching the point of adulation. Such meaningless worship possibly contributed to Debord's suicide simply because his razor sharp perceptions couldn't live with the falsity of such fame. Later too Michele Bernstein was to marry Ralph Rumney and for a time Ralph lived with her in Salisbury in Wiltshire. (One thing I could never get over here was how all these libertarians needed to marry and divorce! I always liked a comment Bruce Elwell threw off when talking to him in the late 1970s concerning somebody belonging to an ultra-leftist outfit called 'Zero Work': Bruce a former American member of the SI quipped: 'He believed in really straight things like divorce'. Bruce was a divorcee!)

At the same time, Ms Bernstein was contributing paid for articles to the newspaper, Liberation in Paris, a hotchpotch of post '68 Mao Spontex leftism and anything else you care to mention ever weakening throughout the years. It was though a relationship based on pre-1968 memories, never facing up to the new complexities and the horrible Pandora's Box of a post 1960s world that was gradually going utterly insane. Seeing nostalgia was really the only basis between Rumney and Michele it couldn't last and the relationship broke up. Neither Michele nor Ralph could abandon or rather supersede art. They couldn't escape its contradictory modernism/anti modernism via a kind of more clued-in post-Dadaism. It simply wasn't sharp-edged enough.

It is said that Ralph Rumney argued with Georges Bataille about eroticism but like EP Thompson previously what was discussed is irretrievably lost. This new mood beginning in the early 1970s, this new darkening, unwelcome passage to Hades found itself mirrored in the writings and interests of the French surrealist, George Bataille. From the late 1950s to the early 1970s his book, 'The Accursed Share' was given great prominence in any discussion of the surplus most societies, primitive or modern, throw up, whether in a potlatch of destruction, festivity or the bestowing of fabulous gifts. The book even celebrated somewhat the contemporary American Marshall Plan! Now Bataille was re-defined and his sadomasochistic researches or obsessions came much more to the fore and were rather more alarming than his growing collection of objet trouve medical experiments like pickled babies in kilner jars. I for one could never forget Andre Breton's pithy but sharp riposte, noting his 'scatological obsessions' which went something, like: 'Bataille loves wallowing in shit. We don't'. The revolutionary side of Bataille was thus eclipsed and ever after there's been a surfeit of 'wallowing' everywhere suiting swathes of pornographic imagery and the language of aggressive marketing (e.g. initiated by the former Benetton ads), as well as more informed Batailleistas like the Chapman Bros commoditizing horror in saleable safe, artistic form, to Stewart Home's novels of sexualised mutilation etc. Bataille's canonisation - if you like - was fully secured in 2006 with the promotional surrealist exhibition at London's Hayward gallery instigated by the art historian, Dawn Ades. For those somewhat more clued in, though still lacking, is it possible to say there's little difference between Bataille's oeuvre and Lautreamont's, 'Songs of Maldoror'? I'd reply saying, though the latter on the surface is a hideous book that's impossible to comfortably like, at the same time, page after page, line after line, there's a subtlety now fully open, now somewhat disguised, shot through with a materially transcending perspective pointing beyond horror. Lautreamont offers unequivocal hopes of revolution, though without deploying the word or concept, Bataille apart from the profundity of 'The Accursed Share' doesn't (though in the 1930s in 'Contra-Attaque' he held Trotskyist sympathies) but I bet Rumney's argument wasn't pitched on this necessary level! Later the latter lamely said about Bataille: 'I didn't agree with his interpretation - but I cannot remember my conversation'. Moreover, remember Lautreamont, to say the least, mocked art's limitations, Bataille revelled in them reviving the novel and praising Francis Bacon's paintings to the skies. No wonder Stewart Home feels so safe with him.

I would have liked to have discussed some of this train of thoughts with Os Cangerceiros that heavily situ-influenced group from France mentioned previously. True you could raise some such thoughts but only go so far sometimes tramping the hills around Halifax as we did especially and so often with the delightful and warm hearted Morgane and sometime with Pete our mutual friend. Morgane was a woman who was only eight years old when May '68 exploded in France remembering really well the kiddy occupation of her school. For sure, she had read every word of Guy Debord but I cannot recall we ever talked about Ralph Rumney looking down on Halifax from windswept moor tops. As for the Kangaroos (as Os Cangaceiros was nicknamed) they were delighted that Michele Bernstein in the pages of Liberation had praised their book, called 'Tendre Venin' (Gentle Poison) on the Chiapas uprising in Mexico in the early 1990s, which was one of the best on the uprising despite a too profiled concentration on the Zapatista army and not enough on the local people. As for myself I always wondered why Michele and Ralph had to live in Salisbury. What was wrong with those really down home hills and the great sites of industrial dereliction?

As for Ralph Rumney having broken up with Ms Bernstein, he went to live in Monasque, a thoroughly bourgeois town in Haute Provence where he continued to paint and continued to drink himself silly (not that there's anything wrong in the latter activity). He died aged 67 in 2002.

For Liverpool Vicki: *David Wise. July 2007*

Footnote On Yves Klein:

It is said that Ralph Rumney introduced the work and thoughts of Yves Klein to London after Klein's exhibition - more publicity coup - in the small Iris Clert gallery on the Rue des Beaux-Arts in Paris in 1958. There's no point here in enumerating in detail what Klein got up to other than to note he played on radical ideas as so many others did around this time and throughout the following decade simply because it was the done thing to do. Most of this was nebulous experimentation that was neither one thing nor another and few pushed things through to an incendiary revolutionary conclusion. Even novelist supreme, Simone de Beauvoir could pontificate endlessly on the end of the novel without taking her conclusions seriously as a jumping off point for something far more cutting edge. (Everywhere much of this critique was deployed opportunistically, though today, of course, there's nothing like this spirit of enquiry around).

Klein tried to encapsulate a modern dialectic of opposites bringing into play ideas redolent of the ancient Greek philosopher, Heraclites as well as modern tomes like Gaston Bachelard's 'The Psychoanalysis of Fire'. These opposites for Klein were presented in a mystical/artistic way and hardly the stuff that had kept Hegel so grounded. Within this 'flow' were incorporated certain absolutes from modern art: Mallarme's blank page, Malevich's 'White on White', Rodchenko's 'Black on Black'; tabla rasas pointing to an end and a new (explosive?) beginning. For Klein this 'new' beginning was initiated by way of 'the void', the immaterial and IKB (International Klein Blue), which was an approximate memory of the intense blue skies above the beach at Nice he felt an intense empathy with as a child. It was though a pseudo beginning, one that was merely pastiche and imitation and none of this 'experimentation' encountered the real subversive drift of the time, which was assiduously avoided. His tabla rasa wasn't a springboard towards a practical 'recovery through transfer' (a profound concept of Marx's I've mentioned elsewhere here in the context of bebop) but the re-definition of the mystical playing to the tune of the death of art whereby 'the ashes of my art' became a requiem put up for sale; part of 'the void' sold for gold rather than taking payment in francs, half thrown into the Seine half kept. Such acts all added to radical image making though with no substance behind them because Klein wasn't anti political economy as such. (At that point in time the Situationist International of 1957 had refused to sell anything and rightly had got Klein's number!)

Throughout part of the Icteric years in Newcastle-upon-Tyne - to be exact from 1965 to early 1967 - we took Yves Klein seriously though this was due more to our youthful uncertainty and naivety than anything else. Ron Hunt of course wrote about him and Klein seemed to mirror our growing wider concerns as we groped towards a revolutionary totality. At the time despite being a distorted perspective, the doors were being opened to dialectics, to bad taste (Klein had said 'I howl it from the rooftops: Kitsch, Corn, Bad Taste' though in truth we preferred Andre Breton's: 'In the bad taste of my epoch I wish to go further than any other' a slogan that was duly spray painted on a wall), the end of art and the wider transformation of the environment. We thus took an interest in Klein's architecture; or rather anti-architectural schemes pointing towards a sophisticated technology discreetly placed underground allowing a naked new Eden to run a mock on top. We were also interested in personalised forms of flying a la Malevich's proposals for slow flying white squares and Klein's attempts to fly like a bird, maybe to replace birds, also grabbed us. We liked his emphasis on the elements; on fire, air and water particularly as Icteric emphasised the other element ' earth - and we can claim the dubious (dis)honour of initiating land art in these islands. By the middle of 1967 all this was definitively pushed aside and very rapidly, as the real perspective of a total revolution revealed its shape. For sure we still wanted the new Eden but by then we knew how to get it and that had more to do with Detroit going up in flames via the re-awakened anger of the exploited, than schemes flattering a particular artistic ego and the growing bank account behind it. (Finally the truth of the matter is, we - about 7 or 8 individuals - in Newcastle's remote urban backwater went on to make theory and action far more coherent than anything Klein or Rumney ever did).

Maybe the above is kind, far too kind to Yves Klein. If the guy had lived - he died at an early age of a heart attack - he would have been pilloried on the barricades of May 1968 and that would have been that. But it wasn't to be and periodically Klein's memory keeps returning in the form of a watered down cultural radicalism pretending to encompass some kind of totality. In the mid 1970s David Jacobs and Chris Winks, wrote a somewhat interesting pamphlet called 'At Dusk' critical of some of the delusions prevalent in the American pro-situationist circles and among other things, broadly the argument fell back heavily on a Freudian interpretation of many of these foibles. A little later meeting Chris Winks in London in the company of one or two others, the conversation somehow got round to Yves Klein and it took me a while to recollect what precisely were my criticisms of the guy. I was quite surprised by the interest shown wondering what was intended. By then Chris Winks was just to say helping play a major part in producing a magazine called 'Processed World' oriented around the early days of the white-collar computer slave interminably nailed down to a re-vamped office desk. Chris had become one such slave himself. Indeed it was a very interesting magazine even if the articles were often uneven but I always looked forward to reading it. Over the years though I couldn't help but notice how the critique of culture contained within its covers was getting sloppier and sloppier.

Then the magazine seemed to fold. Around 2005, a well rehearsed, installation art phenomenon hit the London stage called The Blue Man Group. I couldn't be fooled; the blue was unmistakeably IKB (International Klein Blue) and a little later it came as no real surprise to find that a Chris Wink (the 's' had been dropped) was responsible for much of this display. It was as if the guy was ashamed of his re-accommodation with culture trying perhaps to hide his name? Unmistakeably too, around the same time an ad became prominent on TV promoting Intel Centrino IT technology as the best CPU processor on the market. A blue man flew through the air on a skateboard and the connection with the now defunct 'Processed World' became blindingly obvious. And the man on the skateboard: Why it was a simulation of Yves Klein flying through the air'"

DW: *Early Summer. 2007*

Nietzsche, Revolutionary Subversion And The Contemporary Attack On Music

For American Rebecca:

The following is fragmentary critique - there have been a few minor alterations since - that was sent to a young American woman who is hopefully putting together a re-appraisal oriented around the activities of Black Mask and the Motherfuckers rescuing them (and others?) from the repression and calumnies brutally foisted on them in the United States. It is a grim picture typified by an account of their activities plus relatively recent interview with Ben Morea conducted by an appalling, sneering Harvard professor, name of John McMillian.

I am surprised Black Mask and the Motherfuckers are less well known than King Mob and the French Situationists in the States. Have you seen the recent book by Peter Doggett There's a Riot Going On, published by Canongate (Edinburgh, New York, London) that deals with the 'revolution' in music, the title taken from Sly Stone's album of the same name? There are three pages on Black Mask and the Motherfuckers. Basically the guy deals with the Fillmore East intervention against hip entrepreneur Bill Graham together with pop group MC5 and John Sinclair. Although factually reasonably accurate, Doggett is essentially a musicologist living in Hampshire, England and he just hasn't a clue re wider, world-turned-upside-down perspectives managing to make historically important subversive incidents into very dull reading indeed. It's as though he can make no comment or take sides! The uniqueness of Black Mask/Motherfuckers was that they forthrightly attacked all the most advanced ultra-modern representations of capital that recuperated real living aspects of general creativity emanating from those who wanted to live completely different lives ranging from cultural mausoleums like the Rockefeller Center/Museum of Modern Art, hip police chiefs like Captain Fink and cutting edge pop musicians from Ed Sanders & the Fugs to MC5.

It was a form of subversion unique in dissident 'other' America and has never been repeated there, or its potential remotely fulfilled. My brother David was involved in the Ed Sanders attack just after the Fugs had brought out that record that became a hit with the lyric: 'art is nothing, nothing, nothing' turning living contestation into acceptable, saleable commodity. It meant Sanders quickly figured on the cover of Time magazine. A few days after this Black Mask inspired attack, David bumped into Murray Bookchin on a street on New York's Lower East Side and Murray eagerly grabbed him saying 'Ed Sanders is crying saying he's sold out and can't forgive himself'. David laughed gleefully. It must also be clearly understood that Ben and co were the first to prioritise the role of pop music attacking its pivotal fulcrum in the vista of contemporary alienation, especially the music that specifically said it was on the side of the revolution or indeed was the revolution itself, rightly pointing out it was merely hip performance which, in reality set itself against clued-in intervention from the street and the route that could clearly go somewhere definitively overthrowing the audience/performer estrangement , blocking all paths to social/individual emancipation.

These facts in themselves also point to something else and a wider historical memory or historical subconscious as modern interventions like that outlined above didn't just come from nowhere. It is in this context that we can view the Nietzsche contra Wagner polemic as a seminal document of modern times and of great importance as regards the present musical panorama, for that is what it is 'a visual, wrap around panorama of artistic enactments that endeavours to become all encompassing and that strives, through the aid of the increasingly sophisticated minimalist gadgetry of quantum mechanics, to encompass all of life and eventually become a substitute for life, a 'second life' ' (or 'skin', for quantum mechanics via computing and Craig Venter is on the verge of creating a replicant biology in tandem with implant engineering) - compensating for the absence of the first.

Essentially however it has its (primitive) origins in Wagnerian stage craft that aimed at a similar total immersion, having its roots in the gesamtkunstwerk prefigured by German philosophical idealism and the importance it granted to art and the intuitive imagination as a parallel making of society which had to escape the confines of art for it to become a real force (though it was never stated quite as bluntly as this, all the elements are there that allow one to do so). It was also a response to the revolution of 1848 in some subtle, unremarked measure, and one never given the slightest credence by musicologists influenced by Bakunin and revolutionaries of the same ilk whom for a short time Wagner befriended. In place of the twilight of the gods, the gotterdamerung, there arose the god of music as exclusively masterminded and choreographed by Wagner, that demiurge that Nietzsche denounced as being unable to save music, though without taking his insight to the logical moextremes it patently cries out for. The young Nietzsche idolised Wagner and would embarrassingly abase himself in front of him and for several year was his step 'n' fetch it, before turning on Wagner with a vengeance, which was the most painful blow ever to land on Wagner.

Nietzsche's first book The Birth of Tragedy, brimming with all the naive verve of youth, was effusive in its praise of Wagner. Debord rated the book highly, a fact I have only recently become aware of, and indeed one can see how some of its concepts shaped Debord's theorising. In later introductions to this book penned by Nietzsche it becomes apparent that his aversion to Wagner has become unbearable, though brilliantly obsessive with Nietzsche worrying every detail of Wagner's music, life and the influence of the man himself who now, in Nietzsche's eyes, could not do right for doing wrong.

The intros' stress the immediate background - the Paris Commune of 1871 - though Nietzsche refers to it as the Franco-Prussian war, unaware that this signal event in the history of class struggle had perhaps affected his profound enquiry into the nature of Greek drama and its codicil, the apotheosis of Wagner as a contemporary recreation of the spirit of Greek drama. In the decade long interval between the two intros, something had happened for Nietzsche. Now he was finding the auditorium and the company of performers/singers/actors - 'miming maniacs' - suffocating, and glad to be away from it all in the clean air of mountain passes, humming with the sounds of insects in which he finds a new innocence beyond the Judaic Christian morality that Wagner has become a declining and interminable prisoner of - not least because of his belief in total artistic envelopment as a panacea possessing the power to cure the catastrophic alienation of man under capitalism.

In so far as he once could accurately diagnose alienation, it has to be said that Wagner was closer to Marx than Nietzsche ever was, though neither Marx or Engel's (the latter especially seeing he was contemporaneous with Wagner's greatest triumphs) could even begin to contemplate engaging on a critique of Wagner or even see it as essential. Here Nietzsche, as a reluctant 'communist', increasingly alive to the decay of artistic form, definitely had the drop on both of them.

In any case the growing theatricalisation of music, the triumph of the means of production over performance goes back to Wagner, though no one has the wit today to compare the Live Aid nonsense and Live Earth gore with the sound/performance orgies emanating from Bayreuth, the latter's obvious influence on the Nuremberg rallies and their gradual morphing into today's pop spectaculars with a penetration amounting to billions of viewers that Wagner and Hitler would have died for.

It is unfortunate Nietzsche never had much to say about Hegel. Though describing him somewhere as a 'brother genius' (the other brother being Schopenhauer), it seems at times as if he had only cursorily dipped into Hegel, much preferring Kant. And it is Kant's philosophy that we see peering through the shades of The Birth of Tragedy time and again, particularly the importance Kant grants to the 'thing in itself' and the limitation such a concept imposes on scientific knowledge. As such Nietzsche looks to destructive, galvanic 'creativity', (as prefigured in the drunken Dionysian hordes out of which Greek drama sprang and which is also a mythologisation of the Indo-European migration that, reading between Nietzsche's lines, posed the key question of quiescence - Buddhism - or action) to provide meaning in preference to the knowing - and passive - distance of science .

But it is missing the mark to claim that Nietzsche repudiated science, and that his entire philosophy was a repudiation of reason (as for instance George Lukacs wilfully alleged) in the name of an altogether different epistemology, ultimately derived from a defeated religion and renascent 'art', though one conceived as a principle of life. For instance, he followed with considerable interest Helmholtz's investigations into quicker-than-thought reflex actions, and he was much taken with Nageli's researches into amoebal life forms, the latter in particular prompting thoughts on alimentation and the psychology of hunger that many years later were to knock Freud sideways. However, Nietzsche's claim that these amoebal forms show a rhythmic, aesthetic propensity goes well beyond Kant, even if Nietzsche's assertion that 'life can only be grasped as an aesthetic phenomena' is indebted to Kant - though it clearly transgresses the restricted sense Kant grants to the aesthetic as alone able to bridge the otherwise unbridgeable antinomy of pure and practical reason.

As you are probably aware both David and myself are fascinated by insects particularly butterflies and moths and have been since we were in short trousers.

Rereading The Genealogy of Morals after a time span of thirty years I was particularly struck by the number of references to insects (there is a distinct buzz to the entire book) even going so far as to list the number of occasions insects are mentioned ' and never unfavourably. To my mind it is an altogether less strained work than Thus Spoke Zarathustra (and that reflects Nietzsche's jealously as regards Christianity never entirely able to overthrow the myth of the saviour) where biblical images of eagles and serpents abound, insects rarely appearing in the bible other than negatively, like the plagues of locusts for example. Nietzsche as an entomologist? Why, I even wrote a few lines on the subject several years ago with an eye to the founding fathers of modern entomology like Hooke, Leevanhoek, Ray, Schwammerdam all four coincidental with the rise of Protestantism (described by Marx as 'religion's self-criticism') - and capitalism, insects acting in various ways as living picture writing and one that by emphasising the astonishing formal variety of insect morphology and range of insect behaviours implies a critique of the growing uniformity of life under capitalism. Though, to begin with, this admonition is far from obvious in the work of the aforementioned individuals, by the time Keats came to write his Ode to Psyche it certainly was.

To my mind Nietzsche in The Genealogy of Morals and in other stray references throughout his oeuvre had taken the subject a stage further by impishly, and perhaps involuntarily, linking entomology to a rejection of the past and a rebirth of wonderment, innocence and a freedom from guilt. And, it should be added, to the abolition of money for there is a nascent critique of political economy in The Genealogy of Morals evident from the attention Nietzsche pays language, pointing in particular to the verb 'deber' meaning both to owe a sum of money and to do ones a moral duty. Need I say more? It certainly goes some way in helping elucidate the extraordinary hold entomology has over the both of us. And could the increased interest in insects we see appearing everywhere be a basis for a deeper, more larval, and yet soaring critique of capitalism and which will help this downtrodden, desperately saddened humanity to eventually take wing and become inspired? That Nietzsche was a proto-ecologist is also never noticed. He arraigned industrial capitalism in the'Genealogy' for its hubris in full expectation of the nemesis to follow: 'Our whole attitude to nature, our violation of nature with the help of machines and the heedless ingenuity of technicians and engineers is hubris'. In the next breath he describes god as some putative spider, that spider taking the place of Kant's categorical imperative and forever weaving a web of deception in terms of final causes we must combat and which is our categorical imperative. This is the only time arthropods, as far as I can recall, are treated, if not in a wholly negative manner, then certainly ambiguously in the 'Genealogy'. Otherwise to be in the presence of insects is an ennobling experience, and beyond good and evil as these 'opposites' have hitherto been conceived.

Nietzsche's final work written when he was 'mad' was Ecce Homo. It is a work not easy to come by in this country or in America - and not because it is sacrilegious but because it is vain glorious, especially so to English ears. To me it stinks of religious envy and it might have made more sense to have written a work entitled Ecce Arte - behold the artist or art. Its consequences could have been, would have been, far more profound - and relevant. Zarathustra sought to be a creator of life, of people, rather than art but unfortunately he comes across as something of a crank prophet obsessed with replacing Christ. though unable to do much more than emulate what he was striving to overcome. And with nothing like the equivalent degree of success -

in fact when all is said and done Zarathustra is not much more than a ridiculously still born literary figure. Hegel also made Christ out to be an artist in his Philosophy of the Fine Arts but Hegel, despite paying lip service to Christianity for career reasons, was a less religiously obsessed man than Nietzsche and it never detracted for one moment from his main task which was to historicize the forms of art, a stupendously productive enterprise and which willy-nilly influenced Nietzsche and everyone else who subsequently has given a moment's thought to art's history. And though now conveniently forgotten that is what Hegel wanted to do: make art history.

But to get back to Nietzsche as a critique of art rather than art critic. Would for instance that Nietzsche had been able to update his critique of music with a consideration of Debussy for example, that other founding contemporary musical influence, almost on a par with Wagner and whose importance grows by the minute with each commissioned piece of nature schmaltz especially composed to accompany yet another wild life TV programme. Though often dazzling solely on account of the photography, they still leave the viewer feeling empty, who, even in this moment of direst emergency, is only ever there to be entertained. Nothing unsettling, like incisive critique which could be a prelude to changing nature (i.e. restoring it), must ever be allowed to intrude upon these nature spectaculars.

Debussy like Wagner also anticipates filmic modes, the endless melodies of his tone poem perfectly lending themselves to the minute, never-ending variations required by the serial production of nature films on an industrial scale that caters to a market demand that is now global. Under the weight of formulaic nature recitatives that aspire to outlive nature and narratives both spoken and unspoken that do not have to be anthropomorphic in order to falsify content, nature becomes essentially a fictionalised nature. Without barely a word said in protest, nature ends up succumbing to art long before it is finally destroyed by capitalism and climate change. Considering just how trenchant Nietzsche's critique of Wagner is, and one that is capable of effortlessly spanning the 120 year gap in between, I have often wondered what he would have heard in Debussy that would resonate down to our own times. The sound of silence? For that is more than likely in a musician in which the sounds of nature have a tendency to take over, the medley of rustling leaves continuing where Debussy left off and finally leading to an artistic crisis of vast proportions and consequence.

When did the reclaiming of Nietzsche for the revolution begin and by whom? I think that ultimately we have the Frankfurt School to thank for that, particularly Herbert Marcuse in his book on Freud entitled Eros and Civilization. This book, dotted with numerous references to Nietzsche, certainly changed the way I thought about Nietzsche and led me on to unearth yet more Freudian anticipations in the nooks and crannies and highways and byways of Nietzsche's thoughts than those cited by Marcuse. Though I was then inclined to think that without the scientific grounding that Freud supplied, Nietzsche's intuitions, like his notion of the primal crime on which civilization is based, would forever remain inspired guess work, I also never wavered in my conviction that civilization and its discontents was experienced in an altogether more razor like and total manner by Nietzsche than it ever was by that respectable bourgeois, Sigmund Freud.

Did Georges Bataille help reclaim Nietzsche for the radical revolution envisaged by the International Lettrists, the Situationist International, King Mob and the Motherfuckers and others in America? All three volumes of his The Accursed Share were some of the most influential books of the post war years, though ones that were hopelessly vitiated by a conception of communism that owed everything to Stalin and next to nothing to Marx.

To this arid Russian soviet alternative Bataille counter poses Nietzsche, though recognising that Zarathustra's revolt is also doomed to failure, as fascism has in a sense demonstrated, though he never once unequivocally insists that Nietzsche would have unhesitatingly rejected Hitler with the same vehemence as Marx would have done Stalin. It showed how much Bataille was affected by the ruling discourse, and more's the pity that he did not see fit to attend the seminal discussions around Rouge et Noir and the nascent Socialisme ou Barbarie group who were then beginning to develop a theory of state capitalism. Had Bataille understood the tenor of what they were saying, it could have fundamentally changed everything regarding his reworking of Mauss's Essai sur le Don and what society did with its surplus and which gave humanity its sovereign purpose?

This fundamental, and until Bataille, ignored category of political economy, which is so resistant to analysis in terms of labour value and the reproduction of labour power, took the 'science' well beyond the realm of necessity and mere survival - though it is questionable if Bataille ever really understood what was meant by the abolition of political economy. My history is hazy here and I'm unable to say exactly how Bataille's study of the potlatch contributed to a deeper understanding of the first violent, spontaneous revolts against consumer society and its inevitable corollary : work itself. Or to what degree he influenced Lettrisme, then International Lettrisme and finally the SI. It is a hidden history and one that could do with being exposed to the clear light of day, particularly in the English-speaking world. The Bataille that comes down to us, and that is so big both here and in the States and has such a market appeal, is the one that justifies art (e.g. the Chapman Bros, Genesis P-Orridge etc) and is mired in the aestheticisation of De Sade and Lautreamont, turning them into erotic novelists and instigators of a sadoporn art genre.

Also Bataille cannot escape the charge that he helped prepare the sewer of post modernism, particularly so in Michael Foucault's case. Though Bataille was hostile to academia, his writing often suffers from a typically academic lack of directness and thus prefigures the get-out clauses post-modernism is littered with. Following the Second World War and reflecting the rise of social democracy whether in a 'right' or 'left' form, there was a huge increase in higher education establishments, their baneful influence doing much to weaken and finally destroy revolutionary theory. It is more imperative today than ever to keep clear of academic institutions, even if only for the sake of one's mental health.

Finally there was also a post war Stalinoid rehabilitation of Nietzsche led by Louis Althusser who was in turn much influenced by the philosopher of psychoanalysis, Jacques Lacan, who in the manner of the philosophes attempted to reduce Freud to a series of algebraic equations. However even Lacan drew back from carrying out a similar mathematical diminution on Nietzsche, though Thomas Mann's fictionalised portrait of Nietzsche in the person of Adrian Leverkuhn in Dr Faustus has him steeped in the mathematical relations of music. A more un-Nietzschean preoccupation cannot be imagined and to think, as Mann obviously does, that Nietzsche would have been an aficionado of Schoenberg, is completely mistaken to my mind. No matter whether tonal or atonal, the musical score per se would have come under the philosopher's hammer.

And as to the Stalinoid rehabilitation of Nietzsche ---- I have my own personal story to relate. I doubt if you have heard of Dick Pountain, but suffice to say he is now worth around a cool '100 million and is the business partner of Felix Dennis, currently one of the richest people in Britain, worth just this side of billion, though formerly one of the editors of Oz magazine. (The same company that made 'Notting Hill' is presently making a film of the Oz trial entitled Hippie, Hippie Shake in Notting Hill). Dick in his earlier days hung around with King Mob before abandoning libertarian critiques to embrace 'scientific Marxism' as preached by Louis Althusser. To mark his conversion he pinned up a photograph of---Friedrich Nietzsche! Casual visitors mistakenly took it to be a photograph of Stalin, for by this time Pountain had begun to relate to BICO (British and Irish Communist Party) who were engaged among other things in reprinting transcripts of the Moscow Trials to prove that Stalin was right and that e.g. Bukharin was a running dog lackey of capitalism after all! He was.

But so was Stalin, though under another form that 'bent' the law of value so to speak and suppressed the internal market by bringing commerce completely under the control of the state. (Mark my words this beast is due for a revival). Louis Althusser had built his entire life around the concept of the 'epistemological break' (though 'brake' would more accurately describe this dead-end) to explain the moment Marx broke with Hegel, and on the slenderest evidence from that time forwards, purportedly dropped any mention of dialectics as idealist and pre-scientific. Pountain had intended inscribing his pin up of Nietzsche with the words 'Hegel is dead, killed by Nietzsche' believing him to be a thorough going determinist. But so in a sense was Hegel, who was no stranger to the hidden hand of history, of forces operating behind people's backs. Indeed he could be said to have 'invented' the idea, for it was a notion that was central to his entire system.(1)

Looking back this latter-day adulation of Nietzsche from a Russian soviet perspective could be said to herald the break up of the nomenclature, and marked a transitional stage prior to some members of it becoming filthy rich from Yeltsin's reckless privatisations of state companies. Wallowing in regret - and money - Pountain now lashes himself for ever having supported the soviet system and crying foul whenever the operations of the free market are obstructed. Now both Hegel and Nietzsche are dead - killed by money!

Strange to say Nietzsche's reputation has rarely been higher than it is today, whilst Freud's star continues to decline. He is rated highly by Daniel C. Dennett (Darwin 's Dangerous Idea) and, given that Richard Dawkins has a great regard for Dennett, no doubt also by Dawkins, who in turn has no time at all for the 'soft science' of either Freud or Marx. According to Dawkins, the god delusion can only be dispelled through rigorous scientific demonstration, and the notion that religion is the alienated essence of man is a complete anathema to him. Thus he cannot begin to understand the hold religion has over mankind. The only way to abolish religion is to abolish the conditions that give rise to religion, and that prevent every last one of us from experiencing fulfilment.

To Dawkins capitalism is not a problem, never mind the problem, and the very last thing Dawkins wants to see is the drawing down of heaven to earth, as took place in the Paris Commune of 1871. And so we are back to where we more or less started in the discussion of Nietzsche, the Paris Commune of 1871 and before that in a few remarks on Black Mask and the Motherfuckers, on a developing total intervention against a growing total alienation that demands total revolution. Do we ever really get away from these momentous events, events that will inevitably return to haunt the last days of mankind, if we don't finally succeed in overthrowing this goddamned system?

Alex Trocchi's Hour Upon The Stage

We never met either Ralph Rumney or Alex Trocchi though we easily could have done so and most likely would have been welcomed. But what would have been the point as it would have been no more than gawping at icons surrounded by an increasingly worshipping entourage. Nonetheless I once spoke to Alex, and it was to prove a transcendental moment in my life, getting a telephone call from him one morning angrily wanting to know why his cleaner hadn't turned up to shovel up all the shit. As I was going out with the gal on a casual basis at the time she was in fact in bed recovering from the previous night's drunken spree. He slammed the phone down retorting: "That bloody cleaner is too much".

Alex Trocchi and Ralph Rumney: Their names in the late 1950s/early 1960s conjure each other up as they were the only two British members of the early Situationist International and in many ways they were both rather similar having come from reasonably well-off backgrounds quickly becoming bohemian rebels setting off early in life for the Parisian Left Bank. Historically they have come to be regarded as revolutionaries advancing a contemporary relevant critique of modern society, though in reality neither was able to transcend cultural specialisms and dissident cultural milieus. These two were forever pulling themselves up short, never allowing themselves to fall and fall and fall on through the cultural safety net , constantly afraid their publishers and dealers might no longer have anything to do with them even though this fear was rarely openly acknowledged. Constantly re-working things (e.g. Trocchi's novel Young Adam morphed from its first published edition in 1954 to its final version in 1963 and the same went for some of Rumney's artifacts) their real revolutionary contribution was very patchy. For sure such impulse to constantly change insights and nuances is commendable as why should everything you do be set in amber, but such flow was not applied to that subversive theory fully appropriate to the times.

Trocchi's was a promise which never came to anything like fruition, though it was far more significant than fellow traveller, Ralph Rumney. Both the present critiques of these interesting and noteworthy characters are inevitably contrasted with our own very different experiences relating to a wider, more total critique set unfortunately within the paradigm of much harsher times whereby we had to pick up on the best of their efforts whilst making sure we didn't repeat their compromises with the old world. In fact compare and contrast is the essential underlying motion of these two highly selective portraits of Ralph Rumney and Alex Trocchi as we felt it necessary to make some clear distinction between them, us and those like us who have been forced to be more sternly negative in our approaches to an increasingly alienated existence where even the survival of much sentient life, and not only humanity, has become doubtful.

In his lifetime Trocchi was calumnied more than praised, but this had more to do with his aberrant lifestyle than his artistic/literary product. It is a familiar refrain in the history of some who wrote within what became the cliche of 'outsider rebellion' and perhaps personified most clearly in one of the earliest contributions to 'outsider' rebellion, that of Mary Shelley's Frankenstein. Three to four decades after and you need only think of Lautreamont and the monsters infesting Maldoror to realise the experience was plummeting to ever greater depths. Trocchi's scribbled comments: "Notes towards the making of a monster" fell within such a trajectory as it became the title: The Making Of The Monster of Andrew Murray Scott's rather pedestrian and boring book on Alex Trocchi.

One of Alex's failings which, we will go into at greater length here, was his persistent need to be a showman, which in practise meant encouraging such definitions, lacking a native savvy to keep clear of a media manipulated public gaze inviting such stereotypes. Someone had once warned him: "Be careful that you don't become notorious instead of famous", though in reality these days such labels have kaleidoscoped; indeed some kind of notoriety - usually now a vapid notoriety - is necessary in order to be a bankable asset. It could be said that within this trajectory, Alex was something of a pioneer, notwhithstanding the fact he hardly made a penny out it!

Much of the rubbishing related to Trocchi's scrapes with the law, which were numerous throughout his life - more serious in his youth than later in London's Kensington – and were largely to do with his drug taking, especially his heroin habit. The reaction of the authorities was certainly far heavier than anything deployed against literary precursors such as Baudelaire, Coleridge, De Quincey or even, Branwell Bronte as their opium habits were pretty much ignored by the powers that be, as indeed initially was drug taking amongst the new factory proletariat during their sparse leisure time. But by the 1950s illicit drug taking had combined with a McCarthyite witch hunt against 'commie subversives' , particularly in New York where Trocchi lived for a while, the city legislature having passed a law which could mean 'the chair' for anybody found guilty of selling drugs to minors

. Hardly surprising that Trocchi's drug anguish was therefore far worse than anything Coleridge or De Quincey ever experienced, and he was far more persecuted for it by the state, which is why the Situationist International rightly came to his defence commenting: "that drug taking is without importance" a remark which must be understood within this specific context, and not as a proclamation on the eternal validity of drug taking whatever the circumstances. Furthermore, with a devil may care attitude, Trocchi certainly spectacularised his drug habits, helping further bring the wrath of the moral establishment down around his ears. He was punished and punished and punished again for such transgressions.

As for ourselves, how often have we experienced castigation upon castigation and endless notoriety which, if not for the same reasons - drugs never came into it - comes pretty damn close, not so much using 'monster' as self-definition, but your very body as the worst PC crime in existence and "the biggest cunt of all" , followed by "supreme arsehole" as lesser epithet etc. Both however were involuntary refrains welling up inside whenever the shit was hitting the fan, whenever you'd again put another person's back up who'd decided to have yet another familiar pop in the spirit of "It's time these guys were taught a lesson".

Hadn't you'd had that lesson thrown at you a million times when the inevitable daily chips were down, when one door closed to be followed rapidly by another and then another. Some were worse than others, especially those that came like whistling daggers from your nearest and dearest like Anne Ryder's (Black Mask/UAATWMF) so many, many moons ago when she penned a letter saying she didn't want to be in the company of "a self-destructive ghost" and "an outsider". As bald and as rabid as that as the men of money and opportunity beckoned, never to set eyes on you or contact ever again; indeed to disappear off the edge of the map you were just so bad. Yes, truly 'the supreme cunt' forever hovering and trembling on the precipice of perpetual nervous breakdown. Yes, most certainly monstrous and though for different reasons you recognised Trocchi's introjections under constant attack, and water really does wear away a stone.....

Trocchi's books were burnt, but then our pamphlets and posters were, though for different reasons. Ours because we suggested a peoples' uprising in pretty violent terms that sometimes deployed sexualised graphics, Trocchi's for more simple obscenity, in an injunction brought by the sheriff of Sheffield who seized some of his stuff together with others from local bookshops, to be dumped forthwith into the flames of the municipal incinerator. Sheffield: 1963, ours in Newcastle, 1967, only four years between the fiery furnaces. Harsh, repressive cities? Well no. Sheffield especially gives off an emancipatory air among its people, streets and enclaves like that corner of Castle Market which really is the nearest thing to a humanised odd ball Paradise and perhaps the hellfire attitudes of its great and good helped its population move in these entirely different directions which the libertarian ambience of Castle Market hints at?

Yes for sure, the endless misery and for Alex, the drugs: "I have needed drugs to abolish within myself the painful reflection of the schizophrenia of my times, to quench the impulse to get at once on to my feet and go out into the world and live out some convenient, traditional identity of cunning contrivancy; acting, doing, asserting myself in the world of others, desperately as men do, and competitively against short time. The astronauts who were my heroes moved on trajectories through inner space... I wanted to escape out of the prison of my mind's language; to "make it new". The very concepts in terms of which men still ordered their lives.... and these were the root and fabric of our insanity....the dud coinage of our everyday language was the measure of our imbecility". Yes Alex, what better description could there be and, as fresh as ever, it applies to all of us who try, and still try.....

These are the comments of a guy who tried to live life for real. Trocchi was feisty and a natural rebel from the word go, with a healthy disrespect for the rules of daily commerce, nicking from shops when a kid, and at school engaging in pranks that had a real edge. That's always a good sign. He was to quickly grow up living hard and fast in a then courted bohemian drift, though like his fellow traveller Ralph Rumney, this overlapped with an unfortunate predilection for la dolce vita, and for those who inhabited its circles: One day penniless, the next right in there with an on the lam rich whom you rapidly became unfortunately financially dependent upon.

And never forget whilst at the apex of alternative rebellion Trocchi sent at least one of his off-spring to a private school near Paris. Altogether, it was something post 1968 we couldn't do or fall in with, especially having disappeared through the sieve of the cultural paradigms which were la dolce vita's bottom kowtowing line. Ah that we could have kowtowed like this as things may have been easier, especially survival. None the less there was compensation in trawling the negative, and Rimbaud had come up with one: "I am a thousand times the richer, let us be as miserly as the sea".

But this miserliness wasn't puritanical, repressive or fatalistic as it was sometimes mistakenly characterised, even by erstwhile friends. It's just that you had little or no choice as again you had to set out into the unknown moving onto a clearer though necessarily different terrain and one pointing well beyond the boundaries of art and representation. Just how much of this society did you wish to hang on to in any case? Beyond basics - food, warmth, shelter, physical and mental health etc - did you really want to go in for spectacular consumption? A thousand times: No. No. No....

La boheme in any case had always favoured the wayward refugees from the middle classes. That was also partially Trocchi's misfortune as he'd hailed from the relatively well-off in Glasgow - there had been housemaids in the past - and his upbringing was much more middle class than ours and that of most of our friends who were the products of post second world war social democracy. Indeed one of our close relatives had been a housemaid and maybe it could be said this fixation on social provenance which seems to mark these islands, as it marked us, became something like a Freudian repetition compulsion and just as emotionally inexplicable to ourselves as to others not imprisoned in this often mind-boggling conundrum.

And as if to complicate matters further, Trocchi, though from a more privileged background, wasn't at all well-off, consequently he too was always 'throwing them in' against those in the boheme/ la dolce vita milieu that were more financially secure than him, having dosh and inheritances. Way back then Trocchi had an advantage because guilt tripping worked, though as a tactic, even in the 1950s it never really extended much beyond an experimental bohemian cultured clique. Moreover Trocchi was able to supplement a few freebies with the occasional scholarship and grant. Part and parcel of this was Trocchi's epater le bourgeois stance whereby he could wind up the 'on the lam rich' whilst still making himself acceptable, allowing scope for 'poor me' appeals and occasionally hitting the jackpot. Post '68 and all that was out if you wished to have the honour of cutting edge stuffed under your belt.

Again the bottom line was cultural celebrity. But what would happen if your ideas or your imagination was pushing beyond the cultural realm? Could you then be still on the tap in any serious way? Our experience has proved otherwise. Throughout Trocchi's life the dismissal/transcendence of culture keeps cropping up getting ever more intense as the late 1960s approached. It all began in a rather beautiful, casual way. Completing his enforced national service in the navy in Xmas 1945 in the last moments of the war, and so young, our man was walking at night along Southend pier (it must be the pier) and back to where his frigate was anchored. Fed up, Trocchi had been reading a book of poetry after a dismal night out on the town and in a moment of exasperation threw the book into the sea watching the words first distort then gradually disappear under the gentle swell: "To get away from words that followed him like a footstep down his own mind! To escape from thoughts and ideals and words". (Was this an intimation coming deep from within of the historical necessity to make a final break with the sublimated constraints of written poetry?)

Maybe all such individuals like us have had similar, almost premonition-like illuminations. Ours was meeting Jacques Vache in a Harrogate public library aged fourteen and a half, and four years later having had your mind blown learning about that incident when Charlie Parker, somewhere in the American mid-west played his alto sax up close to the face of a cow in a field - and did this memory morph to the day on Newcastle Town Moor in 1968 when you tried to spray paint the gist of the King Mob leaflet The Death of Art Spells the Murder of Artists onto a poor, unsuspecting grazing cow who looking nonplussed, quickly legged it?

For sure even at this early moment Trocchi was, probably unbeknown to himself, connecting with the movement of negation at the heart of modern poetry, from Gerard de Nerval, to Mallarme, to Appollinare, to Duchamp. But this was Britain and there was the whole ossified weight of Eng Lit hanging about your shoulders and just how far and how thorough was Trocchi's re-evaluation of Eng Lit going to be? Evidently his lecturers thought Trocchi's student essays were ace. It would be interesting to know what Trocchi's take was, fondly imagining they were constructed around the essential dimension of the breakthrough/dissolution of form - maybe following on from Hazlitt, influenced by Lettrism - and not (repeat NOT) pickled in the vinegar of Eng Lit interpretation which resolutely sets itself against the outcome emanating from the explosive revolt of form.

But all this is fanciful. Was it ground breaking? Did Trocchi's developing ideas begin to open up a vista beyond culture, seeing into so many things and the moment where culture could move - and transcend - into a rejuvenated life? What were his student essays like, seemingly so clued in and knowledgeable about the intricacies of past poetic form; things like 'The Development of Ideas in Keats' Poetry', Chaucer's 'The Canterbury Tales', Dryden's satire, Donne's poems and Alexander Pope. What did Trocchi have to say on John Milton and Edmund Spencer's 'The Fairie Queene'? Was his long manuscript - 73 pages long - entitled 'General Theory of Literary Criticism' any good? Perhaps there are more than relevant clues in all of this which need to be disentangled, though perhaps not as the guy finally was to remain stuck fast in the groove of written poetry and that of novelist, though it was more the transcendence of the form of the novel, rather than the form of poetry, that engaged Trocchi. He tried to quit his literary habit as much as his drug habit, but in the end couldn't do either.

Even after Trocchi's excellent contribution to subversion with his 'Invisible Insurrection Of A Million Minds' in 1961, within the space of ten years he was welcoming the publication of much of his past poetry by Tandem Books, which wasn't much more than a celebration of his encyclopaedic knowledge of style ranging from the techniques of Donne, Marvell and other metaphysical poets up to contemporary times and, only adding to the large amount of crap Trocchi wrote, miring himself in further obfuscation. He didn't even consider so much as a forward condemning or maybe self-critiquing his juvenilia.

Trocchi never separated his wheat from his chaff, and that simply wasn't good enough. Obviously no slouch ,Trocchi remarked that "Coleridge was an opium addict and he wrote the greatest literary criticism of all time, 'Biographia Literaria'" yet failed to go beyond this to acknowledge that the Biographia constantly splits open the boundaries of literature, which is why it is an early milestone in the transcendence of art. (Hazlitt had remarked that a good part of the Biographica had been cribbed from German philosophical theory - which again postulated the end of art (our emphasis) - but also that the crib was better than the original!) It might be big headed to intervene here, but did we not push things like this that much farther and more comprehensively, realising that you had to explain more historically, especially as everything was becoming so much more dumbed down in the face of the developing neoliberal economic experiment, and even though such seemingly 'academic' concerns were well 'apres the event' out there on the streets (in the late 1960s)?

Though media heat was directed against Trocchi's contemporaries, The Angry Young Men, it was nothing like the assault against his own person. In any case, that 'heat' was normally followed by a welcoming introduction, as The Angry Young Men were taken up so quickly by a traditionally oriented Eng Lit pantheon, applying as they did an acceptable artistic form to a content the literary establishment knew nothing about, but were more than fascinated by. The writers embrace of Northern Working class culture slotted into a growing programme of social anthropology, helping unveil the mysteries of social apartheid and a different species being, recalling a similar fascination with Mass Observation during the 1930s, and the later war years. (See also "Comparisons from Mass Observation to King Mob".)

The only overlap between the Angry Young Men and Trocchi was an initially vague, but real hatred of the system, with the latter seeing himself more as enrage in the French sense of the term, which only occasionally sliced through to the real negative, though when it did it was to turn into a sharp scalpel indeed. All of them tended to remain on a diffuse 'ban the bomb' level, and even when Trocchi alone among them did briefly wield a very subversive scalpel indeed, his analysis of the recuperative methods of modern day consumer capitalism remained feeble e.g. performing for the TV rather than engage' - the real engage' - in an imaginative intervention against the mode of representation which was coming to imperiously dominate and destroy all our lives.

It was from such engagé perspectives that Trocchi judged Orwell, tending to dismiss his "political" stuff, concentrating on what was leftover, his way of writing as something of an existential individual preparing the ground for much lesser figures such as Albert Camus. It seems Trocchi had little knowledge about leftisms beyond a simplistic anti Communist party stance which, quite crudely, equated communism with the Stalinoid state, and he wasn't up to Orwell's subtleties and experiences of such things, especially his fraternal relationships with the Spanish anarchists during the Spanish revolution of 1936-8, despite belonging to the militias of the Trotskyist POUM.

Beyond that Trocchi probably knew absolutely nothing about the old ultra left represented by individuals such as Bordiga, the early Sylvia Pankhurst, Gorter or Pannekoek etc nor did he probably have much of a clue even about Socialisme ou Barbarie or its off-shoot, Solidarity in Britain. As far as Orwell was concerned, Trocchi found a book like The Road to Wigan Pier something of a mess and that lengthy impassioned, viciously beautiful tirade at the end of the book against a self-important leftist milieu swept right over him. Minutiae like the "mechanical snigger" of the Marxologist would most likely have passed right over Trocchi's head, seeing he'd probably never crossed swords with such obnoxious politicos!

Without resorting to too much repetition, we know that try as he might, Trocchi could not escape the paradigms of culture and everything ineluctably was marked by this. His friendships remained imprisoned within the circle of writers, artists and sculptors, dissident though some were, like his chum Christopher Logue who, to his honour, did spend a few months in prison for his political beliefs. However, by the late 1960s, Logue was nothing more than a Trotskyist hanger-on, contributing to the idiocies of The Black Dwarf around Tariq 'Tin Pan' Ali, and the syndrome of "there's no business like revolutionary show business".

If Trocchi hung around with others who weren't writers, they were most likely culled from the usual con men and flankers who are often attached to these circles, and a presence marking the essential con that it is at the heart of the vast contemporary art world. In retrospect it was a great personal failing in comparison to the life of a fellow Scotsman nigh on two centuries previously; that of the great ploughman Robbie Burns with his friends in the Ayrshire pub, as he supped daily with the likes of Clockie Brown, the Auld Man, Holy Willie among others. Trocchi never had a good friend among the wild working stiffs and their dependents. How different and hard edged might Trocchi have become if some of his best mates had been spreads, sparkies, truck drivers or chippies on drugs for, after all, there's more than enough of them who enjoy the chemical relief from a nightmarish existence?

True, Paris was to finally open up Trocchi's mind in the late 1950s/early 1960s, but only after he'd trawled through all the detritus of the Left Bank scene, and too late, he could never leave it behind. His anchor was the expat American/English literary scene where they pointlessly discussed facets of the oeuvre of Eliot, Pound, Yeats, Joyce, Faulkner and Miller without heading for the heart of the matter. Trocchi's editorship of the magazine Merlin during these years is a mirror up to this ambience, most of the time publishing the successful litterateurs of their age as well as a few old time big names like Genet, Queneau, Eluard, Ionesco, Neruda and Beckett, sometimes connecting somewhat, though in a very tame way, the old Parisian art/anti-art traditions.

The name Merlin was gleaned from Ezra Pound by Logue and the magazine immediately sought to compete with Sartre's Les Temps Modernes. In reality Merlin wasn't much more than run of the mill, hardly venturing into the beckoning, subversive terrain beginning to be felt throughout Paris at the time, but it did rapidly become a springboard to predatory publishers who invariably ripped the writers off and/or forced them to do things they didn't want to do. Maurice Girodias was one, and as a business man persuaded Trocchi to write eight pornographic novels under the pseudonym of Frances Lengel, making Girodias' publishing house, the Olympia Press, a pretty packet over the coming decades.

Not that Trocchi really minded, because unlike today, pornography way back in the 1950s had a hip, artistic, risque, even avant garde character, appearing to take on the state and censorship. Remember France in the 1950s had no censorship, so the hinterland between art and pornography could be safely explored and then, if you like, exported. The whole Left bank scene in the mid 1950s had really gotten off on The Story of O by Pauline Reage or was it Simone de Beauvoir? And here an overlap between Trocchi and Ralph Rumney beckons, with both wanting to prize open the stultifying moralism of Olde Englande, though Alex went farther in this than Ralph, indulging in bouts of mild sado masochism, though you suspect more for the sake of performance, publicity and the spotlights than anything else. Hadn't Alex once said: 'The conquest of a new female, especially a beautiful one, was closer to hate than love'? Whatever, generally The Story of O was regarded as a worthy female addition to De Sade, and the sometimes risque content of Merlin reflected this, though the magazine was immediately welcomed by the British cultural establishment with the likes of Stephen Spender, Bertrand Russell, and Sir Herbert Read singing its praises.

Nevertheless, Trocchi did take the piss out of the literary establishment a little by hoodwinking them with (for the time) two brazen hoaxes, concerning Irish writer Frank Harris, and the Greek poetess Sappho respectively, producing two 'authentic' freshly unearthed books by them: The Lives and Loves of Frank Harris and Sappho in Lesbos. Though based on existing material, Trocchi had fabricated the rest. In our late teens the former certainly had us fooled as we eagerly read and enjoyed 'that book' on Frank Harris in a smutty way. Trocchi had completed the book on Sappho in 1960, and if it had come out then instead of 11 years later it would have had a helluva impact. As for the Frank Harris, the title of the book in a later edition eventually became What Frank Harris Did Not Say.

It's still a great pity that there isn't more of this hoaxing around, especially when art is now something like the omniscient word of god in the late Victorian era, when more Christian churches were built than ever, at the very moment the church was about to really enter the twilight zone, despite all the efforts of the Born Again in recent years to put a humpty dumpty fool of Nazareth back together in one piece.

If such tactics were to be employed again today they would also probably have to be lucidly explained and, fairly quickly after the event simply because every subversive tactic or technique has now been virtually lost. It could perhaps also be said that Trocchi's hoaxes, even his 'pornography', pointed to something like a new innocence among many songs of experience; an emancipation not only from 'honest' writing but from sexual shame and guilt, and still valid, especially in these maimed times when most sexuality, differently inclined or straight, has become lost and fucked-up by ultra-commodification.

Then a dramatic geographical break occurred as Trocchi left Paris for New York. It was a break that seemed to encourage a more profound crisis in everyday life. Penniless, he was forced to find a job, any job, becoming a scow captain with the New York Trap Rock Corporation on the river Hudson. Essentially it meant he was a bargee with zilch status, remarking: "The scow captains were regarded as the rats of the waterfront" and symbolic of the fact he'd rejected literature and literary product. Also, this was a necessary step as it distanced him from a literary/artistic Greenwich Village and the cultural commodity as he confronted the next hurdles on the road to realisation, that of bums and proletarianisation and an overlap with the buildings, as 'the rocks' removed were mainly building materials and, sometime later, we were to pick up these building materials as an ordinary gang collective without the intermediary of the subcontractors we were to hate so much.

Trocchi noted his stint as a scow captain as "a period of extreme alienation" - where "I never came nearer to self-destruction". (In reality, what was wrong with that? Scumbags as we are, we've put up with things like that for decades!) Trocchi had made the necessary step beyond the art scene, maybe feeling it like an absence, though like some fellow traveller American Beats this was to be where it ground to a halt, on the threshold of that open door between art and life. Such rich absence gave Cain's Book something of a radical edge that pointed elsewhere, even towards a veiled revolutionary praxis, but then six months later Alex jacked the job, scurrying back to the literary scene and to another open door, that of The Cedar Bar, that artistic/literary watering hole where Jackson Pollock and his cohorts had hung out.

Cain's Book though wasn't like Young Adam, a novel as such, but a process of moralistic disintegration combining forthright polemics and personal history, and without time sequences, with no beginning, middle or end, independent of novel or manifesto, which is why it still hasn't been made into a film like Young Adam, as film makers understand novels and little else.

In a way the book is a development of a comment of Mayakovsky's: "From the philistinism of living comes the philistinism of politics", though with a more cataclysmic emphasis on ritual mundanity: "He had to spread them thinly over the day, as he spread margarine over his bread, to prevent the collapse of the world". Real revolutionary theoretical films despite the passive audience/screen social relation and cause for condemnation of cinemas entire ouevre are out of the question and Cain's Book is half and half. Also because Cain's Book was neither mickling nor muckling, it was immediately proclaimed by the lions of the literary establishment like Samuel Beckett and Norman Mailer. (That thankfully has never happened to us, but then our publications and films were always beyond the ken of all categorisation and referentials, both cultural and political.)

It took France to make the anti-novel novel, 'le nouveau roman' , into the anti-film film in the shape of the 'nouvelle vague', something which the Anglo-American world has always found difficult to come to terms with. And as is well known, Last Year at Marienbad was a Robbe-Grillet anti novel in motion and rip-off of early International Lettriste anti films. This though was - and still is - beyond the ken of the English speaking world and such experiment always remained very much at the margins of cultural production, most likely because the real subversion at the heart of the revolt of modern art in its classic heyday never really touched these shores, (though it did America in a minor key.) In many ways Trocchi's was a lone voice with perhaps the exception of BS Johnsons', oriented around post Joycean stream-of-consciousness anti-novel novels. But Johnson was unable to take steps towards more coherent revolutionary theory, even though he realised that a lot more was needed than pushing the boundaries of anti art. But instead of searching out the elusive autonomy of the sharp end, Johnson settled for the role of trade union rep. Nevertheless the guy really tried and that incessant cold shouldering, having been 'washed up on these inhospitable shores' (John Dennis) may have been a factor in his suicide.

Now for a further interesting tale. A few years back we once had occasion to mention the film Young Adam based on the novel by Alex Trocchi to our niece Clare, as she had helped facilitate the film's production as part of the management structure of the British Film Institute, raising money for it, so the name was at least familiar to her whilst knowing nothing about the man or what he stood for. (Later we were to seriously fall out with her the more she got into a despicable PFI privatisation at the BFI) A short discussion ensued. We mentioned that Trocchi had been, for a brief period, a member of the situationists and that he was a writer/anti writer, and that this was evident in the film when Adam chucks his typewriter into the canal in the hope that he may eventually become a fully-fledged bargee. The film also contained other art historical references, as when Adam smeared the remains of his breakfast over his estranged girlfriend, a clear allusion to the surrealist, Meret Oppenheim. (The book ends on that ringing anti-climatic half-sentence "and the disintegration was already taking place" a something the film couldn't capture).

As for Clare's brother, the actor Greg Wise and now married to Emma Thompson, it was all lost on him, for he had not even heard of Trocchi, never mind Meret Oppenheim, though he had heard of Ewan McGregor who played young Adam and probably was jealous of his stardom, wishing he could have landed the role seeing his looks were the equal of McGregor's. It also turned out that our thespian had not heard of Thomas Bewick, the wood engraver from Northumberland. We were about to launch into a disquisition on Bewick, on his qualities as a naturalist and how he linked nature and the iniquities visited on the rural poor together, remaining a revolutionary all his life when we decided to call it a day. We were getting nowhere with our bullet-proof conversers and the whole thing was just downright depressing. Better to shut up and say nowt.

Yes our Alex couldn't break free. For sure, he was a scow captain and also willing to sometimes hit the odd job circuit as handyman or gardener, but there it remained. Trocchi's solution: Rather than something egalitarian; a collectivity or a workers' collective versus the boss etc, he instead inclined towards the solipsist loner, tending towards the entrepreneurial, like selling books. (Collectivity as mode of survival - that essential egalitarianism - was unlike us - anathema to Trocchi). Ah yes there was something else: he actually ventured on the dole and social security for a short while. He found it rather demeaning and are we supposed to feel sorry for him? Afraid not, as any self-respecting subversive doesn't give a toss about stints on the dole which once, in any case, held out unlimited possibilities to engage in subversion. Finally, when the literary world failed him and he the literary world, Trocchi no longer looked to casual work or the dole but to that of business man trading in antiquarian books, moving from Portobello Rd and Kensington Market to his final resting place at the Rare Books Antiquarius emporium in Kings Road, Chelsea in the 1970s and interestingly not too far from Maclaren's and Westwood's pre punk SEX boutique down the less salubrious end! Selling wares and performance. Money and performance; always performance! (Scots Alec, Kensington High St?)

The scows had made their subversive mark however, and back in Paris Trocchi was to write - for its time - the remarkable The Invisible Insurrection Of A Million Minds, which was not only published in the Situationist International journal in 1962 and Anarchy mag in London, but the literary New Saltire Review in Edinburgh, whose editor, the later Mastermind's Magnus Magnusson,also demanded to be revised. (Did Alex do as requested: Most likely!) For once biographer Scott Murray grasps things: "This new direction led him away from the concept of novels, stories and scripts - saleable commodities which could be sold to publishers and to the general reading public, and instead led him to challenge the entire nature of literature". That was the whole point ,and is exactly why Alex couldn't stick to the letter of what he'd superbly written in The Invisible Insurrection Of A Million Minds' , because from then on, there would be no financial reward at the end of the emancipatory rainbow.

Interestingly too, William Burroughs didn't really approve of the Invisible Insurrection, seeing the concepts contained in the manifesto as an excuse to avoid the serious task of 'creative' writing by the 'creative' individual genius, and which is why a little later, King Mob's deployment of a Burroughs' one-off "Storm the Reality Studios;

Retake the Universe" on a demonstration banner sent out the wrong signal. Yet immediately you sense Scott Murray deep down doesn't approve in any case of Trocchi's drift, but is too polite and academically cunning to say so, despite his body language betraying him. According to this 'expert', by 1955 Trocchi's letters to his brother had become 'bilious tracts', citing such lines as: "I reject the entire system....the answer is revolution".

In retrospect, you do indeed wonder what all the fuss was about, because in any case Alex immediately betrayed himself,attending the International Writers' conference at the next Edinburgh Festival almost in the same breath as he helped write an editorial for the Situationist International magazine, while also arranging an exhibition at the ICA of his driftwood sculptures, the 'feelies' or "futiques", as he called them. Habits of a lifetime refused to budge and Trocchi in any case always had been writing for official mags beginning with The Scots Review in 1950. If anything his cultural world was expanding, even engaging in a bit of action painting here and there when times were boring and, moreover, selling his paintings to London art dealers. No longer though was it writing or rather a frozen in time painterly action which attracted him, the more the active performing and exhibitionist part of himself found outlet and impact through an ever-enlarging and technically newer, media mode of production. More and more Trocchi looked for media roles, initially as an extension of shock - well for the times - episodes in his writings, like deploying fuck expletives (well before his occasional friend Ken Tynan openly deployed them), remarking: "As artists we situate ourselves at the level of man-at-crap".

First these active, on-the-spot stunts were for shock and sensation, like shooting up on live American TV in 1961 when making a guest appearance on a programme discussing drugs - and paying the price (I mean really paying the price, and not in monetary terms) as the law got heavy. In some ways these actions of Trocchi's were initially rather admirable, but a little later the money angle really began to creep in. Sure many appearances remained provocative, but increasingly with an eye to the irregular cheque in the post, Alex, sensing acceptance wasn't too far away, even gave half hour TV programme interviews which went hand in hand with an emerging lecture circuit, plus a stint as visiting sculpture tutor at St Martin's College of Art, London. The failure that entails in dealing with the media essentially on its own terms was laid bare, as seen in the growing sensationalised tabloid description of Trocchi "as the media's favourite junkie". The guy finally sold himself short, never realising as Nick Brandt was to say some twenty years later, "with ever the best intentions, the media always makes you look a prat".

Yet even here through the distorting, mocking lens of the TV interview, with a ridiculous charlatan of an interviewer doing the business, Trocchi could perceptively say: "We mustn't consider ourselves as professional writers any longer"..... in the literary industry like the "Shakespeare Industry" ... which had to be overthrown as we now approach the time of the.... "millions of individual centres of sensitive men and women all over the world who, if they could only become aware of their identity, and the fact that there were a million such identities who, acting together could create a new world."

The media used Alex Trocchi, he didn't use the media. In contrast, The Situationist International's approach to the media at the time of his cavorting for the TV - his hour upon the stage - was the only possible position to adopt; one of utter negativity, alongside a clear explanation of why you must behave like this, having nothing to do with either newspaper journalists or TV appearances. It was a negativity which after 1968 was practised more and more, especially and, indeed with some longevity, throughout the highly capitalised world, including some interesting developments on this score some time later by Os Cangaceiros, and interventions against television by the strikers of Les Intermittents in 2004.

During the 1980s in France, Os Cangaceiros experimented with different ways of dealing with the media. One of their participants, commenting in a stray thesis in May 1995 (http://www.revoltagainstplenty.com/index.php/archive-global/58-os-cangaceiros.html) said: "The best use of the media (instead of them using you) is to try and bypass them. First, make them unnecessary so they might react as a mere amplifier of what happened and without us deploying their assistance".

And then for Trocchi there was to be Sigma; a collective, ill thought through that rapidly became meaningless, that wasn't necessarily of the old world but neither was it of the new; a product of The Invisible Insurrection of a Million Minds but also a failure of its application too. For starters, Sigma had nothing to do with egalitarian, sharp end collectivism but an artists/writers coming together and ugh with what consequences! Playing on radicalism, its terminology was also a meaningless distortion. Technically, 'sigma' is the symbol used in mathematics for the sum of the whole, and so in this instance representing a deflected acknowledgement of dialectics and the necessity of totality and total critique. Indeed Trocchi referred to Sigma as "a dialectical instrument" though it was anything but.

As a bureaucratic organisation Sigma eschewed the principal of commercial publication, though its practise had nothing to do with a perspective tending towards the transcendence of money, but a 'clearing house for artists to sell their wares, cutting out the agents and middlemen', eg: influencing a few years later a Dutch state initiative whereby all artworks were bought up on a yearly stipend by anybody who wished to call themselves artists in (1970s-80s). You'd hoped at the time that such a scheme might have produced some quality revolutionary reflections, as some more enlightened individuals in disguise could have quickly knocked out some artistic shit giving them time to produce revolutionary theory and action of quality, yet still able to pick up another grant from the Dutch state at the end of the year. No such luck.

The Invisible Insurrection - that record of the explosion of a million minds thinking, experiencing and trying to live in different ways - got sidetracked by the changing face of culture itself, and the manifesto, instead of contributing to contemporary revolutionary critique, helped form the basis of the alternative poetry production of Sigma, spearheaded by the now well forgotten - and deservedly so - figure of Simon Vinkenoog. Sigma was a widened and spread out redefinition of culture, embracing the beginnings of all the shit that is centre stage and so overpowering us today, and is finally a banal acceptance of what is. Needless to say Sigma has nothing to do with revolutionary praxis nor does it provide an opening out onto such hopes, emphasising as it did throughout its heyday in the 1960s, happenings, installations, environment exhibits and all the rest of the crud panoply which somewhat later, people like the Saatchi Bros and henchmen of Thatcher's were to sponsor as social democratic capitalism gave way to the infinitely greater hell of the free market.

Trocchi went on to found the First International of Poetry in 1965, which was itself a sad displacement and recuperation of the first (and best) Workers' International of 1864, founded by English trade unionists and quickly broadened in scope and intention by the likes of Marx and Bakunin. But this kind of radicalism was exactly what Trocchi was now into, distorting and camouflaging revolutionary initiatives, and not searching out new friends - essentially those without professional aspirations - and tapping into the new tremors the times were increasingly revealing. Instead he increasingly associated himself with people like acid media guru Tim Leary, psychiatrist RD Laing with his half-baked grasp of cultural negation together with a none too deep take on Artaud. Other poets like Mike Horowitz and Jeff Nuttal were similarly half-baked. He also liked the novelist William Burroughs though truth to tell, Trocchi like Rumney occasionally, had a far more significant grasp of what was beginning to unfold than all the American Beats, precisely because they did understand something of the terminal crises inherent in artistic form beginning to add the essential dimension missing in social revolutionary praxis.

Within Sigma, everything quickly went awry. The transcendence of art got locked into a perspective of mass democratised art to be placed here, there and everywhere, becoming a harbinger of today's neoliberal or PFI aesthetic economy. Trocchi lamentably commented: "I reject the category of literature because it is highly dangerous and leads to a number extravagances and perversions. What I want to create is an infectious ambience for the revitalisation of art, because art should be something to inform every waking moment" (oh dear, oh dear, oh dear, oh...). As if to reinforce these increasingly vapid notions Trocchi banally suggested to the Postmaster General that a series of stamps be cut featuring and commemorating the work of British sculptors. Hardly the stuff dreams are made of.

Trocchi soon wanted Sigma to become a business, albeit an alternative one (and limited company) before such notions encountered the grim reality whereby counter culture also became a culture counter, extensively refurbished, decades later entering the arena of global market players. The then Labour administration in the 1960s under Harold Wilson took an interest via Ms Jenny Lee, the new Minister for the Arts, and even though Trocchi disliked official institutions, in reality he wanted them in a sensitised, reconstructed form in the shape of a London Free University, the anti-university staffed by anti-lecturers, though stopping well short of that rallying cry of the most radical elements in the uprisings of 1968:'abolish the university'. (1) Trocchi's poorly digested notion of recuperation was becoming all too obvious and he was tending to become all things to all people. After he resigned from the Situationist International in 1964, no wonder Guy Debord was forced to condemn him and 'the mystical cretins' like Alan Ginsberg, Colin Wilson, RD Laing and Tim Leary he was hanging around with. Indeed you get the impression Guy had shown much leniency and patience.

It can be argued though that without Trocchi, the underground of the 1960s/ early 70s, wouldn't have been what it was, together with its related periodicals and pamphlets. Indeed, The International Times, that generally banal, alternative organ of the late 1960s put on the masthead of its first issues that IT was "a sigmatic newspaper", a move instigated by Trocchi's fellow Glaswegian,Tom MaGrath. Moreover, there was also something of an essential drift in these diverse alternatives, happenings and the like as they evolved throughout the years, slipping more and more towards the lower orders, leaving the specialists in art farther and farther behind an increasingly autonomous momentum. That beautiful style of writing that Trocchi was so capable of producing gave way to a rawness and spontaneity when some of these tendencies were taken up by others which courted the semi-literate at times, but whose vitality compensated for loss of stylistic ease when crying out for 'revolution now' together with a renewed passionate life. For having the courage to take this path, Trocchi must be given credit, as we were some of the first also to have the courage to tear its failings and contradictions apart during the moment of King Mob, including a few attacks both theoretical and physical on The International Times. For sure at the time we thought a lot of this alternative culture was complete rubbish but now that the froth has gone, even its ill-defined social egalitarianism, it's as if the 1960s never existed and on this score, we have to agree with some recent comments by Lawrence Ferlinghetti.

By 1968 Trocchi was falling apart on some of its contradictions, as if the ground he'd prepared had become too much for him. More famous than ever, and on the threshold of the big time money-wise, the impetus and ethos of that annus mirabilis was anti art and anti money. It was as if the year had stabbed Trocchi in the back as it superseded his hesitations, bringing about an ennui and lethargy he was henceforth never to escape from, lapsing into a fraught though reasonably comfortable middle class alternative lifestyle. Followers and acolytes, from well-meaning nobodies to the Leonard Cohens, Marianne Faithful's and Mick Jagger's, were welcomed , and even in the aftermath of the late 1960s, a renegade from King Mob's revolutionary perspectives in the shape of Chris Grey. As for us, our lives were to head off in a diametrically opposite direction, eschewing hangers-on, followers and acolytes; unknown and unseen without image and profile. The disappeared -the has beens who never were - "Fame; I knew it yesterday" as Mallarme pregnantly called it.

Almost immediately Alex Trocchi was to encounter searing personal tragedy with the death of loved ones followed by an untimely demise which though clinically diagnosed as cancer was probably more accurately to do with a broken heart. It was April 1984 and just a few weeks into what was to become the epic British miners' strike which, if it had succeeded might - just might - have stalled somewhat the most devastating counter revolution in history. Unfortunately, if Trocchi had survived the guy probably wouldn't have given much of a damn whether the strike succeeded or not as by then he was so out of it having lost all revolutionary coherence years previously.

Though these are arguments and memories outlining a way of seeing essential things about life, and more or less suppressed in the pantheon of English (and American) Lit and among what's left of a radical social perspective, they've wormed and worried their way sideways into aspects of hip Media/Culture. Occasionally in The Sopranos and especially Californication, the role of writer is obliquely portrayed as at an end, becoming nothing but a mockery of its former self. What's leftover are only the entrails, the wordsmiths of one-liners and/or searing blogs to be consumed by alienated replicants colonised by the language of advertising though feeling very uneasy with its blatant lies and disinformation. Artistic expression is virtually dead, though beyond this lies a world getting off on never ending fucks - only it's a souped up, commodified bad sexuality amounting to total disaster, where nothing can be realised, least of all fulfilment and happiness, except because it is

TV, nothing is stated as frankly and truthfully - merely hinted at - and, least of all, providing clear openings assisting the re-vitalising of revolutionary critique.

Which leads to a final point. The really interesting latter years fact about Trocchi was his final inability to do anything, which the more conventional culture bugs (e.g. Barry Miles who is still as big a prat as he ever was) refer to as 'writers' block'. Though easy to dismiss as a simple consequence of Trocchi's well known heroin addiction, maybe it in fact it points to something far more significant: the failure of cultural forms of writing as a vehicle of communication and the end of the writers' role, itself part and parcel of a deeper historical malaise where all officially recognised creativity defined by the artistic embrace has lost its raison d'etre. Does it matter now how well one writes and how seemingly rich is the supposed artistic flair? That old but lost adage is truer today than ever; those who live authentic lives are the ones who write the best. For a long time it's no longer been about a 'good' (i.e. formally correct) command of the English language (or indeed any language) merely that this insight has been brutally eclipsed and vanquished in the perfect storm of the worst counter revolution in history. BRING ON WRITERS' BLOCK EVERYWHERE and therefore by strange default, realising the last inspirational example set by Trocchi himself.

It could be said that Michel Prigent always maintained something of an enthusiasm for Trocchi, though if you came out with some of the arguments outlined here in casual conversation Michel would have readily agreed. True, Alex was more clued-in on the essentials than the somewhat earlier generation of American Beats, but he still couldn't make really essential theoretical breakthroughs like, say, Asger Jorn. It could be said maybe that Michel has a certain Scottish sentimentality towards Alex (Michel's mother was from Glasgow, having met his dad when based in Scotland as part of the Free French squadrons of the RAF during the second world war) together with a kind of emphasis on romantic self-destruction/god's die young syndrome in relation to Trocchi's tragic family life. Michel used to regularly carry around those 1970s video interviews with Trocchi - most likely the ones made by Jamie Wadhawan (https://www.youtube.com/watch?v=ZSS7WqJFPCw) in and around Trocchi's house in Observatory Gardens, Kensington - which Michel would offer to me for free!! (2)

To end at the beginning: Our negativity - and the negativity of those like us - was also based on the reality you'd become a taboo representative of a profound moment, the memory of which must forever be suppressed or, if not that, marked by grotesque distortions, facile interpretation and the no people never to be mentioned again, beyond the pale of humanity and simple decency. An open season declared so subtly yet hunted down like vermin. True, we couldn't write as well as Trocchi (ah the beautiful stylist with that often astonishing ability with words) and if only we had had something of that skill as wordsmiths. Alas, we had little apprenticeship, we were "rough hewn" (Wordsworthsmith) Then again we were trying at times to express the inexpressible, trying to describe the virgin outlines of a path we had to take; a lonely path without recognisable assistance, trying to conceptualise this febrile gossamer we were beginning to feel brush against us ,beckoning from a beyond. At times the gist of this came along as a confused jumble of words and phrases. Trocchi never really got to the point where he was really confronted with this difficult and prolonged experience; the moment of a possible breakdown of words, even though, here and there, he came close enough.

After the late 1960s much emphasis was placed on "clearly sorting out your survival", between the exigencies of the here and now under capitalism and the social revolution we all hoped longingly for and wouldn't perhaps be too far away. We had to find a survival which didn't involve a massive compromise of our minds, thoughts, honesty and feelings, whereby we could be 'free' to say what we had to say. No more writers, artists, musicians and their contracts, appearances, conferences etc. All chains had to be cut and cast asunder. You could see clearly that Ralph Rumney and Alex Trocchi were caught in this spider's web, and a trap that Trocchi particularly hated. In fact this fatal nexus helped kill him off.

Generally though the art scene was to get even worse, emptier and emptier. The more the dog days of 'art' encompassed an expanded reproduction, the more it gradually became the central reference for every event portrayed in the media. At the same moment that powerful undertow; that repressed but profound historical concept that art was dead became nothing more than the ravings of the insane. The result is a situation far worse than that of ancient biblical prophets in the wilderness, because today it defies all empirical daily perceptions, cutting through surface appearances and at the moment of its abolition, the role of art is bigger than ever. The artist has finally telescoped into advertising executive, the contemporary hidden persuader of nothingness, the empty-headed ideas guru looking for that elusive, never-ending sales pitch seeking backers, promotion and media exposure for their latest commodity. The pitch is the gimmick to be talked about for 15 minutes, followed by another 15 minute wonder; ad infinitum. Art is money, art is the bank, art is the hedge fund, art is the imagination of fictitious capital mimicking the processes of the hollowed-out company with hollowed out global aims requiring the 'enforced' wage labour of those at the sharp end to be realised.

Like any on-going business concern, artists are no longer required to do much for themselves now, requiring shedloads of working stiffs to bring their vapid concepts to a miserable fruition. Once even 20 years ago these art finks could at least do something for themselves, having acquired a reasonable practical dexterity with basic ingredients and materials; be it welding, woodworking, plasters and resins, nuts and bolts, saws and glues together with knowledge of basic photography and add-on literary skills. Now the most these people have are a few IT competences allied to a back drop where the imperious edicts of the Health and Safety Executive - itself in thrall to litigation culture - further ensures personal practical tasks can never be carried out.

Cast adrift, ours is the polar opposite, and necessarily without profile, somewhat in the multi-skilled tradition of a William Blake where there's no choice but to learn everything yourself, without that much dosh and no sub-contracted outfits/limited companies to hand. It's a situation where you are more or less forced to learn every technique and practical application you may require, whether it concerns materials, command of the English language and/or knowledge of IT. The results may contain many a rough-hewn edge, becoming an easy target to be mocked by the superficial and plain stupid, but who can only see a few ill-planted trees and not a wood beginning to look really healthy.

D & S W: *Spring 2008*

1) A word to the wise: It's not that the former immense insights and brilliance of English poetry has been cancelled. Rather it's magnificent and often delicate, trembling subtleties tracing the outlines of so many breath-taking perceptions should perhaps now be seen as a potential gateway, even guidance at times, to a reinvigorated life during the moment and aftermath of a profound total social revolution.

2) Ironically and retrospectively, today the times are really dumbed down to the point of a near complete incomprehension. Again there is much room for individuals - nay the mass of the people - to really acquire valuable learning and knowledge. However can this, more than ever be taught at a university more in hoc to quick profits than ever?

3) The truth is Michel Prigent is a more consistently significant figure than Alex Trocchi. However, I never got too close to the guy because I could never really take on board Michel's worshipful awe of Debord which he has since transferred to Moishe Postone. (For my mind Guy Debord is a much more substantial figure - and the debt I owe him is enormous - than a cloistered academic like Postone who simply has never encountered real everyday life). In practise this always meant you could only take a practical/theoretical drift with Michel so far before ideological barriers kicked-in. Postone's infallibility has now replaced Debord's infallibility etc. Still I really like Michel as a person and the guy is always funny and enjoyable company and his latest writings in Principia Dialectica are the best things in the magazine. It has been far too easy to characterise Michel for a certain wild madness but first and foremost one must praise the guy for a relentlessly un-compromised daily life.

Comparisons: From Mass Observation to King Mob.

The changing face of revolutionary elites from the 1930s to the late 1960s and ever after.

(Personal reflections and memories on John Grierson, Humphrey Jennings, Tom Harrison, Bill & Nick Brandt, Don Smith, Barbara Roberts, Chris Grey, Chris Caudwell, Dave Robins, Dick Pountain, Clare Wise and others).

The King Mob elite for a brief moment from 1967-69 did break with the tradition of social reformers and commentators which for so long had tended to be the near unique possession of this particular class fraction. They were unquestionably superior to anything that had come before, and were a sign of the transcendence of this powerful and ever-resurgent class fraction in motion. But flash, bang, wallop and it was gone, and forty years later the reasons for this have to be a contender for the most searching question that can be asked of recent times, and why these individuals numbering four or five at most were incapable of living up to their promise. Overnight they fell silent, having betrayed everything they once stood for until now, these former lilies really do smell far worse than weeds.

We can see antecedents in the first half of the 20th century in the likes of John Grierson, Humphrey Jennings, George Orwell and Tom Harrison, the latter three having attended prep schools and then private schools, and in Orwell's and Harrison's case, the crime of private schools, Eton and Harrow. And all in their own ways were innovators, some related to the Mass Observation movement of the 1930s and people to be still reckoned with, and yet never the revolutionaries the King Mob elite purported to be, and for a few brief years unquestionably were.

So it is necessary we take a step back into the past and say a few more words on some of the people mentioned above, a need made doubly pressing on account of the fact our niece Clare Wise is curator to a heritage that crystallised into the British Film Institute, and whose history she is almost completely ignorant of, having just to say heard of a couple of names but unable to furnish any further details not even biographical ones. When she brushed us to one side like frail midges, she had no idea whatsoever who she was dealing with, and that our critiques left the academic grey beards of the BFI standing, who in turn looked on Clare as the devil-in-prada because of her slavish adherence to everlastingly fashionable neoliberal values and mind numbing philistinism, though an expert in knowing how to gush, curtsey and scrape before her political masters and mistresses.

A person like John Grierson, the documentary film maker in the 1930s-40s, can be compared with Labour party PM Gordon Brown in respect of social provenance, his father being a headmaster whose forebears were lighthouse keepers and his mother the daughter of a shoemaker. At school he steeped himself in the romantic writers and poets like Ruskin, Coleridge and Byron rather like we did. The difference being we had it rammed down our throats by an English Lit pedagogue and correct English snob who described our language as 'that of bus conductors not that of Milton and Shakespeare'! Only later did we find there was a revolutionary edge to the latter two that can still cut deep and that goes straight from the transcendence of written poetry to the creation of determinate situations, which in Hegel's view was the bedrock which led directly to the postscript of art.

Never the historic act itself, it was, when all was said and done, merely an afterthought, and symptomatic of the failure of mankind to achieve fulfilment. Grierson had no familiarity with these ideas and what they drew on and were, a continuation of earth-shattering aspects of romanticism that were now so deeply buried, disinterring them was well nigh impossible, they went so much against the grain. Dying in 1972 Grierson was still less aware that these revolutionary ideas had by then peaked and have been in dire reflux ever since that to even to hint of such a heresy today is to invite a storm of abuse that is jovian in its ferocity.

Grierson had served as a telegrapher in the First World War, a formative experience that showed it was possible to transmit messages other than with a pen. The path to poetry and the trade of writer now blocked by modern machinery and war, this encounter with industry was crucial to his later development and the passage from tapping out Morse to looking at life through a camera lens considerably shortened. On being demobbed he had attended Glasgow University at the very moment of the workers' uprising that became known as Red Clydeside. He showed little sympathy, or appreciation of, the really revolutionary currents embedded in Red Clyde, neither that of 'Marxism' or 'revolutionary syndicalism' with its pronounced anarchist inflection, opting instead to loosely align himself with the Independent Labour party, still however the best of all the social democratic labour parties.

After a stint in America, and gaining his spurs as a film critic for a Chicago newspaper, Grierson was sufficiently well known on returning to England in 1927 to be employed as an assistant film officer for the Empire Marketing Board. Arguing for a new type of documentary film, 'epic cinema' as he called it, he was dead set against fiction films that were beginning to dominate the filmic medium And yet his angle was hardly revolutionary, arguing for a film that would represent the relationship between the citizen and the state, an approach that would not have won him many friends amongst the red Clydesiders, especially the anarcho-syndicalists who would have squirmed at the idea.

When the Empire Marketing Board closed down in 1932, he set up the GPO (General Post Office) film unit producing the films, apart from Drifters (1929), he is now famous for: Industrial Britain (1933) Coal Face (1935) and Night Mail (1936). Frustrated by the mounting constraints within the GPO, he left, encouraging others to do the same, and instead set up independent documentary film making units. This would mean raising money on the open market and going cap in hand to companies or the state, in a world in which state capitalism was on the increase, and therefore fundamentally different from public private financiers of the Film Council and their unquestioning submission to market principles.

We would have liked to have discussed some of the essential questions raised above with our niece, but at every turn we would have encountered a blanket ignorance which would have rendered enlightened debate futile. And that would have the further consequence of destroying at the outset any hope of situating our revolt in a historical context, which would have given it yet further edge and a contemporary relevance.

Take Tom Harrison another notable figure and founder of the Mass Observation movement. If Clare has heard of him it will only be the name that comes up on her internal hard drive that passes for mind amongst today's free marketeers. The son of an (engineering) Brigadier General he was sent to Winchester prep school and thence to Harrow and finally to Pembroke College, Cambridge from where he dropped out. Though I am surmising, I suspect he did so under pressure from the workers' movement and the great catastrophe of the 1930s depression. Anyhow his father never forgave him, and he was disinherited, which can only have done him a power of good. Would that more of this economic chastisement had been the lot of the King Mob elite, for this bread and butter matter could have made all the difference to us and to them and to a developing critique of the totality.

Harrison was also a consummate ornithologist, living with cannibals in the New Hebrides, then still a English colony, before moving to Bolton, Lancashire to get closer to our home grown savages, the industrial working class, turning his bird watching and cannibal watching techniques on the working poor of northern England. And though he took work as a lorry driver, ice cream vendor and shop assistant, discreetly taking notes as he went about his duties, he did so with the eye of the stranger, his retina essentially detached from the lives of ordinary working people. He was an observer, not an active participant and his subjects, sociological objects. He did not 'condemn' himself to their reality - which was the only true path to genuine emancipation and fulfilment - merely chameleon like, appearing to merge with it.

And so the Mass Observation movement was born, no detail of working class life deemed too insignificant to record, though never once knowing in the gut the pathos that lay behind trade ads appearing in shop windows that read 'no job too small'. Volunteers were recruited, the techniques of Mass Observation anticipating that of post war market research, whose detached viewpoint was no different to that of Mass Observation. However the legacy could have been even more dubious and had there been a Bolshevik counter-revolution in this country, the techniques of Mass Observation could have provided all the evidence needed for a Mass Repression of the working class, in particular of those autonomous elements groping toward a rejection of political parties, trade unions and the vast apparatus of apparatchiks that would eventually come to form a 'new class'.

Even many decades later, the self-same reflexes are still palpably there though, whether it has a hope-in-hell of getting anywhere is quite another matter. For one thing I have noticed this Cheka-in-waiting must constantly monitor in one form or another, mentally noting every detail, which is then logged and filed and, given half a chance, used against the lower orders when required. And if, in the interim, you want to enrage the beast, then there is no better strategy than cutting it off from its food source and refusing to supply it with any more 'mass' information of your whereabouts, what you are doing and thinking. Hostile observers in the final analysis of the unpalatable realities of 'working class' lives, above all of their 'moral' lapses, crudities, language, jokes and evasiveness, they are also constantly on guard against themselves, rarely permitting themselves the luxury of a spontaneous outburst of feeling. Is it any wonder that this super-repression has, in no small measure, engendered the art/therapeutic society that has grown in proportion to the translocation of the industrial working class abroad class and which also, especially when in open revolt, had a palliative effect tending to cure them of themselves.

One of the people whose name is indelibly linked to Mass Observation is the photographer Bill Brandt. Bill Brandt was the brother of Rolf Brandt, the illustrator, who had a son called Nick, whom you will all have heard of and was the most consequential upper middle class influenced situationist in Britain. I have at the outset to say I like some of Bill Brandt's photos and those taken by Mass Observation, even though it is possible to see in it as an arty foreshadowing of CCTV which, beyond the shadow of a doubt, will be deployed against the 'mass' come the moment of legitimate revolt and that will be also directed against the hold that the free market has on sections of street youth gone despairingly and uselessly fuckhead.

However the eyes of these photographers had become machine eyes that recorded rather than participated. And so they remained, having somewhere in the background a smart abode they could always run back to and from where they would obsessively put the day's events under a microscope to locate the weakness they were hell bent on finding, and which would provide them with a spurious conviction of their own superiority. However to call them spectators is not entirely accurate. They were voyeurs getting off on what they observed, though never able to completely neither take part in nor experience to the full what they were a witness to but whose attractions they nonetheless felt strongly tempted by.

Nick Brandt was never able to escape from this dilemma. At the same time it has to be said he is a very talented individual and I can only regret he was unable to resolve his contradictions and that there aren't more people of the same calibre around. Though pitched at a far higher level, Nick, just like his uncle Bill, never lived what he was describing or analysing. Always residing a safe distance from it, this distance ultimately vitiated what he had to say and, let's admit it, harmed him, turning him into something of a solipsist of an evening.

But he lapped up news of struggle, worrying the details endlessly, and then, on spotting a mistake, pouncing ferociously. He simply could not grasp, other than in the abstract, that in the heat of the moment one is prone to making mistakes, even serious mistakes. But to him these mistakes were intolerable, flattering himself that had he been there he would never have made them. The trouble was he was nearly always elsewhere. Moreover his rush to pass judgement, constant admonishments and finger wagging, a common enough condition in people who have removed themselves from the actual day to day struggles of ordinary people, made it impossible to be with him for any length of time without feeling the urge to plant one on him.

What ultimately ensnared him was his background and family inheritance and it is doubtful he will ever now be released from its grip. And if he were to lose everything, he would change, not within three months or even three weeks, but within three hours. Really it is all just too sad for words, and critique could be in a much better shape than it is and collaboration still possible had Nick been able to put his past behind him instead of allowing it catch up with him and eventually take him over. For over the past 35 years he was the only member of the upper middle class elite it has proven possible to collaborate with, and who still had a cutting edge critique of art, absolutely essential to an understanding of modern times.

Forty year on I would never have thought it possible in this the direst situation ever faced by mankind, for there to be so little relevant thinking around and for there to be such a reversion to worn out ideas on such a gargantuan scale. I ask myself time and again, however did this conservatism get under way in the first place, and why do I feel so estranged from former comrades in arms? We simply now don't have anything in common, and the mere thought of meeting up with them once more enough to send a bolt of apprehension through me. Despite the limitations of men like Grierson, Jennings and Harrison , whose lives and opinions I have endeavoured to briefly outline, I would not feel anything like foreboding at meeting them, assuming they were still alive of course. There is a greater consistency, honesty and commitment to their lives. However much we may bemoan their illusions and lack of revolutionary clarity, at least they did not betray their ideals when the first chill wind blew. Nor can we say they were made of sterner stuff because that would be to reduce the problem to a matter of strength of character, though it has to be said they put themselves about more than their contemporary backsliders, which was bound to toughen them and expand their horizons.

No, something has changed over the last forty years that has nourished this catastrophic state of affairs and I personally believe it has everything to do with the creeping collapse of class struggle, and in particular the near elimination of industrial class struggle, which, when it did explode, had a percussive effect throughout society, causing conflict to rip far and wide. As the wave of de-industrialization advanced, so the UK turned into a financial casino of speculation, becoming the racketeering capital of the world and, what is worse, more of a corporate success story than anything that had hitherto gone before. As social peace broke out, all avenues of escape became progressively blocked, labour laws tweaked on 13 separate occasions until at long last the judiciary had in its legal arsenal the means of throwing the book at wildcat strikers. A pall of compliance and orthodoxy settled over everything, brains turned to mush, houses at the very least trebled in price and the arty delusion of piddling 'creative industries' as the saviour of a de-industrialized capitalism swept the country.

The individuals I mentioned previously, attached to Mass Observation, felt compelled in one form or another to engage with industry and the industrial working class. This smoking chimney of unknowing had left a question mark in the dark clouds that hung over their entire lives. They felt profoundly threatened by what those clouds were hiding from view and which they knew in their bones they had to eventually confront, even at the risk of losing their identity and being overwhelmed by anonymity. This was their personal and social trauma, the rite of passage that no matter how painful, had to be gone through. It was also a trajectory the ruling class feared, as with when colonials 'went native', but which bit by bit the Victorian imperialists learned how to use, the better to increase their surveillance and control. Kipling's police officer who regularly blacked up to merge with Calcutta's locals can, on one level, be seen as an anticipation of the ambiguous aims that lay behind Mass Observation, which were neither entirely a matter of social control but still less about a genuinely revolutionary liberation of the industrial natives.

There are any number of examples detailing that encounter with northern natives and their southern counterparts, particularly in London's East End, and perhaps one day they should all be collected together because they could set off our own times and be a pointer to what's missing. I need only mention Orwell's Down and Out in London and Paris and of course The Road to Wigan Pier. These were also documentaries, but ones that used a traditional medium. Mass Observation and the documentary filmmakers wanted to make use of the new media, television being the baneful outcome of that trajectory, Grierson ending up as a producer for Scottish TV.

Whether working in old or new media, what was common to both was the impact the north, its industries and working people, had upon the documentarists. When Jennings went north for the first time in 1939, having up until then tossed off around the Cambridge art scene, he described it as the most important turning point of his life. Later in 1943, when making a film in Wales, he wrote: 'I feel we have got close to the men ' not just as individuals - but also as a class - with an understanding between them; so they don't feel we are just photographing them as curios or wild animals'..... Living in Bolton in 1936 Tom Harrison claimed he could, without disguising his accent, blend in with his cotton mill co workers! These are just two, though very revealing examples, of what I mean.

Now fast-forward to 1968 and its immediate aftermath. What I have been describing has never been a problem, with the notable exception of Nick Brandt, with our elite, the question having shifted to focus on youth subcultures, only hippie being sufficiently class neutral to engage with. However there was a gathering storm of revolt on the traditional working class front that our elite was never able to identify with, a fact that ultimately reduced them to a silence that would last a lifetime.

For a time we thought Don Smith might be capable of making a contribution to the understanding of what was unfolding. But though a northerner, having been largely brought up in Southport, even he was traumatised by this eruption, and escaped to America because he really did have some idea about the strength of class feeling that existed in this country. And though he visited striking miners in West Virginia in the 1970s (though revealingly in the company of a French person) , astonished at how closely the mining hollows of West Virginia resembled those of South Wales and Yorkshire. he could not, come the 1980s, have visited the striking miners of this country with anything like the same ease.

Nor would he have been accepted with the same ease either, suspicion attending his every move, a suspicion honed by a century of struggle and handed down from one generation to another. Only Nick Brandt was able to see the miners' strike through, though eventually turning against the defeated miners for having let him down (a familiar disposition in our elite in general) and failing to rescue him from the contradictions of his living situation which he found so unbearable. However he was never once seriously tempted to help matters by relinquishing the keys to the Brandt family trust fund and the lumber room chock a block with inflating assets - i.e. artefacts left by his father and uncle.

In France or Italy in the late 1960s, to be opposed to work and to demand its abolition did not mean being opposed to the working class. In fact a similar anti work impulse was increasingly manifesting itself at the sharp end of production, particularly assembly line production. But here in the UK such impulses tended to do so becoming in no time at all an undiluted class prejudice that dared not speak its name, remaining so often in the cloistered world of an 'on the lam' elite, itself eschewing the popular touch. Looking back it is clear King Mob, though at the time unbeknown to itself, (and how could it have known) was at the forefront of this development, though by 1971 it had become a disparate loose grouping riven with internal class antagonism between the haves and have-nots. However not one of us remotely suspected how complete this victory would be, whereby an abstract rejection of work per se could also be deployed turning into a vengeful attack upon an insurgent industrial working class, so relentless and unforgiving that nothing less than its virtual elimination would assuage the beast. And still it brays for yet more blood.

The result thus far down the line has been the creation of a parasitic, financial services orientated, consumer economy where leisure and work are no longer really perceived as opposites; they have merged to an almost unimaginable degree. And yet there is no sign that the end of a world of exploitation is in sight. In fact it's quite the opposite. If anything the emphasis on leisure; of a capitalised realisation of 'never work' is bringing about a work regime - disguised as 'presenteeism' the likes of which we've hardly known historically - where again, the mass of the population, now unbearably isolated and fragmented, in dismembered untogetherness, are worked to death in meaningless, useless occupations and without the 'solidarity' that was so visible in the days of a massified, industrial working class in these islands. Ironically, this ruse of the history of production has brought back the original message of King Mob into a clearer, subversive focus, ready, yet again, to be applied.

However on the cusp of the 1970s how could we have had such insight? Instead, we were increasingly all at sea. A little detail from this period, made more pertinent because of what has happened since, may help illuminate matters. In the company of Liverpool Barbara whose dad was a municipal gardener in Sefton Park I had chanced on Chris Grey one day. I happened to mention an occupation of Lancaster University asking him if he knew anything about it. Not much, he had replied, except it had been called in support of some 'Mrs Mops' who were on strike. Barbara Roberts froze, for this was like a red rag to a bull, her initial, scarcely concealed hostility doubling in a second, hostility Chris Grey had instantly felt.

He later remarked that he found Barbara very uptight ,which caused me to bristle up because once out of ear shot she had let her anger rip at his remark. But that was Barbara, always po-faced in 'radical' company not saying anything but noting everything, a disregarded wallflower who observed the Angry Brigade and their hangers on out of the corner of her eyes whilst they looked completely through her. However this non-person went on to produce one of the finest critiques of Bolshevik democratic centralism I have ever read, and which would have gone completely over the heads of rather fine committed women like Hilary Anne Creek and Anna Mendelsohn, not to mention journalist / professsorial cop-outs such as Hilary Wainwright or Sheila Rowbotham whom it would have been even more wasted upon.

Emphasising the Bolsheviks' bourgeois presuppositions regarding the freedom to take time off work, it was quite the equal of Alexandra Kollontai or Sylvia Pankhurst and unusual on account of the, to my knowledge, previously overlooked angle. However this pedestrian perspective was instantly leavened by an infectious delight in anonymous, irreverent acts of resistance that also made a knowing point, and altogether a typically Liverpudlian trait - as when she told me of a bust of Lenin that was on display in the foyer of Islington Town Hall, the words 'lotta bottle' having been pencilled across his bald pate. This was in the days of the unspeakable Margaret Hodge and her crew (which included a couple of labour councillors, Tessa Jowell and her future husband David Mills from the adjacent Camden Council) before they too became arriviste privateers like their counterparts in the Soviet nomenclature.

This aside has been necessary in order to show the limitations of the King Mob elite (and others) in not appreciating how brim full of humour the working class is in this country, always ready to take the piss, which is more a sign of their independence (hence a prelude to emancipation) than submission, their instant humour on this latter reckoning being an expression of a constitutional inability to take anything seriously, even their own slavery. Finally, the extent of naked class prejudice cannot be stressed too much and that the most advanced revolutionary theory of all time - at least in this country - contained perhaps within it the seeds of an unthinkable counter-revolution that the country is only just beginning to wake up to. What is now a growing reality can be detected in the storm of reproach and accusations of betrayal that blew King Mob apart: the classless corporatism of a level playing field on which to play situationist influenced games had gone forever, the have-nots awaking brutally to the fact they'd been had. Had we ears to hear, our uneducated mums and dads could have told us well beforehand we would be. ("working class history past could have…"

In newspaper article after article, there is a dawning realization of not only the extent of the neoliberal counterrevolution, but of its atavistic nature, and that far from leading to a classless, globalised capitalism, Britain has 'reverted to type', with the top public schools increasingly coming to dominate political and social life once more. The most striking so far is the Guardian's headline of 20th Oct 2007: 'Riven by class and no social mobility ' Britain in 2007'. That same week the newspaper (17/10/07) had also carried an article by that reasonably intelligent operator of a journalist John Harris which provided valuable details - e.g. had Chris Huhne secured the Lib Dem nomination for party leader a year ago it would have meant the leadership of all three parties were respectively occupied by alumni of Fettes, Eton and Westminster. He concluded that 'for all talk of globalisation and belated arrival of a classless society, something about the modern world seems to be returning us to the ossified class system of yesteryear - sans deference perhaps but there all the same'.

However we would argue that the deference is still there, and that class attitudes have survived economic change. As the Guardian puts it: 'that suggests people are still judged by where they come from rather than how much they earn'.

My brother David sometime in 1968 had come across a remark by the leveller John Lilburn from Sunderland, who during the civil war of the 1640s claimed 'all trouble in England comes from north of The Wash'. David had made play with the slogan, brandishing it humorously like a badge of honour. However it did carry a grain of truth, which though it very definitely did not apply to the most revolutionary moments of the English civil war, has over time become truer. The stark fact is King Mob could not have taken the inter-classist, toxic rather than intoxicating, social mix it did take, and one skewed toward an upper middle class public school elite, in any UK city other than London, though theoretically all the elements were in place in Newcastle by the spring of 1967, a city that latitude wise is just south of the Scottish border.

And it was northerners who were the first to come to their senses, knowing that, if only for the sake of their mental health and survival prospects, it was henceforth necessary to keep clear of this class fraction, otherwise one risked being split in two. In fact the writ of the public school elite extends no further than a few miles north of Northampton, stops in Dorset and does not even gain a toehold in Wales and Scotland. But it can wreak terrible damage on the proletariat of the Home Counties, particularly those who had been dislocated by higher education, some becoming; one is tempted to say, 'ragged trousered philanthropists with degrees'. I could cite a number of instances of this destructive vassalage that carelessly threw self-interest, particularly economic self-interest, to the winds, never giving it a moment's thought, and all coming from the south east.

There are pockets of deference in the north, the most notorious being the Nottinghamshire miners, most of whom scabbed during the 1984-85 miners' strike. Here the mechanism is essentially different, the Notts miners coming under the influence of the much older, unreconstructed subservience characteristic of the Dukeries, though in ways often notoriously difficult to specify, but which the Yorkshire miners were convinced was still making its effect felt. One must not, in this context, overlook that the personification of sexual liberation as conceived by the son of a Nottinghamshire miner during the inter war years, was a gamekeeper on a landed aristocrat's estate, gamekeepers being a figure of loathing to hunting, foraging miners throughout the country.

Though looking back, it is now very clear that it was money, assets and property that destroyed radical theory in this country, at the commencement of this counter-revolution the possession of money for a while ranked second to the signifiers of class distinction, particularly that of a public school education. Despite living in a one bedroom flat and not having much money, Chris Grey was nevertheless able to go out with women we described as 'on the lam' from their upper middle class roots. But as for David, I and others like us, we were non-human excrescences that were hurtful to the eye, Lautreamont-like biological mishaps that slithered around leaving a trail of disgusting slime everywhere. This was rejection, and we knew it, and for the sake of our own humanity and self-worth we were left with no other choice than find our own way ad extempore out of the morass. And to this day, this knee jerk of a judgement, we rapidly became the butt of, is the one that stands. Simply a matter of having a chip on our shoulders - or so we've been accused of having - it robs our revolt of all logic and meaning. To say, in a headmasterly fashion, this is simply not good enough, is to underestimate the powerful forces then only just coming into play and that marked the end of the post war social democratic consensus. And though this was ultimately true of America and all other European countries, here it took on an idiosyncratic class bias that is almost unfathomable to outsiders, though not to second and third generation immigrants.

England has especially prided itself on its liberal traditions and that nowhere on earth was the bourgeoisie more entrenched than here, leading Engels's to describe England as 'this most bourgeois of all nations', possessing both a bourgeois aristocracy and a bourgeois proletariat at the opposite pole. Though throughout the

19th and early 20th century there were siren voices warning this was not quite the case, it took until the post war years for exhaustive studies like 'Power In Britain' to show that the country was in the grip of an old boys network whose vice like grip had to be broken if Britain was to reforge itself anew, or rather refashion itself anew, because art in one form or another would eventually give the impression of rising triumphant over the wreckage of Sheffield's Bessemer converters.

However we knew from our own elder brothers how essentially deferential this new meritocracy was, our eldest brother in his final post as professor of architecture in Newcastle University, happy as a pig in shit when out hobnobbing with his lordship of a vice chancellor and only griping about unearned privilege when safely out of earshot. However it has to be said in his favour that he did turn down invitations to attend the queen's garden parties when Sean Connery did not, though equally he held fast to the ridiculous view that the monarchy was a bulwark against tyranny. And he would have looked askance at the subject of the next couple of paragraphs, Dave Robins regarding him as a dangerous, situationist inspired rebel, though in truth he would turn into an even more active monarchist than our elder brother. And there hangs a tale..........

Some weeks ago a member of our building gang received an urgent phone call to say that Dave Robins had only days to live and could we re-plaster a ceiling that had fallen in? It would have been like walking into the lion's den, and so we nimbly handed the job on to someone else. Imagine what a painful experience that would have been with us up ladders covered in muck while a retinue of the great and good passed under them to pay their last respects to Robins, sneering at us behind our backs as 'sixties casualties'. And it would have been thought bad form if we asked for payment, despite the fact Robins lived in a house easily worth a million. Either way we were on a hiding to nothing, and so why not confirm their worst suspicions that we are 'callous in the extreme' and be hung for a sheep as a lamb?

Dave Robins's obituary in the Guardian (12/8/07) is sub-headed '1960s underground journalist, sociologist and charity worker'. Written by Ian Buruma; a media-hogging litterateur if ever there was one, we learn Robins took part in the 1968 student rebellion (in fact the biggest general strike in French history though this is not mentioned) 'returning to London full of enthusiasm for the situationists, whose ideas about transforming life through spectacle and art appealed to him'. It is difficult to imagine a brief summing up that is more completely wide of the mark and so fundamentally wrong on all counts. (In fact Robins in 1967 had helped prepare for publication an edited version of Ten Days that Shook the University that had appeared in Circuit, a 'radical arts' magazine. Sending a copy to Don Smith, he had been stung by Don's acerbic reply, sadly now lost, denouncing his superficial, radical arts, interpretation of situationist theory. Unfortunately the well deserved savaging was not enough, though Robins did blanch at the mere mention of Don's name for several years afterwards). Buruma also lays stress on the fact that Robins came from a working class background in Willesden, sometimes playing this up 'to his advantage' though neglecting to say this is the classic ploy of an opportunist and kowtowing to power always lead to betrayal.

Several of us were working on a boat in Chelsea harbour the day Robins' obituary appeared. It just so happened that Steva Lapivala, one of the guys we worked with, had lived with Robins for two years and was also 'a nice Jewish boy' from north

London. This was on a Friday, and for the whole of that day and the rest of the weekend, Stevalapivala worried the matter, not letting it drop for a one moment. His unofficial obituary soared with inspired brilliance, each sally more incisive than the last, and I only wish I'd had a voice recorder at hand. We suggested he write his own appraisal of Robins in Wikipedia but unfortunately there is little chance of that. It is not so much that Stevalapivala is afraid to commit himself and speak his mind in public; rather that he eschews the merest hint of becoming a name, opting to shoot from the hip anonymously, though with deadly accuracy. Accustomed to acting on the spur of the moment, his reverence for maximum spontaneity means the loss of anything more durable and which, if written down or recorded in some way, could reach out to a far wider public and be a source of inspiration. Who would ever know that he deliberately spilt a cup of coffee over Sir Norman Foster, told Sir Richard Branson to fuck off (rather than calling the police, Branson offered him a free ticket to a concert) and called Martin Amis a cunt when he chanced on him in a street in Notting Hill. Great stuff.

Proposing to call the day 'Dave Robins Day', we also recollected reading an article in The Economist sometime in the late 1980s in which Robins, pretending to knowledge of building he did not have, quoted an enormously inflated weekend rate for young building workers employed on Canary Wharf 'with their trainers and trainees' which left us gasping and salivating at the mouth. We were at that time working for Dave Beida, the guy who was to contact us to ask if we would repair the damaged ceiling. Mentioning that he would be seeing Robins shortly, Stevalapivala had quickly chipped in 'oh and ask him where these jobs can be had as we'd like some of it'. We knew only too well that building workers were never paid anything like the sums Robins imagined they were, our 'working class hero' merely pandering to bourgeois prejudices as he almost always has done. The last time Stevalapivala had seen Robins was in Swiss Cottage. We were loading up a skip when we noticed Robins coming down the road. He proffered his outstretched hand to Stevalapivala who, instead of shaking it, filled it with pieces of broken plasterboard.

The obituary does say Robins became a director of grants at the John Lyons Charity, dispensing money from Harrow School to youth organisations in London. The public school settlements were a major part of the Victorian charity scene. In terms of salving the conscience of the rich there was nothing more prestigious or 'county'. Nor must we overlook that Cluttons, the ultra posh estate agent, is the property arm of Harrow public school. There never was a time when Robins would have despised such jobs, a bejewelled job description like the above always causing him to go weak at the knees. Notorious Stevalapivala put me right about that. Back in 1972 he had accompanied Robins to the 'left wing' watering hole The Gay Hussar, just for a laugh and to take the piss out of the clientele. He was not to be disappointed for Lord Rothschild and Lord Goodman were there, who, on seeing Robins, greeted him with a very effusive 'Heeeeello David'. Robins spent the rest of the evening apologising for his insolent friend who eventually was thrown out.

My memories of Robins is of a person who saw hierarchies in front of him, not authentic people, so is it any wonder that he should now prostrate himself before a quintessential pillar of the establishment, of Olde Englande. He certainly was not interested in either David or me, because we could not advance his career, and therefore were not worth knowing: things were by now that crude. How different his attitude toward us was from that of Fred Vermorel and Malcolm McClaren who, a mere four years earlier in the late sixties, paid the closest attention to what we had to say. It gives one an idea of the speed of the counter-revolution. For a brief period Robins had shared a flat with Chris Grey already by then turning to the east and the Rajneesh cult. There is no way a 'working class boy' from north London, especially not an educated one, could have related to that d'classe upper middle class milieu, and he would have instantly seen that, despite appearances to the contrary, money, above all inherited wealth, was the ruling deity and the outward show of being above capitalism and the labour market, phoney to the very core.

All Robins stood to inherit was a pile of unpaid bills, and like many another educated 'working class' lad and lass, very quickly realised the only way these people were ever going to respect you was by getting on in the world and climbing the social ladder via a different route. Either that or savage them unremittingly from the sidelines. This was the only real way forward, and Robins was never prepared to play the long game, for it meant going down over. Never a very inviting prospect, but it has its compensations, not least because of the enormous territory it opens up which 'they' can only judge (mainly rebuke) from the outside, lacking all day to day intimacy with it, and hence all feeling, and finally, understanding of it.

There is much more that could be said of the life and times of Dave Robins, of his friendship for instance with Dick Pountain (another situationist influenced person and rather more central to King Mob than Robins), the two of them collaborating on a crap book called Cool Britannia (2000) and who had the cheek to call himself a computer journalist in a supplementary obituary. I don't know any other computer journalist who has a 'cool' '50/'100 million in the bank.

Besides that, for decades he had nothing good to say about the late sixties, becoming an apologist for Stalin in the seventies before finally turning up the free market message full blast as the money rolled in. Pountain's temporary infatuation with Stalin was perplexing, for the cult of Stalin in Britain was never as widespread here as it was in France and Italy. A gal from Liverpool, Freddie Cook, helped me out with this puzzle. The industrial districts of Derbyshire (Pountain came from Chesterfield) she claimed had an unusually pronounced Stalinist legacy differing markedly, say, from that of the northeast: for instance in Co Durham we only ever knew one Stalinist and that was the signalman who lived next door and though the ambience was one hundred percent Labour Party, the adults we tended to seek out as children, it has become clear in retrospect, belonged to the ILP and had Trotskyist and anarchist leanings.

Freddie's observation is illuminating, because it shows a novel familiarity with the difference between regions, and sensitivity to the distinctive characters of northern cities. This was notably lacking in Orwell, Harrison, Jennings etc. who, in the thirties, made the trek north (and Wales, or London's east end, but mainly the north) to confront their 'appointment with the future' in the shape of the industrial working class, rather than a genuinely autonomous revolution made by them (Orwell excepted if his unforgettable account of the workers takeover of Barcelona in Homage to Catalonia is anything to go by.)

Now these men would have been interested in these nuances if told about them: the King Mob elite, once past their unbeatable best, not at all, 'never work' ' as previously pointed out - rapidly and very unfortunately turning into a put down, in particular, of the industrial working class and a byword for the restoration of traditional privileges, though this time the task of 'coupon clipping' would take place in a cloud of cannabis smoke. The same cannot be said of Nick Brandt however, who would avidly soak up such information and which is all to his credit. On the eve of the 1984/85 miners' strike, I well remember him asking about Barnsley, what did it look like etc, every minor detail relating to this town of absorbing interest to Nick and which, situated at the centre of Britain's largest coalfield, was also the headquarters of the NUM. A faraway look crept into his eyes as though we were describing a fabled city at the end of the rainbow. We are not sneering at his response, simply regretting the loss of these glazed awed expressions that stole over a person at the mere mention of a town or region. Happening in tandem with the disappearance of insurrectionary hopes, the world is a much, much poorer place in their absence.

Highlighting Cool Rules, jointly authored by Robins and Pountain, the obituaries in the Independent and the Guardian are nearly as much about Pountain as they are Robins. It was the summaries of the book we obsessed over the most as we felt they most summed up the contradictions, even bare faced hypocrisy, of the authors, both of them to us shining examples of the 'highly competitive and celebrity obsessed culture' they were condemning. Setting off a train of recollections in all of us, I recalled the last time I had seen Robins and Pountain together it was Pountain chasing Robins, the latter the infinitely more pushy of the two, though both were avid for success. This was some time in the early to mid seventies and I was in the company of Madeleine Neenan formerly the most active woman member of King Mob, and she had at once remarked on their 'success ethic'. By now the finer gradations of hierarchies were really clambering into the saddle (though they still had a long way to go to before reaching today's insufferable Louis Quatorze type pettiness and order of rank) with neither of us able to play the game, though Madeleine tried and failed hopelessly, going mad in the process.

I was also led to reflect how little things had changed, and how like a typical northern industrialist Pountain was, issuing disclaimers of his personal wealth and pretending to his former friends to be down to his last twenty pence when he was rolling in money. Meanwhile his boss Felix Dennis, a former editor of the underground newspaper Oz and now overlord of a vast, multi-billion dollar publishing empire spanning Maxim to Computer Buyer (Pountain's particular line of expertise), never passes up an opportunity, Mockney barrow-boy style, of proclaiming himself the 65th richest man in the UK. Pountain would never do this, not because he finds it vulgar, as would former alumni of top public schools, but because of his background that puts a premium on mastery of industrial processes, the shop floor never leaving the millionaire, the millionaire never leaving the shop floor.

This was once a key feature of British industry, the tendency toward a corporatism of skill implicit to it, a factor in preventing industrial unrest. Dennis, back in the seventies, was totally reliant on Pountain's technical grasp of the printing business, Pountain putting the magazines to bed and supervising each stage of the printing process and becoming very appreciative of the skills of printing workers, chatting to them for hours about technical matters which he found calmed him. Sickened by what he mistakenly considered to be the petite bourgeois nature of The Angry Brigade (a superficial comment culled from an increasingly Leninist perspective), the therapeutic nihilism of industrial technique temporarily relieved him of the anguish caused in part by the unwanted attention of the Special Branch. The latter interviewed him on two occasions on account of his links with members of The Angry Brigade and their numerous hangers on, the whole caboodle, surprising though this may now sound, having become a more or less fashionable thing to be a part of and like a new 'in crowd'.

Before dropping out, Pountain had been a physics student at Imperial College, and very quickly saw the potential in personal computers, persuading Felix Dennis to produce Britain's first computer magazine which would make his fortune ' and point Dennis in the right direction, who would eventually amass a treasure trove superior to that of Mick Jagger and the equal of Paul McCartney's. The tables had been turned, and it was now Flash Robins chasing the outwardly Spartan Pountain who, affecting a certain down at the heels drabness, doesn't like it to be known he takes his holidays on Mustique (Dennis, who owns an island in the Caribbean, innocently revealing in his autobiography that he does.) Such holiday venues are solely for the mega-rich who look down on mere millionaires as a sort of underclass.

When he was a student at Imperial College during the sixties, Pountain, rather than walk down King's Road, then the apotheosis of 'swinging' London, would, en route to college, go out of his way to avoid it, he hated it so much. Finding the general ambience of phoney liberation completely depressing, he once took to his bed for two weeks with only a large jar of pickled onions for food. Perhaps it was his visceral rejection of consumerism as epitomised by the fashion industry that drew him to situationist theory, immediately taking to it like a number of other science students did, before rejecting it in favour of an updated Stalinism (as mediated through Althusser) to be ditched in turn for the free market. From this superior vantage point he then proceeded to settle accounts with his past authoritarian errors. Scourging himself with capitalism, he ascended ever higher into the heavens in perfect step with the mounting millions.

Pountain's supplementary obituary marks 'a return of the repressed' ,just as it denies it, wanting to believe the vogue word 'cool' means much the same as it did in the sixties. We never liked the term then and even less now (and, what's more, neither did Pountain) for there is more shit to get hot under the collar about today than ever. 'Cool' today is code for an expanding universe of buying and selling, a fact that Pountain and Robins readily acknowledge, though not the closing off of revolutionary hopes the term now implies, for that dashed hope was meaningless to them when they wrote Cool Rules in the final two years of the 20th century. In the fifties and sixties the word was sufficiently fluid to also vaguely signify opposition to work, exploitation, the stealing of time and so forth.

As a scientist, for a time Pountain, in company with other revolutionary scientists, showed a quick grasp of the revolution of modern art, which can only have come through King Mob and the situationists. One has to go back to Chris Cauldwell in the late twenties/ early thirties to find a comparable synthesis, Cauldwell writing a book on art, Illusion and Reality and on science, The Crisis in Science, the latter a remarkably prescient attempt to come to terms with quantum theory, Cauldwell declaring that the wave and a particle duality (and a boon, incidentally, to the 'naturalizes' of dialectical materialism) was destined to poke a hole in the ordered, commonsensical world of the bourgeoisie that could not be patched up. (Living when he did, Cauldwell could not have foreseen that quantum technology would 'change the world' in order that everything would remain the same, and that the parallel universes announced by quantum theory would find a simulated realization in the 24/7 game playing avatars of cyberspace, the managed inner universes increasingly of use in the maintenance of social order.)

Illusion and Reality however is a pitiful eulogy of soviet style social realism, and therefore totally counter to the subversive intent of The Crisis in Science. There can be no doubt that in the late sixties the synthesis these youthful revolutionary scientists around King Mob were striving for and who had rejected the role of scientist, not one of them able to take up the kind of jobs they had been trained for, was on a much higher level than that of Cauldwell. What's more, they were completely opposed to the usurpation of popular power implicit in Lenin's notion of the need for a vanguard party and therefore way beyond Cauldwell's idolization of Lenin. Phil Meyler - one of the scientists in crises - had written an MA thesis on Cauldwell, whilst laudably copping a state student grant to avoid work, but which he has described as rubbish, although that is very unlikely. No one ever did get to read it and though possibly drawn to Cauldwell on account of his connection with Ireland, there must have been other factors in play, like Cauldwell's botched earlier attempt to unify art and science.

Transcending his background in science, Phil did go on to make very important contributions, perhaps most notably on the Portuguese uprising in the mid 1970s, amongst others. But he was the only one,(amongst the scientists around King Mob) and looking back it is the unproductive waste of talent and insight that is most distressing, and it is now almost too late in the day to make good the absence by having it come from the horse's mouth. Besides the inclination is just no longer there.

 As with King Mob and the surrounding ambience, what is most striking is the sorry fact that so much was promised and so little delivered. And when it did deliver, it was in the opposite perspective, coming gift-wrapped in zillions of pounds. In terms of a rags to riches story that contains a longish chapter describing an encounter with the most revolutionary theory the world was capable of at that time (call it what you will if in need of a name), there is nothing on the continent, or in America, to remotely compare with a figure like Dick Pountain, who flailing around sleeplessly on his diamond encrusted bedstead, still cannot lay to rest the ghost of that radical past, try as he might.

I well remember the conversations about art I had with Dick Pountain sometime around the mid - seventies when he was just beginning to slip into the Althusserian groove. There was a finality about his views on art, particularly music and the pop music scene, which went way beyond anything proffered by his Sorbonne mentor. He was disappointed to find out that a blank album cover by a guitarist, whose name escapes me though it may well have been J J Cale, was a production slip-up. Dick (for then he was still Dick) had mistakenly thought it was a deep comment on the blankness of music, with the refusal to perform and suicide the next step down the line.

He had also been struck, as I had been, by a teen pop idol's comments (David Cassidy to be precise) on the reflex, automata-like behaviour of pop audiences who pissed themselves, screamed and fainted because they were now merely playing out a role, performing to themselves and to others and never at any stage wholly caught up in what they were doing. I recall him also scoffing at some reproduction of paintings by monkeys that an animal behaviourist claimed showed signs of an aesthetic sense. To Dick aesthetics could not be reduced to mere pretty patterns, and to use the term whilst a watertight scientific theory of the aesthetic was lacking, was a meaningless endeavour.

This was where we parted company, because Kant had tried to do precisely that, though Dick would have instantly bridled at the mere suggestion that Kant was scientific, though actually he was the equal in terms of pure science of any scientist then working. (I had just nicked Kant's Critique of Judgement from the Oxford University bookshop in Charing Cross Rd). At any rate, like a scientific judgement, Kant's theory was meant to be applicable to all time and places, and like a scientific judgement, though not independent of history, was not identical with it either, the philosophy of history in Kant something of an afterthought, and of considerable less importance in his overall system than aesthetics.

Hegel had marked a considerable advance on this hypostatisation; historicising everything he got his hands on, arguing that 'laws of art' are much more variable than scientific laws ,and that they are the more immediate products of an unfolding human praxis, or consciousness, which is much the same thing in Hegel's system. Such a conception also differentiates the 'aesthetic' sense of animals from that of humans because it implies a constant discarding and renewal of meaning in accord with humanity's unfolding aspirations ,which does not happen, and cannot happen, in the animal world to anything like the same extent as in the human. Monkey or elephant paintings say more about us than they do monkeys or elephants.

I also remember that I had recently nicked all four volumes of Hegel's Philosophy of the Fine Arts,and I been bowled over by his declaration that the arts were dying. As I recall, the supercession of painting would be replaced either by technical illustration or, temporarily, by the fog of mysticism, before the final triumph of the philosophical life, the only true life according to Hegel. To me lounging in a bedsit in Ladbroke Grove between spells out plastering and getting covered in shit, it summed up perfectly what was happening to Chris Grey and, rather than going back into art, went some way to explaining his flirtation with the abysmal Rajneesh cult. Though I never discussed it with Dick, who was now becoming increasingly hostile to the Hegelian legacy in Marx, treating it as a symptom of scientific immaturity, Hegel's views on art had come as a stunning revelation to me. I have been wrestling with them ever since, trying to give them a contemporary glow, adding bits on here and there as the disintegration of artistic form becomes increasingly mainstream, but its revolutionary implications ever more remote. Dick had wanted to set light to the Hegelian legacy (especially singling out George Lukacs) ,emblazing the pyre with the words: 'Hegel is dead, killed by Nietzsche', a sentiment which also stemmed from Althusser, reflecting the latter day Stalinoid rehabilitation of Freud and his precursors. For a while Dick had pinned up a photo of Nietzsche, that horrified a couple of visitors mistakenly taking it to be that of Stalin for there was a passing resemblance, both sporting moustaches!

Dick was also at this time beginning to radically overhaul what Marx actually said, expelling not only all mention of dialectics in favour of pure science, but rejecting slogans like 'abolition of the wages system', (which Marx had proposed at the time of the First International), declaring money could never be abolished. And the most that could be achieved in this direction----were (would you credit it!) credit cards that were then coming on stream but nothing like as ubiquitous as they are now. This 'credit card communism', relieving people of the burden of carrying money and the guilt of possessing it and, licensing a freedom to purchase recklessly, because of the mistaken notion it gave rise to that it was the plastic and not the consumer that was paying, must be accredited with helping bring down the Soviet Union. Certainly an organisation Pountain was affiliated with, 'The British and Irish Communist Organisation', thought that the Tory Chancellor Lawson's 1987 budget was very influential in undermining the Soviet Union. Britain then possessed large state controlled industries, and though most of them would be shortly privatised, was much closer in every respect to Russia than America. The same organisation had only a few years' earlier published transcripts of the Moscow Trials of the early 1930s that 'proved' the culpability of 'capitalist roaders' like Nickolai Bukharin, and which Pountain had appeared to unhesitatingly agree with. Then living in a two bed roomed flat with a child, he had dreamed of unleashing the 'red terror', and giving firing squads the order to shoot. But by this time it would have been the actual revolution that was first in the firing line, as always is the case whenever a 'red terror' (i.e. ultimately pro-capitalist terror) has been unleashed. Is it to be wondered the guy had to flagellate himself with a free market that, to most others, is turning out to be the worst scourge ever and that will achieve the ultimate purification of the human race by liquidating it.

I do wonder if there were not figures comparable to Dick Pountain in the former Soviet Union around that time. Inevitably they would have belonged to the nomenclature, apparatchiks who would shortly profit from the biggest state sell-offs in history, some becoming billionaires many times over like Yukos magnate, Khordovsky and Chelsea FC's Abramovich. Could they be heard advancing similar arguments in the eighties to Dick, bending Marx to prove their point, in a country that had made a habit of bending Marx to justify every shift in policy? Perhaps one day more light will be shed on this particular period in history and who knows what surprises will be in store for us?

By the late 1970s / early 80s, the breach was almost complete and we no longer sought out each other's company. We met up the last time in a basement flat Pountain had just recently purchased close to Notting Hill tube. He was becoming property conscious, and though I did not quite like to admit it, I thought he was more bothered we didn't drop ash on his antique sideboard than by anything we had to say. Less than a decade earlier he and Phil Meyler (who was present at the last meeting), rebelling against Christmas had shot up a Xmas tree with an air gun, smashing every bauble on it, before driving some 400 miles across America in total silence finally stopping and alighting on what they took to be grass. Finding it was astro-turf Dick had broken the silence to ask, 'Is this the future?' Money and property make a person conservative practically overnight, but even I was shocked to hear that in the 1990s he had objected to someone turning up dressed improperly in everyday clothes at the funeral of a Bunch Books comic illustrator, one of Felix Dennis's earlier publishing ventures.

Nasty Tales had been one of the comic books, which are now collectors' items. Significantly it was never able to change into anything like Puzz, an Italian comic of the mid to late 1970s that did begin to more memorably represent the alienations of modern capitalism, for a brief period, in a popular format, 'Nasty Tales' never getting, manga style, beyond the merely pathological. And had they done so they would never have sold and Felix Dennis was only ever into publishing to make a profit. I remember one strip that dealt with the relationship between a husband and wife and the seriously nasty effect a growth the size of a pumpkin on the wife's face had on those around. Turning out to be a brain tumour, the comic strip ended with her husband saying 'Kill the Whore of Rome' and an acquaintance replying 'Kill Everyone'. Dick thought such nasty tales a sign that pathology, normally the province of the right, had shifted leftwards and that the right would never again be able to use 'evil' as potently as it had once done. All the right could come up with was the prissy morality of the Festival of Light spearheaded by Mary Whitehouse, and that was a real wet blanket. But that was then and the dual heritage of political correctness, a bastard child of free market sensitivities and 'left,' political liberalism, still barely heard of. However in the minds of most people it is firmly identified with the latter and to speak out in utter disregard of an internal censor (and a project dear to surrealism once the stage of poetic archaism the surrealists tended to favour, despite themselves, had been left behind) is to risk being thought, if not a potential fascist, certainly a very brutal, degraded person in sore need of reconstruction and therapy. It all adds up to the fact that the uninhibited, authentic voice of the proletariat has never been so monitored, suppressed, fettered, gagged, manacled and feared, (because the conditions are ripe for it to catch on), as now.

I do recall the last time we saw Dick, there was either a very early desktop computer or word processor on the table, which Phil almost immediately began to practise on. He later commented that he could tell Dick's articles in commuter magazines had been written on a word processor because of the default mode of writing, every unnecessary word having been stripped out. I cannot recall if we discussed computer art on this occasion, but we certainly had on some other, Dick believing the computer held the key to the solution of the antimony between art and science. Though this was well before the creation of Photoshop, even then it was apparent that what Dick now meant by art was a whole load of tricksy paintshop effects delivering old master patinas and smudgy impressionist prints for the masses, to layering and avant-garde collages for the more daring and all just one big load of predictable crap, none of which was worth a second glance. The programs are sold under the command to 'get creative', and though promised, creativity is the last thing they deliver and more disheartened than ever I was distressed by the ease at which Dick had been taken in by this ultra conservative nonsense and the descent into the most banal conformity it seemed to signify. This was not what was meant by the realisation of art, and I felt Dick had been much closer to it earlier on in the seventies when desperately twanging away on his guitar using a test tube as a slide, he seemed to be testing the limits of what a guitar was capable of. Wanting a new life and depressed at the hopelessness of ever producing a new sound he, like Hendrix, whose psychedelic guitar noises were just then being issued and broadcast to an uncomprehending public, sensed that beyond lay a whole territory of new activity outside the scope of 'music' ' the collapse of referentials meant there was much italicising to do - but which was somehow still related to it.

Though the above reflections may seem to have gone off at several tangents, they give an idea of how wide ranging, and challenging, discussions then were and how narrowed down to nothingness they have since become. And so back to the obituaries which prompted the detours------.

Robins at best was only ever marginally aware of the critique of art (he married an art historian) and was working on a grandiose synoptic novel, portentously entitled The Great Willesden Novel, when he died. A sample of his jottings was reproduced in his obituary: 'the libertarian loony left scene of the early seventies was very strong on rogering and leg-over. It was a leg-over based scene. The centrality of leg-over'. The libertine behaviour that Robins describes, and participated in to the full, had by the early seventies become corroded with money and power and essentially available only to those on the make, women as well as men. The occasional egalitarianism that had characterised sex in the sixties vanished almost overnight and it would have been altogether more accurate if Robins had written that by the early seventies the age of fucking and uncomplicated hedonism was rapidly coming to an end, to be replaced by an unnavigable ersatz of sex. Increased commodification stripped sex bare of Eros and henceforth the hideous, chaste union of the two ravening sharks in Maldoror would have been a closer approximation to the truth of relationships generally.

Inevitably, though there are major differences, a person like Robins reminds me of my elder brothers. However they were never as influential as Robins: though my elder brothers were on their knees, they were just too square, too fifties, for them to carry that much weight. When my second eldest brother died there was to be no obituary to him: the guy was just too much of a fuddy-duddy for that. Though very conservative, at least you knew what you were dealing with. However it is a vastly different matter with people like Robins as a reborn establishment needs such figures that once upon a time had dabbled with radical theory to provide it with a renewed legitimacy.

Incomplete: *Stuart Wise September to November 2007*

Following footnote by Dave Wise:

On Ripon Grammar School - which we attended for two nightmarish years after four years in a secondary modern school followed by a year in a technical school.

After the 11+ exam there were only two choices if you weren't in the fee paying category, and that was either the secondary modern or the grammar school. The former was training for manual work, whilst the latter was for professional work. The technical schools were for the 15+ basically the 'brighter' secondary modern pupils, encouraging a technical education up to basic GCE level (General Certificate of Education). During the 1970s after the egalitarian explosion of the late 1960s ' (though the explosion was ten times more than that) ' a system of 'comprehensive schools' came into existence which combined secondary modern and grammar school. Generally they were Labour party inspired, set against the perceived inequities of the 11+ era and crude class divisions. By the end of the 1970s, Thatcherism opposed all of this and though not going back to anything like the old system, desired a populist elitism based more on money than traditional class differences in the UK. The public schools were (and are) the back bone of the real Anglo-Scottish aristocracy and, more essentially, the upper middle class. Thatcher disliked these schools as they stood and wanted to democratise them by way of a Thatcherite inspired nouveau riche that had bought their municipal rented home, becoming self-employed in the process - heading towards rich businessman/woman status - and intelligently working the stock market.

As for the grammar schools Thatcher wanted them to fight back against lowest common denominator Labour party inspired orientation, and retain their traditional aura though becoming less snobbish in the process and where crude business practise wasn't a dirty word. In the late 1950s, Ripon Grammar school was even then a relic of a bygone age (a relic so familiar to Olde Englande) and a former cathedral school harking way back before the Lutheran inspired Reformation of King Henry the Eighth's reign. It was brutal in its respect for traditional hierarchies'. And yet not quite so, as our Eng Lit obsessed headmaster was also a fervent Labour party supporter and thus set against the rampant traditional Toryism of this part of North Yorkshire (we were bussed in daily!) who'd also come from relatively low down the social scale ', probably lower middle class - and through dint of hard work had acquired a scholarship to go to Oxford University. He was just as equally obsessed with Spain in 1936, though filtered through the eyes of the contemporary Oxford poets (Spender and Auden in particular ,though I guess he felt nothing for a CP oriented Marxist writer like Chris Caudwell who was also part of the Oxbridge setup). And when this guy, our headmaster, mentioned George Orwell it was the Orwell of 1984 and Animal Farm and not the superb Homage to Catalonia which he probably instinctively knew to keep away from. He saw in Stuart and I persons somewhat like himself, and therefore pathologically hated us, though this was perhaps expressive of his own self-hatred. Interestingly during the late 1960s this headmaster was to say at a school speech day - and noteworthy because it was reported in the press - that "revolution was something that completely took possession of you and which you were powerless to resist" and he meant by revolution the activities of the Angry Brigade. A really schizoid guy. Little did he know we wanted to go with The Angry Brigade to blow Ripon Grammar School sky high!!

© Revolt Against Plenty 2014

ON WHAT HAPPENED AT SELFRIDGES

For Ms Vicki Maguire:

I just wanted to explain a little more about the anti-Xmas, anti-consumer intervention so that you may be able to correct Jamie Reid's false assumptions. And I hope he doesn't get annoyed with you about it! He in fact quite recently put on a display in a shop window in Westbourne Grove, Notting Hill for Pepe jeans. It was simple consumer advertising but deployed a lot of his old props like the Boredom and Nowhere destination buses he gleaned from Point Blank in California decades ago. As an aside to this did you know that the Blue Man Group performance troupe is a child, or rather offspring, of Point Blank via Chris Winks? He used to visit me in the 1970s and we'd talk about Yves Klien and the use of blue which acquired some mystical potency for the latter. I'd wanted to meet Chris because I did find some interesting things in his At Dusk pamphlet and rather better than all the pro situs I was meeting who simply reiterated verities and whom by then I found wearisome most of the time. (Klein had for a short time been big among us in Newcastle in the Icteric days). After that Winks produced Processed World but his critique of art I noticed was getting sloppier and sloppier throughout the early 1980s. So it came as no surprise when his name resurfaced though this time he calls himself Chris Wink having removed the 's'!

Anyway back to Selfridges. After some rudimentary planning in early December 1968 I informed Maclaren and Vermorel about what we intended doing and could they get plenty of people along to Oxford St. By that time I was very friendly with both of them and they listened a lot to what I had to say which meant I could go on and on and on. I ranged all over putting forward my theories on English romanticism, English philistinism conjoined to British imperialism, Yorkshire and the northeast, plus my knowledge of Russian Constructivism, Surrealism, International Lettrism and the like. Much of the latter - apart from Lettrism - had though come from Ron Hunt in Newcastle. Fred Vermorel was more clued in about tendencies within the workers' movement and knew and could discuss the Friends of Durrutti and the antics of the different Trotskyist sects etc. In that sense he was very 'French' and in any case his mother hailed from the country, and of course Fred had fought splendidly on the barricades in Paris in May 1968. None the less, Malcolm Maclaren had dash and audacity and proved to be very plucky and imaginative darting here, there and everywhere during the battle for Selfridges. (Ashamed to say, I utterly wallowed in the way these two guys listened so attentively. It was very flattering). From an exciting and fulfilled childhood amongst the northern coalfields I too in Newcastle had become very French!

I know Maclaren was particularly fascinated with the concept of the drift, the derive. That allowed me to take-off, not only about Baudelaire but De Quincey especially and how Charles Dickens was influenced by him in his endless walks through London, getting right in a way some wonderful aspects of the cockney character like mispronouncing words that unbeknown to them, end up being very inventive. De Quincey and the old urban rookeries fascinated Maclaren, and the latter's experience of them really got through. (Incidentally one of the most haunting descriptions of

Liverpool is conjured up by De Quincey as he sits in a room for days on end top of Everton Hill looking down on the harbour and listening to all the foreign voices stoned out of his head, motionless. Laudenum of course, or as De Quincey's children delightfully called it 'doddenum'!) Later, much later, Maclaren made an arse of all this in his ill-digested attempt to play for Lord Mayor of London with his programmed version of a drift through cultural events, museums and the like.

The Selfridges intervention was really a disparate, collective effort. No one at the time really thought it was something to be claimed, something to be copyrighted for in any case, that was the enlightened 'no property' spirit of the times. Later Maclaren was to say he was dressed as Santa Claus which wasn't true. A good friend, Peter 'Ben' Trueman, out of his head on speed, did that! In the Oxford St film, 'The Ghosts of Christmas Past' Maclaren voiceovers the leaflet we gave out but it was the Clegg's and myself who wrote that and then I 'designed' it making it into a spoof Christmas card kind of thing. I couldn't help thinking also that Shane MacGowan's performance in the film was meant to be Ben Trueman because Ben lolled, loppeled and rolled, outta control. Maclaren was certainly in awe of the guy. Ben was spectacularised by all the recuperated radicals who were essentially using him as thesis material, advancing their future careers. It was as if the guy was the pure essence of uneducated, wild, pristine hooligan revolt, hailing from a working class background in Winchester. Never a student.

Ah wonderful! Ben was no fool though and rapidly realised he was being used and even set up. We became good friends and had some great times in the pub where he liked to drop a vibrator in pints of beer watching it froth all over the table - to much hilarity. He was a builder too, though half the time you wondered if he was casing the joint or the church next door where he'd nick the lead off the roof. (This happened!)

Around about 1974 I was working with him on a site. It was Xmas Eve (again!) and the boss, after faithfully promising all of us we'd get paid on the dot at 5 in the evening, came up and told us he had no money. Ben knocked him out with a heavy left to the jaw and then proceeded to elegantly seduce his wife who didn't need any enticing. (I think in any case she'd had enough and had probably wanted to engage in some kind of fisticuffs herself as her husband was such an arrogant prat).

The Selfridges intervention was really all about playing with consumerism in a kind of liberated way, by taking apart its essential cash nexus and/or subverting the commodity form, plainly emphasising that everything has to be free. I guess this is why the intervention is still so powerfully remembered years later.

Recently (23.06.07) there was a review in the Saturday Guardian of a book entitled Consumed, by Benjamin Barber with the subtitle of How Markets Corrupt Children, Infantalise Adults and Swallow Citizens Whole. Debord is mentioned for emphasising pseudo-needs alongside Marx, and it looks as though there's some kind of drift to the concept of commodity fetishism within its pages. However, Barber being a professional go-between (The book jacket blurb says: 'He consults with political and civic leaders throughout the world on democracy, citizenship, culture and education') means the guy is a right idiot with absolutely no idea of relevant praxis and how to get out of this shithole? I would however like to think something of that essential impulse is returning. Indeed it must do if the planet isn't to be utterly destroyed through ecological catastrophe.

However, when we started off on our anti-consumer jag in the late 1960s ('consume more, live less' etc) contradictions quickly became apparent. In a way, the Clegg's weren't objecting to consumerism per se, merely cheap consumerism and its extension to the working class. I remember one evening around the same time they started sneering about Blackpool. My beloved Anne was there and she went bananas throwing things around the room. A button had really been pressed. Anne as a kid used to go to Blackpool on her Wakes' Week break with her parents who worked in the Lancashire cotton mills. She remembered the resort with a simple joy. (Wasn't Blackpool called Manchester-on-Sea and Morecambe Bradford-on-Sea?) My sympathies were entirely with Anne as it had also been my experience, though for me it was Bridlington where I built endless sand castles in a state of utter bliss.

The Clegg's though were so snooty they knew nothing about the reality of Wakes' Week. And as for consumerism, for sure they didn't possess fluffy teddy bears or have toby jugs on the mantelpiece but they had property all over the place. An ex-crofter's cottage up in Sutherland near Quinaig and later, a cottage near Penyghent, a house in Leeds, one in Clapham etc. Buy, buy, buy. The hypocrisy was plainly obvious. (Diana Clegg - nee Marquand - was the sister of the Liberal party MP, David Marquand etc). Who you are related to doesn't matter of course, but if one of them happens to be some rich or important fink you have to tell them where to get off.

Undoubtedly with Anne this kind of thing created resentment and unfortunately envy. In no time she sadly began to see in me a loser, a man with no prospects, or as she called me in a letter when in agony we broke up, 'an outsider'. This really hurt particularly as the Special Branch at the time had me watched and visited etc. Jobs became very difficult to get and an employers' blacklist had curtailed any hope of an academic career etc even if I'd wanted one. Since then I'm afraid Anne just went for money and property, becoming a kind of serial divorcee: 'I do thee wed until the inflated price of property doth us part and I need to make a further buck' etc. I'm sorry if this sounds brutally cynical but it's part of the general drift of things in a terminally horrible direction. At the same time it looks as though Anne went from unhappiness to unhappiness, a reflection of the trivial commodity sickness of our epoch noted not only by Barber and people like Oliver James in books like Affluenza, but more and more others.....Maybe Anne couldn't forget the Selfridges intervention as she certainly enjoyed it. Is this a sign of more optimistic times on the horizon?

I also wonder about the ideological effects of background. Anne's parents in Droylesden, Manchester were also Tory voting working class. I'd really never come across this type of thing before as my background had been Labour oriented to the core and my Dad's best friends on the railways were in the Independent Labour party and so much was discussed. I know the signalman next door to us was blanked because he was a Stalinist etc. It all got through, even it took a long time to realise what major strikes our parents had been involved in. Then to hear Anne's poor mother saying in 1969 that two Spanish radicals (Maoists) called Garmendia and Orteaga should be garotted was too much. I know it was genuflecting towards the TV, but I found it difficult to handle and then an uncle coming around saying he hated strikes even though he was only a print worker and the bosses are always right etc. And yet when it was all gone, I missed Droylesden so much, and even now when I go through northwest Manchester past Chadderton, Failsworth, Newton Heath, all the way up to Ancoats, I'm so quiet, internal, so absorbed and Stuart always says to me: 'I know who you are with and what you're thinking.'

Dave Wise : *Spring 2007*

Reflections on "THE LUMP"

Introduction: Spring 2002

Back cover of pamphlet piss-take on sculptor: Carl Andre's, 120 Bricks

The following text was hand written very hastily during a few late nights in March 1997. The gang was knocking out a fair-sized, off the cards, plastering job and exhaustion was the name of the game. It was at the behest of Wildcat in Germany, au ultra-leftist outfit commendably insisting on workers' autonomy superceding leftist and trade union forms of struggle. It was simultaneously translated into German and typed up there while final reflections were added a week or so later. It was put together in a small book alongside a translation of Dave Lamb's Solidarity pamphlet, The Lump, An Heretical Analysis, which came out in Britain in 1974.

Reflections was translated verbatim and some peculiar loop the loops in English grammar should maybe have been altered. No matter, they have been corrected here. One or two new footnotes have been added and some of the German ones - which here need no explanation - have been left out. It was, though, a text for German readers and this accounts for a lot of the many broader generalities which, had it been for home grown consumption, would have been more developed. Some details no longer apply though the broad thrust still very much does.

Much of the pamphlet deals with the often bizarre conflict between rank 'n' file lumpers and rank 'n' file trade unionists, when, often it really isn't or shouldn't be a conflict at all - and most protagonists deep down know it! In particular, the rank 'n' file Building Worker Group was singled out for particular critical attention. More should have been elaborated but time was of the essence as after all, the BWG is certainly better than all others proclaiming independence from the set paradigms of the union. Recently, the Building Worker Group, (BWG) has had a text published by Revolutions Per Minute: RANK AND FILE OR BROAD LEFT: A short history of the Building Worker Group. It certainly makes for interesting reading.

The Building Worker Group (BWG) was formed in 1974 at the behest of the then Trotskyist, International Socialists (later the Socialist Workers Party) as part of their industrial strategy creating base groups in a period of high workers' combativity. These base groups initially attracted a lot of fairly clued-in workers pissed-off in one way or another with the Left Labour/ Communist Party reliance on the workers as nothing more than an actively demonstrating pressure group on left wing MPs and left-leaning union officials. Seemingly, these base groups appeared to be independent bodies with often their own newspaper, relying only on the power of the workers themselves. In reality though, they were nothing more than the hoped for industrial muscle of the party and no autonomy or spontaneous activity was to be given any significant head.

Once Thatcher's dictatorial, anti-working regime came to power, the SWP feeling and anticipating defeat in the air - and well before real bitter defeat became a grim reality - disbanded these caucuses. Some bitter rumblings surfaced from below but most succumbed to this diktat. In July 1982, Tony Cliff, the leading SWP ideologue, ordered the BWG to be disbanded. They rightly refused and those members in the SWP, of whom Brian Higgins was one were expelled from the party. If other industrial branches had possessed the same spirit as Higgins and co, we might now have had a more lively scene industrially, perhaps not unlike the COBAS rank 'n' file bodies in Italy, even though such organisations though more insistent on anti-bureaucratic spontaneous responses, in themselves are also incapable of transcending a trade union form.

This shock certainly helped to broaden minds in realising the enormity of enemies you then faced as the BWG carried on through many disputes, slowly but remorselessly bitterly criticising the Broad Left approach seeing it essentially as a convenient trajectory deployed by the bosses. Rightly the BWG perceived that the SWP had, after appearances to the contrary, fallen in with this trajectory. (mind you, the SWP had always been on this jag) In the following years, the BWG were to come up against most of the far leftist, mainly Trotskyist, parties who rubbished them whenever possible. Prominent among them were the Workers Revolutionary Party though Arthur Scargill's Socialist Labour Party played its part too, knocking them because they wouldn't support a big wig union official who had tried to take Higgins to court.

The BWG slowly produced a very pertinent analysis of Broad Left behaviour in various disputes during the 1980s and since. Among them were the British Library, Southwark Council Direct Building Works Dept, Northampton Labour Council, Hays Wharf and The Laing's Lock Out Committee in 1985/6 which, "set London alight for six months". Historically, they grounded this in a critique of the Building Workers Charter which was at the fulcrum of the 1972 building workers' strike as the first of the Broad Left pressure groups pretending it was a rank 'n' file organisation. No doubt they saw it's menacing shadow at work in the 1980s semi-independent organisations like the Joint Sites Committee and the London Steel Erectors Committee with the latter, having no independence from the London Regional Secretary of the AEU though playing on the appearance of some kind of autonomy. The same goes for OILC (Off Shore Industrial Laison Committee) who were merely a recruiting rank 'n' file outfit organising for the benefit of union officials but forced by their own devious momentum to go on strike. Once things seemed to be getting out of hand they made certain union officials moved in to finish off a potentially momentous oil workers struggle in the North Sea just after the bitter defeat of the miners' strike. If this strike had been allowed to develop - as it had all the spontaneous potential of so doing - it could have reversed the miners defeat. (These particular strikes have been outlined in some detail in two additional texts republished here and which German Wildcat translated in the late 1980s).

Confusion within the BWG really sets in once you realise that its long term aims of a rank 'n' file group are essentially conceived in terms of a trade union form. The reality is you cannot have aims other than upsetting the bosses and their stooges seemingly forever until one day hopefully they finally completely fall apart beset by so many other impossibilities. It's impossible to get "total reform of the union" or to "put the unions under workers' control". At the same time, the BWG desires "new" independent workers organisations seeing them as "almost a necessity". A kind of well meant but incoherent floundering then fills the gap as impasse looms with pointless support for nationalisms (a 32 county Irish Republic, self-government for Scotland and Wales and, no doubt now, for the English regions).

As another aside to this process, interestingly the BWG was quite rightly excited by the fuel protests in 2000 and was "horrified" by the TUC's 2000 conference which called for a mass scabbing of blockades and picket lines. Why though be "horrified" when you know bureaucrats regularly go in for this type of thing? It's that shadow of leftism which all rank 'n' file groupings seem to possess and can never get away from. Moreover, the backbone of these protests were the self-employed, the so-called "small-businessmen" - precisely those types vilified as "lumpers" within the building industry. In the pamphlet, the BWG says, "A rank 'n' file organisation is open to all workers associated with a particular industry or union be they employed or unemployed". This is just not true yet when an earth shattering revolt breaks out they make an identification which they can never follow through trapped within their own lock-jawed syndrome. We were also excited and produced some texts just after the protest was peaking - which unfortunately always seems to be the case - (c/f the one included here which was translated and produced for German Wildcat). We tried to highlight some of the contradictions and complications of this short-lived though exhilarating revolt which purist, dead duck and plain boring groups like Echange et Mouvement panned so completely.

At this impasse we do encounter very real problems though. After such activity and history like the BWG has, it's hardly surprising they're looked up to by the anarcho-syndicalists who, as always, have the eternal solution to hand of the one big union like the CNT or CNT-U. And there you have it - no need for much further thinking. We well know the history of these organisations and there's no need to go into them here other than to say, history didn't produce the new world expected of them. Rank 'n' file bodies like the COBAS in Italy don't have such grandiloquent pretensions and maybe as such are telling as regards the temper of the times. Accounts of COBAS activity in the English language merely go into details about the activity engendered but what about their aims? The crux of the matter seems to be: is it possible at this historical juncture to have aims other than something more nebulous without also, being fluffy in the process? To be sure one can go on about abolition of the wages system and the spectacular commodity economy but what does all that mean in practise when we already know some of these things were already bureaucratically enshrined in the fixed and fast organisations of the old workers' movement. Of course, we ardently desire a world without money but getting from here to there is quite a different matter.

Tub-thumping ways of proceeding at this point don't seem much good and this is where criticism of the BWG's hectoring tone (that kind of Calvinism alluded to elsewhere in the original text is not only ineffective but can be off-putting). The atmosphere thus engendered becomes, a priori, hostile to opening up discussion, where the unmentionable can be mentioned, and where the ability to listen to others allows ourselves to be influenced and changed in turn thus subverting that privatised, armoured psyche preventing an essential, "but what then" drift.

Unofficial movement, rank 'n' file etc over the last 30 years or so have become terms which now lack all meaning unless specified. In the book 'Glorious Summer', Darlington and Lyddon more or less conceptualise the momemtum of the huge wave of strikes in 1972 as pushed by those below and thus essentially defined by the rank 'n' file and as true for the biggest building workers strike in these islands history as for the others. The BWG on the contrary suggest the Broad Left was responsible for sabotaging an outcome on the brink of a more stupendous victory than was achieved.

Certainly at moments of great revolt, officialdom, particularly lower grade officialdom are, willy nilly, dragged along in its wake unable to continue controlling their day to day recuperative routine. If however, that's all that's needed such strategy rapidly runs into a brick wall, as on the morrow, though weakened, the structure remains intact ready to gradually take on its old repressive role all over again. Thus the BWG are right to clinically tear apart all the overt contradictions in the organisations they criticise.

The BWG also utilise the trade union form. Higgins is after all, Gen' Sec' of the Northampton branch of UCATT forced to abide to more than some degree within the union's statutes. No doubt he is able to push the union form to its very limits reinterpreting things to suit better ends. No doubt, hopefully too, he can direct some of the funds to producing strike leaflets etc with real clout and purpose and in effect, related to BWG activity. Often a leaflet is necessary and if there's no ready source to pay for it, a proposed action is severely limited. We must be realistic here. In the text on The Winter Of Discontent, it's noted that union offices were sometimes occupied by members as such venues also provided free phones when most urgently needed etc. On a better level and in a more open organisation, Rene Riesel in France was Gen' Sec' of the Confederacion Paysanne of small farmers when he instigated exemplary and courageous actions against GM contaminated grain and the like. Later though, Riesel felt impelled to resign his post in this new and more relevant organisation (an organisation far in advance of UCATT) precisely because of its bureaucratic structure and the way it was beginning to ape the aims of big agriculture. Does this now mean that Riesel feels more vulnerable and isloted than ever?

German Wildcat did a good job in a rushed situation. One thing however is contentious relating ver much to what has been said in this introduction. A certain important part was cut out relating to criticisms of the anarcho-syndicalists in the building trade, mainly around Black Flag, and their cooperation with the broad perspectives of Brian Higgins and the BWG which nonetheless are in some kind of flux and looking perhaps for some more coherent critique.

Like the anarcho-syndicalists, Revolutions Per Minute, a publishing project which hosts a web site, The Red Star Research, makes no criticism of the general aims of the Building Workers Group. It seems sufficient to be anti the SWP, and approves of Haringey Solidarity Group, with its populist "community" ideologies - in going along with Higgins and co. Criticism is absolutely essential. The issue of the Lump in all its complexities must also be at the centre of such critique which is why the deletion of a pointed part of the original text - and now here reprinted in full - was so irksome. Broadly - and it was no more than broadly - the argument had to do with the anarcho-syndicalists - following through, albeit in a more militant way - the fundamental though now rhetorical aims of the unions. In relation to Higgins, an amusing aside on the man - comparing him with the type of Scottish Calvinist Robbie Burns would have wanly satirised - was also deleted on the grounds that building workers elsewhere wouldn't know who the guy was. Surely a simple footnote would have sufficed pointing out that Burns, an untutored ploughman was an insurrectionary Scottish poet at the time of the French revolution. After that, well it's simple enough to go to a library or the Internet to find out more about what an amazing guy Burns was.

Protecting workers from upsetting facts and too-critical (!) thought is never helpful. If some anarcho-syndicalists had got annoyed - and they undoubtedly would have - well tough! On the simplest level what was published was only the opinion of one person. People are then free to condemn such opinion but at least it's been aired. It seems Wildcat were trying to keep together a heterogeneous bunch of building workers together throughout the world who, over the Internet, were beginning to break away from leftism. It's also the old story of not alienating the most retarded element meaning it's only the lowest common denominator keeping everybody together. The trouble is such strategy never works! Around 1981, we published a translation from Spanish called: The Bankruptcy of Syndicalism and Anarchism. It was a vitriolic attack on the traditions of a libertarian ideology in Spain when a more relevant, contemporary libertarian critique was now urgently needed. It was hated though: it certainly meant a sensitive button had been pressed.

As previously alluded too, included also here are excerpts from a long letter which was published by Wildcat in the late 80s though it was never published in Britain. It explains a few things about coordinations and the shop stewards movement which may be useful in relation to the main text. It also includes descriptions of relatively unknown incidences of some especially violent action by building workers on unionised sites which (strangely?) had been forgotten or repressed in the Reflections.... Though very critical of the "new" rank 'n' filism it is far too optimistic and even we ourselves had underestimated the degree of the remorseless, whittling defeat taking place - the direct obverse of Pannekoek's proclaimed piecemeal whittling in Britain then going in the other direction - which Echange et Mouvement often used in a laudatory way. Well, that is until the social collapse here when they all skidadalled!

The other is again a text quickly thrown together on Robert Tressell for the benefit of those in Germany who were quite unaware of The Ragged Trousered Philanthropists. The relevance to our present period when everything is again at rock bottom was perhaps too simplistic. It was less than a profound attempt to put Tressell into some kind of perspective historically and also to explain how grotesquely

Tressell had been used by Labour Party and TU hacks. It now seems that some of this text has been quoted in a new German edition published in Switzerland. In 1953 evidently an edited version of the book was printed in the former GDR but most likely in response to the East German workers' uprising of that year certain parts of the book were censored -perhaps those parts referring to the abolition of the wages system? It seems this censorship and the reasons for it have been pointed out. Unfortunately, the initial English intro failed to make criticisms of the book itself. One quite blatantly stands out. Owen, the "socialist" hero building worker really is one helluva cardboard cut out figure. He's such a goody goody two shoes it's almost laughable at times. Does the guy have sex, has he ever been bad just for the sake of it? This isn't just a carping criticism because it's precisely such quasi-mythical figures, regaled in moral splendour who are the ideological backbone of that moral puritan force which has such a lamentable trajectory in the history of social insurgency in these islands. It sure is a good time for an end to all that.

REFLECTIONS ON THE LUMP BY DAVE LAMB. (PUBLISHED BY SOLIDARITY. BRITAIN, 1974)

Some thoughts on the pamphlet by Dave Wise - for the use of "Wildcat" in Germany. March, 1997.

Looking back, the Solidarity pamphlet, The Lump, in the building industry from the early 70s (1974) it was well optimistic never mind the more than occasional flights of fancy. But who wasn't optimistic at the time despite the depressions, freak-outs, suicides and the all-pervading sense that the audacious edge of the late 60s rebellions was being whittled away. The atmosphere was strike happy, rebellious, even confident in a battered sort of way and totally un-like the sheer despair, defeat and incipient, if not to say galloping, free market totalitarianism which now stalks Britain.

As far as I was concerned The Lump pamphlet was a delight after a fraught, sometimes OK but nonetheless mutually suspicious relationship with building worker union shop stewards who had been engaged in a number of strikes in the building industry culminating in the 1972 nationwide building strike. Suspicion didn't emanate however, from unionised building workers around the stewards. These people were only too glad to have a pint in a pub where spontaneous friendship mattered the most: the suspicion was inseparable from even the lowest ranks of the union hierarchy. It would manifest itself in telling jibes: seeing you could talk so well, why weren't you writing in union papers or thinking of becoming a very left wing MP in Parliament where you'd really have clout? I regret I was not in the 1972 strike though I had recently been working on a big site run by Gilbert Ash - a company whom later became part of the Bovis Group. The atmosphere there had been very intense; the canteen was so full of passionate talk about so many extreme things that the site agent banged on a table one day calling all of us, young and old alike, "vandals". Even he, I think, was affected by the atmosphere despite his psychotic disposition and would try putting his arm around you in shady corners. It seemed he was a repressed gay who would nonetheless have said, "hang gays". The Timekeeper had in the past been a vicious foreman but a few years previously, some building workers had fitted him up. They'd purposelessly sent him across some scaffolding boards that hadn't been properly secured and he fell, floor by floor, hitting the deck with a sickening crunch. Now crippled and limping badly, his disposition had changed and he said to me: "I'd hire any Trotskyist" - obviously thinking I was one. Seeing the guy was so disarming, it crossed my mind to be equally disarming and I wanted to blurt out something like: "Well, art is dead. You see, I was knocked out by these Situationists who had superceded the Anarchists but that wasn't enough neither as you still had to strive for an even greater authenticity. Abandon all career, set out on the roads, or in this case building the road". He wouldn't have understood so I just left it. What was the point? The guy had become a really nice guy and that's what was important. I left the building industry for a short while on the very eve of the big strike. I greatly regret that.

On a simple level it's very difficult to discuss or assess the building trade from the point of view of the people who work in it with any accuracy. After all, it probably involves about 2 million people in one capacity or another and thus it is so varied. At the present time some building workers have taken time off and have been involved in building some of the tunnels in the eco-protests at Fairmile and Manchester airport. Now what would a union militant think about that. Sadly, probably not that much.

In 1974, I think Dave Lamb was trying to cock a snoop at the union militants and after all my recent personal experiences, it was therefore, a joy to read. But I also felt at the time that Dave Lamb didn't know enough about union sites and therefore, was somewhat biased. It wasn't sufficiently accurate. I also doubt very much if he'd worked on a union site for any length of time - if at all. On the other hand, anti-Lumpism hadn't been that important in the strikes preceding the big 1972 strike. In the previous years, there had been a prolonged, stop and go strike on the Barbican in east London which had occasionally broken out into violence. In the dispute Communist Part shop stewards had a high profile. Nonetheless, while on strike, building workers subsidised their militancy and their drinking which, invariably, seems to go with the job - what with all the shit and dust flying about on sites builders love their ale - by doing small building jobs -"foreigners" as they were called - on the side. Fine. Nothing wrong with that but CP building workers did the same too. A few years later and the same individuals, together with all the burgeoning "new" leftists, were to use the Lump as an ideological stick to often beat others with.

Lump workers often did (and still do) receive higher rates of pay than unionised building workers, though in a more irregular way. This is somewhat unusual and is the complete reverse of say the United States where unionised building workers always seem to get higher rates. Therefore on the simplest of economic levels, it's easy to understand the Lump's attraction in Britain. At that time, Lump workers were getting £2 an hour (skilled rate) compared to the union skilled rate of £1.50p per hour. But then to go on -as Dave Lamb did - and say that Lump workers in the early 70s initiated a lot more strikes than unionised building workers is stretching credibility. When Lump workers did go on strike it was often in order to get union recognition on a particular site. An obvious question begs: why should they want a union if they were getting well paid? Well, sometimes they weren't getting their wages as easily as that. More often than not, wages were irregular, coming in fits and starts which always makes one nervous. Often, union organisation was desired for simple safety reasons - but more on this later. These union recognition strikes took place by and large on big sites and one must never forget the untold but colossal number of "ragouts" (small half day strikes or so) on many a small operation. Simply too, there were those workers who'd down tools on some outfit never to return again!

Many Lump workers did scab during the nationwide building strike of 1972 and that was real bad. It's not so much they crossed picket lines (although this happened) as carried on working oblivious to what was taking place elsewhere. Seeing the strike had nothing to do with their blinkered immediate interests why take any interest? All one can say in mitigation is that unionised workers were striking for wages which were often the norm on Lump sites. On the other hand at the time, or thereabouts, there were disputes where members of a particular building union would cross another union's picket lines (e.g. a scaffolders' strike in Co Durham in the mid 1970s).

Despite the arrests and jail sentences meted out to figures who became prominent in the 1972 dispute, the strike, despite all the spontaneous initiatives within it, never drifted beyond union control and was quite prominently anti-Lump which was also, a factor in contributing to Lump scabbing. In the months after, - nay, perhaps for a few years - those who often made the most noise against the Lump were often middle class - prominently Labour Party voting - professional types who'd never had any day to day contact with building workers apart from employing them to build extensions on their homes in a rising house and property market.

For those who worked at the sharp end of the building trade, the response was much more diverse not to say chaotic. Many building workers, union and non-union alike, were well aware of all the contradictions inherent in the anti-Lump position and that's hardly surprising. Only the real union ideologues (specifically senior shop stewards or branch officials) tenaciously stuck to a strict anti-Lump line - a line which got weaker and weaker generally the lower down you descended in the union hierarchy. Thus you'd find a lower ranking shop steward quite happily talking in the pub to, say, a small time Caribbean sub-contractor (note, not big time - they usually drank in smart pubs and generally were white in any case). I mention Caribbean because maybe there was a common anti-police bond that could have provoked interesting contradictions in themselves. There were (and probably still are), Afro-Caribbean Lump gangs who refuse to do work on any ultra-repressive institution like say a police station, a prison or a magistrate's court. One spray-plastering gang I was friendly with turned down a job on Wakefield prison even though the pay was excellent. It was all very praiseworthy stuff. Yet quite recently, the "radical" Building Worker rank 'n' file paper called for the unionisation of workers engaged in building police stations. Although the person who'd written the article slipped in a line criticising the function of police stations, it would have been a nice idea, if he'd also suggested it would be an ideal situation to engage in some structural sabotage while putting the damn building up, e.g. badly installing a steel RSJ girder or leaving out cement in a brick mortar mix is an easy enough thing to do etc. In his book, The Keys to My Cell, Des Warren, one of the Shrewsbury Three building workers jailed in connection with the '72 strike, recalled how in the late 70s, he put a certain substance in his paint while forcibly employed decorating the prison where he was incarcerated. It meant the paint would never dry! Again commendable but you wonder if it was the extreme circumstances of prison which motivated Des to behave like this and would he have done so as a union activist on the outside?

Don't forget too, that the real anti-Lump thrust had basically nothing to do with workers' real self-interests. Issues like safety and such like were by the by. The real thrust was the economics of the nation state. The Lump meant taxation on wages was not being paid and taxes were a sacred cow for social democrats vis-a-vis the redistribution of wealth channelling funds to a welfare state subsidising council housing, schools and hospitals etc. The union militants only emphasised the more beneficial aspects of state capitalism and in doing so presented a very biased picture of taxation and one which was so demagogic it was all too easy to dispute. Taxation as a means of subsidising the repressive state apparatus; police, prisons, social work institutions, higher education, culture and the arts etc, was never their brief and don't forget their intellectual briefing had basically emanated from an assembly of Labour Party hacks who had a personal vested interest in promoting such a line. At times -and on the dusty site floor - you often wondered if you were talking to a shop steward or a tax inspector and building workers in an admittedly mildly fearful way, often saw "their" representatives as a kind of ersatz tax man. The trouble is during the following years, the tax debate was taken up by the free market right in their even more hideous power plays which meant any more coherent on-the-spot debate was stymied.

Other things were also easy to dispute. Union ideology insisted that people on the Lump were bad trades people and known as "bodgers" for not having gone through the procedurally correct apprenticeships. In short, just cowboys as the saying goes in English. This was always pretty priceless when it came from trade union people, who, over a pint, readily admitted to having learnt their particular trade (steel fixing, carpentry or whatever) by watching other operatives doing it on a site and then trying their hand at it. In time they became good at their chosen trade. Generally a lot of skilled trades people start off by being cowboys or cowgirls. In reality (and everyone knew it) most apprenticeship papers were pretty meaningless in any case as experience was what counted. Only recently, and that's mainly to do with increased bureaucratic accounting and also ever-tightening EU legislation, have correct papers and certification mattered. You were taken on at face value, given a few hours site test and if you knew your trade, were kept on. If you'd been bullshitting, well down the road you took a walk whether the site was union or non-union. In any case, cowboy work was (and is) something endemic, big or small company, union or non-union and it goes way back into the mists of time. Some of the worst cowboy building work our gang has come across was in prestige heritage London buildings in the neo-Palladian style designed by the famous late 18th century architect, John Nash. They're all beautiful facade but contain no real structural substance. Although we winced at some of the really atrocious construction that had been carried out

originally in the guts of the building and now being somewhat modernised and made safer, nonetheless these "cowboy" buildings have survived two centuries.

If the critique of The Lump had been conducted in a more thoughtful, clear and honest way, assessing the pros and cons according to specific situations then things might have turned out somewhat differently. Although it's a big perhaps things might have been somewhat less ideological. The fact that workers often get cheated out of their wages on The Lump (or, at least, part of their wages) by thieving sub-contractors was very low down on the anti-Lump agenda. This thieving has now grown immeasurably.

Again, it's necessary to say the building scene is very varied and no two sites have the same feeling and texture. It's often such things that can make some sites so fascinating. Inevitably this overflows into the many and varied lump situations. Some can be truly hideous. At the time of writing The Lump pamphlet terrible things were happening on some lump sites which were well known and had a kind of folklore status among building workers. Some sites where property developers were speedily building new private housing estates quickly became notorious. Bryant's in Birmingham was such a one. Brutal sub-contractors ruled and the site manager's office one night was blown up which attracted press headlines. It was possibly executed by cheated building workers (there were 10,000 such relatively miniscule explosions throughout England in 1972 alone) and many were to do with intolerable work scenes. The Bryant's bomb however, could also have been the action of Angry Brigade types as it was accompanied by a small manifesto. It was a moment after all when the names of property speculators such as Bryant's, Leech and Barrett's became synonymous with all that was sickening about exploitation.

The problem is, on a big site where there's no basic organisation among those at the sharp end things can quickly get awful and really dangerous. There's nothing worse than having a bullying foreman on your back telling you to do hair raising things like clearing away rubbish from under scaffold while operatives work far above on the scaffold and great nuts and bolts etc thud into the ground near you having just missed your head, or, for example being forced to walk on so-called strengthened glass while loading up a skip. Then there's all the potentially dangerous heavy machinery and if you have an accident it's often mightily difficult to claim compensation or, even if successful, the monetary recompense is pitiful. You can hardly ask the foreman to be nice and reasonable as he'd probably laugh in your face accusing you of cowardice. If you refuse to do his bidding, especially if unskilled, the likelihood is you'll be asked to collect your cards from the site office. And so on. No wonder, in this all too common situation everywhere, there's often a basic cry for some on-site organisation which in this reified time and space expresses itself in a simple but traditional union form. Abstractly we can lament this knowing all too keenly what nonsense unions are and knowing too, that capital needs them ten times more than workers but such insight is naught set against the pressing necessities of immediate practical fears.

Then, having got yourself a union nothing changes much and all the contradictions again arise even over elemental issues regarding safety which was say, the impulse for bringing in the union in the first instance. A unionised site (a Higgs and Hill site?) in West London a few years ago strongly emphasised safety. Remarkably, safety officers stationed there were sent round to all small, non-union sites in the immediate vicinity. In a friendly and concerned way they criticised all safety lapses and invited operatives to safety meetings held on the big site in the evenings. Yet, irony of ironies, it was on this ultra-safety conscious home site off Queensway that a gigantic crane was shortly to keel over killing some building workers.

On the other hand, some of the Lump sites were hilarious, life enhancing and had a fine libertarian disposition, particularly in the 1970s and early 80s. Gangs weren't that uncommon which worked on the principal of equal wages making no economic differential between skilled and unskilled often dividing up the amount later after being paid by a sub-contractor who obviously insisted on the usual wage differentials between skilled and unskilled. Such gangs were egalitarian and had often dispensed with the boss in the shape of a sub-contractor even if they were obviously unable to dispense with other bosses in the industry. In these situations which often usually existed on smallish sites - though not always - there was many a wildcat strike just for the hell of it, simply because you wanted a good drink together, to smoke some dope, or because everyone had a rotten hangover or just generally wanted to fuck about. In such gangs, made up of like-minded individuals -say from 4 to 8 - getting high on the "craic" (in the original Irish language meaning passionate, flowing, unrepressed conversation packed with jokes and wild stories encapsulated within its own eroticism). You could shape your work scene to some degree cutting out some of the more oppressive alienations. Holding a good gang together in a nifty sort of way could be virtually guaranteed to keep a foreman or site manager etc off your back ever wary of upsetting a bunch of mates they knew were skilled at their trades. Such gangs too, would liven up other workers who so often would refer to them as "the union" usually because the craic wound up quite rapidly with a lively, on-going attack on the system generally. None of that meant you didn't do a lot of back-breaking work as these things took place under the constraints of capital and naturally you went for the highest wages on offer - if you could get them. Equally though, horrible gangs existed and sometimes you worked side by side with them: gangs which were uptight, psycho and racist to the core advising you on the best way of say, shooting gypsies in the back etc! When using the past tense here it doesn't mean such scenes don't exist today. They do but good gangs, as well as bad - though we don't miss the latter - are dispersed and increasingly a lot harder to find or keep going. Simply put, reaction puts more blocks in the path of such spontaneous work organisation - a form of togetherness which, as far back as the railway and canal building navvies, were an axiomatic part of subversion in the building trade. It's a testament to the success and strength of the neo-liberal, free market that such gangs have been virtually vanquished by capital.

I would guess this was the type of Lump situation Dave Lamb was involved with though, most likely he wasn't involved with it for too long. After writing The Lump pamphlet, it seems he progressively abandoned a life on the tools for a more acceptable, professional, cadre-type career. He followed it up with a very interesting historical text on forgotten and often officially covered-up soldiers' mutinies in the British army. Nonetheless, this was a step back from something as relevant as The Lump and an on-going development of his ground breaking iconoclastic critique of the building industry would have made a lot more sense. The last I heard, which was quite some time ago, Dave Lamb was writing a book with Chris Pallis (the former main Solidarity organiser) on the philosopher Wittgenstein. It seems he'd become a university lecturer. One cannot help but feel it's a pretty cynical development though fitting well with the demoralising, and destructive go-getting zeitgeist we're all really sickened with.

In fact a proportion of these gangs in the early 1970s were made up of ex-student, drop outs who'd trained in specialisms such as architecture, surveying, town planning and what have you and in the lefty populist mood of the times tried to become workers. Initially they were consciously anti-careerist and had something of a critique of these professions - closely involved with management - as part of the superstructure of the building trade. This was all to the good but then most never deepened their first splendid rejection. They only tried to become workers and although workerism has to be rejected, workers' position in the social structure is still pivotal in the assault on the old world. Once reaction started to really bite, these same people pathetically backtracked into the cadre role they'd half-heartedly tried to overthrow within themselves. If they'd maintained their original negation they could have over the years broadened the building workers' critique into a more comprehensive and subversive totality. They chose not to. Today, everything built is nothing but bullshit in terms even of the simple splendours of the not so recent past and all life-enhancing spatial qualities related to a humane everyday encounter have evaporated. Nothing in its present form will be retained -ousted as it will be - in a thorough going social revolution. The hollowed-out shell of an architect's role will instantly crumble into nothingness as everybody finds there wasn't an ounce of creativity left in their dire designs. From then on the imagination can be given free play probing the possibilities of a new spatial dimension finally inseparable from all desires liberated from the suppression of the monetary economy. Interesting weeds and shrubs creeping up through the motorways, the City of London warrened with mysterious tunnels, clouds of butterflies as part of new eco-systems slowly taking over the shells of former banks. And so on.

But let's not get carried away here. At any rate, the above is merely a fairly banal personal fantasy and a renewed environment may not be anything like that as it will take place through a poetry made by all and not by one as in Lautreamont's maxim. Meanwhile, the conditions are just too grim and getting grimmer. The Lump: genuine waged workers, self-employed or little businessmen? It's now a difficult question. Until quite recently, many Lump workers never bothered to register in any specific economic category. In this respect many didn't exist in terms of official economic statistics, others were signing on the dole and weren't really "casual" in the classic sense of the term having a subversive outlook and life style generally and who were living active critiques of the world of work generally. Accepting the role of self-employment (in the sense of paying a self-employed stamp, keeping accountancy books or paying for the services of an accountant) was regarded as close to nerd status or, at least, "suburban". In short, part of the Lump was an expression of the marginal proletariat's way of life but then it could so easily go ridiculously ideological categorising 5 day a week workers as "straight".

Equally though the 5 day a week union militants repaid this slur with equally blinkered comment never reflecting on all these growing complexities with any sensitivity. Their minds were focussed on the big time sub -contractors hired by Wimpey, John Laing or McAlpine's. Such though was their obsession they tended to look rather paranoically at everything and everyone else that wasn't 100% pure union as "suspect" (a favourite term) which didn't equate with a sub-contractor's aura when that aura plainly was nowhere to be seen. Nonetheless, simple facts forced them to make a distinction between a fat cat sub-contractor and a self-employed worker. Obviously, you couldn't avoid that one. The militants though tended to approve of the respectable, kosher, self-employed trades person who, at the time, had a rather petite bourgeois, mini-capitalist life style and aspirations, often looked down disapprovingly on the wild, mad gang out for a good time and having more of a propensity to riot than strike. Yet the militants and the wild men just couldn't get away from each other. Ironically they were almost constantly in each other's pockets in the pub, unable and even unwilling to get away from each other yet constantly slagging each other off.

Sometimes Lump mini riots were quite impressive. We once worked on a biggish site in the early 1980s in west London which was part official, part unofficial. It was funded by Camden Council and the then functioning, Greater London Council and from the very first day, it was fascinating and crazy. The site boss, related to some posh Irish aristocratic family with an old Norman inflection before his surname, finally went completely over the top in his financial arrangement and massively over-spent on materials needed. We'd shake our head at the piles of sand and cement, at the mountains of Welsh slate and so on. After a few months this social housing project for the poor was near completion. Then came the day he had no money to pay the workers. He tried to borrow some dosh off a local drug dealer known as "Straight Mick" as the number of workers gradually filled up the ground outside the site office anxiously waiting for their wages. Opening the office door he finally admitted he'd got nothing. The whole site erupted as chain saws were deployed on doors and cupboards everywhere, cement mixers destroyed and floors torn up. Wreckage was strewn everywhere. Ironically, we who'd always gloried somewhat in the spontaneous festivity and potlatch of a riot, stood back having qualms about joining in because this street of conversions were for poor people who often anxiously came to visit us inquiring when their homes would be ready for them to move in. Nonetheless, though standing on the sidelines we vicariously felt in a rather shame faced way the exhilaration of the destruction.

These mini-riots have from time immorable always been prevalent on building sites and must surely still be quite frequent. They do however, take place a lot less on the more formally structured union sites but I have heard a shop steward laughing as he recalled a worker in an aggro fit dropping one TV after another down a garbage shute. They'd all been "pinched" from management offices. The ultra-leftist outfit, World Revolution in one of their more entertaining articles on the St Paul's riots in Bristol in 1980 commented upon building workers on a nearby site cheering on the rioters molotoving cops. In a rigidly ideological and as is their want, World Revolution reckoned the builders were remembering the days of 1972 when the cops attacked builders' picket lines. All that though, is fanciful revolutionism, as many building workers tend to get in a lot of trouble with the cops often simply through wild drinking scenes getting out of hand.

Things change - often without you realising it - until it's staring you in the face. Nowadays, self-employment has lost the choice which until quite recently, was associated with it. It's now an economic structure heavily imposed by the state

,changing as it becomes more widespread, downgraded and often not much more than a polite description disguising precarious, part time employment complimenting in some ways, the proletarianisation of a once up-market suburbia as the rich moved back to recolonise the inner cities. Similarly, though rather more desperately, marginality gave way to the often bleak, nether world of the excluded. Moreover, do all the distinctions and separations associated with the early 1970s up to the early 1980s now really apply?

The drive towards self-employment heavily promoted in the very first days of the Thatcher Government in 1979 and as a riposte to The Winter of Discontent had been well prepared in advance during the last days of PM Callaghan's Labour Government with its new monetarist initiatives. It was largely and ironically, an invention by the state as it was also a recuperation of the individualistic and hedonist drives of youth in the sought for new communitarian ways of the late 60s, embraced but essentially altered by a state seeking its own renewed survival. The fresh innovative and individualistic life-blood borne in a social cauldron was rapidly drained away. It wasn't however, until the final catastrophic defeat of the miners after their year long strike that the new panacea of an ersatz self-employment was promoted everywhere over the following years as the be all and end all of everything that work could become. It was presented as the direct inverse of a Stalinist workers' paradise and with the same relentless propaganda. There was the cornucopia of get rich quick, of everyone becoming a capitalist of sorts holding stocks and shares with a personal pension plan courtesy of a kindly faced insurance company. Britain was put on course to become a popular capitalist work utopia.

If the miners had won, it's extremely doubtful this trajectory with all the rest of the bullshit paraphanalia (a crazy house price boom been not the least of them) would have had the same, razor-sharp, cutting edge. The madness of the market would have been considerably curtailed. In retrospect it's fair to say- and one cannot over-emphasise this enough - how the defeat of the miners was one of the most tragic defeats for the working class of the world this century. Initially, it was the prelude to nearly every other defeat in Britain: from health workers to dockers to inner-city rioters. The guts were torn out as humiliation was followed by endless rounds of further humiliation as hardly anybody but the few crudest profiteers were left unscathed. A little later and the dimension of the world historical defeat of the miners became clearer because in a way the defeat of the miners parallels the defeat of the German revolution between 1918-21 in heralding a newly shaped and rather unforeseen totalitarianism. It's extremely doubtful if the state capitalist system of Eastern Europe and Russia would have collapsed - despite the rapacious media onslaught - if there hadn't been Thatcher's example whereby one state industry after another was destroyed and the massed ranks of workers abolished to make way for millions of petty entrepeneurs as a crusading neo-liberal economics was messianically embraced. True, behind Thatcher lay Reagan and a revitalised American form of "capitalisme sauvage" aided fortuitously perhaps by the equally devastating impact of hi-tech pioneered in California's silicone valley but Britain was uniquely the vanguard of the world and the way forward in famously destroying, "the enemy within". Even now, during the recent rebellion by South Korean workers, President Kim Young Sam praised Thatcher's defeat of the miners ardently hoping he could unleash the same repression in one fell swoop.

If that was defeat there also had to be a final, final round of utter degradation: the ransacking of all the mining communities in 1992 carried out not through swords and armed pillage but courtesy of a TV sound bite and a lie mimicking a literary stream of consciousness endlessly promoted which said; "there's no market for coal" when it was plain there was a very big market indeed albeit perhaps adapted more to pharmaceutical production. In reality, it was a cynical plan concocted and executed by MI5 secret services under the leadership of its boss, Stella Rimmington who'd been awarded her counter-insurgency spurs during the miners' strike of 1984-5. Beyond and even further lay an even greater goal: ransacking everybody at the sharp end.

Although the last page or so might seem like a long digression it's been put there to fully emphasise that the defeat of the proletariat here must be placed first and foremost. All the concomitant and more recent horrors like an intensified wave of sub-contracting, contracting out (out-sourcing), spurious self-employment, wiping out a great raft of unemployment and health benefits, pushing through enforced low wages, labour schemes etc, has, as a hellish backdrop, an all pervasive atomisation and an almost total loss of community bringing with it, crack-up and madness everywhere. It's based on one single ringing fact: DEFEAT!

The Lump pamphlet can therefore, without a lot of clarification relating to the here and now only be regarded as an excellent period piece, good as it was for the its time, even though many things should have been gone into in greater depth. As mentioned previously, except occasionally you no longer meet situations in the building trade like during the 1970s. The rebellious edge has been lobotomised. Collective gangs regardless of union status are few and far between and a tradition going back to the railway navvies has been broken. By and large, the bosses decide what the composition of a gang will be - all in the interests of breaking the nuclei and possible spear head of class solidarity. Everything, including the universal panacea of self-employment, fits in with isolation and a subjective solipsism centered round an agonised and screwed-up individual firmly shackled by a class society he or she has now little awareness really still exists. Every effort to think and act collectively is virtually in Britain characterised as criminal set inside a country where even to use the term "working class" can be regarded as bordering on the subversive!
Building workers whether they want to be or not have had self-employment thrust upon them in order to hold down any kind of job or have access to any kind of wage. It's all a chimera however as they're really not working for themselves but for a slave driver generally in the form of a sub-contractor who makes a mint out of them. Some are still fortunate enough to work for a big company but the numbers dwindle daily. Although a sub-contractor directly employs self-employed trades people basically as full time workers they are virtually without any rights or security. They can be dismissed on the spot without recourse to any procedure. The boss doesn't have to pay into any sickness schemes (as that's now up to the worker to make provision for), nor does he have to pay out holiday money. Thus for two weeks over Christmas say, the workers are effectively without any money. After national insurance deductions etc workers on top rates employed by a London sub-contractor get about £75 per day but after all other stoppages (usually mere cons which have more to do with the subby's profit margin), workers take home between £45 to £50 per day. The sub-contractor, on a gravy train just gets richer and, as often as not, deductions are

not handed over to the state anyway. After a decade or so, if the sub-contractor is lucky and ruthless enough, he invariably ends up a millionaire after getting into one scam or another at the expense of the poor. It's easy. You can buy up wholesale low grade fixtures and fittings as against better quality ones agreed in the contracts; merely slap on one coat of paint when three have been promised; paint over wet concrete or plaster; use low-quality tiles; skimp on the roofing as nobody can see that etc. One could go on. It all ends up though as a very long list adding up to a lot of money over time. Often too, the subby is in league with an architect or surveyor or some suit in management and they divide the spoils amongst themselves. It's all well covered up and in the bigoted atmosphere ruling in Britain today, even if they're found out, it doesn't matter in the slightest as it's well known only the poor are corrupt. Few dare then call the boss to account for fear of becoming liable themselves to heavy financial penalties knowing full well that any exposure of a "fat cat" would only result in a mild reprimand. Hardly surprising then economic class polarisation relentlessly intensifies as the gap between rich and poor has become wider than ever. One example will suffice. It was customary up until the mid 1990s for the boss to hand out loyalty bonuses -often around £3000 or more - to reliable building workers at Christmas. Since then all such benevolence has been scrapped as the greed of the rich intensifies. Most self-employed, though not all by any means, don't have a clue how to behave capitalistically and their grasp of economics is usually quite paltry. Their accounting system is often quite rudimentary and despite appearances to the contrary, they're not that good at fiddling. Many cannot afford the services of an accountant and if they get hold of a cheap deal they get a cheap result which just isn't worth it. Punters try it once and then give up. Often they earn just enough so as not to be able to qualify for housing benefit to cover part of the rent on their home or else their books are in such a mess that no Town Hall official could sort them out easily. More often than not in order to get over this hurdle, fear often prevents the individual from presenting an acceptable swindle sheet to the housing authorities. They get frightened of getting found out over minor irregularities just in case a prosecution would be in the offing. Moreover, and to cap it all, sometimes the same person can earn good money in one week and then nothing for the next three weeks. How could all this be explained to a rule-clad petty functionary with a computer? Seeing the computer is infallible the machine doesn't possess the intelligence to explain such vagaries. Fear thus becomes a punishment in itself reinforced by a bottom line adamantly insisting that asking for monetary assistance off the state if you're poor is tantamount to a criminal act.

In London, on the buildings, a wage of £75 per day is a sheer privilege in comparison to many places elsewhere. Plasterers in small country towns like Hebden Bridge in West Yorkshire can earn as little as £15 per day. Contracts between sub-contractors and "reputable" clients (like Housing Associations or Council Depts) which, only a few years ago would have involved some kind of honour and bureaucratic etiquette, are torn up on the spot as the hunt intensifies for the most rapacious exploiter touting the cheapest price which means, in turn, having the cheapest proletarians on offer. In this dog eats dog atmosphere, it's hardly surprising that in some outfits the regime beggars belief. You don't walk about the site, you run. Barrett's, the house builder, systematically fires its workers almost on a daily basis. A carpenter is say, given 24, 4inch, size 8 screws from the materials depot to put together a particular bit of wooden studding. If the carpenter loses any screws or fucks any of them up, he or she has to pay for them. Screws of that size are about 60 pence each so at the end of a bad day, you can easily be down £20. Just what are you supposed to live on? Fresh air? And in the era of the really cleaned-up, po-mo, pristine facade, with an even more pristine interior, some maintenance engineers are expected to forgo the overalls for suits even though constantly handling oily machinery and tools. Looking untidy can result in threats of dismissal (an oily lapel can be a near capital offence!) even though the companies refuse to foot the constant dry cleaning bills. One can go on with these horror stories and they're everywhere.

Though it would take some time, a compilation of true-life tales from the buildings could probably now equal that chilling account of 19th casualism, ironically titled:The Ragged Trousered Philanthropists by Robert Tressell and which became the bible of English trade unions. It's the complex story of a group of workers on a building site on their knees to a merciless free market capitalism. When I first read it many moons ago, a suicidal chill enveloped me: could this become true again? Could people dying of fatal diseases be forced nonetheless to work among the muck and rubble again? Well OK folks, it's back. There are carpenters around now ill with cancer plugging away at the daily grind either because they cannot afford to live on the miserly, basic sickness benefit of about £68 per week or because they cannot take the constant harassment meted out by those state appointed "doctors" known colloquially as the Mengeles. These creeps oversee just who should be allowed sickness benefit these days as their sole aim is to save as much money as possible so that more tax cuts for the rich can be guaranteed. Basically, the state - via these blood-money hacks - believe the sick have a duty to work.... Or perhaps a guy ill with cancer feels confusedly inside that the free market is so death-driven that you may as well be drawn into a contemporary dance of death anyway? And behind that too maybe is the sheer fear of dying alone in the loneliest society ever? Who knows and why now shouldn't such a situation be all of the above and more?

One of the reasons why 19th century casualism has reappeared is directly related to the steadily growing difficulties encountered in trying to get any form of state unemployment benefit and with the new draconian Job Seekers Allowance, it's going to get a lot worse. Furthermore, if you spontaneously walk away from an impossible work scene or if you get dismissed from a job under the cloud of "industrial misconduct" well there ain't going to be any guaranteed survival for you mate for some time. It's as though your being forced on the rob. A sub-contractor on a site can sadistically use such a ruling to threaten a worker for been an hour late because of transport fuck-ups or whatever. Sometimes it really does mean dismissal. These threats and this reality are a constant nightmare for already precariously employed people and on pain of survival they're forced into a submission no matter how much the spirit rebels inside to at least snap back. Hire and fire it seems, becomes all there is to life.

Once it was possible in the building trade, especially when getting older, to fix up employment with the Direct Labour Departments - the DLO's - administered by the local councils to get to grips with all the maintenance work needed on their housing stock and a also, to have on hand, a body of people to build new council house stock. The pace of work was generally more easy going and there was a closed union shop guaranteeing an easier time which meant you could get away with more than a few freebies like sleeping or sunbathing on a roof during a hot summer's afternoon. Now these DLO's have all but been swept away with CCT, the law on Compulsory Competitive Tendering. Strikes against DLO abolition, which admittedly were pretty desultory strikes, have made no difference. During the early 1980s, even some Lump gangs went along to DLO protest meetings to voice their support, though this was a rarity. In their place, sub-contractors have moved in en masse, trade unions have ceased to exist and some fat cats are again (!) making a lot of money. It's not as though things have suddenly become more efficient in terms of getting jobs done, as on the contrary, there's generally been a deterioration in the quality of work executed on council housing. Going along with these "new" found means, an ideology of "new" youth abounds which means getting poorly trained young 'uns to knock out the work as quickly and cheaply as possible, pushing aside the older, more technically experienced, building workers. That informal apprenticeship of site work - where the young learned all the nifty, technically brilliant tricks from old hands at the building trade - has gone along with all the rest.

However, after having said all of this and taking a more, all rounded view, a word of fact and a word of caution is necessary. One cannot simply blame the sub-contractor today as in the past in a time when they had a much greater freedom of movement. Nowadays they are much more at the beck and call of big capital where essentially the whole structure and directive comes down directly from the huge and powerful building companies themselves. The composition of these companies which are some of the most ideologically committed to a free market oriented state, have changed drastically from what they were twenty years ago or so when they directly employed thousands of workers and sub-contracting was relatively minimal in comparison with today's standards. Sub-contracting then was largely a matter of specialised, technical operators advancing new structural innovations which no one else was capable of carrying out. Now the big companies are "hollowed out", existing as client, wining and dining, artistic vending operations shorn of most day to day responsibilities involved in construction. Financially and as mini-global empires, they are richer than ever involved in high profile stock market wheeler-dealing and extremely able to crack the whip on the many backs of the sub-contractors they employ and who essentially organise and administer all their masters' work. Economically, these big guys can destroy these sub-contractors whenever they deem it fit to do so. If say, a sub-contractor makes a complaint against them acting against the pressures foisted on him by the big companies by withdrawing his company and self-employed work force (in a kind of parody of a strike) he can be in deep trouble. Contracts can be immediately cancelled along with money owed to the sub-contracted company that can run into huge sums of money bordering on a million pounds. Consequently, the sub-contractor then faces bankruptcy which means his bank assets are seized if, not, immediately, his flash house and car. He therefore has no ready to cash to pay his workers for work in progress or finished. Probably, he'd like to pay his workers if only because he doesn't want the news to get around locally he's a bad payer and no craftsperson of value will work for him in the future - once, of course, he gets on his feet again! These creeps usually do spring back after a short period of mourning replete with a new name for the new company registered in the wife's or brother's name, fit and fine to let the good old exploitative times role again. If the subby suffers anguish - obviously plainly for all to see in the pub over inability to pay - it's largely for commercial reasons and to prevent himself ending up with more than a thick ear. He cannot really resort to law as the cost of say taking a giant like McAlpine's to court is prohibitive He'd lose anyway and the big guys know this which is why they resort to these foul means in the first place. Inevitably, the workers see the sub-contractors as the big shit giving them as much grief as possible in a clandestine sort of way like doing a bit of damage to their smart houses or torching their flash cars. Fine, but the problem is the biggest shits - - those giant companies who initiate such policies - and from whom the problems really stem - go unscathed. It could be said that the growth of sub-contracting has been very effective in preventing the workers from getting their hands around the throats of the powerful building companies who have such a profound influence over British, free market, neo-liberal economics. These monsters are responsible for so much - a dependency on oil, an obsession with road construction , a hatred of wild nature, rail traffic and travel and so much else beside.

It would be nice to say there's been some reflection on all what's happened on the buildings over the last thirty years or so but it's a sure sign of just how bad times are that there's not even that! There's been little or no change in set attitudes. Ideologies of all types still abound with arguments stuck more or less in the past. An unemployed Irish carpenter friend on the eve of retirement and who'd worked on all types of building scenes, big and small, union and off- the-cards, recently attended a meeting of the inner London, Shepherds Bush branch of UCATT - the builders' union. He honestly stated in relaxed conversation that he did some work on the side now and again to top up his pittance of an unemployment benefit. Some of the members present turned nasty more or less suggesting he was a low down scab even though the guy had never crossed a picket line in his forty years on the sites! When telling me about this incident, with his eyes and head rolling wildly, he was clearly very upset. Really it was too much.

On the other hand, the builders' union from the electricians EPIU to the TGWU (Transport and General Workers' Union) and UCATT (Union of Construction And Technical Trades) have now accepted bona-fide self-employed people into their ranks and it's not difficult now to find fully paid-up union members on an individual basis working for rip-off sub-contractors. They do this however, on the basis of the union being not a means of creating daily workplace organisations but as a form of insurance and legal protection if anything should go wrong at work when, in the present circumstances, free legal aid for the majority of fully employed workers has been abolished. The union thus becomes the workers' insurance company.

This has created a backlash among some union fundamentalists who wish to go back to the days when labour only, sub-contracting was barred from many a site and everyone worked for the one big company making it easier to array a united force against the bosses. To be sure you can well sympathise with such nostalgia and how we miss the constant industrial ferment and it's true we'd all feel a lot happier if strikes of any significance were going on in the building industry. However, most of the workers who go on like this are so completely black listed that there's no way in the present circumstances of head long reaction they're going to get a job on a big site in the foreseeable future. The bricklayer, Brian Higgins of The Building Worker rank 'n' file group is the most notable. He, along with sympathetic others, got together a bricklaying gang in the late 1980s worked on a reasonably sized lump site and then pushed for unionisation. Strikes were called and from some initial small successes snowballed into halting major sites in the very centre of London itself. The giant London Bridge City development came to a standstill. It really was impressive but even the palpable misery of the late 80s - reeking from the defeat of the miners - seems like relative paradise in comparison to now. Higgins has become unemployable but he constantly tries to kick-up untidy increasingly but now squeezed back into a sectarian obsession with the union wanting it transformed into a more "democratic" organisation and more accountable to its members. Desiring "freedom of speech" he mouths off incessantly against "sell-out" union officials. Although some more advanced kind of independent Trotskyist (c/f new intro here) his fervency reminds one of some old time Scottish calvanist who wouldn't be out of place in a satirical aside in a poem by Robbie Burns. Recently, Brian Higgins has been sued by Dominic Hehir - a UCATT union official - for defamation of character. Yes sued! It reveals just how far down the road of money terrorism Britain has gone (despite Hehir being Irish and living in Dublin) when a well-heeled bureaucrat is able to demand compensation from a penniless worker.

Basically, Higgins wants a union fully responsive to its rank 'n' file members, a true union, a fighting union! This demagoguery though appealing can be nothing but simple hogwash. It's the kind of thing though which finds a sympathetic response among that tiny band of anarcho-syndicalists though in a less trade oriented form. It's even a little wider than that. The Crook branch of UCATT in Co Durham has something of an old-style libertarian disposition on these lines often producing somewhat interesting pamphlets and leaflets (e.g a pamphlet on a strike in a factory which produced wallpaper in Bishop Auckland in the early 80s. The instigators, who became known as "The Wallpaper Warriors" rapidly transcended Trotskyism immediately taking to arms killing a cop apocalyptically thinking, after the huge 1981 urban riots, that Britain was on the very edge of revolution. The pamphlet though interesting never made enough of these and other essential connections). Despite all of these anti-bureaucratic sympathies, in reality, the anarcho-syndicalists inevitably go along with a lot of procedural union bureaucracy such as the obscure rituals related to the "star nights" - don't ask me what all this means but most likely has its origins in old time radical free masonry. There is something of an overlap between people like Higgins and the anarcho-syndicalists but it's really only based on mutual respect for the others' on-site militancy rather than moving on to something more coherent. Individually too, some of the anarcho-syndicalist building workers have been very brave in the past and some, particularly during the miners' strike, landed up with heavy jail sentences.

It's doubtful if the supine present-day character of the unions in Britain can continue indefinitely. In America -that other free market Mecca - they're changing and some bureaucrats now issue "fiery" statements like calling for an uprising of the American working class. What in reality though does all this mean as for sure they don't want any such thing? It means wanting some kind of rebellion to break out and then some Young Turk can have some success in seeking to transform the union and get ahead nailing down a power position. Thus illusions multiply all over again as a repetition compulsion is unleashed and any revolutionary breakthrough is again denied.
On a more general level, all this talk of a sustainable capitalist take-off in Britain following a new direction -the third way - is nonsense. Don't be fooled. A lot of this

spin emanates from the media which is more policed by management than most countries in Europe and is merely a front expounding the benefits of neo-liberal economics. Sure there may be some more inward investment by global multi-nationals moving to Britain where labour is cheaper - because more flexible - than in many other countries in Europe or even some Asian countries like South Korea. A car worker can be hired in Wales for £8,000 per year. The equivalent in Seoul would be £10,000 to £12,000, so no wonder Korean multi-nationals take advantage of a capitalist paradise. However, to move on from this and declare that there's an increasing general prosperity is way off the mark. Can one also say unemployment is really falling? For sure there may be more part time work available but there's been no real palpable increase in full time employment. Companies downsize, shedding full-time workers everywhere at the same time as stock market quotations and dividend payments go up and up. Moreover, the Job Seekers Allowance is increasingly sweeping people off all kind of benefits and unemployment statistics here are only calculated for those receiving such benefits and not for those out of work as happens elsewhere in Europe. The official statisticians now find such a situation laughable and are finally saying so because unemployment in Britain could be nearly as high as in Germany but whose to know in a country when lying is sacrosanct? For sure there is a real expansion in prison building and, therefore, a few more building workers are employed, but it's all geared towards a penal system whose intake is rising by 250 inmates a week. Most are banged-up for petty offences like shop lifting, small time burglary, defaulting on fines or spraying up some hip-hop graffiti which are all treated as great crimes. What though are you supposed to do walking around skint in a world where money and consumption is proclaimed everywhere and where endemic rip-offs by the rich are proclaimed everywhere. It feels that naked and together with the ever-extending array of laws and penalties against those at the sharp end, is it surprising that workers are living in fear and dread under the sway of a money terrorism waiting to be unleashed on the rest of our immediate European neighbours.

A powerful fraction of capital here wants to bequeath to the rest of the world an updated version of 19th century "Manchester free trade liberalism". It's ironically focussed on a little Englander mentality, or rather, a home counties mentality, which now wants the world as its oyster, making the obscene heyday of British Imperialism seem enlightened and progressive in comparison. We are the miserable end game which could end up on your doorstep soon if the inevitable insurgency accompanying free market economics isn't fought more lucidly than was the case here. People are thirsting for revenge - scared though they are - and we must finally put our faith in that but when will hope break out again?

Dave Wise. *March 1997*

Some notes on Robert Tressell which may prove helpful in some kind of introduction to the German Wildcat edition of The Ragged Trousered Philanthropists seeing this is the first German translation.

Robert Tressell was writing at a time - the early years of the 20th century - when the workers' movement in Britain and Ireland was at one of its lowest ebbs ever. Not much was taking place. The big and often violent miners' strike of 1896 was nothing but a memory. Reaction was rampant. Laws against workers taking any kind of action, particularly strike action was practically out of the question as such activity at the time was union led. The Asquith Conservative government of the day gave itself powers to sequester all union assets. A lot of the unions were small outfits with not much money and thus they faced bankruptcy and liquidation. Finally, a tiny union at the Taff Vale company in South Wales took on the Taff Vale Railway Co and declared a strike. In response, the government seized all the union funds, the union ceased to exist and the strike collapsed. The shock waves spread like wildfire throughout the employed and the message was loud and clear: either shut up or put up.

This then was the immediate background to Tressell's dark and foreboding book. The workers had given in to this terrible pressure and began to somewhat accept it as their lot. It was therefore easy to characterise them as "mugs" - to use the American expression - and Tressell's Hastings on the south coast of England (and where he'd worked as a painter and decorator) thus becomes Mugsborough. In retrospect, it's perhaps easy to see as somewhat patronising and there's very little scope given in the book to the transformation of the submissive and conned subject once direct action is undertaken.

However, in many respects it was the very misery engendered by such submission that was gradually to galvanise the workers and transform them and, as a by-product, produce a more combative, centralised, as well as a more recuperative trade union movement with something like a "never again" as Taff Vale, casualism and The Ragged Trousered Philanthropists became canonised in a labourist ideology which provided suitable and applicable rhetoric/credentials for any aspiring left wing trade union bureaucrat and leftist Labour politician in an ascendant state capitalism. Quoting Tressell became an almost obligatory career move. Nay, it was even more: an essential under-pinning of the One Nation Toryism which guaranteed some kind of worker protection. And a long-lingering sentiment has remained well into these rampant, neo-liberal times. It's been said that Tressell's book was one of the favourite books of John Major, the last Conservative Prime Minister! But this by then was an exception.
Generally though, the book retained its quasi-mythic status until the 1980s. The laws enacted against workers in the early 70s and which were overthrown by wave upon wave of strikes, in fact reinforced this status (c/f the pamphlet about Tressell commemorating his new statue in Liverpool put out by old-style Liverpool TU members). Finally though the 1980s did produce a more enduring anti-worker legislation which has ferociously remained creating an atmosphere of resignation and stupidity reminiscent of Taff Vale times. In practise though these laws now are far more draconian than ever they were in the early years of the 20th century. Hopefully, we all can remember with what intense fury, violence and even aborted

uprisings these laws helped engender in the Britain of the 1980s. The workers were defeated and the laws increased. The present absence of struggle is, of course, predicated on this defeat. The stakes were high and in retrospect it's easy to see all the manifold failures of our side. Most were blatantly obvious even at the time and a belief in following trade union directives in the final analysis - when the chips were really down - was fatal. It's our fault we lost; nobody else can be blamed. A lot of the miseries a la Tressell have returned with a vengeance and a name you were weary of hearing endlessly repeated, knowing what an opportunistic aura it possessed, has again acquired cutting edge.

What must be remembered about the early 20th century in these islands was that the period of outright repression was a prelude to one of the most explosive periods in our history - what became known as The Great Unrest between 1909 to 1914. Robert Tressell died in Liverpool on the eve of the outbreaks.

However, from 1905 onwards signs of trouble were in the air. The aborted 1905 revolution in Russia caused consternation in ruling circles in Britain. An incoming Liberal government in 1906 (which many said at the time was elected due to the shock waves emanating from Russia) quickly drafted legislation scrapping the nastiest aspects of the previous governments labour laws. It was a palliative to what they perceived to be a changing mood. By 1909, the Liberal government enacted a piece of legislation which became known as The Peoples' Budget. It was the first systematic form of state capitalist protection against the worst ravages of the market on workers' lives that a British government had come up with and old age pensions etc became a statutory right.

It was a case though of the state giving too little too late in an attempt to forestall workers taking independent action... In no time these islands were in uproar from one end to the other. Strikes and riots broke out everywhere. Police were killed and gunboats were sent up the Mersey to put down insurrection in Liverpool. The army shot dead striking miners in West Yorkshire and the city of Hull in east Yorkshire experienced a huge orgiastic riot which sent shock horrors throughout the Christian establishment as not only did they witness the burning of the city but mass fucking in the streets... School kids refused to go to school organising against teachers etc. The accounts of this period are sparse in the annals of English social history and the best is probably Stanley Dangerfield's, The Strange Death of Liberal England... Then in Dublin in 1913, the famous transport workers strike broke out fitfully organised by the anarcho-syndicalists replete with the first armed workers' militia of the 20th century patrolling the streets of the Irish capital for many weeks. (Moscow and St Petersburg had seen armed insurrection without a prior organised militia).

It's been said recently by some of those Anglo-American new breed of academic autonomist historians that the outbreak of hostilities among the belligerent powers in Europe in 1914 wasn't really a war over the carve-up of imperial markets but a dire necessity in order to forestall social revolution. Although this argument has the merit of dethroning the time-honoured Social Democratic and Leninist economic and political perspective, it's possibly over the top. The only proletariats' in Europe on the offensive in the years prior to the inter-imperialist world was were those of Britain, Ireland and Russia and in the latter country, strikes and barricades were only just happening after a lapse of seven years. In the same period, Germany, France and Italy were relatively quiet.

Dave Wise. *1999.*

Excerpts from a letter published in German Wildcat, September 1989 commenting upon a few strikes in Britain.

If it hadn't been for the existence of the most draconian labour laws in Western Europe, almost certainly one would have seen a "repeat" of The Winter of Discontent both in 1988 and 1989. A "repeat" in the sense of strikes all cascading together, tumbling over each other in some rambling sort of way.

However, these present strikes in Britain have been more under union control than those recent strikes in France or Italy -despite the fact that the unions have infiltrated and used the co-ordinations there. But in contrast to France say, where the strikers have won very little and basically nothing in pay rises, despite the existence of "new" organisational forms, here strikers have been remarkably successful this year. Almost every major strike - railway workers, local government officers etc - has been won both in terms of wage increases and in pushing back and even thwarting restructuration, particularly pay bargaining. The only exception - and it was a devastating one - was the defeat of the dockers. The dockers' defeat has had though, amazingly enough, very little real impact on other striking sectors and, it seems, for other sectors preparing to strike. Set against the grim reality that these strikes have been won against the most reactionary regime in Western Europe - now going to lunatic lengths in the proposed poll tax to subjugate the rest of the population - they're no small victory. Ironically, strikers here have been more successful than their French counterparts facing a modern, flexible, social democratic state.

But then, when all is said and done, though glad to see the return of the "English disease", making one feel rather better inside, they're also not very inspiring affairs and quite unlike the ransacking and violence of the miners' strike and the printers etc even though these strikes were defeated. This is not to worship violence for its own sake - a kind of metaphysic of violence - merely to note the rage expressed in these actions really did point to something more than a fairer version of the old order.

As for "new" content, well, I don't know enough about that on that real intimate level which is of course necessary. Most of the time you simply cannot know this vis-a-vis those little changes/facts etc that can potentially open entirely new perspectives as time goes by. Finally you are involved in the relatively limited parameters of your own space. Certainly, there's been the reemergence of rank 'n' file unionism despite having a new name but I'm not sure what it means. It's still after all, rank 'n' file unionism and not "open" in the sense through which the form of a new world -if there is to be one - could come.

For instance, the old shop steward structure among striking steel erectors was thrown out but only in order for a new shop steward structure to be established which was prepared to get rid of a ridiculous two year agreement signed by engineering

(AEU) bureaucrats. The new structure, though more prepared to fight, nonetheless wasn't that different from those they'd overthrown. At one important moment at least, when 16 big building sites were on strike in London in early summer, this stewards committee made decisions behind the backs of striking steel erectors - decisions that it seems - weren't really challenged by striking steel erectors although there was muted anger among a small minority.

Interestingly too (the mood is catching) these organisers no longer called themselves shop stewards but "coordinators", imitating their French counterparts. This has happened not only in the construction industry (maintenance building workers on the North Sea oil platforms used the term too) but also among London Underground train drivers. Indeed, the tube drivers were the first to deploy the tag. A nagging doubt remains. Aren't they just shop stewards under a new guise? We shall see! Certainly there's been an attempt to discipline some of these coordinators - particularly by UCATT officials in the building industry. On the Isle of Grain in the Thames estuary during spring, some union bureaucrats were beaten up and thrown off sites by strikers where previously some heavy action had taken place and railway lines had been uprooted and gantry cranes pushed over etc. It's hardly surprising therefore that the union big wigs came down on them squashing all resistance though getting squashed themselves in the process. Sounds exciting doesn't it? Well, it could have been a splendid precursor to something much bigger but the action remained confined to the Isle of Grain and London sites and limited to steel erectors who never really attempted to generalise their dispute to other building trades - never mind others. When they did make a gesture in that direction it was conceived in such an archaic union manner. A meeting was held at Conway Hall in central London by steel erector coordinators and though other building workers were invited it had to be care of the union card when 70% of building workers aren't in unions. If only they'd made an appeal on pasted up posters to all building workers or, something similar! That perhaps might have meant a new mood was in the air!

On the North Sea oil platforms it was a little better. Building workers involved girl friends/wives in occupations over the appalling safety standards on the rigs and during the dispute began to make appeals to oil production workers. Some responded, but then the action petered out. (Did the coordinators lose their nerve, as after all, they were taking on the mighty oil companies well noted for their brutality? Even so, some maintenance workers were well pissed-off when the strikes - on the eve of getting dramatically bigger - were ended by the coordinators).

Similar things can be said about the tube drivers. They never opened their coodination to other underground workers. They kept their elite role intact vis-a-vis other railway workers. Despite this lack there was also a fair degree of radicalism within that somewhat myopic narrowness. Bureaucrats, mainly belonging to ASLEF were ordered out of meetings and it seems, the coordinators were basically anti-party (some, it was said, had been Tory voters). It was only later that Trotskyists moved in to try and colonise the coordinations. At the end of their long strike, even though finally the strikers had relinquished the running of their dispute to the ASLEF bureaucrats, drivers at a final coordination meeting ferociously refused - deploying the heaviest language -"listen motherfucker" - to talk to any media representative. It was a response not seen since the early, heady days of the miners' strike. All in all, the tube drivers' action was something of a step in the right direction.

Really what's needed is an analysis of the organisational composition of shop stewards over the last 20 years or so evaluating how their role has changed. In the 1960s, the Situationists, most likely prodded by Solidarity in Britain, could hold to the view that shop stewards were basically an autonomous revolutionary body, or, potentially so - if one could only get to them - and clue them into real autonomous theory. Of course, it tended to smack of leftist handing theory down to the masses but there was rather more to it than that. Maybe it was an understandable perspective then at a time when there was hardly a national pay bargaining structure in existence and grabbing what you could (free collective bargaining!) usually depended on how bloody-minded you were prepared to be at a local level. Certainly, the situation was very open and some shop stewards here did latch on quickly to aspects of some of the most advanced and fresh theory in existence. However, 1970s reorganisation and the emergence of a national pay bargaining on a big scale plus a much greater integration of stewards into the union/state hierarchy put paid to what had increasingly become, a mistaken concept though not perhaps, initially.

In a sense, I don't think the fully employed workers have still recovered from that subtly shattering experience. It would be worth investigating how the stewards fragmented throughout the 70s, for example, the substantial increase in the number of senior stewards often on 100% facility time paid for by the company/state dept or multi-national and thus becoming almost as remote from the sharp end of an intensifying workers' alienation as the union bureaucrat in his/her office. During the savage Thatcher years of the 80s you really wonder just how much has that position been reversed. Indeed, some recent statistics and which the Trotskyist SWP eagerly pounced on, say that the number of shop stewards has risen from 300,000 in 1979 to 360,000 now! Basically though, the shop steward apparatus - with all its manipulations, encouraging/derailing struggle syndrome, ignoring mandates, decisions taken by themselves etc - has continued virtually unscathed. Perhaps what one is beginning to see is a union rank 'n' filism powered by those shop stewards at the real bottom end of the union hierarchy who feel sufficiently estranged from this hierarchy to borrow the term coordinator in order to give merely the appearance of something different? It was certainly more than that in the early days of the tube strike. It may be the beginning of something different but there again, probably not as it's going to take some fundamental sea change for this "new" movement to break out of the union carapace.

Dave Wise. *September 1989*
(Apart from the new critical introduction here, all the articles were published in one form or another by Wildcat, the autonomous German revolutionary group). See the following on the Revolt Against Plenty web

Derives, Housing & Real Ecos
Notes Towards the Economics & Aesthetics of the UK's Great Building Disaster
The Lump
Brendon Ward: Builders, Chancers and the Craic
Their Passed-away Builders

© 2015 Revolt Against Plenty

Reflections on Brendan Ward's Builders' Remembered (1984)

….and "Builders, Chancers and the Crack" (1985) together with scattered thoughts on the first and <u>only</u> national building workers' strike of 1972

(It seems the above two books are out of print and no library possesses old copies)

Oh, how the anarcho-syndicalists - though not necessarily other anarchists - hated Brendan Ward's "Builders, Chancers and the Crack" .All they could see was the racism, not the great richness beyond that, and which comes through however narrow his attitude to trade unions are, viewing them mainly as composed of suits in an office situated well away from the work places they claim to represent. Nor could the anarcho-syndicalists appreciate the larger than life characters Brendan Ward was describing. These people were anarchic without being self-styled anarchists, believers who constantly took the piss out of the church and its priests. They rebelled against the subcontractors but were not above being subcontractors themselves, even the Bear O'Shea and the Darky Flynn who have entered into legend because of their honourable mention in "McAlpine's Fusiliers", the song written by the Communist party supporting Dominic Behan and that once, not all that long ago, was the building workers' anthem. (By the way and no offence meant, nowadays the anti-heroic "Cement mixer, putty, putty" by Charlie Parker's side kick Slim Galliard should really be the song of the building trade, and Slim knew both Notting Hill Gate and Kilburn very well - we'd always say "Hi Slim" to him).

But in Brendan's tale they are not fusiliers but "outlaws". And McAlpine's was only one of many building firms they worked for, though Wimpey's and John Laing's are also mentioned in "McAlpine's Fusiliers". Murphy's wasn't and both books by Brendan Ward make much of him and his business.

In quick succession we are introduced to "John Murphy and his outlaws incorporating The Elephant." these outlaws also an army with commanders: gangers who worked for Murphy like the notorious Elephant. So the whole book kicks off with a song of praise to Murphy's, something Dominic Behan would never have done. Brendan Ward was obviously proud to be a personal friend of John Murphy disguising the exploitation of the mainly Irish work force by an appeal to their combined brute strength: "Men are proud they belonged to the toughest army in the world". Some were but many were broken by it and even comparing them to the mighty Fionn MacCumhall of Irish legend who scooped out Lough Neagh in Northern Ireland, could never disguise that.

The Elephant was Murphy's foreman and ganger, a reincarnation of Fionn MacCumhall: "He dug muck with a shovel especially made by a blacksmith outside Sneem. It was the size of four shovels but in the hands of the Elephant it looked only normal. He could dig and fill a lorry as fast as a JCB and that is no exaggeration". This mythic figure was also hated and "the men who worked for him wished him the cruelest death that could be imposed". Perhaps in no other trade in the Britain of the immediate post war years was such mythic corporatism possible and one that so effectively masked the true face of exploitation. Even J Murphy was reputed to be afraid of his pet, the Elephant: "We all know a dog will stand by his master when attacked but on the other hand the master is unsure when the dog will attack him". And no matter how much the subcontractors and the gangers draped themselves in legend, if, on payday, men weren't paid then fists would start to fly and if the ganger did not win the fight his colourful name and reputation was in tatters. Even the mighty Elephant was to eventually get his------".

Though a nasty bit of work, Brendan Ward has something nice to say about the Elephant for he wasn't just pure brute, respecting a witty reply and even displaying on rare occasions a typically Irish sense of humour. Once when working at Heathrow an Aer Lingus plane passed over and the Elephant had gazed at it longingly: Asked if he would like to be on it he answered: "Well it's like this. I would not like to be up there and not be in it". And Ward fawns on his boss the contractor John Murphy: "His many millions have altered his lifestyle alright in that he does not live in the Bush but he is still as happy driving an old banger of a van as a Rolls Royce. – Fair enough John Murphy does not drink in Biddy's on a Saturday but it's a mother who would blame him."

The road-mending firm of Murphy's began as a trench-digging outfit and rapidly rose on the backs of Irish workers. A start up firm in post war Britain with no financial backing, Brendan Ward is proud of John Murphy's success, having become so big by the 1980s it can play the home grown English construction companies at their own game. And as a former Murphy worker – or outlaw – he clearly wants to swap Mc Alpine's Fusiliers for Murphy's Outlaws in Irish building worker legend. John Murphy made his name by driving his men hard. As Brendan Ward says "John (on first name terms indeed!) was mainly involved in laying pipes. It involved water, gas, sewers, electricity and telephone cables. There were no mechanical diggers and after the war a massive construction bonanza hit England". Not having earth-moving equipment the firm made up for in sheer brawn spurred on by the brutal bullying and notorious ganger men like the afore mentioned Elephant. Making a virtue out of necessity there is something John Henry like about the navvying driving down 9ft when the steam hammer only did 7ft except this was not one individual but thousands of workers unable to continue working much after forty – which Brendan freely admits - because they were ruined in body if not in soul. That, and the old myths of Ireland, like the giant Cuchulain able to flatten mountains and fight "the ungovernable sea", (Yeats) their ancient culture being used against them.

In Ireland the punctilio of class does not mean as much as in Britain and a millionaire publican, until recently, could unselfconsciously sit down and play dominos with his regular customers. This just would not happen amongst the English or the Scots and Welsh, though it has to be said Ireland is now rapidly changing in this respect. As a friend, Phil Meyler once acutely remarked of these fast-fading times: "Ireland is sociable but not socialist".

We knew one such person, Mick, who owned the Pelican in the Gate, his wife Jean becoming rather snobbish sending her children to a private nursery school as her husband, a reputedly, tough no nonsense, subcontractor though exceptionally genial, welcoming publican, just got wealthier and wealthier. In the sixties he'd the foresight to buy two pubs one in Kings Cross the other in Notting Hill Gate. Others could have done the same but most just threw their money away like it was paper. At times one sensed they were close to burning it. The Pelican closed down a few years back and opened up as an organic food and drinks bar before flopping completely, then morphing yet again, the one constant being in these new fangled changes that it was anti the poor. Mick unable to be anything else than an un-adapted Irish publican finally cashed in his chips in the late 1990s as time was also called on the unique culture of the Irish building scene which from just before the Second World War had long been a dominant factor in construction in Britain, particularly in London and the south east. Mick was also ashamed of his property wheeler dealing rushing away from those customers who'd got his number, knowing in his heart of hearts it was disgusting.

He must have come from some kind of enlightened family in Kerry as Mick also had a brother, a plasterer, self-educated and of left wing persuasions who would regularly hold forth in the pub on society's inequities often deploying very colourful language. Oddly enough he always carried around with him a really, really bashed-up book of the writings of Emmanual Kant, well under-lined with mucky finger prints on every page. In semi-drunken arguments he'd drag Kant out of his coat pocket, select a quote and fire it across the pub whether it was applicable or not.

Mick's pub was one among thousands to disappear. Biddy's in Kilburn or, to give it its full name, Biddy Mulligan's (or as the locals, drifting with words as the Irish love to do, called it Willy Pulligan's then Willy Tulligan's as Pulligan's was too obvious, the flow of suggestion spiralling crazily) became a smart venue, going by the name of The Australian Bar. Finally, seeing the Kilburn Irish have been pushed too far they've recently gone on something of a low profile offensive to reclaim some pubs they've been evicted from care of the makeover business. Subsequently, Biddy Mulligan's has returned though more as shadow than full-blown reality. The day though has yet to return when Irish labourers would forget where there nearby hole in the road was having supped more than a few jars in Biddy's during lunchtime!

In Brendan's account a continual, though unconscious, critique of money keeps showing through. He says of the Darky Flynn: "I never met a man who had less value on money. He never worried about tomorrow in his life. He always reasoned he could wake up dead and a fat lot of good an accumulation of wealth would be". There are also many other stories about the spendthrift habits of the Irish building workers, money passing through their hands like water. Though never reaching the heights of the Northern Irish protestant Tressell who wrote a book around building sites "The Ragged Trousered Philanthropist" which consciously called for the abolition of money, there is one account of a corn threshing session in old Ireland where his friend "O'Donell from Tir Conail" (no one ever knew his first name) writes "the threshing day was a festive occasion and no money changed hands - It was an honour to be there."

In fact "O' Donell" had entrusted Brendan with the job of being his literary executor after his death, for the man was much addicted to writing and "when funds were low he passed his time by writing". Most of his writing was an undecipherable scrawl but Brendan did manage to interpret a few pieces, mostly on what life was like in the old days and which make fascinating reading. His few paragraphs entitled "Cutting the Turf" is not just about how TV and "the lounge bar had replaced chatting around the open hearth" but also a criticism of industrialized agriculture like the combine harvester and the mechanical turf cutting machines which had destroyed "the mirth that had prevailed" formerly for "the day on the bog was a picnic occasion". He writes beautifully and with feeling about the slean, the tool used for cutting turf: "The slean was a beautiful tool. There was a romance involved with it which brought fatigue, happiness and satisfaction to everybody". Anybody who has worked with hand tools will know what he means but a writer, seeing themselves in the writer's role, never would.

He also tried his hand at writing poetry none of which ever comes off (or could have) and which only adds to the quality of the fragments. Like so many other building workers he hit the bottle but the bottle hit him back, ending up in the gutter and writing of how one day a pig lay down at his feet whilst there when "a city gent came along/And quietly sang his song/ You can tell the one that boozes/By the company he chooses/ The pig got up/ And quickly strode away". The un-metrical twist at the end is what makes it and even the pig could not bear to keep him company. No writer would really know what that feels like either, because the profession of writer stops them sinking that low.

"O' Donell's" writing constantly threatens to fall apart just like the ramblings of the splendid Yorkshire miner, John Dennis also from an Irish background. Back in the seventies we used to frequent a pub in Ladbroke Grove much used by Irish and other building workers, for this was around the time of the national building workers' strike. This pub also has been altered beyond all recognition and is now the Earl Percy Hotel when 30 years ago it was just a cut above a spit and sawdust place. Amongst the usual regulars was a white haired building worker of about sixty whom every night would take out a little book and begin to scribble in it, like he was possessed. Occasionally he would look up, his far-off eyes fixed on the ceiling not on other people. No one ever got to read what he wrote in his little notebook and he rarely spoke to anyone. However by sidling up to him it was possible to make out the lettering – for that was all it was, not even sentences just letters. He was obviously a lettriste in pure form.

There was also a building worker, a brickie, by the name of Huey who could be found there most nights. He was in the habit of suddenly cheeping "cuckoo, cuckoo, cuckoo" in a falsetto voice that would go on all night. No one ever seemed to mind. Apparently he was a real gentleman to work with and his whole demeanour resonated gentleness finally ending up in an old peoples' home bursting out to the carers' every now and then "cuckoo, cuckoo, cuckoo". Really it wasn't a bad comment on the time as the whole world was starting to go really cuckoo, these two little portraits giving a much needed personal touch to the setting of the first national building workers' strike of 1972.

Brendan Ward never once mentions the strike, which is a bad, bad omission. He was an Irish republican imbued with a hatred of England not feeling a scrap of loyalty to the country and taking it for all he was worth by not paying taxes, though never once tempted to join the IRA. Though hardly cool, his discreet republicanism was similar to some of the Scots who played a key role in helping ferment the strike Though sympathetic to the aims of Irish republicanism they were not only intolerant of terrorism but would never agree to subcontracting in the service of the cause. They were also very doctrinaire when it came to the pragmatic use of the lump to keep strikes going, an attitude which caused them to clash with far less "principled" Irish building workers who would unhesitatingly use the lump – and more - if it enabled them to keep a strike going.

The clash between one such Scottish organiser Mac and an Irish building worker, another O'Donnell (actually in the Communist party) used to happen fairly regularly, O' Donnell calling Mac a John Knox puritan and Mac regarding O'Donnell as a gombeen man. O'Donnell was undoubtedly the easier to get on with and very quick to acknowledge the contradictions which, if not recognised, would lead pretty smartly into blatant hypocrisy and even schizophrenia. However he was hated for pointing the obvious out and rapidly condemned as a very suspicious, even perverted, character, a label he fortunately just shrugged off and paid little attention to though it must have hurt.

O' Donnell was also much more aware of the sheer craziness of capitalism and, drug fiend that he was now judged to be, smoked dope fairly regularly, a habit Mac loathed and feared. He also listened to psychedelic music and would occasionally drop some acid, neither of which met with 'union' approval because it was anti the hard drinking Scottish and Irish folk music traditions that in London and the South East in particular was rooted in the Scots/Irish building worker community.

O'Donnell also had a Scottish friend called Finn who played the guitar and had only joined the strike under peer pressure. He also had a beautiful red haired Scottish wife called Dorothy who was forever badgering him to get a better job and wanted nothing to do with strikes. One night Finn broke under the strain and had smashed up his expensive guitars. In fact Finn finally ended up leaving the buildings and getting a degree in philosophy of all things, as did O' Donnell who wound up back in Ireland owning a smallholding, his teaching qualification now enabling him to teach as well as farm. None of this worked out though as finally the guy was to devote himself completely to his core activity of drinking and smoking dope. Neither could stick with the buildings and we last heard that Finn had lost the ability to speak, except in philosophic terms, and had landed a job in a college though managing to hang on to his ambitious wife. It's a fair bet that the both of them, now around sixty, will look back on former times with great nostalgia and deem their subsequent lives a detour in emptiness when compared with the wealth of life they once knew on the buildings.

Most of the Scots we knew came from Kilmarnock, several of them making the trip to London together and quickly becoming domiciled in the same area, even street, as this was London in the sixties and bed-sit accommodation easy to find. This collective behaviour has long since gone, the last occasion being in the seventies when a bunch of lads and lasses all came down from Manchester together, a number of them also ending up on the buildings - and on the bottle and marijuana. They also quickly found accommodation but this time in squats however, for the London property market was then undergoing deep and lasting changes, the increasing emphasis on homeownership in a seemingly endlessly rising market profoundly transforming the nature of building and anchoring it more firmly than ever in the domestic arena.

One of the lads from Kilmarnock was called Jim and he also was employed on the buildings, though never for very long on the same site, skipping from one job to the next. He was a very genial character but regarded with suspicion by his more narrowly militant brethren: as one of his less judgemental acquaintances said "Jim can peel an orange in his pocket with a boxing glove on". He liked to relate how he would go into the miners' welfare in Kilmarnock and deal acid to the local miners and then drop a tab himself and sit back and enjoy the fun as miners morphed into different shapes and colours. This was a couple of years prior to the great miners' strike of the early seventies (1972 and 1974) that brought down the Tory Heath government. Jim also got taken up and went to college wringing his hands over his unpaid taxes and eventually becoming a union bureaucrat. Something must have happened in the meantime for a couple of years' back he was to be seen on Portobello Rd on a Sunday in charge of a stall selling gloves, scarves and underpants. Never a fool, had he, one wonders, arrived at a critique of trade unionism preferring to be a petite bourgeois small trader than living with the dishonour of being a not very effective broker of labour power in these increasingly harsh times.

Jim in the early 1970s among his odd jobs was also a bit of a chauffeur, an occasional driver for another guy from south west Scotland called MacQuinney, and a young trendy businessman in the design field. MacQuinney was one of the guys from the late sixties who used to like smashing up, or at least, pull from their steel cotter pins, wooden Jesus Christ statues nailed on crosses outside churches everywhere. Realising rebellion was all over with he yet needed the pulse of the street to keep him going; a guy who wanted his cake and yet more to eat. Becoming a designer he could converse – just – on the situationists. He needed a mad-cap, libertarian worker like Jim if only as a foil and after the day's business, night after night he would sit slap bang in the middle of all the builders knowing he wasn't trusted yet sensing they were all increasingly at sea too.

Mac also left the buildings after the national building workers' strike returning to Scotland where he took a job on the oilrigs. There was a degree of tension between him and his New Zealand born wife Roz who wanted a baby and would go out on sex strike. Mac never spoke about such intimate things rejecting fatherhood because he feared the responsibility would weaken his militancy as it had done with many another building worker who once they became father's grew mightily afraid of the sack and being blacklisted. However it is easy to be critical of such figures as Mac and, though much admired and respected, his ascetic stance went against the grain of the times, his unbending, repressive demeanour stopping him from ever acknowledging the reality of his sister's suicide, who, shortly after the strike ended, had defenestrated herself in Edinburgh. Henceforth Mac would refer to Mary's death not her suicide.

Mac also would never fix people up with jobs in a trade that was notorious for slipping someone money in order to get a start and subbies never expected to buy a round. It has to be said the Scots and Northerners generally were far more adamant then the Irish in not bowing to this time-honoured custom, which also features prominently in the bible of the builders workers unions' Tressell's "The Ragged Trousered Philanthropists". On the other hand Mac did not like pilfering from sites but even he couldn't help tittering when a building operative had been caught by the agent with a TV on his fork lift truck and rather than say "fair cop guv" had proceeded with it to the rubbish shoot claiming it was broken. Mac also knew many agents were corrupt and would skimp on materials and flog off the surplus. Yet despite this tolerated criminality, coming mainly from the top, and which can have very dangerous consequences indeed in building, sabotage is none the less part of struggle and it always raises a smile and causes a feeling of joy to run through the body.

Some instances are particularly splendidly outrageous like the one recounted by a now dead chippie, Frank, when fitting out the QE2 in Glasgow's shipyards back in the early seventies. A very expensive grand piano had been installed in one of the palatial ballrooms on the liner but unfortunately one of the other chippies employed on the fitting out had managed to severely scratch the piano. Knowing they would be held responsible, and their pay docked, there was nothing else for it. So they set to work with their skill saws and chopped it up, throwing each piece into the Clyde through the portholes. Later the same gang would go on the rampage and gut the interior of the QE2 in protest against the withholding of bonuses. No one was ever brought to book because the yards were so well organised and the Clyde work-in was either still in progress or a recent memory. Meanwhile several flying pickets were shortly to be frog marched off to jail in rural Shrewsbury on trumped-up conspiracy charges.

Frank was by no means a libertarian and was, for instance, very down on squatting, believing squatters liked nothing better than immediately smash toilets when they occupied property and shit on the floor instead. They also had babies just so they could murder them and dispose of the remains under the floorboards! By now living in Kilburn in London, Frank, a Glasgow protestant, liked nothing better than to open the windows of his flat overlooking Kilburn High Road, still then something of an Irish catholic "ghetto", and blast out that belting hymn of the Orange Order: "The Sash my Father Wore." He also had on the walls of his flat a cherished copy of his favourite painting: "When did you last see your Father" which depicts two Royalist children being questioned by a brute of an interrogator looking a shade like Oliver Cromwell during the English Civil War of the 1640s'. Frank never did find out the Pope was on the side of King Billy in the Battle of the Boyne, the founding myths of the orange and the green only just then beginning to be questioned in Britain but which was always the reality in Ireland pace the United Irishmen of the 1790s and whenever the real social shit hits the fan.

A tacit support for Irish republicanism and virtually none whatsoever for Northern Ireland's protestants, even by chapel-goers, was also a factor in the miners' strike of 1984/85, particularly in Yorkshire. Some of these striking miners also worked the Lump, whenever, that is, they could get lump work, receiving cash in hand at the end of the day to help sustain the strike. What did come, as a surprise is that they found the work very heavy and would return home at the end of the day exhausted, though less inclined to think of building workers as having it cushty in comparison with miners.

One of the most interesting features of Brendan Ward's account is the number of Irish immigrants who found work in the mines to then move on to do building work. They tended to work down the mines during the Second World War, presumably alongside the Bevan Boys, though Brendan never mentions any staying on permanently. However the skills they acquired hewing coal served them in good stead for post war navvying work, the ability to shift "muck" having something John Henry like about it, as though an unofficial war had been declared on the JCBs, which were just to say beginning to come on stream and eventually put many of them out of work. Though Mac, the militant building worker mentioned previously, had never worked down the mines, his father had been a coal miner in the Fife coalfield. Mac vividly recalled his father coming home from work to say the mines had been nationalised to then repeatedly break down crying, the bewildered child asking what that meant and his father replying, between his sobs, "it means there will be pit head baths". No one from Ireland would have responded in a similar manner because for them coal mining was only a temporary expedient and filled with a greater wanderlust than ever in post war Britain, would soon be moving on.

When Brendan Ward first came to England he hardly knew the difference between a chain saw and a chain gang. Never in receipt of any training other than what he learned on the job and following the tried and tested principle of "monkey does what monkey sees" i.e. watching other people, over the years he has become "skilled" and it is apparent from the terms he uses he has a wide knowledge of the building trade. This brings us to another, very important point, about the Irish immigration and that is they were as skilled at a broad spectrum of farming as they were at building. This is what he writes about his friend "O'Donnel from Tir Conail" on the rare occasions he went back home "He knew every sheep intimately—He noticed the turf rick was well covered and the pikes of hay were thatched and well held down with scallops". As well as scribbling profusely, the memories pouring out of him, of a way of life that had gone forever, he had also been a miner in Yorkshire.

By the end of his life this cat certainly knew a thing or two and it would have been a pleasure to have met him, provided he had been able to stay sober. Though forever in each other pockets and rucking constantly this jack-of-all-trades approach of the Irish was also a bone of contention with the Scots who, hailing from the land of Adam Smith, were more adapted to the division of labour and far more inflexible when it came to trying there hand at things different from what they had been trained to do. Bad workmanship was a mark of shame with the Scots whereas with the Irish it was almost a badge of honour. It was certainly an indication of a will to live and a sign they had got their priorities right, Brendan saying of The Darky Flynn: "Work was incidental to him". Flan (or The Flower) from the Burren was also similarly disposed: "work interfered in a big way with his leisure."

However there is more to it than this: in a country they hated, building became a form of guerrilla activity and legging it down the street, when a house front collapsed, all part of a war carried out by other means. Brendan described himself as a professional "but alas, not in the art of construction, but destruction" saying in his life he had variously "tried to pass as a labourer, a plumber, a brickie, a lift engineer, a plasterer, a chippie, a paper hanger and a tacker." What's more in 1985 he is proud to shout it out loud but over twenty years on the numbers who once would have revelled in such a frank admission have dwindled to practically nothing. It is not just that the controls have tightened since then but attitudes to work have become more serious, taking away all pleasure in work and robbing us of the laughs when things go wrong big time.

This brings us to Brendan's discussion of Irish humour perhaps the most unique humour to be found anywhere and which was once such a feature of the building scene and sorely missed now that it has gone. It is a humour that never ceases to surprise the Irish either because it put things in another perspective or causes us to look at things differently. For example Brendan suddenly breaks off to say it is already three in the morning and he "is expected at Reading by 7 30 am by his good employer" adding "he might not miss me if I'm late but then on the other hand British Rail might, and the train could be held up for an hour awaiting my arrival". We miss the train but to an Irish person the train misses you. However it was the Irish speakers whose language chiefly impressed Brendan – in particular the Connemara men: "They talked in Irish and they definitely had a way of conversing in the English language. For instance Flaherty was asked how long his mother was dead. He replied: "If she was alive tomorrow she would be one year dead." Another of his descriptions concerned a dog he had trained back home "the dog could be in the air while his hind legs were on the ground." But there were times when he got his terms wrong like the time he rose early to go mowing: "I was putting the winkers on the sun when the mare was rising". It is definitely the sort of inversion a surrealist in the heyday of surrealism as a way of life would have responded to and inevitably one thinks of Synge captivated a century ago by the many layered language of the peoples' of the Aran Islands like it was the realisation of symbolism in a land beyond poetry on the far shores of western Europe.

The logic of this anti-logic could - and can - catch authority off guard and many a building worker was saved from a smack on the head by the quick wittedness of their replies. One of Brendan's friends, The Chancer, was caught by the brutal ganger The Elephant carrying one bags of cement at a time while his mate was carrying two: "How come you're only carrying one bag, Chancer, when the other man carries two"- "Oh he's too lazy to go back for the other one" answered The Chancer."

If Brendan is to be believed one of them, The Flower, had a remarkable capacity for ad-libbing and we never pass a Trollope and Coles sign without being reminded of the Flower's ad-lib: "A glass with holes for Trollope and Coles" nor his ad lib on the "pincher laddies" (i.e. the building workers who would return at night and have equipment away, even JCBs) "A rum and black for the pincher Mac". He also ad-libbed around the name of Mulvaney, a subbie who did workers out of money right left and centre and was reputed to be gay: "A half of beer for Mulvaney the queer". In any case the ad-lib was not nearly as good as when we once, in the company of a good man of the buildings, fell to thinking about the number of gay plumbers we knew: "perhaps it's all those pipes" he ventured. The person is Jewish not Irish but had been brought up in Holloway surrounded by the Irish, though it must be admitted the Jews have their own capacity for word play based more on assonance and alliteration. We were once working on a flat belonging to a musical journalist when I happened on the lyrics of a rap song that ended "the stick-up kids are out to tax" to which our ad-libber immediately replied "and when I get rich I'll send you a fax".

Many of the thrifty Irish have become property millionaires in the last 30 years both here and in Ireland some many times over – and probably astonished at their "good fortune" for they brought property when it was going cheap. One such person was Donegal Jack, a ganger man who always succeeded in having three or four wage packets for himself. In order to achieve this he drove the men to the utmost and booked in another few ghost names on the timesheet. His employers were aware of the fiddle but seemed to tolerate it as long as he still made a good profit for them. It is hard to understand how his men despised him so much but yet continued to work for him year after year. Donegal Jack, as Ward says "was a loathsome creature all right. Anyway he saved his money and bought three houses in Kilburn, which he let out to tenants despite the fact that he owned three houses, he squatted in a flat along with two black men. – Despite the fact he was squatting he still charged them rent." We (not Brendan Ward) knew a Donegal Joe who died recently of drink. He could easily have been a victim of Donegal Jack as a tenant and as a building worker – whenever he was not drunk that is.

Sean the Fisherman, and unlike Donegal Jack was it seems a really nice guy, perpetually able to create a fantasy construct of the life he left behind in Ireland the recollection of which starts as he notices a seagull winging over a trench he is about to dig: "His mind wandered to his youth as soon as he learned to walk he accompanied his brothers on fishing trips. He became an excellent boatman and could make a currach in three days. His descriptions of nature are something else: "In summer time the setting was idyllic. The heather behind the house blew in gentle waves in the wind, exposing its multicolours as it rose and fell. The sheep bleated for their lambs as they searched out a bit of grass. They were like white dots on a floral carpet". Sean was as efficient in farming as he was in seafaring.

Rather similar it seems was Flan from the Burren: "The Burren is one of the most fantastic places on earth. The breathtaking scenes, the rare flowers and grasses are enjoyed and appreciated from people all over the world. That is lovely but the scenery seldom pays the rates….." Then there's a comment on Achill: "People emigrated from Achill without ever setting foot on the mainland. The island of Innis Kee was shrouded in sorrow through drowning….." It reminds you of Yeats's: "Holy Isle of Innisfree"…..

There is in "Builders Remembered" (1984) a chapter on Terry who became known as "Terry the Philosopher" rather than Terry Clifden, the place of his birth though "he recalled being reared near Clifden" like he'd now half forgotten. It was plain to see he was a man who had thought long and hard about many things and though it is not always possible to agree with his conclusions they are always full of interest. He had a critique of money from the start, even if not, by any means, a fully worked out one, – as indeed do a lot of people who have lived long enough to remember a childhood, even in Britain, were money was all but absent from the lives of children and young adults. As he said to Brendan "money was scarce but nobody went without. Life was lived to the full with money necessity remaining at a minimum."

Ah yes to be one of the dwindling few who know in their bones what that means. This attitude to money followed the Irish to England especially those that became building workers, who were impressed more by how much they earned than the paper notes that made it up and as Terry profoundly observed: "When the pay packet came Paddy held up the packet and threw away the contents". He had also pondered long on the different attitudes of the Irish and English toward property. "Security is something the Irishman in England desires. Most emigrants have worked hard very hard to own their own houses. The Englishman is content to live in a council flat round the corner from mum's council flat and again around the corner from his mum in-law's council flat. He never considers helping himself to some of his employers property as dishonesty. He more or less treats it as a bonus. On the other hand Paddy is careful with his employer's property." And it is true that many an Irishman saved hard so he could buy a pub, a farm, a house back home, Ireland being an altogether more petite bourgeois nation than Britain at that time.

This is not intended as a put down, simply an acknowledgement of different levels of development with property and the means of production far less concentrated in a few hands in Ireland. However the same cannot be said of now and in the past twenty years the economies have converged leading to an amelioration of the underlying tension between the Irish and the English – certainly on building sites. There was even something of a reverse migration English building workers sucked in by Ireland's stupendous property boom. This of course has come to end with Ireland throwing open its door to the new Europe and the wave of immigration that followed undermining wages and working conditions on the buildings just as in Britain.

Terry the Philosopher had thought about the Irish attitude to tax stating that: "Paddy never minded paying indirect tax on his drink and tobacco but income tax was another day's work." Moreover, "he certainly objected to his money being used to pay for Downing St, Westminster, Kensington, Balmoral or Mustique." By Westminster he obviously meant the Houses of Parliament so in addition to the usual stab at the aristocracy and Queen Bessy he was also having a go at parliamentary democracy though without being able to draw more radical conclusions and put things on a revolutionary footing.

Terry the Philosopher had also interesting comments to make about the spread of subcontracting in Britain after World War Two and obviously this thinking working man made a huge impression on Brendan his theorising helping shape Brendan's opinions. "London is full of subcontractors," he said. "Before the seventies all work was carried out by direct labour. Companies were forced into massive investment in plant machinery and materials. They cut their overheads by subcontracting out the various stages of the work."

There is however a crucial omission in all this and which Brendan does not expand on by starting out from where "The Philosopher" left off. And that is to what extent did the huge amount of disruptive strike activity during the 1960s, leading eventually up to the first national building strike, have upon the increase in subtracting during the 1970s? Subcontracting never was just a means of defraying the costs of huge capital outlays onto other shoulders. It is also an extremely effective means of creating division amongst workers and destroying resistance. To neoliberalism subcontracting is an article of faith. And nor must we forget that throughout the 1970s the seeds of neoliberalism were already beginning to sprout within the Treasury and already put into practise in South America with a military coup in Chile leading the rout.

We recognised the characters and the half insights in Brendan Ward's books and as he generalises in Builders Remembered, "The characters are real, living and adventurous and will never be replaced. There could never be such a cross section of humanity encountered in any other walk of life". We could have added so many passages ourselves regarding all the particular characters we met. So, let's have a go as thousands upon thousands could (and can) also do.

There was Tommy Sweeney, The Glaswegian, and the man who built London single-handedly. But obviously that was now all in the past because he spent most of the day hanging around telling others what to do He was also a very rich man but could never quite retrieve his fortune; the trouble was he couldn't access his account for one lay under the pavement on Sochiehall street in Glasgow and the other was buried under the walls of Mountjoy jail in Dublin. As a brickie he'd built all the arches at the top end of Kilburn High Rd as it proceeds towards Shoot Up Hill - a name and description Tommy inevitably loved. He could also stop a bus or car by just putting his arm resolutely onto the bonnet and growling: the one occasion we witnessed he was run down and had to be sent immediately to an A&E unit. He wore a Scottish federation of anarchist badge saying he was friendly with the renowned Scottish anarchist, Stuart Christie, though friendly too with the hardman Jimmy Boyle in Glasgow and claimed: "I culda hadim". (There was always a close link between Glasgow hoodlums and its militant socialist tradition, anarchism and the working class, more so than anywhere else in Britain).

Then there was Smitty and the coppers' pub. Smitty, the son of a Yorkshire miner who worked at Manvers Main colliery, spent more time honing up his plastering tools than plastering – they became as sharp as a knife and the sun would glint off them – and you got a trifle nervous working side by side with him wondering where that trowel might go! He and Sweeney would drink together ending up fighting with each other at the end of the night. It was Sweeney that called time on it. So Smitty would then have to go to the coppers' pub by himself then telling us the next day on the building site how many coppers he had beaten up the night before, once claiming he had pulled the rib cage out of one copper, and this well before the 1984 miners' strike. (Such colour recalls Brendan Ward's memories of The Elephant whether fact or fiction; knocking out 12 coppers at one go).

Then there was Terry the peg-leg Irish plumber who drunk one night was stopped by the police who asked what he did for a living: "I'm a submarine captain" came the reply. The police would on occasion turn up on the site, which would be empty of building operatives half a minute later. And the last heard of Terry: Why, following Synge, though eighty years later, he'd become the only plumber on the Aran Islands! Terry even then working on a London building site could understand work and sleep governed by the seasons and the sounds of nature and not by the clock. Talking to him, Terry would say how he understood the hour at which Irishmen and women in the far-flung countryside arose in the morning. The small farmer was awakened not by the alarm clock but by the lowing of cattle, ever depending when that lowing would be. When he returned from England back to Ireland he was up at cockcrow but within a few days could sleep as well as if he had never been away.

And finally to the crack which according to Brendan "immediately starts and bunches of men gather round to listen to impromptu delivery of yarns." And he is so right about that but it then tales off and though "production immediately falls" initially because of the enthusiastic exchanges when first seeing so and so on site after a long period the good feeling may in fact increase productivity the chatter becoming like a work song though never quite. A clean site is a safe site and a friendly site is a productive site, so goes the litany of management, the state and unions combined. But behind this another reality looms: Brendan Ward was also very mistrustful of the Health & Safety Executive whom he reckoned were very bribebal having being present when officers had been called to a site only to be paid money to then declare the site safe. None of this has changed though bribery is no longer courtesy of discreet brown paper envelopes though it exists on a much vaster, more digital scale.

It seems fitting to conclude these brief remarks with a list of the names Brendan Ward knew: **Stoneface/Treble B/ Big Bad Bob/ Giant Lynch/ Lovely Leitrim/ Monkey Face/ The Bonecrusher/The Chancer/The Bushwhacker and Knobby/ The Flower/ Two Ton Bill/ Sledgehammer/Mick the Jovial/The Darky Flynn/and finally the three animals: The Elephant/ The Bear O'Shea/ The Pig O'Dwyer.**

(By: Stuart Wise with a wee bit of help from Dave: *Summer 2007*)

King Mob : The Posters, Leaflets, Cartoons.

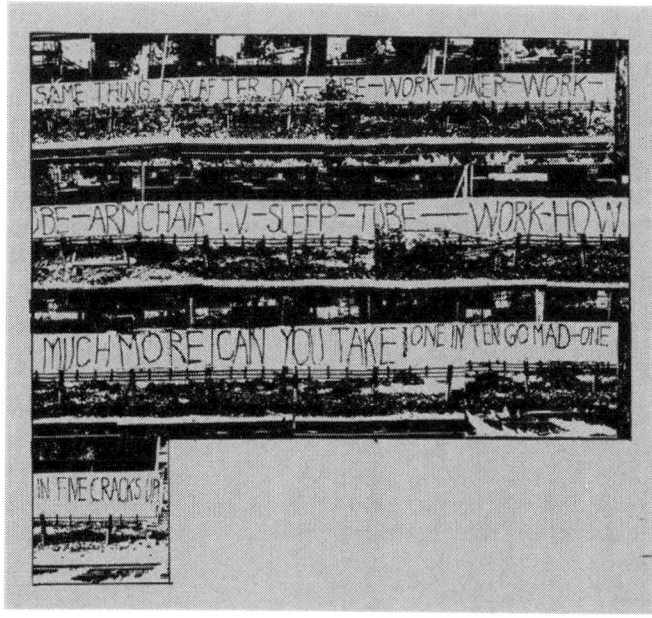

Above: The slogan that adorned the Hammersmith & City tube line at Westbourne Park, West London for many years before being obliterated by tag banality.

Above: some of the stickers mocking the "I'm Backing Britain" campaign initiated by the then Labour PM, Harold Wilson.

 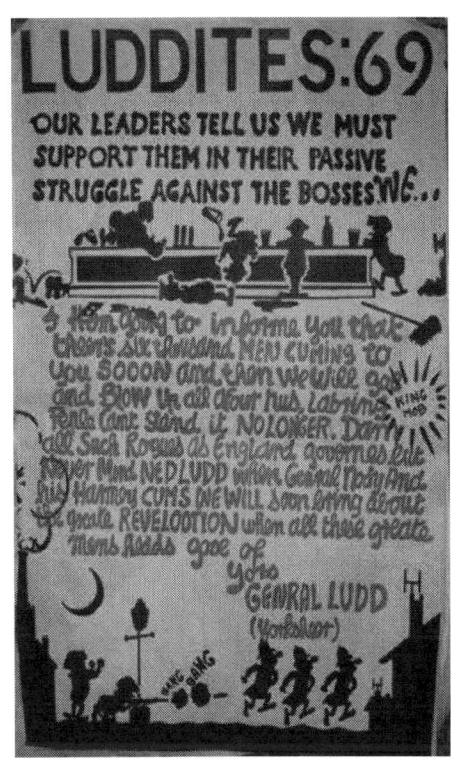

Above: Two King mob posters (The Luddite letter was a found object in EP Thompson's "The Making of the English Working Class").

(The above illustrated an English, King Mob translation of the Situationists: "Thesis on the Paris Commune").

There follows what was soon to be regarded as sexist and crude by the first wave of nice, refined feminists who alarmingly quickly dismissed King Mob in a simplistic way as male chauvinist. Had they never been in a public urinal (?) to find this is the type of stuff which goes down - often more in women toilets than men's - though most of this now in our cleansed day and age is instantly wiped clean by hired firms of graffiti busters. These cartoons were of course a detournemont of bog-wall style and deployed precisely for shock value in relation to a fairly dire occupation at the London School of Economics heavily manipulated by the paid-up intellectuals of New Left Review.

The guy who did this never got anywhere though later his lovely partner from down home Liverpool did say the basis of feminist hate was the white working class male which, only changed after the feminists experienced - what were then called - third world males! The original feminists never knew a thing about what could be achieved by deploying crude diversion but there again they were antipathetic to the spirit of '68, instantly intent on re-vamping a Labour party hostile to concepts of autonomy and open assemblies never mind the death of art!

Yes, the cartoons were crude but they were meant to be. Finally though, you couldn't have met a nicer, more caring, penniless, hurt guy than our friend, Richard 'Irish' Bell, who did these drawings! In the years to come, the all-pervasive feminist ambience made sure these drawings were never ever reproduced though for Malcolm Mclaren they mightily helped influence the outlines of Punk and its imagery. And where would all women punk groups like The Slits have been, which feminists then opportunistically raved about, without these much more profound indicators pointing to an entirely different reality to that of radical image making?

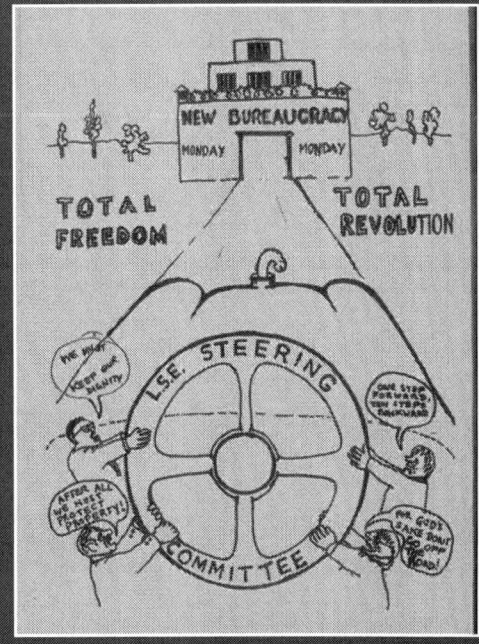

Accompanying Irish's cartoons the tract below - written by Dave Wise - was handed out a day later at the occupation of the London School of Economics. It ended up getting published in David Widgery's The Left in Britain (Penguin books 1976) under the title "Situationlist [sic] diatribe, LSE 1968, Vietnam Occupation."

Everyone was just starting to settle in / talking to each other /thinking about the coming night's playful exploration of the desolate academic labyrinth when the platform bureaucrats took over finally and irrevocably. From then on imagination and creativity were out. Frozen talk / frozen responses were the rule – hecklers mauled – the lot. A tyrannical discussion (speaker versus audience) followed, providing the framework for the professional revolutionary to enact the parliamentary power game and administer in the safest way possible the functioning of the building. Lenin's little homily was pasted up...."guard as the apple of your eye your tools etc" therefore "guard the LSE etc" – a statement which may have been relevant fifty years ago but which is desperately inappropriate to technological regression and the conditions of a claustrophobic consumerism. What do you want to guard....teaching as a commodity totally removed from life? No one suggested fighting against the irrelevancy of what was being taught – maybe burning a few files, facts, statistics or whatever. Instead we were entertained with seminars. "The Sociology of the Revolution etc. (WOW!) We were occupied – by the phantoms of an alienated education system – the situation was created in the name of the revolution and yet the relationships, language, and bodies were the reincarnation of the authoritarian ghosts who have buggered us already. How often must it be said that any true expression of a revolutionary libido now must necessarily involve a subversion of the 'tools': tools devoted today largely to the creation and maintenance of false needs and desires. A building as dry and cold as the LSE under such revolutionary circumstances would be radically deranged, charred, fucked etc. in the process of cathecting with a liberated psyche.....on reflection, this may have been deep down what the Committee of Public Safety feared...perhaps they too realise soccer hooligans are the most militant group within the British working class.

Below: Further stickers etc from Irish.

FEE FI FIDDLE DI FAD I SMELL THE BLOOD OF A WORKING CLASS LAD
BE HE GOOD OR BE HE BAD WE'LL FUCK HIM UP JUST LIKE HIS DAD

DILLY
NO!
DILLY
WE DON'T GIVE A FUCK FOR LABELS AN' LIES.
WE'RE NOT SELLIN' ANY ALIBIS
WE JUS' WAN' TO LIVE OUR LIVES.
WE CAN'T WAIT UNTIL YOUR OLD WORLD SICKENS AND DIES.
WE ARE THE WRITING ON YOUR WALL

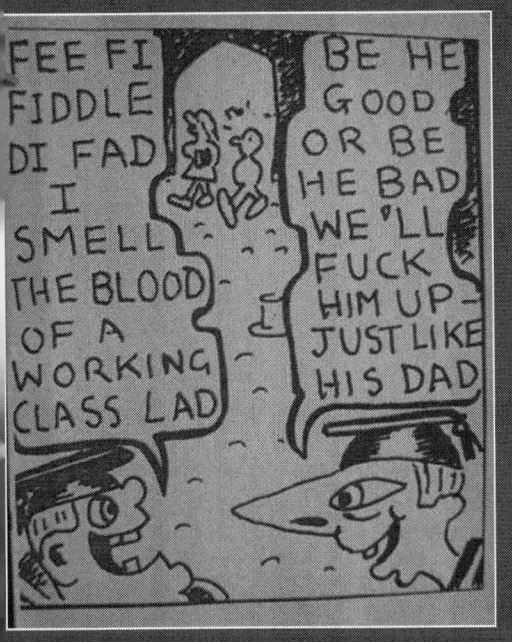

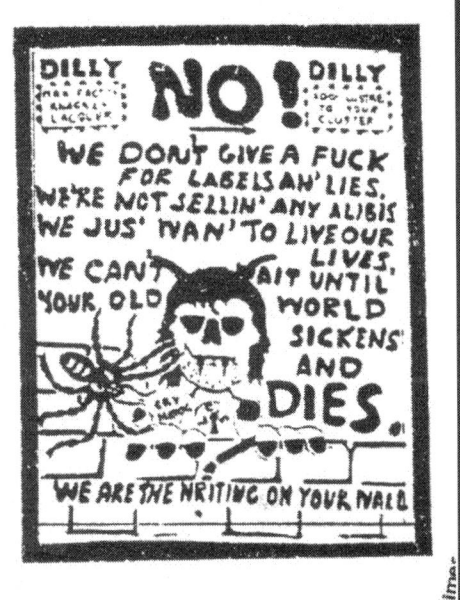

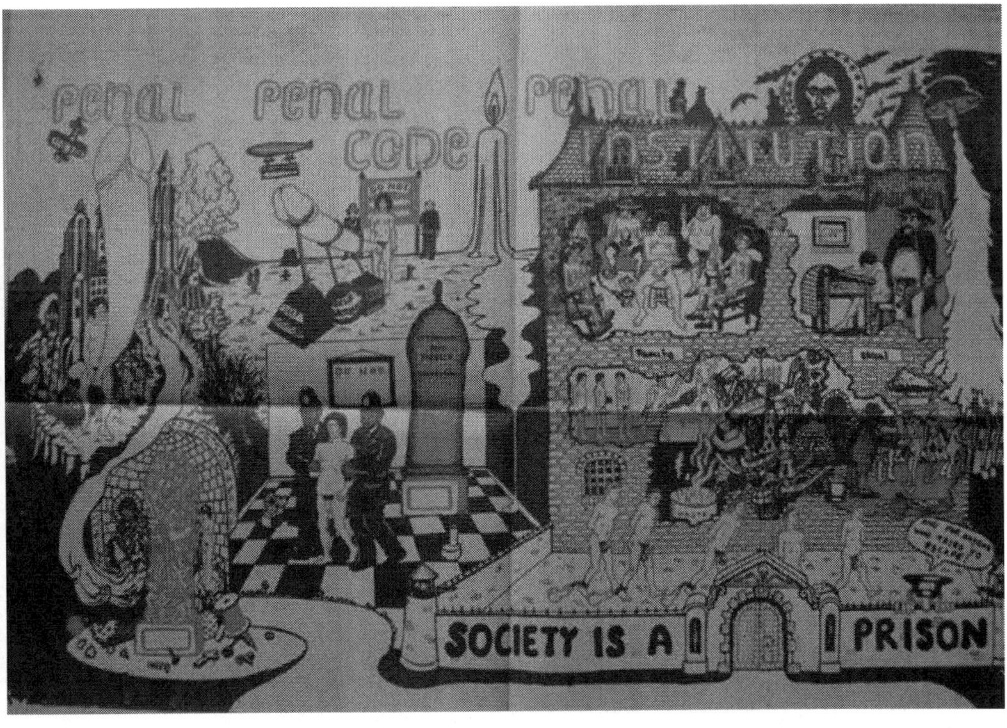
penal penal penal
code
INSTITUTION
SOCIETY IS A PRISON

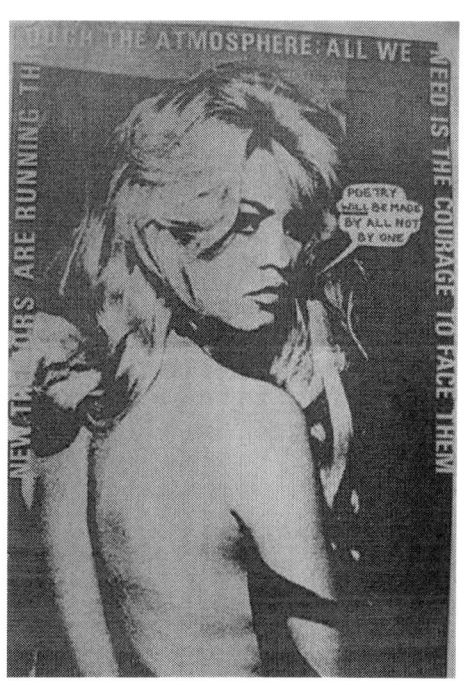

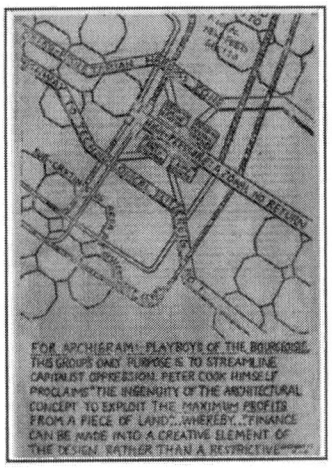 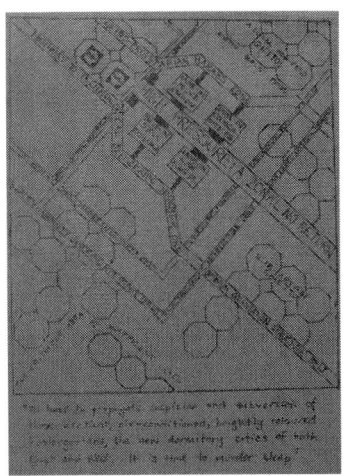

Above: A piss take on the technocratic and future ultra capitalised city centre of Newcastle as conceived by the planners in 1968. Reproduced in a local gestetnered mag

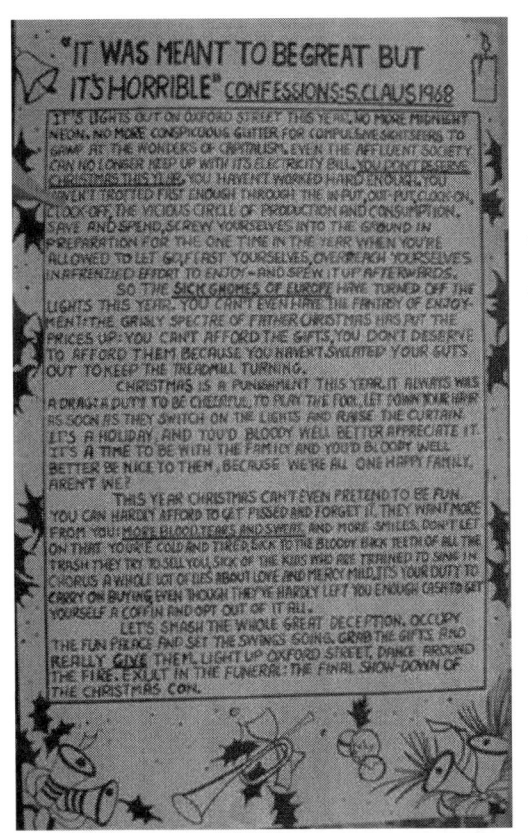

Xmas leaflet which accompanied the invasion of Selfridges in 1968. Many were handed out to shoppers and many scattered across Oxford St

Below: Detourned comix from the first Dublin based Gurriers mag (A "gurrier" was Dublin lingo for a teddy boy)

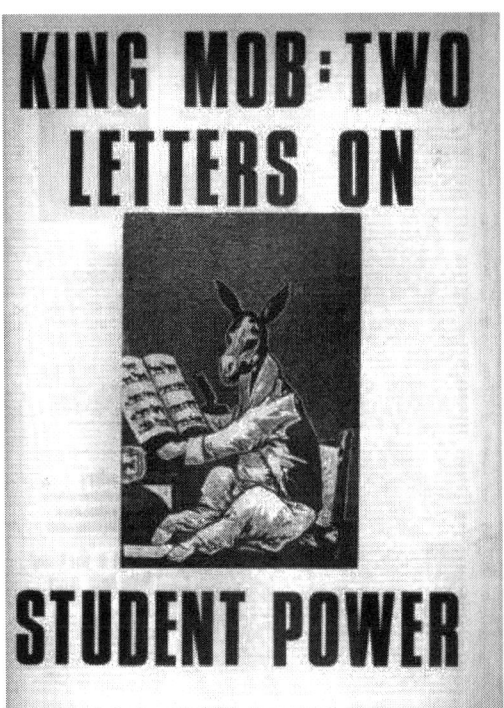

Left. Comment below porno photo in *King Mob 2* on *Student Power*

"Wordsworth and his exquisite sister are with me [This was in June 1797]. She is a woman indeed: in mind I mean, and heart; for her person is such that if you expected to see a pretty woman, you would think her ordinary; if you expected to see an ordinary woman you would think he pretty! But her manners are simple, ardent, impressive. In every motion her most innocent soul beams out so brightly, that who saw her would say "Guilt was a thing impossible in her." Here information various. Her eye watchful in minute observation of nature, and her taste a perfect electrometer. It bends, protrudes and draws in, at subtlest beauties and most recondite faults."

Coleridge: letter to Joseph Cottle

The illustrations above demonstrate how we used (and abused) the past history of poetry and painting. Obviously Coleridge's letter on Wordworth's sister Dorothy is ironically and provocatively related to today's prevailing, denuded pornographic imagery...As for the diverting of Peter Paul Ruben's Head of Medusa, the bubble-speak suggested a more Lautreamont-like take -"as beautiful as the trembling of an alcoholic's hand" etc. and with the word 'beauty' deliberately misspelt suggesting a language beyond an Oxford educated English.....

The above Mickey Mouse spoof was done (we believe) at the behest of Charlie Radcliffe and was not part of King Mob though most of us thought it was terrific and copied it and handed it out.